# Barron's Regents Exams and Answers

## Three-Year Sequence for High School Mathematics (Course I)

### Sequential Integrated Mathematics

**LESTER W. SCHLUMPF**

Retired Principal
John Adams High School, Queens

Former Lecturer in Mathematics, Queens College

**Barron's Educational Series, Inc.**
Woodbury, N.Y. • London • Toronto • Sydney

# Three-Year Sequence
# for High School
# Mathematics
# (Course I)

International Standard Book No. 0-8120-3205-5

PRINTED IN THE UNITED STATES OF AMERICA

789    100    987654321

# Contents

Regents Examinations and Answers

# Preface

A helpful word to the student:

This book is designed to strengthen your understanding and mastery of the ninth year mathematics curriculum as exemplified in the New York State syllabus for the Three-Year Sequence in High School Mathematics — Course I. The book has been specifically written to assist you in preparing for the Regents examination covering this syllabus.

Special features include:

**Complete sets of questions from 10 previous Regents examinations in this subject.** Attempting to solve these will make you familiar with the topics tested on the examination and with the degree of difficulty you are expected to master in each topic. Solving the questions on many tests will provide drill, improve your understanding of the topics, and increase your confidence as the nature and the language of the questions become more familiar.

**Solutions to all Regents questions with step-by-step explanations of the solutions.** Careful study of the solutions and explanations will improve your mastery of the subject. Each explanation is designed to show you how to apply the facts and principles you have learned in class. Since the explanation for each solution has been written with emphasis on the reasoning behind each step, its value goes far beyond the application to that particular question. You should read the explanation of the solution even if you have answered the question correctly. It gives insight into the topic that may be valuable when answering a more difficult question on the same topic on the next test you face.

**A Practice Section at the front of the book consisting of questions taken from former Regents, each with a completely explained step-by-step solution.** The questions are classified into 25 topic groups.

**A specially prepared Self-Analysis Chart following each Regents.** The chart is keyed to the Practice Section questions to direct you to concentrated study on those topics where you discover you have weaknesses.

Follow the procedures in the section entitled "How to Use This Book"—*and watch that mark grow.*

# How to Use This Book

This book has a built-in program to identify your areas of strength and weakness, and to guide you in concentrating your study on those topics where you most need assistance. The first part of the book consists of Practice Exercises. The section contains 153 questions, all selected from former Regents. The questions are classified into 25 topics, and a completely explained solution is provided for each question.

The second part of the book contains 10 of the most recent Regents examinations with completely explained solutions for each question. A Self-Analysis Chart has been constructed for each examination. By following the procedure below you can use it to locate your strong and weak points, and to direct you to the proper topics in the Practice Exercises where you need additional study:

1. Do a complete Regents examination, answering *all* questions (even though you will have a choice on the actual Regents).
2. Compare your answers with those in the explained solutions.
3. On the Self-Analysis Chart, find the topic under which each question is classified, and enter the number of points you earned if you answered it correctly.
4. Obtain your percentage for each topic by dividing your earned points by the number of test points on that topic, carrying the division to two decimal places.
5. If you are not satisfied with your percentage on any topic, turn to that topic in the Practice Exercises in the front of the book and answer all the questions there, comparing your results with the explained solutions.
6. If you still need additional practice on a particular topic, locate appropriate questions in other Regents examinations by using their Self-Analysis Charts to see which questions are listed for this topic.
7. Repeat the first six steps, using other complete Regents examinations, until you are satisfied with your percentages in all the topic classifications.

# Test Techniques — Practice Makes Perfect

## TAKING MATH EXAMS

Success on any examination, including those in the field of mathematics, is dependent on three factors:

1. Competence in the subject matter tested.
2. "Test wiseness," that is, understanding what to expect as to the nature of the test and the conditions under which it is to be given.
3. Emotional attitude or degree of self-confidence in taking the examination.

This book is designed to improve your effectiveness in all three of the above factors. To improve your mathematics competence, practice by answering a number of the past Regents examinations and afterward studying the explained solutions to the questions. Follow the directions in the section on "How to Use This Book" to focus your study on those topics where you need the most attention.

Any nervousness you may have will disappear and your self-confidence will grow as your record on the Self-Analysis Charts improves and as you become familiar with the nature of the Regents examination through practicing on several of them from prior years.

You can also improve your "test wiseness" by developing a practice strategy that will build habits that can serve you well when you take the actual Regents examination. Some suggestions for such a strategy follow.

## TIPS FOR PRACTICE

### How to Handle Individual Problems

1. **READ** the problem through the **FIRST TIME** to get a *general idea* of what you are asked to find; determine what question is being asked.
2. **READ** the problem through a **SECOND TIME** to *identify* and *relate* information or data.
3. **READ** the problem through a **THIRD TIME** to pick out specific facts and decide on a method for solving the problem.

4. **DRAW A SKETCH OR DIAGRAM**, if appropriate. A diagram will help you organize the given information. Some problems give very little information, whereas others give a great deal. A sketch or diagram will help you identify and relate the *pertinent* information.
5. **ESTIMATE THE ANSWER.**
6. **WRITE AN EQUATION.**
7. **SOLVE THE EQUATION.**
8. **CHECK THE ANSWER BY COMPARING IT WITH YOUR ESTIMATE.**
9. **REREAD THE QUESTION** to make sure you have answered what was asked.

**How to Practice Effectively and Efficiently.** To use your time most efficiently when taking an examination, do the following:

1. Do not spend too much time on one question if you cannot come up with a method to be used or if you cannot complete the solution. Instead, put a slash through the number of any question you cannot complete. When you have completed as many questions as you can you will be able to return quickly to the unanswered questions and try them again.
2. After trying the unanswered questions again, check the answer key for the entire test.
3. Circle the number of each question you answered incorrectly.
4. Study the explained solutions for those questions you answered incorrectly. (If the solution employs a formula or rule you do not know, write it on a piece of paper and attach the paper to the inside of your review book cover.)
5. Enter the points for your correct answers on the Self-Analysis Chart following the Regents you tried, and follow the procedure in the section on "How to Use This Book" to direct your remedial study.

## LET'S PRACTICE

**Part I.** Let's do your first practice Regents together. Allow yourself between one hour and one and one-half hours to do Part I. Follow the steps outlined under "Tips for Practice." Answer *all* 35 of the Part I questions even though you will be required to choose only 30 of them on the actual Regents — those on which you believe you can get correct answers. By completing all 35 questions on the practice exams and using the Self-Analysis Charts you will be able to establish a pattern of your strong and weak areas. You may find, for instance, that you usually solve the probability questions correctly but have difficulty with questions on logical implication. Remember your Self-Analysis Chart results, and you will know which 30 questions to choose on the actual Regents.

On the actual Regents, if you have difficulty in finding at least 30 questions on which you are reasonably sure of your ability, it is advisable to choose some multiple-choice questions on which you can eliminate one or more of the choices as obviously incorrect. There is no penalty for guessing, but do not guess until you have first tried to solve the question. If you can validly eliminate some choices, your guess from among the remaining choices will stand a better chance of being correct. Practice this technique as you answer all the Part I questions on practice exams so that you can use it to advantage if you have to resort to it in choosing the questions you will answer on the actual exam.

**Part II.** Spend one and one-half hours doing *all* seven Part II questions. Follow the same steps as you did in Part I.

On the actual Regents you will have to complete only four of the seven Part II questions — those on which you believe you can score the highest (partial credit is allowed on Part II for solutions that are not completely correct if major parts are accurate).

## THE ACTUAL REGENTS

In the weeks before the Regents, you should plan to spend one-half hour preparing each night. It is better to spread out your preparation time this way than to prepare for, say, three hours in one evening.

On the night before the Regents, read over the formulas you have attached to the review book cover. If you have prepared each night for a month or so, this is a good time to study calmly for about an hour and go to bed reasonably early.

You will have three hours to do the Course I Math Regents. After you have practiced on a number of the past examinations, you will be able to complete the actual Regents in about one and one-half hours. Even so, spend the full three hours. It is better to be correct than to be fast.

**Answering the Questions.** Follow steps similar to those you used for the practice exams. Before going on to Part II, go back over Part I, making sure you have answered 30 questions. Go over any of the 30 you were unsure of (those whose numbers you have marked with a slash) and try them again. If you answered more than 30 questions, cross out the ones you do not wish to have counted.

At the end of the first hour of the exam, go on to Part II. Read all the questions completely and select the four question types you have had the most success with on practice exams according to your Self-Analysis Charts. Work out each problem on scrap paper in pencil, and when you feel confident about the solution, copy it into the answer booklet *in ink*. Show all work. If you cannot completely solve four questions, pick the four that will give you the potential for the most credit.

**Time Schedule.** The Course I Math Regents exam is a three-hour examination. Below is a suggested schedule to follow when taking this Regents:

First Hour:
- Complete 30 Part I questions.
- Return to troublesome questions (those you have marked with slashes) and try them again.
- In multiple-choice questions, rule out any obviously impossible choices and then guess if you absolutely cannot answer.

Second Hour:
- Complete four Part II questions.

Next 25 Minutes:
- Redo the 30 questions selected from Part I. Do not refer to the scrap paper because it is unlikely you will spot an arithmetic error by scanning your computation. Re-solve the problems instead; it is unlikely you will make exactly the same errors again.
- If any answers differ the second time around, redo these questions a third time. You still may not be able to decide which is the correct answer—in this case, choose the answer that seems more reasonable to you.

Next 25 Minutes:
- Redo the four Part II questions you chose.
- If you arrive at a different answer, redo the question a third time as you did with Part I.

Last 10 Minutes:
- Check that 30 Part I questions and four Part II questions are answered.
- Check that Part II answers are labeled and that you have included your scrap paper in the booklet.

- If you answered more than 30 Part I questions or more than four Part II questions, write *OMIT* on any you do not wish to be marked.
- Make sure all answers are *in ink* in the answer booklet.

# Practice Exercises

This section of the book consists of 153 questions selected from former Regents examinations and classified into 25 topic groups. Solutions are provided for each of the questions with a step-by-step explanation given for each solution. The 25 topic groups are keyed to the Self-Analysis Charts that follow each of the 10 complete Regents examinations. This enables you to make use of these Practice Exercises to overcome any weaknesses that are revealed through the use of the Self-Analysis Charts.

## 1. QUESTIONS ON NUMBERS (RATIONAL, IRRATIONAL); PERCENT

**1.** Which is an irrational number?

(1)  0      (2)  $\frac{1}{2}$      (3)  $\sqrt{3}$      (4)  $\sqrt{4}$

**2.** Which represents an irrational number?

(1)  $-\frac{4}{5}$      (2)  $\pi$      (3)  $\sqrt{9}$      (4)  0

**3.** If $p$ represents "$x$ is a prime number," and $q$ represents "$x$ is an even number greater than 2," which of the following must be true?
(1)  $p \rightarrow q$      (2)  $p \vee q$      (3)  $p \wedge q$      (4)  $q \rightarrow \sim p$

**4.** What is 2.5% of 1,000?
(1)  2,500      (2)  250      (3)  25      (4)  2.50

**5.** If 30 students took an examination and 24 passed, what percent of the students passed the examination?

**6.** The top 12% of the class is placed on the honor roll. If 42 students are on the honor roll, how many students are in the class?

**Solutions to Questions on Numbers (rational, irrational); Percent**

**1.** An irrational number *cannot* be expressed in the form $\frac{p}{q}$ where $p$ and $q$ are integers.

Consider each choice in turn:

(1) 0: 0 can be expressed in the form $\frac{p}{q}$ as $\frac{0}{1}$ or $\frac{0}{3}$ or $\frac{0}{68}$, etc. Therefore, 0 is a rational number.

(2) $\frac{1}{2}$: $\frac{1}{2}$ is in the form $\frac{p}{q}$ and 1 and 2 are integers. Therefore, $\frac{1}{2}$ is a rational number.

(3) $\sqrt{3}$: $\sqrt{3}$ *cannot* be expressed as the ratio of two integers. As a decimal it would be a nonrepeating, nonterminating number, approximately equal to $0.1732\ldots$ Such a number *cannot* be expressed in the form $\frac{p}{q}$ where $p$ and $q$ are integers. Therefore, $\sqrt{3}$ is an irrational number.

(4) $\sqrt{4}$: $\sqrt{4} = 2$. 2 can be expressed in the form $\frac{p}{q}$ as $\frac{2}{1}$ or $\frac{6}{3}$ or $\frac{10}{20}$, etc. Therefore, $\sqrt{4}$ is a rational number.

The correct choice is **(3)**.

**2.** An irrational number is a number which *cannot* be written in the form $\frac{p}{q}$, where $p$ and $q$ are integers.

Consider each choice in turn:

(1) $-\frac{4}{5}$ is already in the form $\frac{p}{q}$ with $p = -4$ and $q = 5$. Therefore, $-\frac{4}{5}$ is a rational number.

(2) $\pi$ is a nonterminating, nonrepeating decimal. Such a decimal *cannot* be written as the quotient of two integers. Therefore, $\pi$ is an irrational number.

(3) $\sqrt{9} = 3$. 3 can be written in the form $\frac{p}{q}$ as $\frac{3}{1}$ with $p = 3$ and $q = 1$. Therefore, 3 is a rational number.

(4) 0 can be written in the form $\frac{p}{q}$ as $\frac{0}{1}$ with $p = 0$ and $q = 1$. Therefore, 0 is a rational number.

The correct choice is **(2)**.

**3.** A prime number is a number which is divisible only by itself and 1. Any even number greater than 2 is divisible by 2.

Consider each choice in turn:

(1)  $p \rightarrow q$ is the *implication* that if $p$ is true then $q$ is also true. But if $x$ is a prime number then it cannot also be divisible by 2. Hence, the implication $p \rightarrow q$ is false.

(2)  $p \vee q$ is the *disjunction* of $p$ and $q$. It states that either $p$ is true or $q$ is true or both are true. But if $x$ is some number chosen at random, say 9, it may be neither a prime number nor an even number greater than 2. Therefore, the disjunction $p \vee q$ is not always true.

(3)  $p \wedge q$ is the *conjunction* of $p$ and $q$. It states that both $p$ and $q$ are true. But if $x$ is a prime number it cannot also be a number which is even (that is divisible by 2) and greater than 2. Hence, the disjunction $p \wedge q$ can never be true.

(4)  $q \rightarrow \sim p$ is the *implication* that if $q$ is true the *negation* of $p$ is true, that is, if $q$ is true $p$ is not true. If $x$ is an even number greater than 2 it is certainly true that it cannot be a prime number. Hence, the implication $q \rightarrow \sim p$ is true.

The correct choice is **(4)**.

**4.**  2.5% of 1,000

2.5% can be represented as the decimal .025 (the percent sign stands for two decimal places; removing the percent sign thus requires that the decimal point be moved 2 places to the left).

To multiply a number by 1,000, the decimal point is moved 3 places to the right. Thus, $.025 \times 1,000 = 25$.

The correct choice is **(3)**.

**5.**  Of the 30 students who took the examination, 24 passed.

The percent of students who passed equals the number who passed divided by the total number of students who took the test:    $\dfrac{24}{30}$

Reduce the fraction to lowest terms by dividing both numerator and denominator by 6:    $\dfrac{4}{5}$

Convert the fraction to a percent, either by remembering that $\dfrac{4}{5} = 80\%$ or by dividing 5 into 4.00 to get two decimal places, that is .80:    80%

The percent of students who passed the examination is **80**.

**6.**  Let $x =$ the number of students in the class.

Since 12%, written as a decimal is 0.12, we have the equation:    $0.12x = 42$

Clear decimals by multiplying both sides
of the equation by 100:

$$100(0.12x) = 100(42)$$
$$12x = 4200$$

Divide both sides of the equation by 12:

$$\frac{12x}{12} = \frac{4200}{12}$$
$$x = 350$$

There are **350** students in the class.

## 2. QUESTIONS ON PROPERTIES OF NUMBER SYSTEMS

**1.** If $a$ and $b$ are integers, which statement is *always* true?

(1) $a - b = b - a$     (2) $a + b = b + a$     (3) $\dfrac{a}{b} = \dfrac{b}{a}$

(4) $a + 2b = b + 2a$

**2.** Which of the following is illustrated by the equation $x + y = y + x$?
(1) the commutative law for addition
(2) the associative law for addition
(3) the distributive law
(4) the identity property for addition

**3.** For what value of $x$ is the expression $\dfrac{8}{x - 7}$ undefined?

**4.** For which value of $x$ is the expression $\dfrac{x - 6}{x + 5}$ undefined?

(1) $-6$     (2) $-5$     (3) $5$     (4) $6$

**5.** Which expression is undefined or meaningless when $x = 3$?

(1) $x^0$     (2) $x^{-3}$     (3) $\dfrac{1}{x - 3}$     (4) $\dfrac{1}{x + 3}$

**Solutions to Questions on Properties of Number Systems**

**1.** Consider each of the choices in turn:
(1) $a - b = b - a$ is a statement that subtraction is commutative.
But this is not true of integers in general. For example, $8 - 3 \neq 3 - 8$.
(2) $a + b = b + a$ is a statement that addition is commutative. This
is always true for any values of the integers $a$ and $b$.

(3) $\dfrac{a}{b} = \dfrac{b}{a}$ is a statement that division is commutative. But this is not true of integers in general. For example, $\dfrac{4}{2} \neq \dfrac{2}{4}$.

(4) $a + 2b = b + 2a$ is a statement that the sum of one integer and double another is the same no matter which is doubled. This is not true in general. For example, $4 + 2(3) \neq 3 + 2(4)$ since $4 + 6 \neq 3 + 8$.

The correct choice is (2).

**2.** The equation $x + y = y + x$ illustrates the fact that the sum of two quantities is the same no matter in which order they are added. This is the commutative law for addition.

Consider why the other choices must be ruled out. The associative law for addition states that $a + (b + c) = (a + b) + c$, that is, the sum of three quantities is the same no matter how they are grouped in pairs (associated) in the process. The distributive law states that $a(b + c) = ab + ac$, that is, in multiplying the sum of two numbers by a multiplier, the multiplier is "distributed" to each of the terms in the sum. The identity property for addition states that if the identity element, 0, is added to any number, the sum is identical to the original number, that is, $0 + a = a$ or $a + 0 = a$.

The correct choice is (1).

**3.** Division by 0 is undefined. Hence, $\dfrac{8}{x - 7}$ is undefined if the denominator, $x - 7$, equals 0: $\qquad\qquad x - 7 = 0$

Add 7 (the additive inverse of $-7$) to both sides of the equation: $\qquad\qquad\qquad\qquad\qquad\qquad \dfrac{7 = 7}{x \quad\ = 7}$

The expression is undefined if $x = 7$.

**4.** Division by 0 is undefined. Hence, $\dfrac{x - 6}{x + 5}$ is undefined if the denominator, $x + 5$, equals 0: $\qquad\qquad x + 5 = \ \ 0$

Add $-5$ (the additive inverse of 5) to both sides of the equation: $\qquad\qquad\qquad\qquad\qquad\qquad \dfrac{-5 = -5}{x \quad\ = -5}$

Note that the value of the numerator, $x - 6$, has no effect on the question of whether the expression is undefined. Choice (4) concerns $x = 6$. If 6 is substituted for $x$ the expression becomes $\dfrac{6-6}{6+5}$ or $\dfrac{0}{11}$, which is equal to 0. The expression is thus defined to equal 0 when $x = 6$.

The correct choice is **(2)**.

5.   When $x = 3$:

(1)   $x^0$ becomes $3^0$ which is equal to 1. $x^0$ is equal to 1 for all values of $x$ except $x = 0$.

(2)   $x^{-3}$ becomes $3^{-3}$ which is defined as $\dfrac{1}{3^3}$ or $\dfrac{1}{27}$.

(3)   $\dfrac{1}{x-3}$ becomes $\dfrac{1}{3-3}$ or $\dfrac{1}{0}$. But $\dfrac{1}{0}$ is undefined or meaningless since division by 0 is undefined.

(4)   $\dfrac{1}{x+3}$ becomes $\dfrac{1}{3+3}$ which is equal to $\dfrac{1}{6}$.

The correct choice is **(3)**.

## 3. QUESTIONS ON OPERATIONS ON RATIONAL NUMBERS AND MONOMIALS

1.   The product of $6x^3$ and $5x^4$ is
(1)   $11x^{12}$     (2)   $11x^7$     (3)   $30x^{12}$     (4)   $30x^7$

2.   Express $\dfrac{15x^2}{-3x}$ in *simplest form.*

3.   The expression $(3x^2y^3)^2$ is equivalent to
(1)   $9x^4y^6$     (2)   $9x^4y^5$     (3)   $3x^4y^6$     (4)   $6x^4y^6$

4.   The value of $3^{-2}$ is

(1)   $-9$     (2)   $-6$     (3)   $-\dfrac{1}{9}$     (4)   $\dfrac{1}{9}$

5.   The product of $(-2xy^2)(3x^2y^3)$ is
(1)   $-5x^3y^5$     (2)   $-6x^2y^6$     (3)   $-6x^3y^5$     (4)   $-6x^3y^6$

6.   When $4x^3y^3$ is multiplied by $8xy^2$, the product is
(1)   $12x^3y^6$     (2)   $12x^4y^6$     (3)   $32x^3y^6$     (4)   $32x^4y^5$

Solutions to Questions on Operations on Rational Numbers and Monomials

1.　　　　　　　　　　　　　　　　　　　　$(6x^3)(5x^4)$

To multiply two monomials, first multiply their coefficients to get the coefficient of the product:　　　　　　　　　　　$6 \cdot 5 = 30$

Multiply literal factors with the same base by adding the exponents of that base to get the exponent of the product:　　　　　　　$x^3 \cdot x^4 = x^7$

Putting the two together:　　　　$(6x^3)(5x^4) = 30x^7$

The correct choice is (4).

2.　　　　　　　　　　　　　　　　　　　　$\dfrac{15x^2}{-3x}$

To divide two monomials, first divide their numerical coefficients to find the numerical coefficient of the quotient:　　　$(15) \div (-3) = -5$

Divide the literal factors to find the literal factor of the quotient. Remember that powers of the same base are divided by subtracting their exponents:　　　　　$(x^2) \div (x^1) = x^1$

Putting the two results together:　　　$\dfrac{15x^2}{-3x} = -5x$

The fraction in simplest form is $-5x$.

3.　$(3x^2y^3)^2$ means $(3x^2y^3)(3x^2y^3)$

The numerical coefficient of the product is the product of the two numerical coefficients:　　　$(3)(3) = 9$

In multiplying powers of the same base, the exponents are added to obtain the exponent for that base in the product:　　$(x^2y^3)(x^2y^3) = x^4y^6$

Hence:　　　　　　　　　　$(3x^2y^3)^2 = 9x^4y^6$

The correct choice is (1).

4.　By the definition of a negative exponent, $x^{-n} = \dfrac{1}{x^n}$. Therefore,

$3^{-2} = \dfrac{1}{3^2}$ or $\dfrac{1}{9}$.

The correct choice is (4).

**5.**                               $(-2xy^2)(3x^2y^3)$

To find the product of two monomials, first find the numerical coefficient of the product by multiplying the two numerical coefficients together:

$$(-2)(3) = -6$$

Find the literal factor of the product by multiplying the literal factors together. The product of two powers of the same base is found by adding the exponents of that base:

$$(x^1y^2)(x^2y^3) = x^3y^5$$

Putting the two results together:    $(-2xy^2)(3x^2y^3) = -6x^3y^5$

The correct choice is (3).

**6.**   Indicate the product as:         $(4x^3y^3)(8xy^2)$

First find the numerical coefficient of the product by multiplying the two numerical coefficients together:

$$(4)(8) = 32$$

Find the literal factor of the product by multiplying the literal factors together. The product of two powers of the same base is found by adding the exponents of that base:

$$(x^3y^3)(x^1y^2) = x^4y^5$$

Putting the two results together:    $(4x^3y^3)(8xy^2) = 32x^4y^5$

The correct choice is (4).

## 4. QUESTIONS ON OPERATIONS ON POLYNOMIALS

1.   Subtract $4m - h$ from $4m + h$.

2.   Find the sum of $2x^2 + 3x - 1$ and $3x^2 - 2x + 4$.

3.   Perform the indicated operations and express the result as a trinomial:
$$3x(x + 1) + 4(x - 1)$$

4.   Express the product $(2x - 7)(x + 3)$ as a trinomial.

5.   If the product $(2x + 3)(x + k)$ is $2x^2 + 13x + 15$, find the value of $k$.

6.   When $3x^3 + 3x$ is divided by $3x$, the quotient is
(1)   $x^2$      (2)   $x^2 + 1$      (3)   $x^2 + 3x$      (4)   $3x^3$

## Solutions to Questions on Operations on Polynomials

**1.** Subtraction is the inverse operation of addition. Thus, to subtract we add the additive inverse of the subtrahend (expression to be subtracted) to the minuend (expression subtracted from). Therefore, to subtract $4m - h$ from $4m + h$, we add $-4m + h$ to $4m + h$:

Subtract:  $4m + h$    means    add:    $4m + h$
          $\underline{4m - h}$                        $\underline{-4m + h}$
                                                $2h$

The difference is $2h$.

**2.** Write the second trinomial under the first, placing like terms in the same column:

$$2x^2 + 3x - 1$$
$$3x^2 - 2x + 4$$

Add each column by adding the numerical coefficients algebraically and bringing down the literal factor:

$$5x^2 + \ \ x + 3$$

The sum is $5x^2 + x + 3$.

**3.**                                   $3x(x + 1) + 4(x - 1)$

Remove parentheses by applying the distributive law of multiplication over addition (multiply each term in the parentheses by the factor outside):         $3x^2 + 3x + 4x - 4$

Combine like terms:                     $3x^2 + 7x - 4$

The trinomial is $3x^2 + 7x - 4$.

**4.**                                      $(2x - 7)(x + 3)$

Apply the distributive law by multiplying each term of $(2x - 7)$ by $(x + 3)$:        $2x(x + 3) - 7(x + 3)$

Again apply the distributive law by multiplying each term in the parentheses by the factor outside:       $2x^2 + 6x - 7x - 21$

Combine like terms:                     $2x^2 - x - 21$

The trinomial is $2x^2 - x - 21$.

ALTERNATIVE SOLUTION: The product of two binomials may be found by multiplying each term of one by each term of the other, using a procedure analogous to that used in arithmetic to multiply multidigit numbers:

$$2x - 7$$
$$\underline{x + 3}$$
$$2x^2 - 7x$$
$$\underline{\qquad 6x - 21}$$

Combine like terms:                     $2x^2 - \ \ x - 21$

**5.**

Apply the distributive law by multiplying $(x + k)$ by each term of $(2x + 3)$:

Again apply the distributive law by multiplying each term in parentheses by the factor outside:

Factor $x$ from the two middle terms:

Since this product is equal to $2x^2 + 13x + 15$, the coefficients of $x$ must be equal and the constant terms must be equal:

Solve either of these equations for $k$:

$$(2x + 3)(x + k)$$

$$2x(x + k) + 3(x + k)$$

$$2x^2 + 2kx + 3x + 3k$$
$$2x^2 + x(2k + 3) + 3k$$

$$2k + 3 = 13 \qquad 3k = 15$$
$$\underline{\phantom{2k} -3 = -3} \qquad \dfrac{3k}{3} = \dfrac{15}{3}$$
$$2k \phantom{+3} = 10 \qquad$$
$$\dfrac{2k}{2} = \dfrac{10}{2} \qquad k = 5$$
$$k = 5$$

The value of $k$ is **5**.

**6.** Indicate the division in fractional form:

$$\dfrac{3x^3 + 3x}{3x}$$

Apply the distributive law by dividing each term of $3x^3 + 3x$ in turn by $3x$. Remember that in dividing powers of the same base, the exponents are subtracted. Also note that $3x \div 3x = 1$:

The correct choice is **(2)**.

$$x^2 + 1$$

## 5. QUESTIONS ON SQUARE ROOT; OPERATIONS ON RADICALS

**1.** The expression $\sqrt{300}$ is equivalent to

(1) $50\sqrt{6}$     (2) $12\sqrt{5}$     (3) $3\sqrt{10}$     (4) $10\sqrt{3}$

**2.** Which is equivalent to $\sqrt{40}$?

(1) $20$     (2) $2\sqrt{10}$     (3) $10\sqrt{2}$     (4) $4\sqrt{10}$

**3.** The expression $\sqrt{27} + \sqrt{12}$ is equivalent to

(1) $\sqrt{39}$     (2) $13\sqrt{3}$     (3) $5\sqrt{6}$     (4) $5\sqrt{3}$

**4.** The sum of $2\sqrt{3}$ and $\sqrt{12}$ is

(1) $4\sqrt{6}$     (2) $8\sqrt{3}$     (3) $3\sqrt{15}$     (4) $4\sqrt{3}$

**5.** The expression $\sqrt{50} + 3\sqrt{2}$ can be written in the form $x\sqrt{2}$. Find $x$.

## Solutions to Questions on Square Root; Operations on Radicals

**1.** $\sqrt{300}$

Simplify $\sqrt{300}$ by finding two factors of the radicand, 300, one of which is the highest perfect square that divides into 300:

$\sqrt{100(3)}$

Take the square root of the perfect square factor, 100, and place it outside the radical sign as the coefficient, 10:    $10\sqrt{3}$

The correct choice is **(4)**.

**2.** $\sqrt{40}$

Factor out any perfect square factors in the radicand (the number under the radical sign):

$\sqrt{4(10)}$

Remove the perfect square factor from under the radical sign by taking its square root and writing it as a coefficient of the radical:    $2\sqrt{10}$

The correct choice is **(2)**.

**3.** $\sqrt{27} + \sqrt{12}$

We cannot add $\sqrt{27}$ and $\sqrt{12}$ in their present form because only *like radicals* may be combined. Like radicals have the same radicand (number under the radical sign) and the same index (here, understood to be 2, representing the square root). A radical can be simplified by finding two factors of the radicand, one of which is the highest possible perfect square.

$\sqrt{27} + \sqrt{12}$

STEP 1: Factor the radicands, using the highest possible perfect square in each:    $\sqrt{9 \cdot 3} + \sqrt{4 \cdot 3}$

STEP 2: Simplify by taking the square root of the perfect square factor and placing it outside the radical sign as a coefficient of the radical:    $3\sqrt{3} + 2\sqrt{3}$

STEP 3: Combine the like radicals by adding their coefficients to get the new coefficient:    $5\sqrt{3}$

The given expression is equivalent to $5\sqrt{3}$.

The correct choice is **(4)**.

**4.** $2\sqrt{3} + \sqrt{12}$

Only *like radicals* can be added. Like radicals must have the same root (here both are square roots) and must have the same radicand (the number under the radical sign). Factor out any perfect square factor in the radicands:    $2\sqrt{3} + \sqrt{4(3)}$

Remove the perfect square factors from under the radical sign by taking their square roots and writing them as coefficients of the radical:

$$2\sqrt{3} + 2\sqrt{3}$$

Combine the like radicals by adding their numerical coefficients and writing the sum as the numerical coefficient of the common radical:

$$4\sqrt{3}$$

The correct choice is (4).

**5.**

$$\sqrt{50} + 3\sqrt{2}$$

Factor out any perfect square factors in the radicand (the number under the radical sign):

$$\sqrt{25(2)} + 3\sqrt{2}$$

Remove the perfect square factors from under the radical sign by taking their square roots and writing them as coefficients of the radical:

$$5\sqrt{2} + 3\sqrt{2}$$

Combine the like radicals by combining their coefficients and using the sum as the numerical coefficient of the common radical:

$$8\sqrt{2}$$

$8\sqrt{2}$ is in the form $x\sqrt{2}$ with $x = 8$.

$$x = 8.$$

# 6. QUESTIONS ON EVALUATING FORMULAS AND EXPRESSIONS

1. If $b = -2$ and $c = 3$, find the value of $b^2 + c$.

2. Find the value of $6b^2 - 4a^2$ when $b = 2$ and $a = 1$.

3. If $x = 3$ and $y = -1$, find the value of $2x + y^2$.

4. Using the formula $V = x^2h$, find $V$ when $x = 6$ and $h = 2$.

5. Given the formula $F = \dfrac{9}{5}C + 32$, find $F$ when $C = 15$.

6. If $xy^2 = 18$, find $x$ when $y = -3$.

## Solutions to Questions on Evaluating Formulas and Expressions

**1.**      $b^2 + c$     $b = -2, c = 3$

Substitute $-2$ for $b$ and $3$ for $c$ in the given expression:

$$(-2)^2 + 3$$

Simplify:

$$4 + 3$$
$$7$$

The value is **7**.

2.         $6b^2 - 4a^2$             $b = 2$    $a = 1$

Substitute 2 for $b$ and 1 for $a$ in the given expression:

$$6(2)^2 - 4(1)^2$$
$$6(4) - 4(1)$$
$$24 - 4$$
$$20$$

The value is **20**.

3.

Since $x = 3$ and $y = -1$, substitute these values for $x$ and $y$ respectively:          $2x + y^2$

Perform the indicated multiplications:           $2(3) + (-1)^2$

Combine like terms:             $6 + 1$

The value is **7**.              $7$

4.

Since $x = 6$ and $h = 2$, substitute 6 for $x$ and 2 for $h$ in the formula:       $V = x^2 h$

Square 6:                  $V = (6)^2(2)$

Perform the indicated multiplication:     $V = 36(2)$

$V = $ **72**.                    $V = 72$

5.                $F = \dfrac{9}{5} C + 32$

Substitute 15 for $C$ in the formula:     $F = \dfrac{9}{5}(15) + 32$

Divide the factor 5 out of numerator and denominator of the first term on the right side of the equation:     $F = \dfrac{9}{\cancel{5}}(\cancel{15})^{3} + 32$

$$1$$

Multiply 9 by 3:            $F = 27 + 32$

Combine like terms:         $F = 59$

$F = $ **59**.

6.

Substitute $-3$ for $y$:         $xy^2 = 18$

Square $-3$:            $x(-3)^2 = 18$

                     $9x = 18$

Divide both sides of the equation by 9:     $\dfrac{9x}{9} = \dfrac{18}{9}$

$x = $ **2**.                    $x = 2$

## 7. QUESTIONS ON SIMPLE LINEAR EQUATIONS (INCLUDING PARENTHESES)

1. Solve for $x$: $4x = x + 21$

2. Solve for $x$: $8x = 2(x + 15)$

3. Solve for $x$: $3(x + 4) - x = 18$

4. Solve for $x$: $2(x + 3) = 12$

5. Solve for $x$: $3(2x - 5) = 9$

6. Solve for $y$: $6(y + 3) = 2y - 2$

**Solutions to Questions on Simple Linear Equations (including parentheses)**

1.
Add $-x$ (the additive inverse of $x$) to both sides of the equation:

$$4x = x + 21$$
$$\underline{-x = -x\phantom{00}}$$
$$3x = \phantom{00}21$$

Divide both sides of the equation by 3:

$$\frac{3x}{3} = \frac{21}{3}$$
$$x = 7$$

The solution is 7.

2. Remove parentheses by using the distributive property of multiplication on the right side:

$$8x = 2(x + 15)$$
$$8x = 2x + 30$$

Add $-2x$ (the additive inverse of $2x$) to both sides:

$$\underline{-2x = -2x\phantom{0}}$$
$$6x = 30$$

Multiply both sides by $\frac{1}{6}$ (the multiplicative inverse of 6):

$$\frac{1}{6}(6x) = \frac{1}{6}(30)$$

The solution is $x = 5$.

$$x = 5$$

3.
Remove parentheses by using the distributive property of multiplication:

$$3(x + 4) - x = 18$$
$$3x + 12 - x = 18$$

Combine like terms:
Add $-12$ (the additive inverse of 12) to both sides of the equation:

$$2x + 12 = 18$$

$$\underline{-12 = -12}$$

$$2x \quad\;\; = 6$$

Multiply both sides by $\dfrac{1}{2}$ (the multiplicative inverse of 2):

$$\frac{1}{2}(2x) = \frac{1}{2}(6)$$

$$x = 3$$

The value of $x$ is 3.

**4.**

$$2(x + 3) = 12$$

Remove parentheses by applying the distributive law of multiplication over addition:

$$2x + 6 = 12$$

Add $-6$ (the additive inverse of 6) to both sides of the equation:

$$\underline{-6 = -6}$$

$$2x \quad\;\; = 6$$

Divide both sides of the equation by 2:

$$\frac{2x}{2} = \frac{6}{2}$$

$$x = 3$$

The solution is 3.

**5.**

$$3(2x - 5) = 9$$

Apply the distributive law of multiplication over addition in order to remove parentheses:

$$6x - 15 = 9$$

Add 15 (the additive inverse of $-15$) to both sides of the equation:

$$\underline{15 = 15}$$

$$6x \quad\;\; = 24$$

Divide both sides of the equation by 6:

$$\frac{6x}{6} = \frac{24}{6}$$

$$x = 4$$

The solution is 4.

**6.**

$$6(y + 3) = 2y - 2$$

Remove parentheses by applying the distributive law of multiplication over addition:

$$6y + 18 = 2y - 2$$

Add $-18$ (the additive inverse of 18) and also add $-2y$ (the additive inverse of $2y$) to both sides of the equation:

$$-2y - 18 = -2y - 18$$
$$4y = -20$$

Divide both sides of the equation by 4:

$$\frac{4y}{4} = \frac{-20}{4}$$
$$y = -5$$

The solution is $y = -5$.

## 8. QUESTIONS ON LINEAR EQUATIONS CONTAINING DECIMALS OR FRACTIONS

1. Solve for $y$: $\frac{y}{3} + 2 = 5$

2. Solve for $a$: $\frac{a}{2} + \frac{a}{6} = 2$

3. Solve for $h$: $\frac{24}{h} = \frac{16}{4}$

4. Solve for $x$: $0.4x + 2 = 12$

5. Solve for $x$: $1.04x + 8 = 60$

6. Solve for $n$: $3n + 1.4n = 8.8$

**Solutions to Questions on Linear Equations Containing Decimals or Fractions**

**1.**
To clear fractions in the equation, multiply each term by the least common denominator, in this case, by 3:

$$\frac{y}{3} + 2 = 5$$
$$3\left(\frac{y}{3}\right) + 3(2) = 3(5)$$

Simplify: $y + 6 = 15$

Add $-6$ (the additive inverse of 6) to both sides:

$$-6 = -6$$
$$y = 9$$

The solution for $y$ is 9.

**2.** To clear fractions in an equation, multiply each term on both sides by the

$$\frac{a}{2} + \frac{a}{6} = 2$$

lowest common denominator, in this case, 6:

$$6\left(\frac{a}{2}\right) + 6\left(\frac{a}{6}\right) = 6(2)$$

$$3a + a = 12$$

Combine like terms:
Multiply both sides by $\frac{1}{4}$ (the multiplicative inverse of 4):

$$4a = 12$$

$$\frac{1}{4}(4a) = \frac{1}{4}(12)$$

$$a = 3$$

The solution is $a = 3$.

**3.**
Reduce the fraction on the right side to lowest terms by dividing numerator and denominator by 4:

$$\frac{24}{h} = \frac{16}{4}$$

$$\frac{24}{h} = \frac{4}{1}$$

The equation is a *proportion*. In a proportion, the product of the means equals the product of the extremes. Therefore, cross-multiply:

$$4h = 24$$

Multiply each side by $\frac{1}{4}$ (the multiplicative inverse of 4):

$$\frac{1}{4}(4h) = \frac{1}{4}(24)$$

$$h = 6$$

The solution is **6**.

**4.**
To clear decimals, multiply each term on both sides of the equation by 10:

$$0.4x + 2 = 12$$

$$10(0.4x) + 10(2) = 10(12)$$

$$4x + 20 = 120$$

Add $-20$ (the additive inverse of 20) to both sides of the equation:

$$\underline{\quad -20 = -20 \quad}$$

$$4x \quad\quad = 100$$

Multiply both sides of the equation by $\frac{1}{4}$ (the multiplicative inverse of 4):

$$\frac{1}{4}(4x) = \frac{1}{4}(100)$$

$$x = 25$$

The solution for $x$ is **25**.

**5.**
Clear decimals by multiplying each term on both sides of the equation by 100:

$$1.04x + 8 = 60$$

$$100(1.04x) + 100(8) = 100(60)$$

$$104x + 800 = 6{,}000$$

Add $-800$ (the additive inverse of 800) to both sides of the equation:

$$\frac{-800 = -800}{104x \qquad = 5,200}$$

Divide both sides of the equation by 104:

$$\frac{104x}{104} = \frac{5,200}{104}$$

$$\begin{array}{r} 50 \\ 104\overline{)5,200} \\ \underline{5\ 20} \end{array}$$

$$x = 50$$

The solution is **50**.

**6.**

$$3n + 1.4n = 8.8$$

Clear decimals by multiplying each term on both sides of the equation by 10:

$$10(3n) + 10(1.4n) = 10(8.8)$$
$$30n + 14n = 88$$
$$44n = 88$$

Combine like terms:
Divide both sides of the equation by 44:

$$\frac{44n}{44} = \frac{88}{44}$$

$$n = 2$$

The solution is **2**.

## 9. QUESTIONS ON GRAPHS OF LINEAR FUNCTIONS (INCLUDING SLOPES)

**1.** Which point lies on the graph of $2x + y = 10$?
(1)  (0,8)     (2)  (10,0)     (3)  (3,4)     (4)  (4,3)

**2.** A point on the graph of $x + 3y = 13$ is
(1)  (4,4)     (2)  (−2,3)     (3)  (−5,6)     (4)  (4,−3)

**3.** What is the slope of the line whose equation is $4y = 3x + 16$?

**4.** What is the slope of the graph of $y = 2x + 3$?

**5.** The graph of $y = 3x - 4$ is parallel to the graph of
(1)  $y = 4x - 3$     (2)  $y = 3x + 4$     (3)  $y = -3x + 4$
(4)  $y = 3$

**6.** The equation of a line whose slope is 2 and whose $y$-intercept is $-2$ is

(1) $2y = x - 2$     (2) $y = -2$     (3) $y = -2x + 2$

(4) $y = 2x - 2$

## Solutions to Questions on Graphs of Linear Functions (including slopes)

**1.**    $2x + y = 10$

If a point lies on the graph of the equation above, its coordinates must satisfy the equation. Therefore, test each point in turn by substituting its coordinates for $x$ and $y$ to see if the equation is satisfied:

(1)   (0,8):    $2(0) + 8 \overset{?}{=} 10$

             $0 + 8 \overset{?}{=} 10$

               $8 \neq 10$     (0,8) does *not* check.

(2)   (10,0):   $2(10) + 0 \overset{?}{=} 10$

             $20 + 0 \overset{?}{=} 10$

              $20 \neq 10$     (10,0) does *not* check.

(3)   (3,4):    $2(3) + 4 \overset{?}{=} 10$

              $6 + 4 \overset{?}{=} 10$

            $10 = 10\checkmark$     (3,4) is on the graph.

(4)   (4,3):    $2(4) + 3 \overset{?}{=} 10$

              $8 + 3 \overset{?}{=} 10$

              $11 \neq 10$     (4,3) does *not* check.

The correct choice is (3).

**2.** If a point is on the graph of $x + 3y = 13$, then its coordinates must satisfy this equation.

Try each choice in turn by substituting the coordinates in the equation $x + 3y = 13$:

(1)   (4,4):    $4 + 3(4) \overset{?}{=} 13$

             $4 + 12 \overset{?}{=} 13$

            $16 \neq 13$     (4,4) is *not* on the graph.

(2)   (−2,3):   $-2 + 3(3) \overset{?}{=} 13$

            $-2 + 9 \overset{?}{=} 13$

             $7 \neq 13$     (−2,3) is *not* on the graph.

(3)   (−5,6):   $-5 + 3(6) \overset{?}{=} 13$

            $-5 + 18 \overset{?}{=} 13$

           $13 = 13\checkmark$     (−5,6) *is* on the graph.

(4)  (4,−3):   $4 + 3(-3) \overset{?}{=} 13$

$4 - 9 \overset{?}{=} 13$

$-5 \neq 13$     (4,−3) is *not* on the graph.

The correct choice is (3).

**3.**  $4y = 3x + 16$

If an equation of a straight line is in the form $y = mx + b$, then $m$ represents its slope.

To get $4y = 3x + 16$ into the $y = mx + b$ form, divide each term by 4:

$$y = \frac{3}{4} x + 4$$

Here, $m = \dfrac{3}{4}$.

The slope is $\dfrac{3}{4}$.

**4.**  If the equation of a straight line is in the form $y = mx + b$, then $m$ represents the slope.

$y = 2x + 3$ is in the form $y = mx + b$ with $m = 2$; therefore, the slope is 2.

The slope is **2**.

**5.**  If two lines are parallel, they must have the same slope.

If the equation of a line is in the form $y = mx + b$, then $m$ represents the slope. The given equation, $y = 3x - 4$, is in the $y = mx + b$ form with $m = 3$. Its slope is 3.

Examine each choice in turn to see which one also has a slope of 3:

(1)  $y = 4x - 3$ is in the $y = mx + b$ form with $m = 4$.
    Therefore, it is *not* parallel to $y = 3x - 4$.

(2)  $y = 3x + 4$ is in the $y = mx + b$ form with $m = 3$.
    Therefore, it *is* parallel to $y = 3x - 4$.

(3)  $y = -3x + 4$ is in the $y = mx + b$ form with $m = -3$.
    Therefore, it is *not* parallel to $y = 3x - 4$.

(4)  $y = 3$ can be written in the $y = mx + b$ form as $y = 0x + 3$. From this form, $m = 0$. Therefore, $y = 3$ is *not* parallel to $y = 3x - 4$.

The correct solution is (2).

**6.**  An equation of a line whose slope is $m$ and whose $y$-intercept is $b$ can be written in the form $y = mx + b$.

In this case, $m = 2$ and $b = -2$. Hence, an equation of the line is $y = 2x - 2$.

The correct choice is (4).

## 10. QUESTIONS ON INEQUALITIES

1.  Which inequality is represented by the accompanying graph?

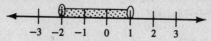

(1)  $-2 < x < 1$     (2)  $-2 < x \leq 1$     (3)  $-2 \leq x < 1$
(4)  $-2 \leq x \leq 1$

2.  Which graph shows the solution to $(x < 3) \vee (x \geq 5)$?

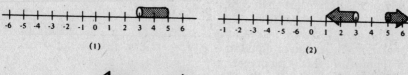

(1)

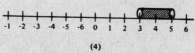

(2)

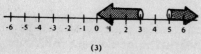

(3)

(4)

3.  The inequality $2x > x + 3$ is equivalent to

(1)  $x > 1$     (2)  $x > \dfrac{3}{2}$     (3)  $x = 3$     (4)  $x > 3$

4.  What are the numbers in the solution set of $4 \leq x < 7$ if $x$ is an integer?
(1)  5,6     (2)  5,6,7     (3)  4,5,6     (4)  4,5,6,7

5.  The inequality $2x + 5 > x + 3$ is equivalent to
(1)  $x > -2$     (2)  $x > 2$     (3)  $x > 8$     (4)  $x > 4$

6.  Given the replacement set $\{5,6,7,8\}$. Which member of the replacement set will make the statement $(x < 6) \vee (x < 8)$ false?

### Solutions to Questions on Inequalities

1.  The graph shows an inequality extending from $-2$ to $+1$. The heavy, shaded circle at $-2$ indicates that $-2$ is included, that is, that the inequality represents some numbers greater than or equal to $-2$. The unshaded, open circle

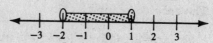

at $+1$ indicates that $+1$ is not included, that is, that the inequality represents some numbers less than $+1$, but not including $+1$. The inequality is therefore $-2 \leq x < 1$.

The correct choice is **(3)**.

2.  $(x < 3) \lor (x \geq 5)$ stands for the set of values of $x$ for which $x$ is either less than 3 or greater than or equal to 5.

Choice (1) shows $x$ greater than 3 and less than or equal to 5. Therefore, this is incorrect.

Choice (2) shows $x$ less than 3 (the darkened line extending to the left of 3) or $x$ greater than or equal to 5 (the darkened line extending to the right of 5 and including 5). This is the correct choice.

Choice (3) shows $x$ less than 3 or $x$ greater than 5. The open circle at $x = 5$ denotes the fact that $x = 5$ is *not* included. Therefore, this choice is incorrect.

Choice (4) shows $x$ greater than 3 and less than 5. Therefore, this choice is incorrect.

The correct choice is **(2)**.

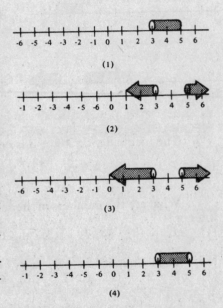

3.

$$2x > x + 3$$

Add $-x$ (the additive inverse of $x$) to both sides of the inequality:

$$-x = -x$$
$$x > \phantom{0}3$$

The correct choice is **(4)**.

4.  $4 \leq x < 7$          $x$ is an integer

The given relationship means that $x$ is greater than or equal to 4 but less than 7.

The only set of integers that fits these requirements is {4,5,6}. The correct choice is (3).

**5.**

$$2x + 5 > x + 3$$

Add $-5$ (the additive inverse of 5) and also add $-x$ (the additive inverse of $x$) to both sides of the inequality:

$$\frac{-x - 5 = -x - 5}{x \quad > \quad -2}$$

The correct choice is (1).

**6.** $(x < 6) \vee (x < 8)$ is the *disjunction* of $(x < 6)$ and $(x < 8)$. The disjunction is true if either $(x < 6)$ or $(x < 8)$ or both are true. Hence, it is false if neither $(x < 6)$ nor $(x < 8)$ is true.

Consider the elements in the replacement set {5,6,7,8}. $(x < 6)$ is false if $x = 6$, 7, or 8. $(x < 8)$ is false if $x = 8$. Hence, both $(x < 6)$ and $(x < 8)$ are false if $x = 8$. Thus, $(x < 6) \vee (x < 8)$ is false if $x = 8$.
8 will make it false.

## 11. QUESTIONS ON SYSTEMS OF EQUATIONS AND INEQUALITIES (ALGEBRAIC AND GRAPHICAL SOLUTIONS)

**1.** Solve for $x$:    $x + y = 7$
$2x - y = 2$

**2.** Which ordered pair is the solution to the following system of equations?

$$3x + 2y = 4$$
$$-2x + 2y = 24$$

(1) $(2,-1)$     (2) $(-4,8)$     (3) $(-4,-8)$     (4) $(2,-5)$

**3.** Solve algebraically for $x$ and $y$ and check:

$$2x + y = 6$$
$$x = 3y + 10$$

**4.** Solve graphically and check:

$$y = x - 3$$
$$2x + y = 3$$

**5.**   a.   On the same set of coordinate axes, graph the following system of inequalities:

$$y > x + 4$$
$$x + y \leq 2$$

b.   Which point is in the solution set of the graph drawn in answer to part a?

(1)  (2,3)     (2)  (−5,2)     (3)  (0,6)
(4)  (−1,0)

6.   On the same set of coordinate axes, graph the following system of inequalities and label the solution set A:

$$2y \geq x - 4$$
$$y < 3x$$

**Solutions to Questions on Systems of Equations and Inequalities (algebraic and graphical solutions)**

1.

Adding the two equations together will eliminate $y$:

Multiply both sides by $\dfrac{1}{3}$ (the multiplicative inverse of 3):

$$x + y = 7$$
$$2x - y = 2$$
$$\overline{\phantom{xxx}3x \phantom{xxx} = 9}$$
$$\frac{1}{3}(3x) = \frac{1}{3}(9)$$
$$x = 3$$

The solution for $x$ is **3**.

2.                              $3x + 2y = 4$
                               $-2x + 2y = 24$

Subtracting the second equation from the first will eliminate $y$.

To subtract, change the signs of each term in the equation being subtracted and proceed as in addition:

$$3x + 2y = 4$$
$$+ \quad - \quad -$$
$$\underline{\ominus 2x \oplus 2y = \oplus 24}$$
$$5x \phantom{xxx} = -20$$

Multiply both sides by $\dfrac{1}{5}$ (the multiplicative inverse of 5):

$$\frac{1}{5}(5x) = \frac{1}{5}(-20)$$
$$x = -4$$

Substitute $-4$ for $x$ in the first equation:

$$3x + 2y = 4$$
$$3(-4) + 2y = 4$$
$$-12 + 2y = 4$$

Add 12 (the additive inverse of $-12$) to both sides of the equation:

$$\underline{12 \phantom{xxx} = 12}$$
$$2y = 16$$

Multiply both sides by $\frac{1}{2}$ (the multiplicative inverse of 2):

$$\frac{1}{2}(2y) = \frac{1}{2}(16)$$
$$y = 8$$

The solution to the system is $x = -4$, $y = 8$ or $(-4,8)$.
The correct choice is (2).

ALTERNATIVE SOLUTION:   The correct ordered pair may be found by trying each of the four choices in turn. The values of $x$ and $y$ from each choice would have to be substituted in *both* equations; the correct ordered pair must satisfy *both* equations. Note that this procedure might require 8 testings (the 4 choices tried in each of the two equations).

3.
$$2x + y = 6$$
$$x = 3y + 10$$

Rearrange the second equation by adding $-3y$ (the additive inverse of $3y$) to both sides:

$$x = 3y + 10$$
$$\underline{-3y = -3y}$$
$$x - 3y = 10$$

Multiply each term in the first equation by 3:  $6x + 3y = 18$
Add the new form of the second equation, thus eliminating $y$:

$$\underline{x - 3y = 10}$$
$$7x \qquad = 28$$

Multiply both sides by $\frac{1}{7}$ (the multiplicative inverse of 7):

$$\frac{1}{7}(7x) = \frac{1}{7}(28)$$

$$x = 4$$

Substitute 4 for $x$ in the first equation:    $2(4) + y = 6$
$$8 + y = 6$$

Add $-8$ (the additive inverse of 8) to both sides:

$$\underline{-8 \qquad = -8}$$
$$y = -2$$

The solution is $x = 4$, $y = -2$.
CHECK:   Substitute 4 for $x$ and $-2$ for $y$ in both original equations to see if they are satisfied:

$$2x + y = 6 \qquad\qquad x = 3y + 10$$
$$2(4) - 2 \overset{?}{=} 6 \qquad\qquad 4 \overset{?}{=} 3(-2) + 10$$
$$8 - 2 \overset{?}{=} 6 \qquad\qquad 4 \overset{?}{=} -6 + 10$$
$$6 = 6 \checkmark \qquad\qquad 4 = 4 \checkmark$$

4.                           $y = x + 3$
                              $2x + y = 3$

To solve graphically, the graphs of both equations are drawn on the same set of axes. The coordinates of the point of intersection of the two graphs represent the solution to the system.

STEP 1:    Draw the graph of $y = x + 3$. Set up a table of values by choosing 3 convenient values for $x$ and substituting them in the equation to find the corresponding values of $y$:

| $x$ | $x + 3$ | $= y$ |
|-----|---------|-------|
| 0 | $0 + 3$ | $= 3$ |
| 3 | $3 + 3$ | $= 6$ |
| $-3$ | $-3 + 3$ | $= 0$ |

Plot the points $(0,3)$, $(3,6)$, and $(-3,0)$. They should lie on a straight line. Draw this line; it is the graph of $y = x + 3$.

STEP 2:    Draw the graph of $2x + y = 3$. To do this, it is advisable to first rearrange the equation so that it is in a form in which it is solved for $y$ in terms of $x$:

$$2x + y = 3$$

Add $-2x$ (the additive inverse of $2x$) to both sides:

$$\frac{-2x \qquad = \quad -2x}{y = 3 - 2x}$$

Set up a table of values by choosing 3 convenient values for $x$ and substituting them in the equation to find the corresponding values of $y$:

| $x$ | $3 - 2x$ | $= y$ |
|-----|----------|-------|
| 0 | $3 - 2(0) = 3 - 0$ | $= 3$ |
| 3 | $3 - 2(3) = 3 - 6$ | $= -3$ |
| $-3$ | $3 - 2(-3) = 3 + 6$ | $= 9$ |

Plot the points $(0,3)$, $(3,-3)$, and $(-3,9)$. They should lie in a straight line. Draw a line through them; this line is the graph of $2x + y = 3$.

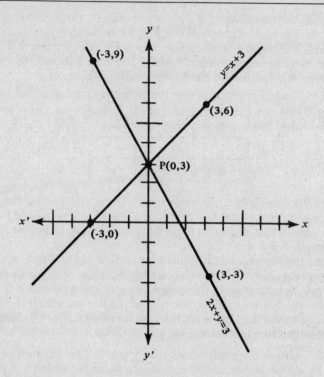

STEP 3: The common solution is represented by $P$, the point of intersection of the two graphs. The coordinates of $P$ are $(0,3)$ or $x = 0$ and $y = 3$.

The solution to the system is $x = 0$, $y = 3$ or $\{(0,3)\}$.

CHECK: The solution is checked by substituting 0 for $x$ and 3 for $y$ in *both* of the two *original* equations to see if they are satisfied:

$$
\begin{array}{ll}
y = x + 3 & 2x + y = 3 \\
3 \overset{?}{=} 0 + 3 & 2(0) + 3 \overset{?}{=} 3 \\
3 = 3 \checkmark & 0 + 3 \overset{?}{=} 3 \\
& 3 = 3 \checkmark
\end{array}
$$

5.    a.    $y > x + 4$
          $x + y \leq 2$

STEP 1: Graph the solution set of the inequality $y > x + 4$. The graph of the inequality $y > x + 4$ is represented by all the points on the coordinate plane for which $y$, the ordinate, is greater than $x + 4$. Hence, first draw the graph of the line for which $y = x + 4$; having this graph will permit locating the region for which $y > x + 4$.

Select any three convenient values for $x$ and substitute in the equation $y = x + 4$ to find the corresponding values of $y$:

| $x$ | $x + 4$ | $= y$ |
|:---:|:---:|:---:|
| 0 | $0 + 4$ | $= 4$ |
| 3 | $3 + 4$ | $= 7$ |
| $-4$ | $-4 + 4$ | $= 0$ |

Plot the points $(0,4)$, $(3,7)$, and $(-4,0)$. Draw a *dotted line* through these three points to get the graph of $y = x + 4$. The dotted line is used to signify that points on it are *not* part of the solution set of the inequality $y > x + 4$.

To find the *region* or *half-plane* on one side of the line $y = x + 4$ which represents $y > x + 4$, select a test point, say $(1,8)$, on one side of the line. Substituting in the inequality $y > x + 4$ gives $8 > 1 + 4$, or $8 > 5$, which is true. Thus, the side of the line on which $(1,8)$ lies (above and to the left) is the region representing $y > x + 4$. Shade it with cross-hatching extending up and to the left.

STEP 2: Graph the solution set of $x + y \leq 2$. This graph is represented by all the points on the coordinate plane for which $x + y < 2$ in addition to those points on the line for which $x + y = 2$. Hence, the line $x + y = 2$ is first graphed. To make it convenient to find points on the line, solve for $y$ in terms of $x$:

$$x + y = 2$$

Add $-x$ (the additive inverse of $x$) to both sides of the equation:

$$\frac{-x \qquad = -x}{y = 2 - x}$$

Set up a table by selecting any three convenient values for $x$ and substituting in the equation $y = 2 - x$ to find the corresponding values of $y$:

| $x$ | $2 - x$ | $= y$ |
|:---:|:---:|:---:|
| 0 | $2 - 0$ | $= 2$ |
| 3 | $2 - 3$ | $= -1$ |
| 5 | $2 - 5$ | $= -3$ |

Plot the points $(0,2)$, $(3,-1)$, and $(5,-3)$. Draw a *solid line* through these three points to get the graph of $x + y = 2$. The solid line is used to signify that points on it are part of the solution set of $x + y \leq 2$.

To find the *region* or *half-plane* on one side of the line $x + y = 2$ for which $x + y < 2$, select a test point, say $(-2,-1)$ on one side of the line. Substituting $(-2,-1)$ in the inequality $x + y < 2$ results in $-2 - 1 < 2$, or $-3 < 2$, which is true. Thus, the side of the line where $(-2,-1)$ is located (below and to the left) is the region representing $x + y < 2$. Shade this region with cross-hatching extending down and to the left.

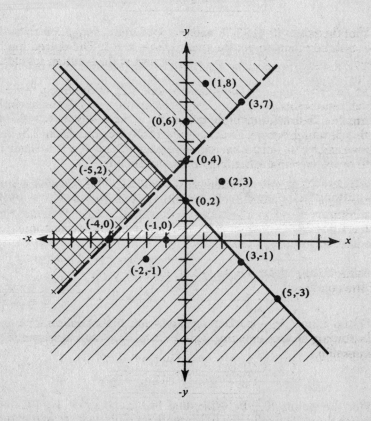

b.   If a point is in the solution set, it will lie in the region in which the graph shows *both* sets of cross-hatching; points in this region

satisfy *both* inequalities. Test each point in turn by locating it on the graph:
(1)　(2,3) does not lie in the cross-hatched area at all.
(2)　(−5,2) lies in the region with both sets of cross-hatching. Therefore, it is in the solution set of the graph.
(3)　(0,6) lies in a region cross-hatched only for $y > x + 4$; it satisfies this inequality but not the other.
(4)　(−1,0) lies in a region cross-hatched only for $x + y \leq 2$; it satisfies this inequality but not the other one.

The only point in the solution set of the graph is (−5,2).

6.　$2y \geq x - 4$
　　$y < 3x$

To find the solution set, both inequalities are represented on the same set of coordinate axes. Each will be represented by a region on the plane; the solution set is the overlapping portion of the two regions.

STEP 1:　To draw the graph of $2y \geq x - 4$, first draw the graph of the equation $2y = x - 4$.

Solve the equation for $y$ by dividing by 2: $y = \dfrac{1}{2} x - 2$.

Set up a table of values by choosing 3 convenient values for $x$ and substituting in the equation to find the corresponding values of $y$:

| $x$ | $\dfrac{1}{2} x - 2$ | $= y$ |
|---|---|---|
| 0 | $\dfrac{1}{2}(0) - 2 = 0 - 2$ | $= -2$ |
| 4 | $\dfrac{1}{2}(4) - 2 = 2 - 2$ | $= 0$ |
| 6 | $\dfrac{1}{2}(6) - 2 = 3 - 2$ | $= 1$ |

Plot the points (0,−2), (4,0), and (6,1), and draw a *solid* line through them. The solid line indicates that points on it are part of the solution set of $2y \geq x - 4$; in fact, they constitute the part repre-sented by $2y = x - 4$.

Now the points on the graph represented by $2y > x - 4$ must be indicated. Points that satisfy the inequality occupy an entire region on one side of the line $2y = x - 4$. Such a region is called a *half-plane*. To find which side of the line represents the half-plane $2y > x - 4$, select a test point, say $(2,2)$. Substituting in the inequality gives:

$$2(2) \overset{?}{>} 2 - 4$$
$$4 > -2 \text{ which is true.}$$

Therefore, $(2,2)$ lies within the region for which $2y > x - 4$. This region is shaded with cross-hatching extending up and to the right.

STEP 2:  To draw the graph of $y < 3x$, first draw the graph of the equation $y = 3x$.

Set up a table of values by choosing 3 convenient values for $x$ and substituting in the equation to find the corresponding values of $y$:

| $x$ | $3x$ | $= y$ |
|---|---|---|
| 0 | 3(0) | = 0 |
| 2 | 3(2) | = 6 |
| 3 | 3(3) | = 9 |

Plot the points $(0,0)$, $(2,6)$, and $(3,9)$. Draw a *dotted* line through these points; the dotted line indicates that points on it are *not* part of the graph of $y < 3x$ (the line is actually the graph of $y = 3x$). Now it must be determined on which side of the line $y = 3x$ the points lie which represent the graph of $y < 3x$. Select a test point on one side, say the point $(2,2)$. Substituting in the inequality $y < 3x$ gives:

$$2 \overset{?}{<} 3(2)$$
$$2 < 6 \text{ which is true.}$$

Therefore, $(2,2)$ lies within the region for which $y < 3x$. This re-gion is shaded with cross-hatching extending down and to the right.

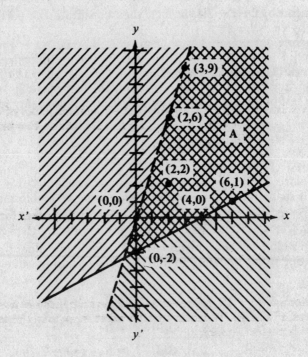

STEP 3: The solution set of the system of inequalities is the region covered by both sets of cross-hatching, including the solid line along one boundary; this region is labeled **A**.

## 12. QUESTIONS ON FACTORING

1. Factor: $x^2 - 7x$

2. Factor: $x^2 - 5x$

3. Factor: $x^2 - 49$

4. Factor: $x^2 - 36$

5. Factor: $x^2 + x - 30$

6. Factor: $x^2 + 5x - 14$

## Solutions to Questions on Factoring

1. $x^2 - 7x$

The two terms in the given binomial have a *common factor* of $x$. The other factor is obtained by dividing $x$ into each of the two original terms, yielding $x - 7$.

Therefore: $\qquad\qquad x^2 - 7x = x(x - 7)$

The factored form is $x(x - 7)$.

2. $x^2 - 5x$

$x^2$ and $5x$ contain a *highest common factor* of $x$. The other factor is determined by applying the distributive law, dividing each of $x^2$ and $-5x$ in turn by $x$: $\qquad\qquad x(x - 5)$

The factored form is $x(x - 5)$.

3. $x^2 - 49$

The binomial, $x^2 - 49$, represents the *difference between two perfect squares*, $x^2$ and 49. To factor such an expression, take the square root of each perfect square:

$$\sqrt{x^2} = x \qquad\qquad \text{and} \qquad\qquad \sqrt{49} = 7$$

One factor will be the sum of the respective square roots and the other factor will be the difference of the square roots:

$x^2 - 49 = (x + 7)(x - 7)$

The correct answer is $(x + 7)(x - 7)$.

4. $x^2 - 36$

The binomial, $x^2 - 36$, represents the *difference between two perfect squares*, $x^2$ and 36. Take the square root of each perfect square:

$$\sqrt{x^2} = x \qquad\qquad \text{and} \qquad\qquad \sqrt{36} = 6$$

One factor is the sum of the respective square roots and the other factor is the difference of the square roots: $\qquad (x + 6)(x - 6)$

The correct answer is $(x + 6)(x - 6)$.

5. The given expression is a *quadratic trinomial*:

$\qquad\qquad\qquad x^2 + x - 30$

The factors of a quadratic trinomial are two binomials.

The factors of the first term, $x^2$, are $x$ and $x$, and they become the first terms of the binomials:

$(x \quad )(x \quad )$

The factors of the last term, $-30$, become the second terms of the binomials but they must be chosen in such a way that the product of the inner terms and the product of the outer terms add up to the middle term, $+x$, of the original trinomial. Try $+6$ and $-5$ as the factors of $-30$:

$+6x =$ inner product

$(x + 6)(x - 5)$

$-5x =$ outer product

Since $+6x$ and $-5x$ add up to $+x$, these are the correct factors:

$(x + 6)(x - 5)$

The factored form is $(x + 6)(x - 5)$.

**6.** The given expression is a *quadratic trinomial:*

$x^2 + 5x - 14$

The factors of a quadratic trinomial are two binomials. The first terms of the binomials are the factors of the first term, $x^2$, of the trinomial:

$(x \quad )(x \quad )$

The second terms of the binomials are the factors of the last term, $-14$, of the trinomial. These factors must be chosen in such a way that the sum of the product of the inner terms and the product of the outer terms is equal to the middle term, $+5x$, of the original trinomial. $-14$ has factors of 14 and $-1$, $-14$ and 1, $+7$ and $-2$, and $-7$ and $+2$. Try $+7$ and $-2$:

$+7x =$ inner product

$(x + 7)(x - 2)$

$-2x =$ outer product

Since $(+7x) + (-2x) = +5x$, these are the correct factors:

$(x + 7)(x - 2)$

The factored form is $(x + 7)(x - 2)$.

## 13. QUESTIONS ON QUADRATIC EQUATIONS

1. The solution set of the equation $x^2 - 3x = 0$ is
(1) $\{3\}$    (2) $\{-3\}$    (3) $\{3,-3\}$    (4) $\{0,3\}$

**2.** The solution set of $x^2 - x - 6 = 0$ is
(1) $\{1, -6\}$     (2) $\{-3, 2\}$     (3) $\{3, -2\}$     (4) $\{5, 1\}$

**3.** The solution set of the equation $x^2 - 7x + 10 = 0$ is
(1) $\{2, 5\}$     (2) $\{2, -5\}$     (3) $\{-2, 5\}$     (4) $\{-2, -5\}$

**4.** The solution set of the equation $x^2 - 2x - 3 = 0$ is
(1) $\{-1, -2\}$     (2) $\{-2, -3\}$     (3) $\{-1, 3\}$     (4) $\{1, -3\}$

**5.** What is the solution set for the equation $x^2 + 2x - 15 = 0$?
(1) $\{3, -5\}$     (2) $\{3, 5\}$     (3) $\{-3, -5\}$     (4) $\{-3, 5\}$

**6.** Which is a root of the equation $x^2 = 3x + 10$?
(1) $-1$     (2) $2$     (3) $5$     (4) $4$

## Solutions to Questions on Quadratic Equations

**1.** The solution set consists of those values of $x$ which satisfy the equation. To find the solution set, solve the equation:

$$x^2 - 3x = 0$$

Factor the left side:

$$x(x - 3) = 0$$

When the product of two factors is 0, either one, or both, must be 0:

$$x = 0 \ or \ x - 3 = 0$$

Solve the right equation by adding 3 (the additive inverse of $-3$) to both sides:

$$\frac{3 = 3}{x = 3}$$

The solution set is $\{0, 3\}$.
The correct choice is **(4)**.

**2.** $x^2 - x - 6 = 0$
The solution set is found by solving the equation. This is a *quadratic equation* which can be solved by factoring. The left side is a *quadratic trinomial* which can be factored into two binomials.

$$x^2 - x - 6 = 0$$

STEP 1: The factors of the first term, $x^2$, are $x$ and $x$, and they constitute the first terms of each binomial factor:

$$(x \quad )(x \quad ) = 0$$

STEP 2: The last term, $-6$, must be factored into two factors which will be the second terms of the binomials. The factors must be chosen in such a way that the product of the two inner terms added to the product of the two outer terms equals the

middle term of the original trinomial. Try
$-6 = (-3)(+2)$:

$-3x =$ inner product

$(x - 3)(x + 2) = 0$

$+2x =$ outer product

The sum of the inner and outer products is $-3x + 2x$ or $-x$, which is equal to the middle term of the original trinomial; thus, the correct factors have been chosen and the equation can be written as:

$(x - 3)(x + 2) = 0$

Since the product of two factors is zero, either factor may be equal to zero:

$x - 3 = 0$ or $x + 2 = 0$

Add the appropriate additive inverse to both sides, $+3$ in the case of the left equation and $-2$ in the case of the right one:

$$\frac{3 = 3}{x = 3} \qquad \frac{-2 = -2}{x = -2}$$

Thus, the solution set is $\{3, -2\}$.
The correct choice is **(3)**.

3. The given equation is a *quadratic equation*:

$x^2 - 7x + 10 = 0$

The left side is a *quadratic trinomial* which can be factored into the product of two binomials. The factors of the first term, $x^2$, are $x$ and $x$, and they become the first terms of the binomials:

$(x \qquad)(x \qquad) = 0$

A pair of factors of the last term, $+10$, become the second terms of the binomials. $+10$ has several pairs of factors; the pair chosen must be such that the sum of the product of the inner terms and the product of the outer terms equals the middle term, $-7x$, of the original trinomial. Try $-5$ and $-2$ as the factors of $+10$:

$-5x =$ inner product

$(x - 5)(x - 2) = 0$

$-2x =$ outer product

Since $(-5x) + (-2x) = -7x$, these are the correct factors:

$(x - 5)(x - 2) = 0$

If the product of two factors is 0, either factor may equal 0:

$x - 5 = 0$ or $x - 2 = 0$

Add the appropriate additive inverse to both sides of the equation, 5 in the case of the left equation and 2 in the case of the right equation:

$$5 = 5 \qquad 2 = 2$$
$$x \qquad = 5 \qquad x \qquad = 2$$

The solution set of the equation is $\{2,5\}$.
The correct choice is (1).
ALTERNATIVE SOLUTION:   The question may also be solved by substituting each pair of numbers from the four choices to see which has two roots both of which satisfy the equation.

4.   The given equation is a *quadratic equation*:

$$x^2 - 2x - 3 = 0$$

Factor the *quadratic trinomial* on the left side. It factors into the product of two binomials. In choosing the factors check to see that the product of the inner terms of the binomials added to the product of the outer terms equals the middle term, $-2x$, of the original trinomial:

$$-3x = \text{inner product}$$
$$(x - 3)(x + 1) = 0$$
$$+x = \text{outer product}$$

Since $(-3x) + (+x)$ add up to $-2x$, these are the correct factors:

$$(x - 3)(x + 1) = 0$$

If the product of two factors equals 0, either factor may equal 0:

$$x - 3 = 0 \; or \; x + 1 = 0$$

Add the appropriate additive inverse to both sides of the equation, 3 in the case of the left equation and $-1$ in the case of the right equation:

$$3 = 3 \qquad -1 = -1$$
$$x \qquad = 3 \qquad x \qquad = -1$$

The solution set is $\{-1,3\}$.
The correct choice is (3).

5.   The given equation is a *quadratic equation*:

$$x^2 + 2x - 15 = 0$$

The *quadratic trinomial* on the left side can be factored into the product of two binomials. In choosing the factors, check to see that the sum of the product of the inner terms of the binomials and the product of the outer terms equals the middle term, $+2x$, of the original trinomial:

$+5x =$ inner product

$(x + 5)(x - 3) = 0$

$-3x =$ outer product

Since $(+5x) + (-3x) = 2x$, these are the correct factors:

$(x + 5)(x - 3) = 0$

If the product of two factors is zero, either factor may equal zero:

$x + 5 = 0 \ or \ x - 3 = 0$

Add the appropriate additive inverse to both sides of the equation, $-5$ in the case of the left equation and $3$ in the case of the right equation:

$$\frac{-5 = -5}{x \quad = -5} \qquad \frac{3 = 3}{x \quad = 3}$$

The solution set is $\{-5, 3\}$.
The correct choice is (**1**).

**6.** $\hspace{5cm} x^2 = 3x + 10$

If a number is a root of an equation it must satisfy the equation when substituted for $x$. Try each of the choices in turn:

(1) $\ -1$: $\ (-1)^2 \overset{?}{=} 3(-1) + 10$
$\hspace{2.5cm} 1 \overset{?}{=} -3 + 10$
$\hspace{2.5cm} 1 \neq 7$
$\hspace{2cm} -1$ is not a root.

(2) $\ 2$: $\ (2)^2 \overset{?}{=} 3(2) + 10$
$\hspace{2.3cm} 4 \overset{?}{=} 6 + 10$
$\hspace{2.3cm} 4 \neq 16$
$\hspace{2cm} 2$ is not a root.

(3) $\hspace{0.5cm} 5$: $\ (5)^2 \overset{?}{=} 3(5) + 10$
$\hspace{2.5cm} 25 \overset{?}{=} 15 + 10$
$\hspace{2.5cm} 25 = 25 \checkmark$
$\hspace{2.2cm} 5$ is a root.

(4) $\ 4$: $\ (4)^2 \overset{?}{=} 3(4) + 10$
$\hspace{2.3cm} 16 \overset{?}{=} 12 + 10$
$\hspace{2.3cm} 16 \neq 22$
$\hspace{2cm} 4$ is not a root.

The correct choice is (**3**).

ALTERNATIVE SOLUTION: Since $x^2 = 3x + 10$ is a *quadratic equation* it may be solved by factoring. The equation will first have to be rearranged into the form $x^2 - 3x - 10 = 0$ with all terms on one side equal to 0 on the other side. The left side can then be factored. A solution by factoring will yield two roots, one of which should be among the four choices.

## 14. QUESTIONS ON VERBAL PROBLEMS

1. If 19 is subtracted from three times a certain number, the difference is 110. What is the number?

2. The sum of the squares of two positive consecutive odd in-

tegers is 74. What are the integers? [*Only an algebraic solution will be accepted.*]

**3.** Find three consecutive positive odd integers such that the square of the smallest exceeds twice the largest by 7. [*Only an algebraic solution will be accepted.*]

**4.** The length of a rectangle is 1 centimeter less than twice the width. If the perimeter of the rectangle is 76 centimeters, find the number of centimeters in *each* dimension of the rectangle. [*Only an algebraic solution will be accepted.*]

**5.** In triangle *ABC*, angle A is 30° more than angle B. Angle C equals the sum of angle A and angle B. Find the measures of *each* of the three angles. [*Only an algebraic solution will be accepted.*]

**6.** The measure of the base of a parallelogram is 4 meters greater than the measure of the altitude to that base. If the area of the parallelogram is 32 square meters, find the number of meters in the measures of the base and altitude.

## Solutions to Questions on Verbal Problems

**1.** Let $x$ = the number.
Three times a certain number minus 19 is 110.

$$3x \qquad - \quad 19 = 110$$

The equation to be used is:                              $3x - 19 = 110$
Add 19 (the additive inverse of $-19$) to both
sides of the equation:

$$\underline{\phantom{3x} \qquad 19 = 19}$$
$$3x \qquad = 129$$

Multiply both sides by $\dfrac{1}{3}$ (the multiplicative
inverse of 3):

$$\frac{1}{3}(3x) \; = \frac{1}{3}(129)$$

$$x = 43$$

The number is **43**.

**2.** Let $x$ = the first positive odd integer.
Then $x + 2$ = the next consecutive odd integer.
The square of one plus the square of the other is 74.

$$x^2 \qquad + \qquad (x + 2)^2 \qquad = 74$$

The equation to be used is:

$$x^2 + (x+2)^2 = 74$$

Multiply out $(x+2)^2$:

$$
\begin{array}{r}
x + 2 \\
x + 2 \\
\hline
x^2 + 2x \\
2x + 4 \\
\hline
x^2 + 4x + 4
\end{array}
$$

Replace $(x+2)^2$ in the equation by its expanded value:

$$x^2 + x^2 + 4x + 4 = 74$$

Combine like terms:

$$2x^2 + 4x + 4 = 74$$

Add $-74$ (the additive inverse of 74) to both sides:

$$
\begin{array}{r}
-74 = -74 \\
\hline
2x^2 + 4x - 70 = 0
\end{array}
$$

Divide each term on both sides by 2:

$$x^2 + 2x - 35 = 0$$

The left side is a *quadratic trinomial* which can be factored into 2 binomials. The factors of the first term, $x^2$, are $x$ and $x$, and they represent the first terms of each binomial factor:

$$(x\quad)(x\quad) = 0$$

The factors of the last term, $-35$, must be chosen in such a way that the product of the 2 outer terms of the binomials added to the product of the 2 inner terms equals the middle term, $2x$, of the trinomial. Try $-35 = (+7)(-5)$:

$$-5x = \text{outer product}$$
$$(x + 7)(x - 5) = 0$$
$$7x = \text{inner product}$$

This factoring is correct since $(-5x) + (7x) = 2x$.

Since the product of two factors is zero, either one or both of the factors must be zero:

$$x + 7 = 0 \; or \; x - 5 = 0$$

Add the appropriate additive inverse to each side, $-7$ in the case of the left equation, and $+5$ in the case of the right:

$$
\begin{array}{cc}
\begin{array}{r} -7 = -7 \\ \hline x = -7 \end{array} &
\begin{array}{r} 5 = 5 \\ \hline x = 5 \end{array}
\end{array}
$$

Reject $-7$ since the question calls for a *positive* number:

$$x = 5$$
$$x + 2 = 7$$

The integers are **5** and **7**.

3. An example of consecutive odd integers is 5, 7, 9, . . . . Each consecutive odd integer can be obtained by adding 2 to the previous odd integer.

Let $n$ = first odd integer.
Then $n + 2$ = second consecutive odd integer.
And $n + 4$ = third consecutive odd integer.
The square of the smallest equals twice the largest plus 7.

$$n^2 \qquad = \qquad 2(n + 4) \qquad + 7$$

The equation to be used is:

$$n^2 = 2(n + 4) + 7$$

Remove parentheses by using the distributive property:

$$n^2 = 2n + 8 + 7$$

Combine like terms:

$$n^2 = 2n + 15$$

Add $-2n$ (the additive inverse of $2n$) and also add $-15$ (the additive inverse of 15) to both sides:

$$\frac{-2n - 15 = -2n - 15}{n^2 - 2n - 15 = 0}$$

This is a *quadratic equation* which can be solved by factoring. The left side is a quadratic trinomial. Its factors are two binomials. The factors of the first term, $n^2$, are $n$ and $n$, and they become the first terms of each binomial factor:

$$(n \quad )(n \quad ) = 0$$

The factors of the last term, $-15$, become the other terms of the two binomials. The factors of $-15$ must be selected in such a way that the inner product of the binomial terms added to the outer product equals the middle term, $-2n$, of the trinomial. Try $-15 = (-5)(+3)$:

$$-5n = \text{inner product}$$
$$(n - 5)(n + 3) = 0$$
$$+3n = \text{outer product}$$

Since $(-5n) + (+3n) = -2n$, these are the correct factors.

Since the product of two factors is zero, either factor may be equal to zero:

$$n - 5 = 0 \text{ or } n + 3 = 0$$

Add the appropriate additive inverse to both sides, $+5$ in the case of the left equation and $-3$ in the case of the right:

$$\frac{5 = 5}{n = 5} \qquad \frac{-3 = -3}{n = -3}$$

$-3$ must be rejected since the problem requires *positive* integers. If $n = 5$, then $n + 2 = 7$, and $n + 4 = 9$.

The three consecutive odd integers are 5, 7, and 9.

4.   Let $x$ = the width of the rectangle in centimeters.
Then $2x - 1$ = the length of the rectangle in centimeters.
The perimeter of a rectangle is equal to the sum of the four sides.
Since the opposite sides of a rectangle are equal, the perimeter is
twice the width plus twice the length, or $P = 2W + 2L$

In this case, $P = 76$, $W = x$, and $L = 2x - 1$. Therefore, the equation to be used is:

$$2(x) + 2(2x - 1) = 76$$

Remove parentheses by applying the
distributive law:

$$2x + 4x - 2 = 76$$

Combine like terms:

$$6x - 2 = 76$$

Add 2 (the additive inverse of $-2$) to
both sides:

$$\underline{\qquad\qquad 2 = 2}$$
$$6x = 78$$

Multiply both sides by $\dfrac{1}{6}$ (the multiplicative inverse of 6):

$$\frac{1}{6}(6x) = \frac{1}{6}(78)$$

$$x = 13$$
$$2x - 1 = 25$$

The width is **13** centimeters; the
length is **25** centimeters.

5.   Let $x$ = the measure in degrees of $\measuredangle B$.
Then $x + 30$ = the measure in degrees of
$\measuredangle A$.
And $2x + 30$ = the measure in degrees of
$\measuredangle C$.

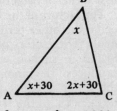

The sum of the measure of the three angles of a triangle is $180°$.
Therefore, the equation to be used is:

$$x + x + 30 + 2x + 30 = 180$$

Combine like terms:

$$4x + 60 = 180$$

Add $-60$ (the additive inverse
of 60) to both sides:

$$\underline{-60 = -60}$$
$$4x = 120$$

Multiply both sides by $\dfrac{1}{4}$ (the
multiplicative inverse of 4):

$$\frac{1}{4}(4x) = \frac{1}{4}(120)$$

$$x = 30 \ (\measuredangle B)$$
$$x + 30 = 60 \ (\measuredangle A)$$
$$2x + 30 = 90 \ (\measuredangle C)$$

$\measuredangle A = 60°$, $\measuredangle B = 30°$,
$\measuredangle C = 90°$.

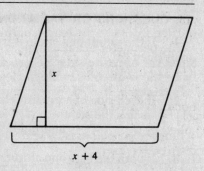

**6.** Let $x$ = the measure of the altitude.

Then $x + 4$ = the measure of the base.

The area of a parallelogram is equal to the product of the measure of the base and the measure of the altitude to that base:

$$x(x + 4) = 32$$

Remove parentheses by applying the distributive law of multiplication over addition:

$$x^2 + 4x = 32$$

The equation is a *quadratic equation*. Rearrange it so that all terms are on one side equal to zero by adding $-32$ (the additive inverse of 32) to both sides:

$$\frac{-32 = -32}{x^2 + 4x - 32 = 0}$$

The left side is a *quadratic trinomial* which can be factored into the product of two binomials. Be sure to check that the sum of the product of the inner terms of the binomials and the product of the outer terms equals the middle term, $+4x$, of the original trinomial:

$+8x$ = inner product

$$(x + 8)(x - 4) = 0$$

$-4x$ = outer product

Since $(+8x) + (-4x) = +4x$ these are the correct factors:

$$(x + 8)(x - 4) = 0$$

If the product of two factors equals zero, either factor may equal zero:

$$x + 8 = 0 \ or \ x - 4 = 0$$

Add the appropriate additive inverse to both sides of the equation, $-8$ in the case of the left equation and 4 in the case of the right equation:

$$\frac{-8 = -8}{x = -8} \qquad \frac{4 = 4}{x = 4}$$

Reject the negative value as meaningless for a length:

$$x = 4$$
$$x + 4 = 8$$

The measure of the altitude is 4 meters and the measure of the base is 8 meters.

## 15. QUESTIONS ON VARIATION

1.   If the radius of a circle is tripled, then the area of the circle is multiplied by
(1)  27      (2)  9      (3)  3      (4)  6

2.   If each side of a square is tripled, the perimeter of the square
(1)  remains the same      (2)  is increased by 3      (3)  is multiplied by 3      (4)  is multiplied by 9

3.   If both the base and altitude of a triangle are doubled, the area of the triangle will be multiplied by

(1)  $\dfrac{1}{2}$      (2)  2      (3)  $\dfrac{1}{4}$      (4)  4

4.   The area of a triangle is $\dfrac{1}{2} bh$. If the base of the triangle is doubled and the height of the triangle is multiplied by 3, then the area is
(1)  multiplied by 6      (2)  multiplied by 3      (3)  increased by 6      (4)  increased by 3

5.   If each side of a square is doubled, then its area
(1)  is doubled      (2)  is multiplied by 4      (3)  is halved
(4)  stays the same

### Solutions to Questions on Variation

1.   The area, $A$, of a circle is given by the formula $A = \pi r^2$, where $r$ is the length of the radius.
If the radius is tripled, then $r$ is replaced by $3r$. Calling the new area $A'$ (to distinguish it from the old area, $A$):

$$A' = \pi(3r)^2$$
$$A' = 9\pi r^2$$

The new area, $A'$, is thus 9 times as large as the old area, $A$.
The correct choice is (2).
ALTERNATIVE SOLUTION:   Choose a convenient value for the length of the radius, say $r = 2$, and use it to compute the corresponding area of the circle:

$$A = \pi r^2$$
$$A = \pi(2)^2$$
$$A = 4\pi$$

If the radius of 2 is tripled, it becomes $3 \times 2 = 6$. Now compute the area of this larger circle:

$$A' = \pi r^2$$
$$A' = \pi(6)^2$$
$$A' = 36\pi$$

Comparing the old area of $4\pi$ with the new area of $36\pi$, it is seen that the area has been multiplied by 9.

Again, the correct choice is (2).

**2.** Since all four sides of a square are equal in measure, the perimeter, $p$, of a square equals 4 times the length of one side, $s$:  $\quad p = 4s$

If the side of length $s$ is tripled, the length becomes $3s$. The perimeter, $p'$, of the enlarged square will then be given by the formula:  $\quad p' = 4(3s)$

Remove the parentheses:  $\quad p' = 12s$

$12s$ is 3 times $4s$, that is, the new perimeter, $p'$, is 3 times as large as the original perimeter, $p$.

The correct choice is (3).

ALTERNATIVE SOLUTION:  Choose a convenient value for the measure of the side of the square, say 5. Then the perimeter = $4(5)$ or 20.

If the side is tripled, its measure becomes 15. The new perimeter is $4(15)$ or 60. 60 is 3 times as large as the old perimeter, 20.

**3.** The area, $A$, of a triangle is equal to one-half the product of its base, $b$, and altitude, $h$:  $\quad A = \dfrac{1}{2}\, bh$

If the base and altitude are both doubled, the new base can be represented by $2b$ and the new altitude by $2h$. If $A'$ represents the area of the enlarged triangle, then:  $\quad A' = \dfrac{1}{2}\,(2b)(2h)$

Remove the parentheses:  $\quad A' = 2bh$

$2bh$ is 4 times $\dfrac{1}{2}\, bh$, that is, the enlarged area, $A'$, is 4 times the original area, $A$.

The correct choice is (4).

ALTERNATIVE SOLUTION:  The question may be solved by choosing arbitrary values for the base and altitude, say $b = 3$ and $h = 2$. Then, since $A = \frac{1}{2} bh$:

$$A = \frac{1}{2} (3)(2)$$

$$A = \frac{1}{2} (6)$$

$$A = 3$$

Doubling the base and altitude will make them 6 and 4 respectively. The new area, $A'$, will be:

$$A' = \frac{1}{2} (6)(4)$$

$$A' = \frac{1}{2} (24)$$

$$A' = 12$$

Since 12 is 4 times the old area, 3, the area of the triangle has been multiplied by 4.

4.   Represent the area of the original triangle by $A$:

$$A = \frac{1}{2} bh$$

If the base is doubled, the new base is $2b$. If the height is multiplied by 3, the new height is $3h$. If $A'$ represents the new area, then:

$$A' = \frac{1}{2} (2b)(3h)$$

$$A' = \frac{1}{2} (6bh)$$

$$A' = 3bh$$

$3bh$ is 6 times as large as $\frac{1}{2} bh$. Therefore, the area has been multiplied by 6.

The correct choice is (**1**).

ALTERNATIVE SOLUTION:   The question may be solved by choosing arbitrary values for the base and height of the triangle, say $b = 2$ and $h = 3$. Then the original area, $A$, is:

$$A = \frac{1}{2} (2)(3)$$

$$A = 3$$

If the base is doubled, the new base is 4. If the height is multiplied by 3, the new height is 9. Then the area, $A'$, of the enlarged triangle is:

$$A' = \frac{1}{2} (4)(9)$$

$$A' = \frac{1}{2} (36)$$

$$A' = 18$$

Since the new area, 18, is 6 times the old area, 3, the area has been multiplied by 6.

**5.** The area, $A$, of a square whose side has length $s$ is:

$$A = s^2$$

If the side is doubled, its length becomes $2s$. Then the area, $A'$, of the enlarged square is:

$$A' = (2s)^2$$

Remove the parentheses:

$$A' = 4s^2$$

Since $4s^2$ is 4 times $s^2$, the new area, $A'$, is 4 times as large as the original area, $A$.

The correct choice is (2).

ALTERNATIVE SOLUTION:   Choose an arbitrary value for the length of the side of the square, say $s = 5$:

$$A = 5^2$$
$$A = 25$$

If the side is doubled, it becomes 10. The new area, $A'$, is then:

$$A' = 10^2$$
$$A' = 100$$

Since the new area, 100, is 4 times the original area, 25, the area has been multiplied by 4.

## 16. QUESTIONS ON LITERAL EQUATIONS; EXPRESSING RELATIONS ALGEBRAICALLY

**1.** Solve for $x$ in terms of $a$, $b$, and $c$:   $ax - b = c$

**2.** Solve for $B$ in terms of $V$ and $h$:   $V = \dfrac{1}{2} Bh$

**3.** The length of a rectangle is 5 more than its width. If the width is represented by $w$, which expression represents the area of the rectangle?
(1)  $w^2 + 5w$     (2)  $w^2 + 5$     (3)  $5w^2$     (4)  $4w + 10$

**4.** The perimeter of a square is represented by $12x - 4$. Express the length of one side of the square in terms of $x$.

**5.** The length and width of a rectangle are represented by $(x + 7)$ and $(x - 3)$. If the area of the rectangle is 24, which equation can be used to find $x$?
(1)  $(x + 7) + (x - 3) = 24$     (2)  $2(x + 7) + 2(x - 3) = 24$
(3)  $(x + 7)^2 + (x - 3)^2 = 24$     (4)  $(x + 7)(x - 3) = 24$

**6.**  As shown in the accompanying diagram, a square with side $s$ is inscribed in a circle with radius $r$. Which expression represents the area of the shaded region?

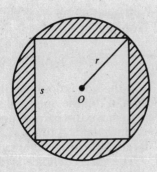

(1)  $s^2 - \pi r^2$     (2)  $\pi r^2 - s^2$     (3)  $\pi r^2 - 4s$     (4)  $4s - \pi r^2$

**Solutions to Questions on Literal Equations; Expressing Relations Algebraically**

**1.**
Add $+b$ (the additive inverse of $-b$) to both sides of the equation:

$$ax - b = c$$

$$\underline{+b = \quad +b}$$

$$ax \quad = b + c$$

Multiply both sides of the equation by $\frac{1}{a}$ (the multiplicative inverse of $a$):

$$\frac{1}{a}(ax) = \frac{1}{a}(b + c)$$

The correct answer is $\dfrac{b+c}{a}$.

$$x = \frac{b+c}{a}$$

**2.**
Clear fractions by multiplying both sides of the equation by 3:

$$V = \frac{1}{3}Bh$$

$$3(V) = 3\left(\frac{1}{3}Bh\right)$$

$$3V = Bh$$

Divide both sides of the equation by $h$:

$$\frac{3V}{h} = \frac{Bh}{h}$$

$$\frac{3V}{h} = B$$

$$B = \frac{3V}{h}.$$

**3.**  Since the length is 5 more than the width, $w$, the length is represented by $w + 5$.

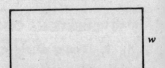

The area of a rectangle equals its length times its width. Therefore, the area is given by:

$$w(w + 5)$$

Remove parentheses by applying the distributive law of multiplication: $w^2 + 5w$

The correct choice is (**1**).

**4.** Let $s =$ the length of one side of the square. The perimeter of a square is the sum of the lengths of all 4 sides. Since the 4 sides of a square are all equal:

$$4s = 12x - 4$$

Multiply both sides by $\frac{1}{4}$ (the multiplicative inverse of 4):

$$\frac{1}{4}(4s) = \frac{1}{4}(12x - 4)$$

$$s = 3x - 1$$

The length of one side of the square is $3x - 1$.

**5.** The area of a rectangle is equal to the product of its length and width:
$(x + 7)(x - 3) = 24$
The correct choice is (**4**).

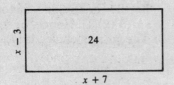

**6.** The area, $A$, of a circle whose radius is $r$ is given by the formula:

$$A = \pi r^2$$

The area, $A$, of a square whose side is $s$ is given by the formula:

$$A = s^2$$

The shaded area is the area of the circle minus the area of the square:

$$\pi r^2 - s^2$$

The correct choice is (**2**).

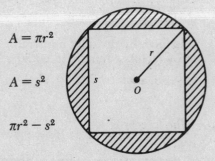

## 17. QUESTIONS ON FACTORIAL *n*

**1.** The symbol for "factorial 4" is 4! What is the value of 4!?
(1)  24     (2)  16     (3)  8     (4)  4

2.  An expression equivalent to 3! is
(1)  3(2)(1)      (2)  3(3)      (3)  3(2)(1)(0)      (4)  3(3)(3)

3.  The expression 5! is equivalent to
(1)  5      (2)  15      (3)  20      (4)  120

4.  What integer does $\dfrac{4!}{3!}$ equal?

**Solutions to Questions on Factorial $n$**

1.  By definition, factorial $n$, or $n!$, equals $n(n-1)(n-2)$
. . . $(3)(2)(1)$. Hence, $n! = 4(3)(2)(1) = 24$.
The correct choice is (1).

2.  Factorial $n$ is the product of $n$ and each of the integers less than
$n$ down to and including 1. Hence, $3! = 3(2)(1)$.
The correct choice is (1).

3.  By definition, factorial $n$, or $n!$, equals $n(n-1)(n-2)$
. . . $(3)(2)(1)$. Hence, $5! = 5(4)(3)(2)(1) = 20(6)(1) = 120$.
The correct choice is (4).

4.  By definition, $n! = n(n-1)(n-2)$ . . . $(3)(2)(1)$

Therefore:
$$\frac{4!}{3!} = \frac{4(3)(2)(1)}{3(2)(1)}$$

Reduce, by dividing numerator and denominator by factors common to both:
$$\frac{4!}{3!} = \frac{4(\cancel{3})(\cancel{2})(1)}{\cancel{3}(\cancel{2})(1)}$$

$$\frac{4!}{3!} = 4$$

The integer is 4.

## 18. QUESTIONS ON AREAS, PERIMETERS, CIRCUMFERENCES OF COMMON FIGURES

1.  The perimeter of a square is 36. What is the length of one side of the square?

2.  Find the area of the triangle whose vertices are $(0,0)$, $(0,4)$, and $(5,0)$.

**3.** What is the area of a circle whose radius is 5?
(1) $100\pi$    (2) $25\pi$    (3) $10\pi$    (4) $5\pi$

**4.** The area of a triangle is 24 square centimeters and the base measures 6 centimeters. Find the number of centimeters in the measure of the altitude to that base.

**5.** In the accompanying diagram, $ABCD$ is a rectangle. Diameter $\overline{MN}$ of circle $O$ is perpendicular to $\overline{BC}$ at $M$ and to $\overline{AD}$ at $N$, $AD = 8$, and $CD = 6$. (Answers may be left in terms of $\pi$.)

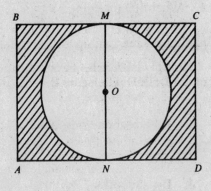

    **a.** What is the perimeter of rectangle $ABCD$?

    **b.** What is the circumference of circle $O$?

    **c.** What is the area of rectangle $ABCD$?

    **d.** What is the area of circle $O$?

    **e.** What is the area of the shaded region of the diagram?

**6.** In the accompanying diagram, arcs $\overset{\frown}{AB}$, $\overset{\frown}{BC}$, and $\overset{\frown}{CD}$ are semicircles with diameters $\overline{AB}$, $\overline{BC}$, and $\overline{CD}$, respectively. $ABCD$ is a rectangle, $BC = 28$, and $AB = 14$. (Answers may be left in terms of $\pi$.)

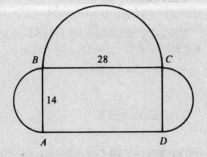

    **a.** Find the area of $ABCD$.

    **b.** Find the area of the region enclosed by diameter $\overline{BC}$ and semicircle $\overset{\frown}{BC}$.

    **c.** Find the area of the region enclosed by diameter $\overline{AB}$ and semicircle $\overset{\frown}{AB}$.

    **d.** Find the area of the entire region.

Solutions to Questions on Areas, Perimeters, Circumferences of Common Figures

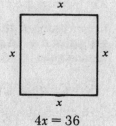

1.   Let $x$ = the length of one side of the square.
The perimeter of any polygon equals the sum of all the sides; in a square, all 4 sides are equal:            $4x = 36$

Multiply both sides of the equation by $\frac{1}{4}$ (the multiplicative inverse of 4):            $\frac{1}{4}(4x) = \frac{1}{4}(36)$

$$x = 9$$

The length of one side is **9**.

2.   The area, $A$, of a triangle is given by $A = \frac{1}{2}bh$ where $b$ is the length of the base and $h$ is the length of the altitude to that base.

If the base is considered to lie on the $x$-axis, then $b = 5$; the altitude (which is perpendicular to the base) will lie on the $y$-axis, with $h = 4$.

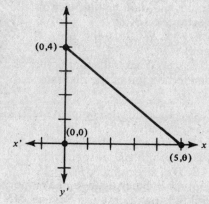

$$A = \frac{1}{2}(5)(4)$$

$$A = \frac{1}{2}(20)$$

$$A = 10$$

The area is **10**.

3.   The area, $A$, of a circle is given by the formula $A = \pi r^2$, where $r$ is the length of the radius.
Here, $r = 5$:            $A = \pi(5)^2$
                          $A = 25\pi$

The correct choice is **(2)**.

4. The area, A, of a triangle is given by the formula $A = \frac{1}{2} bh$ where $b$ is the measure of the base and $h$ is the measure of the altitude to that base. Since it is given that $A = 24$ and $b = 6$, substitute these values in the formula:

$$24 = \frac{1}{2}(6)h$$

Perform the indicated multiplication: $\qquad 24 = 3h$

Divide both sides of the equation by 3: $\qquad \dfrac{24}{3} = \dfrac{3h}{3}$

$$8 = h$$

The measure of the altitude is **8**.

5. a. The opposite sides of a rectangle are equal:
$BC = AD = 8$; $AB = CD = 6$
The perimeter of a rectangle equals the sum of lengths of all four sides:

Perimeter = $AB + BC$
$\qquad\qquad + CD + AD$
Perimeter = $6 + 8 + 6$
$\qquad\qquad + 8$
Perimeter = 28

The perimeter is **28**.

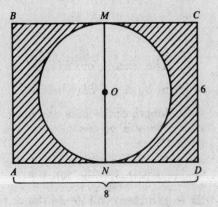

b. Since diameter $\overline{MN}$ is perpendicular to $\overline{BC}$ and $\overline{AD}$, it is parallel to $\overline{CD}$. Hence, $MN = CD = 6$.
The length, $r$, of the radius $\overline{MO}$ is one-half the diameter: $\qquad r = 3$
The circumference, $c$, of a circle is given by the formula $c = 2\pi r$ where $r$ is the length of the radius: $\qquad c = 2\pi(3)$
$$c = 6\pi$$

The circumference is **6π**.

c. The area of a rectangle is equal to the product of its length and width: $\qquad$ Area of $ABCD = (8)(6)$
$\qquad\qquad\qquad$ Area of $ABCD = 48$

The area of $ABCD$ is **48**.

**d.** The area, $A$, of a circle is given by the formula $A = \pi r^2$ where $r$ is the radius:

$$A = \pi(3)^2$$
$$A = 9\pi$$

The area of the circle is $9\pi$.

**e.** The area of the shaded region is equal to the area of the rectangle minus the area of the circle:    $48 - 9\pi$

The area of the shaded region is $48 - 9\pi$.

**6. a.** The area of a rectangle is equal to the product of its length and width:

$$\begin{array}{r} 28 \\ \times 14 \\ \hline 112 \\ 28 \\ \hline 392 \end{array}$$

Area of $ABCD = 14(28)$
Area of $ABCD = 392$

The area of rectangle $ABCD$ is **392**.

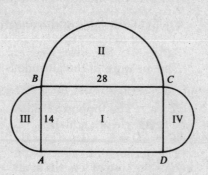

**b.** The area, $A$, of a circle is given by the formula $A = \pi r^2$ where $r$ is the radius. Since $\overline{BC}$ is a diameter, the radius of region $II = \frac{1}{2}(BC) = \frac{1}{2}(28) = 14$. Since region $II$ is half a circle, its area is $\frac{1}{2}A$ or $\frac{1}{2}\pi r^2 = \frac{1}{2}\pi(14)^2$.

$$\begin{array}{r} 14 \\ \times 14 \\ \hline 56 \\ 14 \\ \hline 196 \end{array}$$

$$\frac{1}{2}\pi(14)^2 = \frac{1}{2}\pi(196) = 98\pi$$

The area of region $II$ is $98\pi$.

**c.** Since $\overline{AB}$ is a diameter, the radius of region $III = \frac{1}{2}(AB) = \frac{1}{2}(14) = 7$. Since region $III$ is half a circle, its area $= \frac{1}{2}\pi r^2 = \frac{1}{2}\pi(7)^2 = \frac{1}{2}\pi(49) = \frac{49\pi}{2}$.

The area of region III is $\dfrac{49\pi}{2}$.

   **d.**   The area of region IV is the same as the area of region III or $\dfrac{49\pi}{2}$.

The area of the entire region = area of I + area of II + area of III + area of IV:    Total area $= 392 + 98\pi + \dfrac{49\pi}{2} + \dfrac{49\pi}{2}$

Combine the last two fractions:    Total area $= 392 + 98\pi + 49\pi$
Combine like terms:    Total area $= 392 + 147\pi$
The area of the entire region is $\mathbf{392 + 147\pi}$.

## 19. QUESTIONS ON GEOMETRY (≅, ∠ MEAS., ∥ LINES, COMPLS., SUPPLS., CONST.)

   **1.**   The angles of a triangle are in the ratio of $\overset{\frown}{1:2:3}$. Find the measure of the *smallest* angle.

   **2.**   If two angles of a triangle measure 30° and 70°, what is the number of degrees of the third angle of the triangle?

   **3.**   As shown in the accompanying figure, $\overleftrightarrow{AB}$ is parallel to $\overleftrightarrow{CD}$, and $\overleftrightarrow{AB}$ and $\overleftrightarrow{CD}$ are cut by transversal $\overleftrightarrow{EF}$ at $E$ and $F$, respectively. If the measure of $\angle AEF$ equals $x + 30°$, and the measure of $\angle DFE$ equals $70°$, find $x$.

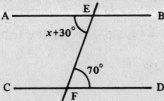

   **4.**   In the accompanying figure, arc $AC$ measures $150°$. Find the number of degrees in inscribed angle $ABC$.

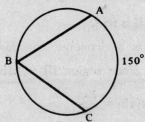

**5.** In the accompanying figure, $\triangle ABC$ is inscribed in circle $O$. Arc $AB$ measures $120°$, and arc $BC$ measures $60°$. Find the number of degrees in angle $B$.

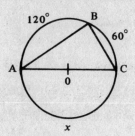

**6.** If two angles of a triangle are complementary, find the number of degrees in the third angle of the triangle.

**7.** Two complementary angles are in the ratio of $1:4$. Find the measure of the *smaller* angle.

**8.** Using line segment $\overline{AB}$ as the base, construct an isosceles triangle whose equal sides are congruent to $\overline{CD}$. (Use compasses and straight-edge.)

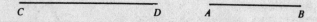

| $C$ | $D$ | $A$ | $B$ |

**Solutions to Questions on Geometry** ($\cong$, $\angle$ meas., ∥ lines, compls., suppls., const.)

**1.** Let $x =$ the measure of the *smallest* angle.

Then $2x =$ the measure of the next angle.

And $3x =$ the measure of the third angle.

Since the sum of the measures of the 3 angles of a triangle is $180°$:

Combine like terms:

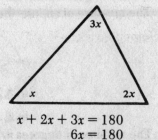

$$x + 2x + 3x = 180$$
$$6x = 180$$

Multiply both sides by $\frac{1}{6}$ (the multiplicative inverse of 6):

$$\frac{1}{6}(6x) = \frac{1}{6}(180)$$

$$x = 30$$

The measure of the *smallest* angle is **30°**.

2. Let $x$ = the measure in degrees of the third angle.

Since the sum of the measures of the three angles of a triangle is 180°, the equation to be used is:

$$30 + 70 + x = 180$$
$$100 + x = 180$$

Combine like terms:
Add $-100$ (the additive inverse of 100) to both sides of the equation:

$$\frac{-100 \qquad = -100}{x = 80}$$

The number of degrees in the third angle is **80**.

3. $\angle AEF$ and $\angle DFE$ are alternate interior angles.

If two parallel lines are cut by a transversal, the alternate interior angles are congruent.

Therefore, the measure of $\angle AEF$ equals the measure of $\angle DFE$:

Add $-30$ (the additive inverse of 30) to both sides:

The value of $x$ is **40**.

$$x + 30 = \quad 70$$
$$\frac{-30 = -30}{x \qquad = 40}$$

4. $\qquad m\widehat{AC} = 150°$

The measure of an inscribed angle is equal to $\frac{1}{2}$ the measure of its intercepted arc:

$$m\angle ABC = \frac{1}{2} m\widehat{AC}$$

$$m\angle ABC = \frac{1}{2}(150)$$

$$m\angle ABC = 75$$

The number of degrees in angle $ABC$ is **75**.

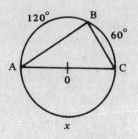

**5.** Let $x$ = the number of degrees in arc $AC$.

Since the sum of the measures of all the arcs comprising a circle = 360°:

Combine like terms:

Add −180 (the additive inverse of 180) to both sides:

$$x + 120 + 60 = 360$$
$$x + 180 = 360$$

$$\underline{-180 = -180}$$
$$x \qquad = 180$$

$\measuredangle B$ is an inscribed angle. The measure of an inscribed angle = $\dfrac{1}{2}$ the measure of its intercepted arc:

$$\text{m} \measuredangle B = \frac{1}{2} \, \text{m}\widehat{AC} = \frac{1}{2}(180) = 90$$

The number of degrees in angle $B$ is **90.**

**6.** If two angles are complementary, the sum of their measures is 90°.

The sum of the measures of all 3 angles of a triangle is 180°.

If the sum of the measures of 2 angles is 90°, then 90° is left as the measure of the remaining angle.

The number of degrees in the third angle is **90.**

**7.** Let $x$ = the measure of the smaller angle.

Then $4x$ = the measure of the larger angle.

The sum of the measures of two complementary angles is 90°:

Combine like terms:

$$x + 4x = 90$$
$$5x = 90$$

Divide both sides of the equation by 5:

$$\frac{5x}{5} = \frac{90}{5}$$

$$x = 18$$

The *smaller* angle has a measure of **18°.**

**8.** STEP 1: Open the compasses to the distance *CD*. With the center of the compasses at *A*, draw an arc of radius *CD*.

STEP 2: With center at *B*, draw an arc of radius *CD* intersecting the arc made in Step 1 at a point *E*.

STEP 3: Draw $\overline{AE}$ and $\overline{EB}$.

△*ABE* is the required isosceles triangle.

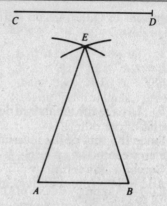

## 20. QUESTIONS ON RATIO AND PROPORTION (INCLUDING SIMILAR TRIANGLES)

**1.** In the accompanying diagrams of triangles *RST* and *UVW*, $\angle R \cong \angle U$ and $\angle S \cong \angle V$. If *RS* = 4, *ST* = 6, and *UV* = 8, find *VW*.

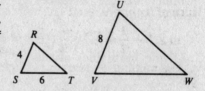

**2.** Right triangles *ABC* and *DEF* are similar. In △*ABC*, the lengths of the legs are 3 and 4. In △*DEF*, the length of the longer of the two legs is 12. What is the length of the shorter leg of △*DEF*?

**3.** The lengths of the sides of a triangle are 24, 20, and 12. If the longest side of a similar triangle is 6, what is the length of its *shortest* side?

**4.** A person 5 feet tall casts a shadow of 12 feet at the same time that a tree casts a shadow of 60 feet. Find the number of feet in the height of the tree.

**5.** A tree casts a 20-meter shadow at the same time that a 6-meter pole casts an 8-meter shadow. Find the height of the tree in meters.

**6.** If a car can travel 51 kilometers on 3 liters of gasoline, how many kilometers can it travel under the same conditions on 7 liters?

### Solutions to Questions on Ratio and Proportion (including similar triangles)

**1.** Since it is given that $\angle R \cong \angle U$ and $\angle S \cong \angle V$, $\triangle RST \sim \triangle UVW$ (two triangles are similar if two angles of one are congruent to two angles of the other).

Let $x = VW$.

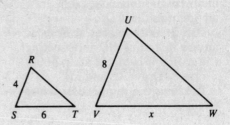

Corresponding sides of similar triangles are in proportion:

In a proportion, the product of the means equals the product of the extremes (cross-multiply):

$$\frac{x}{6} = \frac{8}{4}$$

$$4x = 6(8)$$
$$4x = 48$$

Divide both sides of the equation by 4:

$$\frac{4x}{4} = \frac{48}{4}$$

$$x = 12$$

$VW = 12$.

**2.** Since the triangles are similar, the longer leg, 12, of $\triangle DEF$ will correspond to the longer leg, 4, of $\triangle ABC$.

Let $x =$ the length of the shorter leg of $\triangle DEF$.

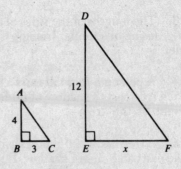

If two triangles are similar, the lengths of their corresponding sides are in proportion:

$$\frac{x}{3} = \frac{12}{4}$$

In a proportion, the product of the means equals the product of the extremes (cross-multiply):

$$4x = 3(12)$$
$$4x = 36$$

Divide both sides of the equation by 4:

$$\frac{4x}{4} = \frac{36}{4}$$
$$x = 9$$

The length of the shorter leg is 9.

3.  Let $x =$ the length of the *shortest* side.

The measures of the corresponding sides of similar triangles are in proportion. Note that 6 corresponds to 24 (the *longest* side of the first triangle) and $x$ corresponds to 12 (the *shortest* side of the first triangle):

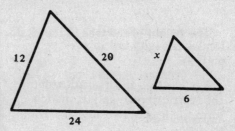

$$\frac{6}{24} = \frac{x}{12}$$

Reduce the fraction, $\frac{6}{24}$, by dividing the numerator and denominator by 6:

$$\frac{1}{4} = \frac{x}{12}$$

In a proportion, the product of the means equals the product of the extremes (cross-multiply):

$$4x = 12$$

Multiply both sides by $\frac{1}{4}$ (the multiplicative inverse of 4):

$$\frac{1}{4}(4x) = \frac{1}{4}(12)$$

The length of the *shortest* side is 3.

$$x = 3$$

4.  The standing person and the tree are vertical; their shadows are horizontal (along the ground). The person and his shadow and the tree and its shadow form the vertical and horizontal legs of two similar triangles:

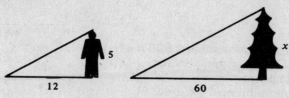

Let $x$ = the number of feet in the height of the tree.

The corresponding sides of similar triangles are in proportion. That is, the ratio of a pair of corresponding sides is the same as the ratio of another pair of corresponding sides:

$$\frac{x}{5} = \frac{60}{12}$$

In a proportion, the product of the means equals the product of the extremes (cross-multiply):

$$12x = 300$$

Multiply each side by $\frac{1}{12}$ (the multiplicative inverse of 12):

$$\frac{1}{12}(12x) = \frac{1}{12}(300)$$

$$x = 25$$

The height of the tree in feet is **25.**

**5.** The tree and its shadow and the (vertical) pole and its shadow form the legs of two similar right triangles.

Let $x$ = the height of the tree in meters.

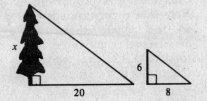

If two triangles are similar, the measures of their corresponding sides are in proportion:

$$\frac{x}{6} = \frac{20}{8}$$

In a proportion, the product of the means equals the product of the extremes (cross-multiply):

$$8x = 6(20)$$
$$8x = 120$$

Divide both sides of the equation by 8:

$$\frac{8x}{8} = \frac{120}{8}$$

$$x = 15$$

The height of the tree is **15** meters.

**6.** Let $x$ = the number of kilometers the car can travel on 7 liters of gas.

The number of kilometers traveled is proportional to the number of liters of gas used:

$$\frac{x}{7} = \frac{51}{3}$$

In a proportion, the product of the means is equal to the product of the extremes (cross-multiply):

$$3x = 7(51)$$
$$3x = 357$$

Divide both sides of the equation by 3:

$$\frac{3x}{3} = \frac{357}{3}$$
$$x = 119$$

The car can travel 119 kilometers on 7 liters of gasoline.

## 21. QUESTIONS ON THE PYTHAGOREAN THEOREM

1.   The lengths of the legs of a right triangle are 2 and 5. Find, in radical form, the length of the hypotenuse.

2.   The length of the hypotenuse of a right triangle is 8 and the length of one leg is 5. The length of the other leg is

(1)  $\sqrt{39}$      (2)  $\sqrt{89}$      (3)  3      (4)  13

3.   In the accompanying diagram of rectangle $ABCD$, $AB = 5$ and $BC = 12$. What is the length of $\overline{AC}$?

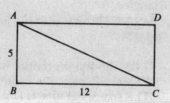

4.   What is the length of a diagonal of a rectangle whose dimensions are 5 by 7?

(1)  5      (2)  8      (3)  $\sqrt{24}$      (4)  $\sqrt{74}$

5.   Express in radical form the length of the diagonal of a square whose sides are each 2.

**Solutions to Questions on the Pythagorean Theorem**

1.   Let $x =$ the length of the hypotenuse. By the Pythagorean Theorem, in a right triangle, the square

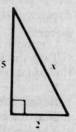

of the length of the hypotenuse equals the sum of the
squares of the lengths of the two legs:

$$x^2 = 5^2 + 2^2$$
$$x^2 = 25 + 4$$
$$x^2 = 29$$

Take the square root of both sides:          $x = \pm\sqrt{29}$
Reject the negative value as meaningless:          $x = \sqrt{29}$
The length of the hypotenuse is $\sqrt{29}$.

2.

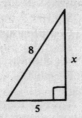

Let $x = $ the length of the other leg.
By the Pythagorean Theorem, the sum of the
squares of the measures of the two legs of a right
triangle = the square of the measure of the hypotenuse:

$$x^2 + 5^2 = 8^2$$
$$x^2 + 25 = 64$$

Add $-25$ (the additive inverse of 25) to both
sides:

$$\underline{-25 = -25}$$
$$x^2 \quad\;\; = 39$$

Take the square root of both sides:          $x = \pm\sqrt{39}$
Reject the negative value as meaningless:          $x = \sqrt{39}$
The correct choice is (**1**).

3.   Since all angles of a rectangle are
right angles, $\angle B$ is a right angle and
thus $\triangle ABC$ is a right triangle.
Let $x = $ the length of $\overline{AC}$.
By the Pythagorean Theorem, in a
right triangle the square of the length of
the hypotenuse equals the sum of the
squares of the lengths of the legs:

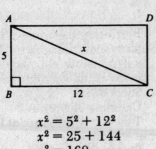

$$x^2 = 5^2 + 12^2$$

Square 5 and square 12:          $x^2 = 25 + 144$
Combine like terms:          $x^2 = 169$
Take the square root of both sides of
the equation:

$$x = \pm\sqrt{169}$$
$$x = \pm 13$$

Reject the negative value as meaningless for a length:          $x = 13$
The length of $\overline{AC}$ is **13**.

**4.** Each angle of a rectangle is a right angle. Therefore, the diagonal forms a right triangle with two of the sides.

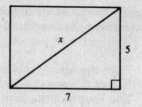

Let $x =$ the length of the diagonal.

By the Pythagorean Theorem, in a right triangle the square of the length of the hypotenuse equals the sum of the squares of the lengths of the legs:

$$x^2 = 7^2 + 5^2$$

Square 7 and square 5:

$$x^2 = 49 + 25$$

Combine like terms:

$$x^2 = 74$$

Take the square root of both sides of the equation:

$$x = \pm\sqrt{74}$$

Reject the negative value as meaningless for a length:

$$x = \sqrt{74}$$

The correct choice is (4).

**5.** All angles of a square are right angles. Therefore, a diagonal forms a right triangle with two sides of the square.

Let $x =$ the length of the diagonal.

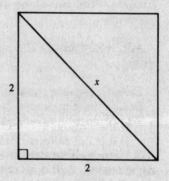

By the Pythagorean Theorem, in a right triangle the square of the length of the hypotenuse equals the sum of the squares of the lengths of the legs:

$$x^2 = 2^2 + 2^2$$

Square 2:

$$x^2 = 4 + 4$$

Combine like terms:

$$x^2 = 8$$

Take the square root of both sides of the equation:

$$x = \pm\sqrt{8}$$

Reject the negative value as meaningless for a length:

$$x = \sqrt{8}$$

This answer may be written in simpler form by factoring out the perfect square factor from the radicand:

$$x = \sqrt{4(2)}$$

Remove the perfect square factor from under the radical sign by taking its

square root and writing it outside as a
coefficient of the radical: $\qquad x = 2\sqrt{2}$

The length of the diagonal is $\sqrt{8}$ or
$2\sqrt{2}$.

## 22. QUESTIONS ON LOGIC (SYMBOLIC REP., LOGICAL FORMS, TRUTH TABLES)

1.  $P$ represents "It is cold" and $Q$ represents "I will go skiing."
Using $P$ and $Q$, write in symbolic form: "If it is cold, then I will *not* go skiing."

2.  If $p$ represents "He is tall," and $q$ represents "He is handsome," write in symbolic form using $p$ and $q$: "He is *not* tall, and he is handsome."

3.  Let $p$ represent "The polygon has exactly 3 sides," and let $q$ represent "All angles of the polygon are right angles." Which is true if the polygon is a rectangle?
(1)  $p \wedge q$      (2)  $p \vee q$      (3)  $p$      (4)  $\sim q$

4.  This sentence is true: "If it is raining, then the ground gets wet." Which sentence must also be true?
(1)  If the ground gets wet, then it is raining.
(2)  If it is not raining, then the ground does not get wet.
(3)  If the ground gets wet, then it is not raining.
(4)  If the ground does not get wet, then it is not raining.

5.  What is the converse of $\sim p \rightarrow q$?
(1)  $p \rightarrow q$      (2)  $p \rightarrow \sim q$      (3)  $\sim q \rightarrow p$      (4)  $q \rightarrow \sim p$

6.  Which is the inverse of $\sim p \rightarrow q$?
(1)  $p \rightarrow \sim q$      (3)  $\sim p \rightarrow \sim q$
(2)  $q \rightarrow \sim p$      (4)  $\sim q \rightarrow \sim p$

7.  What is the inverse of the statement, "If $n$ is an odd integer, then $n + 2$ is an odd integer"?
(1)  If $n$ is an odd integer, then $n + 2$ is not an odd integer.
(2)  If $n$ is not an odd integer, then $n + 2$ is not an odd integer.
(3)  If $n + 2$ is an odd integer, then $n$ is an odd integer.
(4)  If $n + 2$ is not an odd integer, then $n$ is not an odd integer.

**8.** Which is the contrapositive of the statement, "If today is Monday, then tomorrow will be Tuesday"?
(1) Tomorrow is Tuesday if today is Monday.
(2) If tomorrow is Tuesday, then today is Monday.
(3) If today is not Monday, then tomorrow is not Tuesday.
(4) If tomorow is not Tuesday, then today is not Monday.

**9. a.** On your answer paper, copy and complete the truth table for the statement
$(\sim p \to q) \leftrightarrow (p \lor q)$.

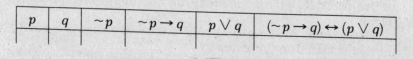

| $p$ | $q$ | $\sim p$ | $\sim p \to q$ | $p \lor q$ | $(\sim p \to q) \leftrightarrow (p \lor q)$ |
|---|---|---|---|---|---|
| | | | | | |

**b.** Is $(\sim p \to q) \leftrightarrow (p \lor q)$ a tautology?
**c.** Let $p$ represent: "I do my homework."
Let $q$ represent: "I get into trouble."
Which sentence is equivalent to $(p \lor q)$?
(1) If I do not do my homework, I will get into trouble.
(2) I do my homework or I do not get into trouble.
(3) If I do my homework, I get into trouble.
(4) I do my homework and I get into trouble.

**10. a.** Copy and complete the truth table for the statement $(p \to q) \leftrightarrow (q \lor \sim p)$.

| $p$ | $q$ | $p \to q$ | $\sim p$ | $q \lor \sim p$ | $(p \to q) \leftrightarrow (q \lor \sim p)$ |
|---|---|---|---|---|---|
| | | | | | |

**b.** Why is $(p \to q) \leftrightarrow (q \lor \sim p)$ a tautology?
**c.** In $(p \to q) \leftrightarrow (q \lor \sim p)$, let $p$ represent "We pollute the water," and let $q$ represent, "The fish will die."
Which statement is logically equivalent to "If we pollute the water, then the fish will die"?
(1) The fish will die or we do not pollute the water.
(2) We pollute the water and the fish will die.
(3) If we do not pollute the water, then the fish will not die.
(4) If the fish die, then we pollute the water.

**Solutions to Questions on Logic (symbolic rep., logical forms, truth tables)**

1. $P$ represents "It is cold."
   $Q$ represents "I will go skiing."
   "I will *not* go skiing" is the negation of $Q$, which is represented by $\sim Q$.
   "If it is cold, then I will *not* go skiing" is the implication, $P$ implies the negation of $Q$, which is represented by $P \rightarrow \sim Q$.
   The symbolic form is $P \rightarrow \sim Q$.

2. $p$ represents "He is tall" and $q$ represents "He is handsome"
   "He is *not* tall" is the *negation* of $p$; the negation of $p$ is represented by $\sim p$.
   "He is *not* tall, and he is handsome" is the *conjunction* of $\sim p$ and $q$; the conjunction is represented by $\wedge$.
   "He is *not* tall, and he is handsome" is represented by $\sim p \wedge q$.
   The symbolic representation is $\sim p \wedge q$.

3. $p$ represents "The polygon has exactly 3 sides."
   $q$ represents "All angles of the polygon are right angles."
   If the polygon is a rectangle, it has 4 sides; therefore, $p$ is false. The angles of a rectangle are all right angles; therefore, $q$ is true.
   Consider each choice in turn:
   (1) $p \wedge q$ is the *conjunction* of $p$ and $q$. If it is true, it asserts that $p$ and $q$ are *both* true. It has been shown above that $p$ is false; hence, choice (1) is *not* correct.
   (2) $p \vee q$ is the *disjunction* of $p$ and $q$. If it is true, either $p$ or $q$, or both, are true. This agrees with the discussion above in which it has been shown that $p$ is false but $q$ is true. Hence, choice (2) is correct.
   (3) If this choice is accepted as true, it asserts that $p$ is true. This contradicts the reasoning above that $p$ is false. Hence, choice (3) is *not* correct.
   (4) $\sim q$ is the *negation* of $q$. If $\sim q$ is true, it states that "not all angles of a rectangle are right angles." This contradicts the facts concerning a rectangle. Hence, choice (4) is *not* correct.
   The correct choice is (2).

4. The given true statement is "If it is raining, then the ground gets wet."
   Consider each choice in turn:
   (1) "If the ground gets wet, then it is raining" is the *converse* of the given statement since it has been formed by interchanging the antecedent (hypothesis) and consequent (conclusion) of the given statement. If a statement is true, its converse may or may not be true.

(2) "If it is not raining, then the ground does not get wet" is the *inverse* of the given statement since it has been formed by negating the antecedent and consequent of the given statement. If a statement is true, its inverse may or may not be true.

(3) "If the ground gets wet, then it is not raining" has been formed by interchanging the negation of the original antecedent with the original consequent. This statement is false; its *contrapositive* (to which it is logically equivalent) would be "If it is raining, then the ground does not get wet" which contradicts the given statement.

(4) "If the ground does not get wet, then it is not raining" is the *contrapositive* of the given statement since it has been formed by negating both the original antecedent and the original consequent and then interchanging them. A statement and its contrapositive are logically equivalent, that is, if one is true, the other is also true. Thus, the statement of choice (4) is always true.

The correct choice is (4).

**5.** $\sim p \rightarrow q$ is an implication which states that the negation of $p$ implies $q$. $\sim p$ is the antecedent of the implication and $q$ is the consequent.

The *converse* of an implication is formed by interchanging the antecedent and the consequent of the given implication. In the converse, $q$ becomes the antecedent and $\sim p$ becomes the consequent:

The converse of $\sim p \rightarrow q$ is $q \rightarrow \sim p$.

The correct choice is (**4**).

**6.**
$$\sim p \rightarrow q$$
The inverse of a statement is formed by negating both its antecedent (hypothesis or "if clause") and its consequent (conclusion or "then clause").

The negation of $\sim p$ is $p$.

The negation of $q$ is $\sim q$.

Therefore, the inverse of $\sim p \rightarrow q$ is $p \rightarrow \sim q$.

The correct choice is (**1**).

**7.** The *inverse* of a statement is formed by changing the antecedent (hypothesis or "if clause") to its negation, and also changing the consequent (conclusion or "then clause") to its negation.

The negation of "$n$ is an odd integer" is "$n$ is not an odd integer."

The negation of "$n + 2$ is an odd integer" is "$n + 2$ is not an odd integer."

Therefore, the inverse of "If $n$ is an odd integer, then $n + 2$ is an odd integer" is "If $n$ is not an odd integer, then $n + 2$ is not an odd integer."

The correct choice is (**2**).

**8.** The given statement is "If today is Monday, then tomorrow will be Tuesday."

The *contrapositive* of a statement is formed by negating its antecedent (hypothesis or "if clause"), negating its consequent (conclusion or "then clause"), and then interchanging the two resulting statements.

The negation of "Today is Monday" is "Today is not Monday."

The negation of "Tomorrow will be Tuesday" is "Tomorrow is not Tuesday."

Thus, the contrapositive of "If today is Monday, then tomorrow will be Tuesday" is "If tomorrow is not Tuesday, then today is not Monday."

The correct choice is (4).

**9. a.** STEP 1: Let T represent "true" and F represent "false." Fill in the columns for $p$ and $q$ with all possible combinations of T and F; this will require 4 lines.

STEP 2: For each line, fill in the column for $\sim p$ with the opposite of the entry for $p$, since $\sim p$ is the negation of $p$.

STEP 3: Use the 2nd and 3rd columns to determine the appropriate entry, T or F, for the column headed $\sim p \rightarrow q$, which means "the negation of $p$ implies $q$."

STEP 4: Use the entries for $p$ and $q$ to determine the appropriate entry, T or F, for each line of the column headed $p \vee q$. This column represents the *disjunction* of $p$ and $q$, that is, it states that either $p$ or $q$ or both are true.

STEP 5: Determine the appropriate entry, T or F, for each line of the final column, $(\sim p \rightarrow q) \leftrightarrow (p \vee q)$ by using the entries in the two preceding columns. The final column states that the two preceding columns are equivalent, that is, that both are true or both are false.

| $p$ | $q$ | $\sim p$ | $\sim p \rightarrow q$ | $p \vee q$ | $(\sim p \rightarrow q) \leftrightarrow (p \vee q)$ |
|---|---|---|---|---|---|
| T | T | F | T | T | T |
| T | F | F | T | T | T |
| F | T | T | T | T | T |
| F | F | T | F | F | T |

**b.** A *tautology* is a statement formed by combining other propositions or statements $(p, q, r, \ldots)$ which is true regardless of the truth or falsity of $p, q, r, \ldots$. Since all entries in the column for $(\sim p \rightarrow q) \leftrightarrow (p \vee q)$ are T, this is a tautology.

The statement **is a tautology.**

c.    $p$ represents "I do my homework."

q represents "I get into trouble."

$(p \vee q)$ stands for the *disjunction* of $p$ and $q$, that is, "I do my homework or I get into trouble." Either $p$ and $q$ are both true, or at least one of them is true.

(1)    "If I do not do my homework, I will get into trouble" is equivalent to saying if $p$ is false, $q$ must be true. This is equivalent to the disjunction $(p \vee q)$.

(2)    "I do my homework or I do not get into trouble" says that either $p$ is true or $q$ is false. This is *not* equivalent to $(p \vee q)$.

(3)    "If I do my homework, I get into trouble" says that if $p$ is true, $q$ is also true. This is *not* equivalent to $(p \vee q)$.

(4)    "I do my homework and I get into trouble" says that $p$ is true and $q$ is true. It is not an implication, and is *not* equivalent to $(p \vee q)$.

The correct choice is (1).

**10. a.** STEP 1:  Using "T" to represent true and "F" to represent false, fill in the columns for $p$ and $q$ with all possible combinations of T and F; this will require 4 lines.

STEP 2:  The third column, $p \rightarrow q$, stands for the *implication*, $p$ implies $q$. For each line under this column, determine the appropriate entry, "T" or "F", according to the values shown in the columns for $p$ and $q$.

STEP 3:  The fourth column, $\sim p$, represents the *negation* of $p$. The entry for each line in this column should be the opposite of the entry in the column for $p$.

STEP 4:  The column, $q \vee \sim p$, represents the *disjunction* of $q$ and the negation of $p$. It asserts that either $q$ or not $p$, or both, are true. Use the entries in the columns for $q$ and $\sim p$ to determine the appropriate entry for each line under $q \vee \sim p$.

STEP 5:  The last column, $(p \rightarrow q) \leftrightarrow (q \vee \sim p)$, stands for the *equivalence* of $p \rightarrow q$ and $q \vee \sim p$. Its value will be "T" if the values of $p \rightarrow q$ and $q \vee \sim p$ are the same as each other; its value will be "F" if their values are different from each other.

| $p$ | $q$ | $p \rightarrow q$ | $\sim p$ | $q \vee \sim p$ | $(p \rightarrow q) \leftrightarrow (q \vee \sim p)$ |
|---|---|---|---|---|---|
| T | T | T | F | T | T |
| T | F | F | F | F | T |
| F | T | T | T | T | T |
| F | F | T | T | T | T |

b. A *tautology* is a statement formed by combining other propositions or statements, $p, q, r, \ldots$, which is true regardless of the truth or falsity of $p, q, r, \ldots$

In the table above, the truth values for $(p \rightarrow q) \leftrightarrow (q \vee \sim p)$ are all "T" no matter what the truth values are for $p$ and $q$ on the same line of the table. Hence, $(p \rightarrow q) \leftrightarrow (q \vee \sim p)$ is a tautology.

    c.   $p$ represents "We pollute the water."
       $q$ represents "The fish will die."

The given statement, "If we pollute the water, then the fish will die" is represented symbolically by the *implication*, $p \rightarrow q$.

In parts a and b above, it has been shown that $(p \rightarrow q) \leftrightarrow (q \vee \sim p)$ is a tautology, that is, that $p \rightarrow q$ is *logically equivalent* to $q \vee \sim p$.

For what statement is $q \vee \sim p$ the symbolic representation? $\sim p$ is the *negation* of $p$ and therefore stands for "We do not pollute the water." $q \vee \sim p$ is the *disjunction* of $q$ and $\sim p$, and therefore stands for "The fish will die or we do not pollute the water." This is choice (1).

The correct choice is (**1**).

## 23. QUESTIONS ON PROBABILITY (INCL. TREE DIAGRAMS, SAMPLE SPACES)

1. The mail consists of 3 bills, 2 advertisements, and 1 letter. If the mail is opened randomly, what is the probability that an advertisement is opened first?

2. If the probability of an event happening is $\frac{2}{5}$, what is the probability of the event *not* happening?

3. Two fair dice are tossed. Each die has six faces numbered 1 to 6. What is the probability that each die shows a 5?

4. A box contains 4 nickels, 3 dimes, and 2 quarters. One coin is drawn, put aside, and then another coin is drawn. What is the probability that the two coins total 9¢?

5. The probability of the Bears beating the Eagles is $\frac{1}{2}$. The probability of the Bears beating the Cubs is $\frac{3}{5}$. What is the probability of the Bears winning both games?

6. From an ordinary deck of 52 cards, one card is drawn. What is the probability that the card drawn is either a king or a seven?

(1) $\dfrac{26}{52}$    (2) $\dfrac{13}{52}$    (3) $\dfrac{8}{52}$    (4) $\dfrac{2}{52}$

7. A die and a coin are tossed simultaneously. The die is fair and has six faces.

    a. Draw a tree diagram or list the sample space of all possible pairs of outcomes.

    b. What is the probability of obtaining a 6 on the die and a head on the coin?

    c. What is the probability of obtaining an odd number on the die and a tail on the coin?

    d. What is the probability of obtaining a head on the coin?

8. The first step of an experiment is to pick one number from the set {1,2,3}. The second step of the experiment is to pick one number from the set {1,4,9}.

    a. Draw a tree diagram or list the sample space of all possible pairs of outcomes.

    b. Determine the probability that:

(1) both numbers are the same
(2) the second number is the square of the first
(3) both numbers are odd

**Solutions to Questions on Probability (incl. tree diagrams, sample spaces)**

1. Probability of an event $= \dfrac{\text{number of favorable cases}}{\text{total number of cases}}$.

There are 2 advertisements in the mail; these represent the 2 favorable cases for opening an advertisement first.

Three bills, 2 advertisements, and 1 letter constitute 6 pieces of mail, any one of which could be the first to be opened. Thus, the total number of cases is 6.

Probability of opening an advertisement first $= \dfrac{2}{6}$.

The probability is $\dfrac{2}{6}$.

2. Probability of an event $= \dfrac{\text{number of favorable cases}}{\text{total number of cases}}.$

Since the probability of the event happening is $\dfrac{2}{5}$, the event has 2 ways to happen (favorable cases) out of a total of 5 possible cases.

The number of cases in which an event will *not* happen = the total number of cases minus the number of cases in which it will happen. Here, the number of cases in which the event will *not* happen = $5 - 2 = 3$.

Probability of an event *not* happening =
$\dfrac{\text{number of cases in which event will } not \text{ happen}}{\text{total number of cases}} = \dfrac{3}{5}.$

The probability of the event not happening is $\dfrac{3}{5}.$

ALTERNATIVE SOLUTION: An event happening or *not* happening covers all possible cases. Therefore, the probability of an event happening added to the probability of it *not* happening equals certainty, which is represented by 1. Hence, the probability of an event *not* happening = 1 − the probability of it happening. In this case, the probability of the event *not* happening $= 1 - \dfrac{2}{5} = \dfrac{3}{5}.$

3. Probability of an event $= \dfrac{\text{number of favorable cases}}{\text{total number of cases}}.$

Since there is only one 5 on each of the die faces, there is only 1 way in which both dice can show 5. Each die by itself can show any of 6 possible faces. Any one of the 6 possibilities for the first die may be matched with any one of the 6 possibilities for the second die, making a total of $6 \times 6 = 36$ ways in which the two dice may be tossed.

Probability of two 5's $= \dfrac{1}{36}.$

The probability that each die will show a 5 is $\dfrac{1}{36}.$

4. Probability of an event $= \dfrac{\text{number of favorable cases}}{\text{total number of cases}}.$

There is *no* way to obtain a total of 9¢ by using nickels, dimes, and quarters. Hence, the number of favorable cases for such an event is 0. There is no need to compute the total number of cases, $t$, as long as it is realized that $t \neq 0$.

Probability of a total of 9¢ $= \dfrac{0}{t} = 0$.

*Note:* The reason it is important to realize that $t \neq 0$ is so that it is possible to divide 0 by $t$; division by 0 is undefined.

The probability is **0**.

**5.** The probability of $\dfrac{1}{2}$ means that the Bears will beat the Eagles in $\dfrac{1}{2}$ of the games they play against the Eagles. Similarly, the probability of $\dfrac{3}{5}$ means that the Bears will beat the Cubs in $\dfrac{3}{5}$ of the games they play against the Cubs. If a Bears-Eagles game is followed by a Bears-Cubs game, then the $\dfrac{1}{2}$ of the times the Bears win the first game will be followed $\dfrac{3}{5}$ of the time by their winning the second game.

Thus, the probability that the Bears will win both games is $\dfrac{1}{2} \times \dfrac{3}{5} = \dfrac{3}{10}$.

The probability is $\dfrac{3}{10}$.

**6.** Probability of an event $= \dfrac{\text{number of favorable cases}}{\text{total number of cases}}$.

In an ordinary deck of cards, there are 4 kings and 4 sevens, giving 8 favorable cases for the drawing of either a king or a seven. Since any one of the 52 cards in the deck may be drawn, the total number of possible cases is 52.

Thus, the probability of drawing either a king or a seven $= \dfrac{8}{52}$.

The correct choice is **(3)**.

**7. a.** A fair die toss has an equal chance of turning up a 1, 2, 3, 4, 5, or 6. To represent this, the die toss is shown by 6 branches on the tree diagram.

Each die toss may be matched with either a head (H) or a tail (T) resulting from the coin toss. Thus, the tree diagram represents the coin toss by two branches above each of the die toss branches, one for H and one for T.

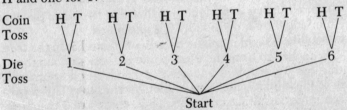

The results of a simultaneous toss of a die and a coin may also be listed in a sample space. The die toss result is shown in the left column; the coin toss result in the right. Each of the 6 possible results for the die toss is paired with the 2 possible results (**HEADS** or **TAILS**) for the coin toss. There are thus 12 lines, each representing a different possible pair, in the sample space:

| Die Toss | Coin Toss |
|:--------:|:---------:|
| 1 | H |
| 1 | T |
| 2 | H |
| 2 | T |
| 3 | H |
| 3 | T |
| 4 | H |
| 4 | T |
| 5 | H |
| 5 | T |
| 6 | H |
| 6 | T |

**b.** In the tree diagram, there is only one branch from the Start that leads to a "6" for the die toss. From the "6" there is only one branch that leads to "H" for the coin toss. Thus, there is only one path that produces a die showing "6" and a coin showing **HEADS**. There are 12 possible paths in all. If the sample space is used to determine the answer, only 1 line of the 12 contains both a "6" and an "H."

Probability of an event $= \dfrac{\text{number of favorable cases}}{\text{total number of cases}} = \dfrac{1}{12}$.

Probability of a "6" and a HEAD $= \dfrac{1}{12}$.

**c.** There are 3 odd numbers on a die: 1, 3, and 5. In the tree diagram, 3 branches go from the Start to one of these odd numbers, representing the 3 possible die tosses that result in odd numbers. From each of these 3 branches, one branch extends to a "T," representing a coin toss resulting in TAILS. Thus, there are 3 complete paths satisfying the two requirements of the question. There is a total of 12 possible paths. If the sample space is used, it will be noted that 3 of the 12 lines contain an odd number and a "T."

Probability of an event $= \dfrac{\text{number of favorable cases}}{\text{total number of cases}} = \dfrac{3}{12}$.

Probability of an odd number and TAILS $= \dfrac{3}{12}$.

**d.** All 6 branches from the Start to the die toss result can be used as the first step toward ultimately reaching a branch leading to "H" for the coin toss. For each of these 6 lower branches, there is only one branch leading to a coin toss of HEADS. Thus, there are 6 paths from the Start leading to possible HEADS. The total number of all possible paths is 12. If the sample space is used to solve, note that there are 6 lines out of the 12 containing an "H"; it does not matter what is shown in the "Die Toss" column.

Probability of an event $= \dfrac{\text{number of favorable cases}}{\text{total number of cases}} = \dfrac{6}{12}$.

Probability of obtaining a HEAD $= \dfrac{6}{12}$.

**8. a.** The tree diagram is shown first. The tree diagram contains 3 branches leading from the Start to represent the first step since either 1, 2, or 3 may be picked on the first step. For each of the "first step" branches, 3 "second step" branches lead to 1, 4, or 9 as the possible second number to be picked:

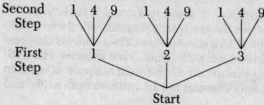

The sample space contains two columns, one for each of the two steps in the experiment. The column for the first step shows the possible numbers, 1, 2, and 3, for that step. Each number in the first column is paired with 1, 4, and 9, in the second column; 1, 4, and 9 are the possible numbers that may be picked in the second step following the first pick of 1, 2, or 3:

| First Step | Second Step |
|:---:|:---:|
| 1 | 1 |
| 1 | 4 |
| 1 | 9 |
| 2 | 1 |
| 2 | 4 |
| 2 | 9 |
| 3 | 1 |
| 3 | 4 |
| 3 | 9 |

**b.**   Probability of an event $= \dfrac{\text{number of favorable cases}}{\text{total number of cases}}$.

(1)   The only way in which both numbers can be the same is if "1" is chosen both times. Using the tree diagram, there is only one path leading to both selections of "1"—the leftmost path. There are 9 possible paths in all. If the sample space is used, there is only one line in which both columns contain a "1"—the first line. There are 9 lines in all. Therefore, the probability that both numbers are the same $= \dfrac{1}{9}$.

The probability is $\dfrac{1}{9}$.

(2)   If the second number is the square of the first, the possible selections may be 1 and $1^2$ (that is, 1 and 1), 2 and $2^2$ (that is, 2 and 4), or 3 and $3^2$ (that is, 3 and 9). Using the tree diagram, one path leads to 1 and 1, a second path leads to 2 and 4, and a third path leads to 3 and 9. Thus, 3 paths out of the total possible of 9 are favorable cases. If the sample space is used to obtain the information, the combinations of 1 and 1, 2 and 4, and 3 and 9 are shown on one line each, a total of 3

lines (favorable cases) out of the 9 possible lines. Therefore, the probability that the second number is the square of the first $= \dfrac{3}{9}$.

The probability is $\dfrac{3}{9}$.

(3) Using the tree diagram, the paths leading to both odd numbers are the paths $1 - 1, 1 - 9, 3 - 1$, and $3 - 9$. Thus, there are 4 possible paths out of the total of 9 which represent favorable cases. Using the sample space, the lines containing 1 and 1, 1 and 9, 3 and 1, and 3 and 9 are the 4 favorable cases of lines containing both odd numbers. There are 9 lines in all. Therefore, the probability that both numbers are odd is $\dfrac{4}{9}$.

The probability is $\dfrac{4}{9}$.

## 24. QUESTIONS ON COMBINATIONS (ARRANGEMENTS, PERMUTATIONS)

**1.** If a boy has 5 shirts and 3 pairs of pants, how many possible outfits consisting of one shirt and one pair of pants can be chosen?

**2.** A school cafeteria offers 6 kinds of sandwiches and 3 kinds of beverages. If a lunch consists of a sandwich and a beverage, how many different lunches can a student choose?

**3.** A boy has 3 shirts, 2 pairs of slacks, and 3 pairs of shoes. Find the total number of possible outfits he can wear consisting of a shirt, a pair of slacks, and a pair of shoes.

**4.** How many four-digit numbers can be formed from the digits 3, 4, 5, and 6 if no repetition is allowed?

**5.** In how many different ways can 4 students be arranged in a row?

**6.** What is the total number of possible 5-letter arrangements of the letters $D, I, S, C,$ and $O$, if each letter is used only once in each arrangement?

Solutions to Questions on Combinations (arrangements, permutations)

1. The boy has 5 choices for shirts. For each of these 5 choices, he has 3 choices of pairs of pants. The total number of possible outfits is therefore $5 \times 3 = 15$.

The number of possible outfits is **15**.

2. A lunch consists of a sandwich and a beverage. There are 6 different sandwiches from which to choose. Each of these 6 ways to choose a sandwich may be matched with each of the 3 kinds of beverages.

Therefore, the number of different lunches $= 6 \times 3 = 18$.

The number of different lunches is **18**.

3. With each of the 3 shirts, either one of the 2 pairs of slacks may be worn. Thus, $3 \times 2$ or 6 shirt-slacks outfits are possible.

With each of the 6 shirt-slacks outfits, there are 3 possible choices for pairs of shoes. Thus, $6 \times 3$ or 18 possible shirt-slacks-shoes outfits can be worn.

There are **18** possibilities.

4. There is a choice of 4 digits (3, 4, 5, or 6) for filling the first place of the four-digit number. For filling the second place, there is a choice of 3 digits (since one has been used for the first place and may not be repeated). Similarly, there is a choice of 2 digits for the third place. The one remaining digit must be used to fill the fourth place. Thus, there are $4 \times 3 \times 2 \times 1$ or 24 different four-digit numbers that can be formed.

**24** numbers can be formed.

5. An arrangement of 4 students in a row is made by selecting one of the 4 students for the first place, one of the remaining 3 for the second place, one of the 2 remaining for the third place, and then putting the one that is left in the last place.

There are thus 4 choices for the first place; and for each of these, there are 3 choices for the second place; for each of these, there are 2 choices for the third place; finally, there is only 1 choice for the last place. In other words, there is a total of $4 \times 3 \times 2 \times 1 = 24$ different arrangements in all.

There are **24** different arrangements.

6. Each arrangement of the letters *D, I, S, C,* and *O* forms a 5-letter "word." Forming such a word may be considered to be the successive acts of choosing the first letter in it, then the second letter, etc., until finally the fifth letter is filled in.

The first letter may be chosen in 5 different ways. Since the letter chosen for the first place cannot be used again, there are 4 choices left for the second place. Then, 3 letters remain as choices for the third place, 2 for the fourth, and 1 for the fifth. Thus, the total number of possible arrangements $= 5 \times 4 \times 3 \times 2 \times 1 = 120$.

The number of possible 5-letter arrangements is **120**.

## 25. QUESTIONS ON STATISTICS

1. If student heights are 176 cm, 172 cm, 160 cm, and 160 cm, what is the mean height of these students?

2. What is the mode of the following data?

2.6, 2.8, 2.8, 2.7, 2.9, 2.4

3. Five girls in a club reported on the number of boxes of cookies that they sold: 20, 20, 40, 50, and 70. Which is true?
(1) The median is 20.
(2) The mean is 20.
(3) The median is equal to the mean.
(4) The median is equal to the mode.

4. Given the following table:

| Interval | Frequency |
|----------|-----------|
| 91–100   | 2 |
| 81–90    | 2 |
| 71–80    | 3 |
| 61–70    | 4 |

Which interval contains the median?
(1)  91–100     (2)  81–90     (3)  71–80     (4)  61–70

5. The following data are heights (in centimeters) of a group of 15 students: 165, 160, 173, 150, 188, 150, 173, 155, 163, 152, 175, 183, 151, 163, 178.

a. On your answer paper, copy and complete the table below.

| Interval | Number (frequency) |
|----------|--------------------|
| 180–189  |                    |
| 170–179  |                    |
| 160–169  |                    |
| 150–159  |                    |

b. On graph paper, construct a frequency histogram based on the grouped data.

c. In what interval is the median for the grouped data?

6. The following data represent the heights (in inches) of 14 students in a certain class: 65, 63, 68, 59, 74, 59, 68, 61, 64, 60, 69, 72, 55, 64.

a. On your answer paper, copy and complete the table below.

| Interval | Number (frequency) |
|----------|--------------------|
| 55–58    |                    |
| 59–62    |                    |
| 63–66    |                    |
| 67–70    |                    |
| 71–74    |                    |

b. On graph paper, construct a frequency histogram based on the data.

c. The median is contained in which interval?

7. The Play-Craft Company, maker of table tennis paddles, listed the following salaries in its annual report:

| Employee | Position | Salary |
|----------|----------|--------|
| Pat Thomas | Manager | $100,000 |
| Don Pierce | Assistant manager | $50,000 |
| Linda Jones | Foreman | $25,000 |
| Jim Jeffrey | Skilled worker | $16,000 |
| Donna Love | Skilled worker | $15,000 |

| John Hanna | Skilled worker | $14,000 |
|------------|----------------|---------|
| Jill Walker | Skilled worker | $14,000 |
| Ben Black | Skilled worker | $13,000 |
| Tony Burch | Secretary | $11,750 |
| John Slack | Custodian | $10,000 |

    a.   Using all ten salaries,

(1)   find the mean,

(2)   find the median,

(3)   find the mode.

    b.   How much more than the mean is the manager's salary?

    c.   If an employee is selected at random, what is the probability that this person's salary is greater than the mean?

## Solutions to Questions on Statistics

    **1.**   The *mean* is obtained by adding all the items and dividing their sum by the number of items (in this case, by 4):

$$\begin{array}{r} 176 \\ 172 \\ 160 \\ \underline{160} \\ 4\overline{)668} \\ 167 \end{array}$$

The mean height is **167** cm.

    **2.**   The mode is the item of data occurring most frequently. In 2.6, 2.8, 2.8, 2.7, 2.9, 2.4, the item 2.8 occurs twice while all others appear only once. Hence, 2.8 is the mode.

The mode is **2.8**.

    **3.**   20, 20, 40, 50, 70

The *median* is the middle item when items are arranged in order of size. Here, the third item, which is 40, is the median. This rules out choice (1) which asserts that 20 is the median.

The *mean* is the sum of all the items divided by the number of items. In this case, mean $= \dfrac{20 + 20 + 40 + 50 + 70}{5} = \dfrac{200}{5} = 40.$

This rules out choice (2) which asserts that the mean is 20.

The preceding calculations have shown that the median is 40 and also that the mean is 40. Therefore, choice (3) is true since it asserts that the median is equal to the mean.

The *mode* is the item which appears most frequently. In this case, 20 is the mode since it appears twice while each of the other items appears only once. The median has already been calculated to equal 40; hence, choice (4) is false since it asserts that the median is equal to the mode.

The correct choice is (3).

4. The median is the middle item when a set of data is arranged in order of size.

First add the frequencies: $2 + 2 + 3 + 4 = 11$. Therefore, the middle item is the 6th; there are 5 items above it and 5 items below it. Counting down from the top, the $91 - 100$ interval contains 2 items and the $81 - 90$ interval contains 2, making a total of 4. 2 more are needed to reach the 6th item. Since the $71 - 80$ interval contains the next 3 items, the 6th is contained within the $71 - 80$ interval.

The correct choice is (3).

5.   a.

| Interval | Number (frequency) |
|----------|--------------------|
| 180 – 189 | 2 |
| 170 – 179 | 4 |
| 160 – 169 | 4 |
| 150 – 159 | 5 |

b.

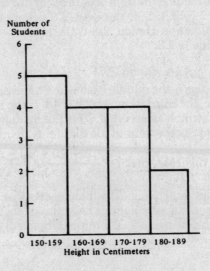

c.  The *median* is the middle item when items are arranged in order of size. Since there are 15 heights given, the eighth one would represent the median; there are 7 items on each side of it.

Counting down from the top of the table shown in part a, the first two intervals, 180–189 and 170–179, account for 2 + 4 = 6 items. Thus, 2 more items are needed to reach the eighth. Both the next two would lie in the 160–169 interval since it contains 4 items.

The median lies in the **160–169** interval.

6.  a.

| Interval | Number (frequency) |
|----------|--------------------|
| 55–58 | 1 |
| 59–62 | 4 |
| 63–66 | 4 |
| 67–70 | 3 |
| 71–74 | 2 |
| Total | 14 |

b.

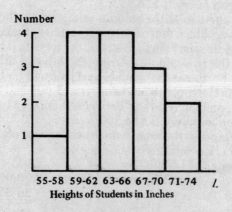

Heights of Students in Inches

c.  The *median* is the middle score when the scores are arranged in order of size. When the number of scores is even (as in this case), there are two middle scores, and the median is midway between them. Since there are 14 items of data in this case, the median lies between the 7th and 8th in order of size.

Counting from the lowest height (top of the table), the first two intervals, 55–58 and 59–62, together contain 1 + 4 = 5 items.

Thus, 2 more items must be counted off to reach the 7th item and 3 more must be counted off to reach the 8th. Since the next interval, 63–66, contains 4 items, the 7th and 8th both lie within this interval. Therefore, the median, which is midway between the 7th and 8th items, lies within this interval.

The median is contained in the **63–66 interval.**

7.  **a.**  (1) The mean is obtained by adding all the salaries and dividing by their number, 10:

$$
\begin{array}{r}
100,000 \\
50,000 \\
25,000 \\
16,000 \\
15,000 \\
14,000 \\
14,000 \\
13,000 \\
11,750 \\
\underline{10,000} \\
10)\overline{268,750} \\
\overline{26,875}
\end{array}
$$

The mean salary is **\$26,875.**

(2)  The median is the middle salary when they are arranged in order of size. Since there is an even number of salaries, 10, there is no single middle salary. In such a case, the median is taken to be midway between the two middle salaries (the 5th and 6th); half the salaries will then be above the median and half will be below it. Counting down from the top, the 5th salary is \$15,000 and the 6th is \$14,000. Thus, the median (midway between them) is \$14,500.

The median salary is **\$14,500.**

(3)  The mode is the salary which occurs most often. \$14,000 occurs twice; all other salaries occur once each.

The mode is **\$14,000.**

     **b.**                Manager's salary = \$100,000

                         Mean          = $\underline{\quad 26,875}$

                         Difference  = \$ 73,125

The manager's salary is **\$73,125** more than the mean.

   **c.**  Probability of an event $= \dfrac{\text{number of favorable cases}}{\text{total possible number of cases}}$.

There are only two employees (the manager and the assistant manager) with salaries greater than the mean. The number of favorable cases for selecting an employee with a salary greater than the mean is thus 2.

The total number of cases for the random selection of an employee is 10.

The probability of selecting an employee with a salary greater than the mean is $\frac{2}{10}$.

The probability is $\frac{2}{10}$.

# Examination June, 1982

## Three Year Sequence for High School Mathematics—Course 1

### PART ONE

DIRECTIONS: *Answer 30 questions from this part. Each correct answer will receive 2 credits. No partial credit will be allowed. Write your answers in the spaces provided. Where applicable, answers may be left in terms of π or in radical form.*

$3y = 48$
$y = 16$

1 Solve for $y$: $\dfrac{y}{12} = \dfrac{4}{3}$

1. $\underline{16}$

2 In the accompanying figure, triangle $ABC$ is similar to triangle $DEF$. If $AC = 6$, $AB = 7$, $DE = 28$, $\angle B \cong \angle E$, and $\angle C \cong \angle F$, find $DF$.

2. $\underline{24}$

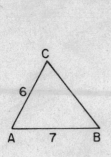
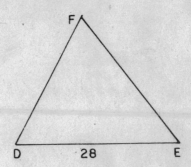

1

3 The graph below shows the distribution of scores on a math test. How many students took the math test?

3.

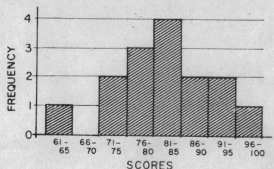

4 Solve for $x$:  $4(2x - 1) = 20$

4. $X = 3$

5 Solve for $x$:  $0.02x = 32.6$

5. $1630$

6 In a class of 20 students, 12 are boys and 8 are girls. If a student is randomly selected, what is the probability that the student will be a boy?

6. $\dfrac{12}{20}$

7 If $p$ represents the perimeter of a square, represent the length of a side of the square in terms of $p$.

$\dfrac{p}{4}$  7. $p = 4$

8 Express the mean of $(2x + 1)$, $(x + 1)$, and $(3x - 8)$ in terms of $x$.

8. $2x - 2$

9 The probability that an event will *not* occur is $\frac{7}{12}$. What is the probability that the event will occur?

$7 \to 12 = 5$

9. $\dfrac{5}{12}$

10 The circumference of a circle is $12\pi$. What is the radius of the circle?

10. $6$

11 What percent of 30 is 9?

11. $30$

12 Let $p$ represent the statement "The base angles are congruent," and let $q$ represent the statement "A triangle is isosceles." Using $p$ and $q$, write in symbolic form: "A triangle is isosceles if and only if the base angles are congruent."

12. _____

13 Express $\dfrac{2a}{3} - \dfrac{a}{4}$ as a single fraction.

13. _____

14 If the point $(2,3)$ lies on the graph of the equation $2x + ky = -2$, find the value of $k$.

14. _____

15 Factor:   $25x^2 - 16$

15. _____

16 How many different arrangements of four digits can be formed from the digits 2, 5, 6, and 7, if each digit is used only once in each arrangement?

16. _____

17 Solve for $b$ in terms of $V$ and $h$:   $V = \dfrac{bh}{3}$

17. _____

18 The test scores for a group of students are 70, 80, 30, 80, 60, 65, and 90. What is the median score for this group of students?

18. _____

19 Solve the following system of equations for $x$:
$$3x + y = 5$$
$$y = 5x - 3$$

19. _____

20 The lengths of two legs of a right triangle are 3 and 5. Find, in radical form, the length of the hypotenuse.

20. _____

21 The length of a rectangle is represented by $(x + 3)$, and the width of the rectangle is represented by $(x - 8)$. Express the area of the rectangle as a trinomial in terms of $x$.

21. _____

22. If two angles of a triangle are complementary, find the number of degrees in the third angle of the triangle.

22. _90_

23. In the accompanying diagram, triangle BCE is inscribed in square ABCD. If the length of side $\overline{BC}$ is 4 centimeters, what is the area in square centimeters of the shaded portion of the diagram?

23. _8_

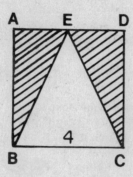

24. As shown in the accompanying diagram, angle QPR is inscribed in circle O. If arc QR measures 38°, what is the measure in degrees of angle QPR?

24. _19_

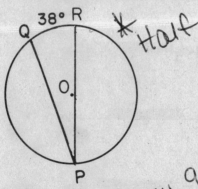

✗ Half

25. Factor:   $x^2 - 6x + 9$

Multiply 9
Add 6

$(x-3)$
$(x-3)$

25. _____

DIRECTIONS (26–35): *For each question chosen, write in the space provided the* numeral *preceding the word or expression that best completes the statement or answers the question.*

26 The product $(-4x^2)(3x^3)$ is equal to
  (1) $-12x^5$          (3) $12x^5$
  (2) $-12x^6$          (4) $12x^6$                                26. __1__

27 Which is an irrational number?

  (1) $\sqrt{9}$                    (3) $\dfrac{2}{3}$ $\Big\}$ rational

  (2) $\sqrt{2}$                    (4) $0$                        27. __2__ ~~4~~

28 The expression $6 \le x + 4$ is equivalent to
  (1) $x \ge 2$          (3) $x \le -2$
  (2) $x \le 2$          (4) $x \ge 10$                            28. __1__

29 Which graph represents the solution set of
  $-2 \le x < 1$?

(1)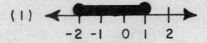

(2)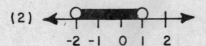

(3)

(4)                                           29. __3__

30 Which expression is undefined or meaningless when
$x = 5$?

(1) $x^{\frac{0}{5}}$

(3) $\dfrac{1}{x - 5}$

(2) $x^{-5}$

(4) $\dfrac{1}{x + 5}$

30.

31 Let $p$ represent the statement: "$x$ is even." Let $q$
represent the statement: "$x \leq 12$." Which is true if
$x = 20$?
(1) $p \rightarrow q$        (3) $\sim p \vee q$
(2) $p \wedge q$        (4) $p \wedge \sim q$

31.

32 Which is the equation of a line parallel to the line
whose equation is $y = 3x + 1$?

opposite

(1) $y = -\dfrac{1}{3}x + 1$    (3) $y = 3x - 1$

(2) $y = 2x + 1$        (4) $y = -3x + 1$

32.

33 One of the factors of $3x^3 - 6x^2$ is
(1) $3x^2$        (3) $-6x^2$
(2) $3x^3$        (4) $(x - 6x^2)$

33.

34 Which is *always* false?
(1) $p \rightarrow q$        (3) $\sim p \rightarrow \sim q$
(2) $q \rightarrow p$        (4) $p \wedge \sim p$

34. 4

35 The solution set of $x^2 - 7x + 10 = 0$ is
(1) $\{2, -5\}$        (3) $\{-2, 5\}$
(2) $\{2, 5\}$         (4) $\{-2, -5\}$

35. 3

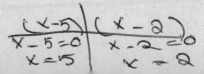

**PART TWO**

DIRECTIONS (36-42):  *Answer four questions from this part. Show all work unless otherwise directed.*

36 *a* On your answer paper, copy and complete the truth table for the statement  $\sim q \rightarrow [(p \rightarrow q) \wedge \sim p]$   [8]

| $p$ | $q$ | $p \rightarrow q$ | $\sim p$ | $\sim q$ | $(p \rightarrow q) \wedge \sim p$ | $\sim q \rightarrow [(p \rightarrow q) \wedge \sim p]$ |
|---|---|---|---|---|---|---|
| T | T | T | F | F | F | T |
| T | F | F | F | T | F | F |
| F | T | T | T | F | T | T |
| F | F | T | T | T | T | T |

*b* Is  $\sim q \rightarrow [(p \rightarrow q) \wedge \sim p]$  a tautology?   [1]   NO

*c* Justify the answer you gave in part *b*.   [1]   T F T T

37 *a* Solve the following system of equations algebraically:

$$x - y = 1$$
$$3x + y = 9$$   [4]

*b* On a set of coordinate axes, graph the system of equations in part *a*.   [6]

38 An architect wants to design a rectangular room so that its length is 8 meters more than its width, and its perimeter is greater than 56 meters. If each of the dimensions of the room must be a whole number of meters, what are the *smallest* possible measures in meters of the length and width? [*Only an algebraic solution will be accepted.*]   [5,5]

39 Mary chose one of the four numbers, 1, 2, 3, and 6, at random. She then chose one of the two numbers, 1 and 5, at random.

*a* Draw a tree diagram or list the sample space of all possible pairs of numbers that Mary could choose.   [3]

*b* Find the probability that Mary chose an even number first followed by an odd number. [2]

*c* Find the probability that Mary chose *at least* one even number. [2]

*d* Find the probability that both choices were the same number. [2]

*e* Find the probability that Mary chose two even numbers. [1]

40 Find three consecutive odd integers such that the square of the first is equal to the second plus twice the third. [*Only an algebraic solution will be accepted.*] [5,5]

41 In the diagram of parallelogram *ABCD*, $\overline{DE}$ is perpendicular to $\overline{AB}$, *AD* = 15, and *AE* = 9.

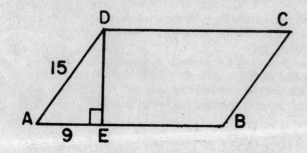

*a* Find *DE*. [2]

*b* If *BE* is 2 less than twice *AE*, find *BE*. [1]

*c* Find *AB*. [1]

*d* Find the area of triangle *AED*. [2]

*e* Find the area of *ABCD*. [2]

*f* Find the area of trapezoid *EBCD*. [2]

$$15^2 + 9^2 = c^2$$
$$225 + 81 = c^2$$
$$\sqrt{306} = c^2$$
$$c =$$

42 The diagram below is a cumulative frequency histogram of raw scores on a mathematics examination.

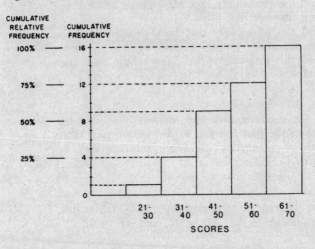

a How many students took the examination?  [2]
b How many students had a score less than or equal to 60?  [2]
c What percent of the students had a score less than or equal to 60?  [2]
d Which interval contains the median?  [2]
e Which interval contains the lower quartile?  [2]

# Answers June, 1982

## Three-Year Sequence for High School Mathematics—Course 1

### ANSWER KEY

### PART ONE

| | | | | | | | |
|---|---|---|---|---|---|---|---|
| 1. | 16 | 11. | 30 | 21. | $x^2 - 5x - 24$ | 31. | 4 |
| 2. | 24 | 12. | $q \leftrightarrow p$ | 22. | 90 | 32. | 3 |
| 3. | 15 | 13. | $\dfrac{5a}{12}$ | 23. | 8 | 33. | 1 |
| 4. | 3 | 14. | $-2$ | 24. | 19 | 34. | 4 |
| 5. | 1630 | 15. | $(5x + 4)(5x - 4)$ | 25. | $(x - 3)(x - 3)$ | 35. | 2 |
| 6. | $\dfrac{12}{20}$ | 16. | 24 | 26. | 1 | | |
| 7. | $\dfrac{p}{4}$ | 17. | $\dfrac{3V}{h}$ | 27. | 2 | | |
| 8. | $2x - 2$ | 18. | 70 | 28. | 1 | | |
| 9. | $\dfrac{5}{12}$ | 19. | 1 | 29. | 3 | | |
| 10. | 6 | 20. | $\sqrt{34}$ | 30. | 3 | | |

**Part Two**—*See answers explained.*

### ANSWERS EXPLAINED

### PART ONE

1. The given equation is in the form of a proportion:

$$\frac{y}{12} = \frac{4}{3}$$

In a proportion, the product of the means equals the product of the extremes (cross multiply):

$$3y = (12)(4)$$
$$3y = 48$$

Multiply both sides of the equation by $\frac{1}{3}$ (the multiplicative inverse of 3):

$$\frac{1}{3}(3y) = \frac{1}{3}(48)$$
$$y = 16$$

The solution is **y = 16**.

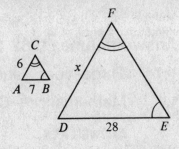

**2.** Let $x = DF$.

In similar triangles, corresponding sides are in proportion, that is, the ratio of any pair of corresponding sides is equal to the ratio of any other pair of corresponding sides (note that corresponding sides are opposite equal angles):

$$\frac{x}{6} = \frac{28}{7}$$

Reduce the fraction on the right side by dividing numerator and denominator by 7:

$$\frac{x}{6} = \frac{4}{1}$$

In a proportion, the product of the means equals the product of the extremes (cross multiply):

$$1 \cdot x = 6 \cdot 4$$
$$x = 24$$

$DF = 24$.

**3.**

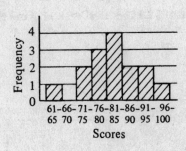

Scores

The number of students who took the math test is the sum of the frequencies for each group of scores:

| Score | Frequency |
|-------|-----------|
| 61–65 | 1 |
| 66–70 | 0 |
| 71–75 | 2 |
| 76–80 | 3 |
| 81–85 | 4 |
| 86–90 | 2 |
| 91–95 | 2 |
| 96–100 | 1 |
| Total: | 15 |

**15** students took the math test.

**4.**

$$4(2x - 1) = 20$$

Remove parentheses by applying the distributive law of multiplication over addition:

$$8x - 4 = 20$$

Add 4 (the additive inverse of $-4$) to both sides of the equation:

$$\frac{4 = 4}{8x \quad = 24}$$

Multiply both sides of the equation by $\frac{1}{8}$ (the multiplicative inverse of 8):

$$\frac{1}{8}(8x) = \frac{1}{8}(24)$$
$$x = 3$$

The solution is $x = 3$.

**5.** Clear decimals by multiplying both sides of the equation by 100:

$$0.02x = 32.6$$
$$100(0.02x) = 100(32.6)$$
$$2x = 3260$$

Multiply both sides of the equation by $\frac{1}{2}$ (the multiplicative inverse of 2):

$$\frac{1}{2}(2x) = \frac{1}{2}(3260)$$
$$x = 1630$$

The solution is $x = 1630$.

**6.** Probability of an event occurring =

$$\frac{\text{number of favorable cases}}{\text{total number of possible cases}}.$$

There are 12 boys in the class, so the number of favorable cases for the selection of a boy is 12.

The total number of possible cases is 20 since any member of the class of 20 can be chosen in a random selection.

Probability of selecting a boy $= \frac{12}{20}$.

The probability is $\frac{12}{20}$.

**7.** Let $x =$ the length of a side of the square.

Since all four sides of a square are equal, and since the perimeter, $p$, is the sum of all four sides: $\quad 4x = p$

Multiply both sides of the equation by $\frac{1}{4}$ (the multiplicative inverse of 4):

$$\frac{1}{4}(4x) = \frac{1}{4}(p)$$
$$x = \frac{p}{4}$$

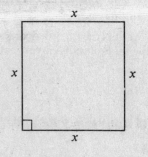

The length of a side of the square in terms of $p$ is $\frac{p}{4}$.

**8.** The mean of three items is the sum of the three items divided by 3:

$$\text{Mean} = \frac{2x + 1 + x + 1 + 3x - 8}{3}$$

Combine like terms:

$$\text{Mean} = \frac{6x - 6}{3}$$

Divide numerator and denominator by 3:

$$\text{Mean} = 2x - 2$$

The mean is $2x - 2$.

**9.** Probability that an event will *not* occur =

$$\frac{\text{number of } \textit{un}\text{favorable cases}}{\text{total number of possible cases}}.$$

Since the probability that the event will *not* occur is $\frac{7}{12}$, we may assume that there are 7 *un*favorable cases for every 12 possible cases. Then the number of favorable cases is $12 - 7$, or 5, for every 12 possible cases.

$$\text{Probability of an event occurring} = \frac{\text{number of favorable cases}}{\text{total number of possible cases}}.$$

$$\text{Probability of this event occurring} = \frac{5}{12}.$$

The probability is $\frac{5}{12}$.

**10.** The circumference, $c$, of a circle is given by the formula, $c = 2\pi r$, where $r$ = the radius.

In this case: $\qquad\qquad 2\pi r = 12\pi$

Multiply both sides of the equation by $\frac{1}{2\pi}$ (the multiplicative inverse of $2\pi$):

$$\frac{1}{2\pi}(2\pi r) = \frac{1}{2\pi}(12\pi)$$
$$r = 6$$

The radius is **6**.

**11.** To determine what percent 9 is of 30, divide 9 by 30 to 2 decimal places:

$$\begin{array}{r} .30 \\ 30\overline{)9.00} \\ \underline{9\ 0\phantom{0}} \\ 00 \end{array}$$

Convert the decimal, .30, to a percent by moving the decimal point 2 places to the right and adding the percent sign: $\qquad .30 = 30\%$

9 is **30%** of 30.

**12.** "A triangle is isosceles if and only if the base angles are congruent" is an *equivalence relation* between "The base angles are congruent" and "A triangle is isosceles." The symbol, $\leftrightarrow$, represents an equivalence relation. In symbolic form, the statement is $q \leftrightarrow p$.

The statement is $q \leftrightarrow p$ in symbolic form.

**13.** In order to combine fractions, they must have a common denominator. The least common denominator (L. C. D.) is the smallest number into which all the denominators will divide evenly; the L. C. D. for 3 and 4 is 12.

$$\frac{2a}{3} - \frac{a}{4}$$

Convert each fraction to an equivalent fraction having the L. C. D. by multiplying the first fraction by 1 in the form $\frac{4}{4}$ and the second fraction by 1 in the form $\frac{3}{3}$:

$$\frac{4(2a)}{4(3)} - \frac{3(a)}{3(4)}$$

$$\frac{8a}{12} - \frac{3a}{12}$$

Fractions with a common denominator may be combined by combining their numerators over the common denominator:

$$\frac{8a - 3a}{12}$$

Combine like terms:

$$\frac{5a}{12}$$

The single fraction is $\frac{5a}{12}$.

**14.** If the point $(2, 3)$ lies on the graph of the equation, $2x + ky = -2$, its coordinates must satisfy the equation when they are substituted for $x$ and $y$:

$$2(2) + k(3) = -2$$

Add $-4$ (the additive inverse of 4) to both sides of the equation:

$$4 + 3k = -2$$
$$\underline{-4 \qquad = -4}$$
$$3k = -6$$

Multiply both sides of the equation by $\frac{1}{3}$ (the multiplicative inverse of 3):

$$\frac{1}{3}(3k) = \frac{1}{3}(-6)$$

$$k = -2$$

The value of $k$ is $-2$.

**15.** The given expression is the *difference of two perfect squares*, $25x^2$ and 16. Take the square root of each perfect square:

$$25x^2 - 16$$

$$\sqrt{25x^2} = 5x; \sqrt{16} = 4$$

The factors of the difference of two perfect squares are two binomials; one binomial is the sum of the two square roots and the other is the difference of the two square roots:

$$(5x + 4)(5x - 4)$$

The factored form is $(5x + 4)(5x - 4)$.

**16.** The number of different arrangements of the four digits is the number of permutations of 4 things, taken all 4 at a time.

$nP_n$, the number of permutations of $n$ things $n$ at a time, is given by the formula:     $nP_n = n!$     where $n!$ is factorial $n$.

In this case, $n = 4$:     $4P_4 = 4! = 4 \cdot 3 \cdot 2 \cdot 1 = 24$

There are **24** different arrangements.

**17.**

$$V = \frac{bh}{3}$$

Clear fractions by multiplying both sides of the equation by 3:

$$3(V) = 3\left(\frac{bh}{3}\right)$$

$$3V = bh$$

Multiply both sides of the equation by $\frac{1}{h}$ (the multiplicative inverse of $h$):

$$\frac{1}{h}(3V) = \frac{1}{h}(bh)$$

$$\frac{3V}{h} = b$$

The solution for $b$ is $b = \dfrac{3V}{h}$.

**18.** The *median* score is the middle score when all the scores are arranged in order of size.

First arrange the scores in order of size: 30, 60, 65, 70, 80, 80, 90.

There are 7 scores, so the middle score is the 4th score (there are 3 scores on either side of it). The 4th score is 70; thus, the median is 70.

The median is **70**.

**19.** Since the second equation is solved for $y$ in terms of $x$, it is easiest to solve the system by the method of substitution.

$$3x + y = 5$$
$$y = 5x - 3$$

Substitute the expression, $5x - 3$, for $y$ in the first equation:

$$3x + 5x - 3 = 5$$

Combine like terms:

$$8x - 3 = 5$$

Add 3 (the additive inverse of $-3$) to both sides of the equation:

$$\underline{\phantom{8x} 3 = 3}$$
$$8x = 8$$

Multiply both sides of the equation by $\frac{1}{8}$ (the multiplicative inverse of 8):

$$\frac{1}{8}(8x) = \frac{1}{8}(8)$$

$$x = 1$$

The solution for $x$ is **1**.

**20.**   Let $x$ = the length of the hypotenuse.

By the Pythagorean Theorem, the square of the length of the hypotenuse equals the sum of the squares of the lengths of the legs:  $x^2 = 3^2 + 5^2$

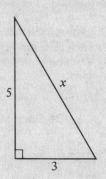

Square 3 and square 5:  $x^2 = 9 + 25$

Combine like terms:  $x^2 = 34$

Take the square root of both sides of the equation:  $x = \pm\sqrt{34}$

Reject the negative value as meaningless for a length:  $x = \sqrt{34}$

Note: Be careful not to assume that the triangle is a 3-4-5 right triangle; in a 3-4-5 right triangle, the side whose length is 5 must be the hypotenuse since the hypotenuse is always the longest side in a right triangle.

The length of the hypotenuse is $\sqrt{34}$.

**21.**

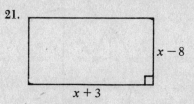

The area of a rectangle is equal to the product of its length and width:

$$\text{Area} = (x + 3)(x - 8)$$

To express this product as a trinomial, multiply the two binomials together:

$$\begin{array}{r} x + 3 \\ \underline{x - 8} \\ x^2 + 3x \\ \underline{-8x - 24} \\ x^2 - 5x - 24 \end{array}$$

The area is $x^2 - 5x - 24$.

**22.**   Let $x$ = the number of degrees in the third angle of the triangle. Let $\angle 1$ and $\angle 2$ represent the two angles which are complementary. The sum of the measures of the three angles of a triangle = $180°$:

$$m\angle 1 + m\angle 2 + x = 180$$

But the sum of the measures of two complementary angles is $90°$:

$$m\angle 1 + m\angle 2 = 90$$

Substitute 90 for $m\angle 1 + m\angle 2$:  $90 + x = 180$

Add $-90$ (the additive inverse of 90) to both sides of the equation:

$$\begin{array}{r} -90 \qquad = -90 \\ \hline x = 90 \end{array}$$

The number of degrees in the third angle is **90**.

**23.** The shaded area = area of square $ABCD$ − area of triangle $BEC$.

The area of a square = the square of the length of one side; area of $ABCD$ = $4^2 = 16$.

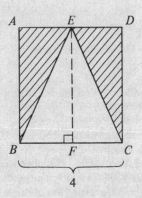

Draw altitude $\overline{EF}$ perpendicular to base $\overline{BC}$ of triangle $BEC$. Since $ABCD$ is a square, $AB = BC = 4$, and $EF = AB = 4$.

The area of a triangle = one-half the product of its base and altitude; area of triangle $BEC = \frac{1}{2}(4)(4) = 2(4) = 8$.

Area of shaded portion = $16 - 8 = 8$.

The area of the shaded portion is **8**.

**24.** $\angle QPR$ is an *inscribed angle*.

The measure of an inscribed angle is equal to one-half the measure of its intercepted arc:

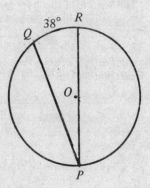

$$m \angle QPR = \frac{1}{2}(38)$$
$$m \angle QPR = 19$$

The measure of $\angle QPR$ is **19°**.

**25.** The given expression is a *quadratic trinomial*:

$$x^2 - 6x + 9$$

A quadratic trinomial factors into two binomials. The factors of the first term, $x^2$, are $x$ and $x$, and they become the first terms of the binomials:

$$(x \qquad)(x \qquad)$$

The factors of the last term, $+9$, become the second terms of the binomials, but they must be chosen in such a way that the sum of the product of the inner terms and the product of the outer terms equals the middle term,

−6x, of the original trinomial. Try $(-3)(-3)$ as the factors of +9:

$-3x =$ inner

$$(x - 3)(x - 3)$$

Since $(-3x) + (-3x) == -6x$, these are the correct factors:

$-3x =$ outer

$$(x - 3)(x - 3)$$

The factored form is $(x - 3)(x - 3)$ or $(x - 3)^2$.

**26.** To multiply two monomials, first multiply their numerical coefficients to get the numerical coefficient of the product:

$$(-4x^2)(3x^3)$$

$$(-4)(3) = -12$$

Multiply their literal factors to get the literal factor of the product. Note that when multiplying two factors which are powers of the same base, the exponents are added:

$$(x^2)(x^3) = x^5$$

Putting the two results together gives the product:

$$-12x^5$$

The correct choice is **(1)**.

**27.** An irrational number is a number that cannot be represented as the quotient or ratio of two integers.

Examine each of the choices in turn:

(1) $\sqrt{9} = 3$ which can be represented as the ratio, $\frac{3}{1}$.

(2) $\sqrt{2}$ is approximately equal to 1.4142, but is a non-repeating, nonterminating decimal, and hence cannot be represented as the ratio of two integers.

(3) $\frac{2}{3}$ is in the form of the ratio of 2 to 3.

(4) 0 can be represented in the form of a ratio as $\frac{0}{1}$.

The correct choice is **(2)**.

**28.** Add −4 (the additive inverse of 4) to both sides of the inequality:

$$6 \leq x + 4$$
$$\underline{-4 \qquad -4}$$
$$2 \leq x$$

This inequality states that 2 is less than or equal to $x$. This is equivalent to saying that $x$ is greater than or equal to 2, that is, $x \geq 2$.

The correct choice is **(1)**.

29.

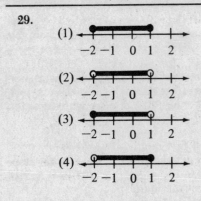

(1)
(2)
(3)
(4)

The solution set of $-2 \leq x < 1$ is the set of numbers which are greater than or equal to $-2$ and less than 1.

All four graphs represent solution sets extending from $-2$ to 1, but they differ in whether $-2$ and/or 1 are included in the set.

Choice (1) has solid shaded circles at both $-2$ and 1, indicating that both $-2$ and 1 are included in the solution set. However, the solution set of $-2 \leq x < 1$ does not include 1.

Choice (2) has open (unshaded) circles at both $-2$ and 1, indicating that neither $-2$ nor 1 is included in the solution set. However, the solution set of $-2 \leq x < 1$ must include $-2$.

Choice (3) has a solid shaded circle at $-2$ indicating that $-2$ is included in the solution set, and an open (unshaded) circle at 1 indicating that 1 is not included in the solution set. This is a correct representation of the solution set of $-2 \leq x < 1$.

Choice (4) has an open (unshaded) circle at $-2$ indicating that $-2$ is not included in the solution set, and a solid shaded circle at 1 indicating that 1 is included in the solution set. However, the solution set of $-2 \leq x < 1$ does include $-2$ but does not include 1.

The correct choice is (3).

30.   When $x = 5$:

(1) $x^{0/5}$ becomes $5^0$ which is equal to 1.

(2) $x^{-5}$ becomes $5^{-5}$ which is equal to $\frac{1}{5^5}$.

(3) $\frac{1}{x-5}$ becomes $\frac{1}{5-5}$ or $\frac{1}{0}$. This is undefined or meaningless since division by 0 is undefined.

(4) $\frac{1}{x+5}$ becomes $\frac{1}{5+5}$ which is equal to $\frac{1}{10}$.

The correct choice is (3).

31.   Since $p$ represents "$x$ is even," $p$ is true if $x = 20$.

Since $q$ represents "$x \leq 12$," $q$ is false if $x = 20$.

(1) $p \rightarrow q$ is the *implication*, "If $p$ is true, then $q$ is true." Since $p$ is true and $q$ is false, $p \rightarrow q$ cannot be true.

(2) $p \wedge q$ is the *conjunction* of $p$ and $q$. It is true only if both $p$ and $q$ are true. Since $p$ is true and $q$ is false, $p \wedge q$ cannot be true.

(3) $\sim p \vee q$ is the *disjunction* of the *negation* of $p$ with $q$. It is true if either the negation of $p$ (that is, not $p$) is true, or $q$ is true, or both. Since $p$ is true, "not $p$" is false. Since $q$ is also false, the disjunction $\sim p \vee q$ cannot be true.

(4) $p \wedge \sim q$ is the *conjunction* of $p$ and the *negation* of $q$ (that is, not $q$). $p$ is true, and the negation of $q$ is also true since $q$ is false. The conjunction of $p \wedge \sim q$ is true if both $p$ and the negation of $q$ are true; since this is the case, the conjunction is true.

The correct choice is (4).

**32.** If the equation of a line is in the form, $y = mx + b$, the slope is given by $m$. $y = 3x + 1$ is in the form, $y = mx + b$, with $m = 3$. Therefore, its slope is 3.

Any line parallel to $y = 3x + 1$ must have the same slope, 3. Examine each choice to see which has a slope of 3:

(1) $y = -\frac{1}{3}x + 1$ is in the form, $y = mx + b$, with $m = -\frac{1}{3}$. Its slope is therefore $-\frac{1}{3}$ and it is *not* parallel to $y = 3x + 1$.

(2) $y = 2x + 1$ is in the form, $y = mx + b$, with $m = 2$. Its slope is therefore 2 and it is *not* parallel to $y = 3x + 1$.

(3) $y = 3x - 1$ is in the form, $y = mx + b$, with $m = 3$. Its slope is therefore 3, the *same* as the slope of $y = 3x + 1$ and hence it is parallel to $y = 3x + 1$.

(4) $y = -3x + 1$ is in the form, $y = mx + b$, with $m = -3$. Its slope is therefore $-3$ and it is *not* parallel to $y = 3x + 1$.

The correct choice is (3).

**33.** $3x^3 - 6x^2$ has a *common monomial factor* of $3x^2$.
The other factor is obtained by dividing $3x^2$ into each term of $3x^3 - 6x^2$, applying the distributive law of division: $3x^3 - 6x^2 = 3x^2(x - 2)$
Of our four choices, the only correct factor is $3x^2$.

The correct choice is (1).

**34.** Consider each choice in turn:
(1) $p \to q$ is the *implication*, if $p$ is true then $q$ is true. An implication may or may not be true, depending on the truth values of $p$ and $q$.

(2) $q \to p$ is the *implication*, if $q$ is true then $p$ is true. As above, an implication may or may not be true, depending on the truth values of $q$ and $p$.

(3) $\sim p \to \sim q$ is the *implication*, if the *negation* of $p$ is true then the *negation* of $q$ is true (that is, "not $p$" true makes "not $q$" true). As above, such an implication may or may not be true.

(4)   $p \wedge \sim p$ is the *conjunction* of $p$ and the *negation* of $p$ (that is, "not $p$"). The conjunction is true only if both $p$ and "not $p$" are true. But $p$ and "not $p$" cannot both be true at the same time. Therefore, $p \wedge \sim p$ is *always* false.

The correct choice is (4).

**35.** The given equation is a *quadratic equation*:

$$x^2 - 7x + 10 = 0$$

The equation may be solved by factoring the left side which is a *quadratic trinomial*. A quadratic trinomial factors into two binomials. The factors of the first term, $x^2$, are $x$ and $x$, and they become the first terms of the binomials:

$$(x \quad)(x \quad) = 0$$

The factors of the last term, $+10$, become the second terms of the binomials, but they must be chosen in such a way that the sum of the product of the inner terms and the product of the outer terms equals the middle term, $-7x$, of the original trinomial. Try $(-5)(-2)$ as the factors of $+10$:

$$-5x = \text{inner product}$$
$$(x - 5)(x - 2) = 0$$
$$-2x = \text{outer product}$$

Since   $(-5x) + (-2x) = -7x$, these are the correct factors:

$$(x - 5)(x - 2) = 0$$

If the product of two factors equals 0, either factor may equal 0:

$$x - 5 = 0 \qquad \text{OR} \qquad x - 2 = 0$$

Add the appropriate additive inverse, 5 in the case of the left equation, and 2 in the case of the right equation:

$$\frac{5 = 5}{x \quad\quad = 5} \qquad\qquad \frac{2 = 2}{x \quad\quad = 2}$$

The solution set is $\{2,5\}$.

The correct choice is (2).

ALTERNATE SOLUTION: This question can be solved by substituting each of the numbers in each solution set in the equation to see if the equation is satisfied. If any number in a solution set fails to check in the equation, the set can be ruled out without further testing. However, as many as 8 substitutions may be necessary before locating the solution set in which both numbers check.

### PART TWO

**36**   **a.**

| $p$ | $q$ | $p \rightarrow q$ | $\sim p$ | $\sim q$ | $(p \rightarrow q) \wedge \sim p$ | $\sim q \rightarrow [(p \rightarrow q) \wedge \sim p]$ |
|---|---|---|---|---|---|---|
| T | T | T | F | F | F | T |
| T | F | F | F | T | F | F |
| F | T | T | T | F | T | T |
| F | F | T | T | T | T | T |

STEP 1:   Fill in the appropriate truth value entry, T or F, on each line of the column headed "$p \rightarrow q$." $p \rightarrow q$ is the *implication*, if $p$ is true then $q$ is true. It has the truth value, T, whenever $q$ has the value, T, or whenever $p$ and $q$ both have the value, F; it has the truth value, F, when $p$ is T and $q$ is F.

STEP 2:   The column headed "$\sim p$" is the *negation* of $p$, or "not $p$." The truth value to be filled in for each line is the opposite of the truth value on that line for $p$.

STEP 3:   The column headed "$\sim q$" is the *negation* of $q$ or "not $q$." The truth value to be filled in for each line is the opposite of the truth value on that line for $q$.

STEP 4:   The column headed "$(p \rightarrow q) \wedge \sim p$" is the *conjunction* of $p \rightarrow q$ and $\sim q$. The conjunction has the truth value, T, only when both $p \rightarrow q$ and $\sim p$ have the truth value, T; in all other cases, the conjunction has the truth value, F.

STEP 5:   The column headed "$\sim q \rightarrow [(p \rightarrow q) \wedge \sim p]$" is the *implication* that if $\sim q$ is true then $[(p \rightarrow q) \wedge \sim p]$ is true. The implication has the truth value, T, whenever $[(p \rightarrow q) \wedge \sim p]$ has the value, T, or whenever $\sim q$ and $[(p \rightarrow q) \wedge \sim p]$ both have the value, F; it has the truth value, F, when $\sim q$ is T and $[(p \rightarrow q) \wedge \sim p]$ is F.

**b.**   $\sim q \rightarrow [(p \rightarrow q) \wedge \sim p]$ *is not a tautology.*

**c.**   A *tautology* is a statement formed by combining other propositions or statements ($p, q, r, \ldots$) which is true regardless of the truth or falsity of $p, q, r, \ldots$ Since the truth values in the table in part $a$ show that $\sim q \rightarrow [(p \rightarrow q) \wedge \sim p]$ has the truth value, F, for certain values of $p$ and $q$, it cannot be a tautology.

**37**   **a.**

$$x - y = 1$$
$$3x + y = 9$$

Adding the two equations together will eliminate $y$:

$$4x \quad = 10$$

Multiply both sides of the equation by $\frac{1}{4}$ (the multiplicative inverse of 4):

$$\frac{1}{4}(4x) = \frac{1}{4}(10)$$
$$x = \frac{10}{4}$$

Reduce $\frac{10}{4}$ by dividing numerator and denominator by 2:

$$x = \frac{5}{2}$$

Substitute $\frac{5}{2}$ for $x$ in the first equation:

$$\frac{5}{2} - y = 1$$

Add $y$ (the additive inverse of $-y$) and also add $-1$ (the additive inverse of 1) to both sides of the equation:

$$-1 + y = -1 + y$$

Since $1 = \frac{2}{2}$, $\frac{5}{2} - 1 = \frac{5}{2} - \frac{2}{2} = \frac{3}{2}$:

$$\frac{3}{2} = y$$

The solution is $x = \frac{5}{2}$, $y = \frac{3}{2}$ or $\left(\frac{5}{2}, \frac{3}{2}\right)$.

    **b.** To graph $x - y = 1$, first rearrange the equation into the form in which it is solved for $y$, by adding $-1$ (the additive inverse of 1) and $y$ (the additive inverse of $-y$) to both sides:

$$x - y = 1$$
$$-1 \quad + y = -1 + y$$
$$\overline{-1 + x \quad = \quad y}$$

Thus, $y = x - 1$.

Set up a table of values for $x$ and $y$ by choosing three convenient values for $x$ and substituting in the equation to determine the corresponding values of $y$:

| $x$ | $x - 1$ | $=$ | $y$ |
|-----|---------|-----|-----|
| $-3$ | $-3 - 1$ | $=$ | $-4$ |
| $0$ | $0 - 1$ | $=$ | $-1$ |
| $2$ | $2 - 1$ | $=$ | $1$ |

Plot the points $(-3, -4)$, $(0, -1)$, and $(2, 1)$ and draw a straight line through them. The straight line is the graph of $x - y = 1$.

    To graph $3x + y = 9$, first rearrange the equation into the form in which it is solved for $y$, by adding $-3x$ (the additive inverse of $3x$) to both sides:

$$3x + y = 9$$
$$-3x \quad = \quad -3x$$
$$\overline{\quad y = 9 - 3x}$$

Set up a table of values for $x$ and $y$ by choosing three convenient values for $x$ and substituting in the equation to determine the corresponding values of $y$:

| $x$ | $9 - 3x$ | $= y$ |
|---|---|---|
| $-1$ | $9 - 3(-1) = 9 + 3$ | $= 12$ |
| $0$ | $9 - 3(0) = 9 - 0$ | $= 9$ |
| $3$ | $9 - 3(3) = 9 - 9$ | $= 0$ |

Plot the points $(-1,12)$, $(0,9)$, and $(3,0)$ and draw a straight line through them. The straight line is the graph of $3x + y = 9$.

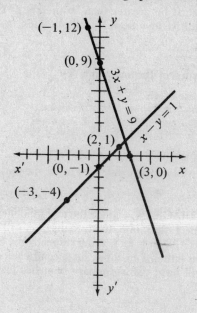

38.  Let   $x$ = the   width   in
meters.
   Then   $x + 8$ = the   length   in
meters.
   Since the perimeter equals the
sum of all four sides, the perimeter = $x + 8 + x + 8 + x + x$,
or, by combining like terms, the
perimeter = $4x + 16$.

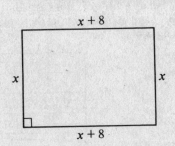

The perimeter must be greater than 56 meters:   $4x + 16 > 56$
   Add $-16$ (the additive inverse of 16) to both sides
of the inequality:

$$\frac{-16 = -16}{4x \qquad > 40}$$

Multiply both sides of the inequality by $\frac{1}{4}$ (the

multiplicative inverse of 4):   $\qquad \frac{1}{4}(4x) > \frac{1}{4}(40)$

$$x > 10$$

Since $x$ must be greater than 10, the *smallest* whole number value for
$x$ is 11.
   If $x = 11$, $x + 8 = 19$.
   The *smallest* possible measures are **19 m** for the length and **11 m** for
the width.

39  a.  TREE DIAGRAM:  Since the first random choice is for one
of the four numbers, 1, 2, 3, or 6, the tree diagram will have 4 branches
leading from the START to 1, 2, 3, and 6 respectively. Since each initial
choice may lead to either 1 or 5 on the second choice, each of the 4
initial branches will have two secondary branches leading to 1 and 5
respectively.

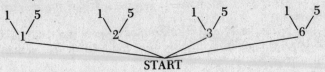

SAMPLE SPACE:  The sample space will have two columns, one showing the number selected on the first choice, and the other showing the
number selected on the second choice. Each of the first choice numbers,
1, 2, 3, and 6, must be listed twice since each may be paired with either
a 1 or a 5 resulting from the second choice.

| First Choice | Second Choice |
|:---:|:---:|
| 1 | 1 |
| 1 | 5 |
| 2 | 1 |
| 2 | 5 |
| 3 | 1 |
| 3 | 5 |
| 6 | 1 |
| 6 | 5 |

**b.**   Probability of an event occurring =

$$\frac{\text{number of favorable cases}}{\text{total number of possible cases}}.$$

Using the tree diagram, there are 4 paths leading first to an even number and then to an odd number: START—2—1, START—2—5, START—6—1, and START—6—5. Using the sample space, there are 4 lines having an even number in the first choice column and an odd number in the second choice column: 2—1, 2—5, 6—1, and 6—5. Thus, there are 4 favorable cases for the choice of an even number first followed by an odd number.

The total number of possible cases is the total number of complete paths from START through the second choice on the tree diagram or the total number of lines in the sample space; in both cases, this number is 8.

Probability of choosing an even number first followed by an odd number = $\frac{4}{8}$.

**c.**   For the probability that Mary chose *at least* one even number, the number of favorable cases is the number of complete paths on the tree diagram which contain *at least* one even number. There are 4 such paths: START—2—1, START—2—5, START—6—1, and START—6—5. In the sample space, there are 4 lines containing *at least* one even number: 2—1, 2—5, 6—1, and 6—5. Thus, the number of favorable cases is 4.

As in part b, the total number of possible cases is the total number of complete paths in the tree diagram (8) or the total number of lines in the sample space (8).

The probability that Mary chose at least one even number = $\frac{4}{8}$.

**d.**   To find the number of favorable cases for the probability that both choices were the same number, look for complete paths on the tree diagram that pass through the same number; there is only one, represented by START—1—1. Similarly, in the sample space there is only one line which contains the same number in both columns: 1—1. The number of favorable cases is thus 1.

The total number of possible cases is 8 (see part *b*).

The probability that both choices were the same number = $\frac{1}{8}$.

    **e.** To find the number of favorable cases for the probability that Mary chose two even numbers, look for complete paths on the tree diagram that pass through two even numbers. There are none; as a matter of fact, since the second choice is either 1 or 5, there can be no even number on the second choice. Similarly, the sample space does not contain any line in which both numbers are even. Thus, the number of favorable cases is 0.

The total number of possible cases is 8 (see part *b*).

The probability that both choices were even numbers = $\frac{0}{8}$ or **0**.

**40.**   Let $x$ = the first odd integer.
Then $x + 2$ = the second consecutive odd integer.
And $x + 4$ = the third consecutive odd integer.
The square of the first equals the second plus twice the third.

$$x^2 \quad = \quad x + 2 \quad + \quad 2(x + 4)$$
$$x^2 = x + 2 + 2(x + 4)$$

The equation to use is:
Remove parentheses by applying the distributive law of multiplication over addition:
Combine like terms:

$$x^2 = x + 2 + 2x + 8$$
$$x^2 = 3x + 10$$

This is a *quadratic equation*. To solve, rearrange it so all terms are on one side equal to 0; add $-3x$ (the additive inverse of $3x$) and also add $-10$ (the additive inverse of 10) to both sides:

$$\frac{-3x - 10 = -3x - 10}{x^2 - 3x - 10 = 0}$$

The left side is a *quadratic trinomial*. It factors into two binomials. The factors of the first term, $x^2$, are $x$ and $x$, and they become the first terms of the binomials:

$$(x \quad )(x \quad ) = 0$$

The factors of the last term, $-10$, become the second terms of the binomials, but they must be chosen in such a way that the sum of the product of the inner terms and the product of the outer terms equals the middle term, $-3x$, of the quadratic trinomial. Try $(-5)(+2)$ as the factors of $-10$:

$$-5x = \text{inner}$$

$$(x - 5)(x + 2) = 0$$

$$+2x = \text{outer}$$

Since $(-5x) + (+2x) = -3x$, these are the correct factors:

$$(x - 5)(x + 2) = 0$$

Since the product of two factors equals 0, either factor may equal 0:

$$x - 5 = 0 \qquad \text{OR} \qquad x + 2 = 0$$

Add the appropriate additive inverses, 5 in the case of the left equation, and $-2$ in the case of the right equation:

Reject the solution, $x = -2$, since $-2$ is not an odd integer:

$$\frac{5 = 5}{x \quad = 5}$$

$$\frac{-2 = -2}{x \quad = -2}$$

$$x = 5$$

$$x + 2 = 7$$

$$x + 4 = 9$$

The three consecutive odd integers are **5**, **7** and **9**.

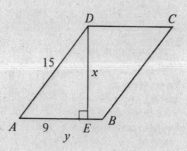

**41 a.** Let $x = DE$.

Since $\overline{DE}$ is perpendicular to $\overline{AB}$, $\angle AED$ is a right angle and triangle $AED$ is a right triangle.

By the Pythagorean Theorem, in a right triangle, the sum of the squares of the lengths of the legs equals the square of the length of the hypotenuse:

Square 9 and square 15:

$$x^2 + 9^2 = 15^2$$

$$x^2 + 81 = 225$$

Add $-81$ (the additive inverse of 81) to both sides of the equation:

$$\frac{-81 = -81}{x^2 \quad = 144}$$

Take the square root of both sides of the equation:

Reject the negative value as meaningless for a length:

$$x = \pm\sqrt{144}$$

$$x = \pm 12$$

$$x = 12$$

$DE = 12$.

**b.** Let $y = BE$.
Since $BE$ is 2 less than twice $AE$:

$$y = 2(9) - 2$$
$$y = 18 - 2$$
$$y = 16$$

$BE = 16$.

**c.** $AB = AE + EB$
$AB = 9 + 16$
$AB = 25$.

**d.** The area of a triangle equals one-half the product of its base and altitude. In $\triangle AED$, $AE$ is the base and $DE$ is the altitude to that base:

$$\text{Area of } \triangle AED = \frac{1}{2}(AE)(DE)$$

$$\text{Area of } \triangle AED = \frac{1}{2}(9)(12)$$

$$\text{Area of } \triangle AED = (9)(6)$$
$$\text{Area of } \triangle AED = 54$$

The area of triangle $AED$ is **54**.

**e.** The area of a parallelogram equals the product of its base and altitude.

In parallelogram $ABCD$, $AB$ is the base and $DE$ is the altitude to that base:

$$\text{Area of } ABCD = (AB)(DE)$$
$$\text{Area of } ABCD = (25)(12)$$
$$\text{Area of } ABCD = 300$$

The area of parallelogram $ABCD$ is **300**.

**f.** The area of trapezoid $EBCD$ = the area of parallelogram $ABCD$ − the area of triangle $AED$: Area of trapezoid $EBCD = 300 - 54 = 246$

The area of trapezoid $EBCD = $ **246**.

**42 a.** The number of students who took the examination is the total cumulative frequency: 16.

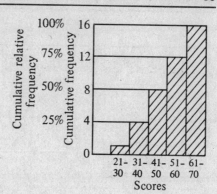

**16** students took the examination.

**b.** The cumulative frequency that includes scores through 60 is 12.

**12** students had a score less than or equal to 60.

**c.** The cumulative frequency of 12 corresponds to a cumulative relative frequency of 75%.

**75%** of the students had a score less than or equal to 60.

**d.** The *median* is the score such that one-half of all scores are above it and one-half of all scores are below it.

There are 16 scores in all. Since there are an even number of scores, the median score is midway between the 8th and 9th scores (there will be 8 scores above it and 8 scores below it). From the cumulative frequency scale, the 8th and 9th scores are both in the 41–50 interval. Therefore, the median is in the 41–50 interval.

The **41–50** interval contains the median.

**e.** The *lower quartile* is the score such that one-fourth of all scores are below it and three-fourths of all scores are above it.

Since there are 16 scores in all, $\frac{1}{4}$ of 16 or 4 scores are below the lower quartile and $\frac{3}{4}$ of 16 or 12 scores are above it. Thus, the lower quartile is at the cumulative frequency 4 mark (note that this is the 25% cumulative relative frequency). The 31–40 interval contains the cumulative frequency 4 mark. Therefore, the 31–40 interval contains the lower quartile.

The **31–40** interval contains the lower quartile.

| Topic | Question Numbers | Number of Points | Your Points | Your Percentage |
|---|---|---|---|---|
| 1. Numbers (rat'l, irrat'l); Percent | 11, 27, 42c | $2 + 2 + 2 = 6$ | | |
| 2. Properties of No. Systems | 30 | 2 | | |
| 3. Operations on Rat'l Nos. and Monomials | 13, 26 | $2 + 2 = 4$ | | |
| 4. Operations on Polynomials | — | 0 | | |
| 5. Square root; Operations involving Radicals | — | 0 | | |
| 6. Evaluating Formulas and Expressions | — | 0 | | |
| 7. Linear Equations (simple cases incl. parentheses) | 4 | 2 | | |
| 8. Linear Equations containing Decimals or Fractions | 1, 5 | $2 + 2 = 4$ | | |
| 9. Graphs of Linear Functions (slope) | 14, 32 | $2 + 2 = 4$ | | |
| 10. Inequalities | 28, 29 | $2 + 2 = 4$ | | |
| 11. Systems of Eqs. & Inequal. (alg. & graphic solutions) | 19, 37a, 37b | $2 + 4 + 6 = 12$ | | |
| 12. Factoring | 15, 25, 33 | $2 + 2 + 2 = 6$ | | |
| 13. Quadratic Equations | 35 | 2 | | |
| 14. Verbal Problems | 38, 40, 41b | $10 + 10 + 1 = 21$ | | |
| 15. Variation | — | 0 | | |
| 16. Literal Eqs.; Expressing Relations Algebraically | 7, 8, 17, 21 | $2 + 2 + 2 + 2 = 8$ | | |
| 17. Factorial n | — | 0 | | |

31

| Topic | Question Numbers | Number of Points | Your Points | Your Percentage |
|---|---|---|---|---|
| 18. Areas, Perims., Circums., Vols. of Common Figures | 10, 23, 41c, 41d, 41e, 41f | 2 + 2 + 1 + 2 + 2 + 2 = 11 | | |
| 19. Geometry (≅, ∠ meas., ‖ lines, compls., suppls., const.) | 22, 24 | 2 + 2 = 4 | | |
| 20. Ratio & Proportion (incl. similar triangles) | 2 | 2 | | |
| 21. Pythagorean Theorem | 20, 41a | 2 + 2 = 4 | | |
| 22. Logic (symbolic rep., logical forms, truth tables) | 12, 31, 34, 36a, 36b, 36c | 2 + 2 + 2 + 8 + 1 + 1 = 16 | | |
| 23. Probability (incl. tree diagrams & sample spaces) | 6, 9, 39a, 39b, 39c, 39d, 39e | 2 + 2 + 3 + 2 + 2 + 2 + 1 = 14 | | |
| 24. Combinations (arrangements, per-mutations) | 16 | 2 | | |
| 25. Statistics (central tend., freq. dist., his-tograms) | 3, 18, 42a, 42b, 42d, 42e | 2 + 2 + 2 + 2 + 2 + 2 = 12 | | |

# Examination January, 1983
## Three-Year Sequence for High School
## Mathematics—Course I

### PART ONE

DIRECTIONS: *Answer 30 questions from this part. Each correct answer will receive 2 credits. No partial credit will be allowed. Write your answers in the spaces provided. Where applicable, answers may be left in terms of π or in radical form.*

1 The probability of rain tomorrow is 40%. What is the probability that it will *not* rain tomorrow?

1. _60%_

2 Solve for $y$:  $3(y - 1) = 9$

2. _4_

3 Solve for $m$:  $\dfrac{m}{15} = \dfrac{2}{3}$

3. _10_

4 If $x = 6$ and $y = 3$, what is the sum of $\dfrac{4}{x} + \dfrac{1}{y}$?

4. _1_

1

5 A tree 10 meters in height casts a shadow 25 meters long. At the same time, a person casts a shadow 5 meters long. What is the number of meters in the height of the person?

5._____

6 Solve for $y$ in terms of $a$, $b$, and $x$:
$$ay - bx = 2$$

6._____

7 Solve for $x$:    $0.03x = 36$

7._1200_

8 There are 3 ways of going from town $A$ to town $B$ and 6 ways of going from town $B$ to town $C$. Find the total number of ways a person can go from town $A$ to town $B$ to town $C$.

8._18_

9 Express the *sum* of $(4x - 2)$ and $(3 - x)$ as a binomial.

9._____

10 A bag contains 2 green marbles, 4 blue marbles, and 5 red marbles. If one marble is drawn at random from the bag, what is the probability that it will be green?

10._$\frac{2}{11}$_

11 In the accompanying diagram, the measure of arc $AB$ in circle $O$ is $46°$. Find the measure in degrees of angle $AOB$.

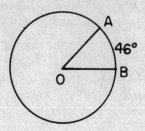

11. $46$

12 Solve the following system of equations for $x$:

$$3x + y = 5$$
$$2x - y = 0$$

12._____

13 Factor:     $x^2 - 7x + 10$

13._____

14 The measures of the angles of a triangle are represented by $x$, $2x$, and $(x + 20)$. Find the number of degrees in the measure of the *smallest* angle of the triangle.

14._____

15 Express as a binomial:     $3x^2(2x - 5)$

15._____

16 Two angles are supplementary and congruent. How many degrees are in the measure of each angle?

16. $90$

17 What percent of 200 is 14?

17. _7%_

18 The length of the edge of a cube is represented by $e$. Express the volume of the cube in terms of $e$.

18. _$e^3$_

19 Factor:      $9x^2 - 1$

19. _$(3x+1)(3x-1)$_

20 Find the length of the radius of a circle whose circumference is $18\pi$.

20. _9_

21 A fair coin and a fair die are tossed simultaneously. What is the total number of possible outcomes in the sample space?

21. _12_

DIRECTIONS (22–35): *For each question chosen, write in the space provided the* numeral *preceding the word or expression that best completes the statement or answers the question.*

22 The value of $\pi$ is
   (1) rational and equal to 3.14
   (2) irrational and equal to 3.14
   (3) rational and between 3.14 and 3.15
   (4) irrational and between 3.14 and 3.15

22. _4_

23 The largest possible value of $x$ in the solution set of $2x + 1 \le 7$ is
   (1) 6        (3) 3
   (2) 2        (4) 4

23. _4_

24 Let $p$ represent "I am 18," and let $q$ represent "I am going to college." Which statement is represented by $p \rightarrow q$?

(1) I am 18 and I am not going to college.
(2) If I am 18, then I am going to college.
(3) I am not 18 and I am not going to college.
(4) If I am going to college, then I am 18.

24._____

25 If $p$ represents the statement "It is cold" and $q$ represents the statement "It is winter," which represents "It is cold and it is not winter"?

(1) $p \rightarrow q$        (3) $p \wedge q$
(2) $p \vee \sim q$        (4) $p \wedge \sim q$

25._____

26 The inverse of $\sim p \rightarrow q$ is

(1) $p \rightarrow \sim q$        (3) $\sim q \rightarrow p$
(2) $\sim p \rightarrow \sim q$        (4) $q \rightarrow \sim p$

26.__4____

27 The graph of which equation has a slope of 2?

(1) $y = 2x - 3$        (3) $y = 3x - 2$
(2) $y = -2x + 3$        (4) $y = -3x + 2$

27._____

28 Which point does *not* lie on the graph of $x - 2y = 10$?

(1) $(0, -5)$        (3) $(5, 0)$
(2) $(2, -4)$        (4) $(6, -2)$

28._____

29 If two rectangles have equal perimeters, which statement *must* be true?

(1) The rectangles have equal areas.
(2) The rectangles are squares.
(3) The lengths of the rectangles are equal.
(4) The sum of the length and width of one rectangle is equal to the sum of the length and width of the other.

29._____

30 The equation $5x + 10 = 55$ has the same solution set as the equation

(1) $x = 45$      (3) $5x = 65$
(2) $x + 10 = 11$      (4) $5x + 15 = 60$

30._____

31 The scores on a test were 75, 75, 85, 90, and 100. Which statement about these scores is true?

(1) The mean and the median are the same.
(2) The mode is greater than the median.
(3) The mode is greater than the mean.
(4) The mean is less than the median.

31._____

32 When $3x^2$ is multiplied by $-5x^3$, the product is

(1) $-15x^6$      (3) $-8x^5$
(2) $-15x^5$      (4) $15x^5$

32._____

33 Which inequality is represented by the graph below?

(1) $2 < x \leq -3$      (3) $-3 < x \leq 2$
(2) $-3 \leq x < 2$      (4) $-3 \leq x \leq 2$      33._____

34 The solution set of $x^2 - 2x - 8 = 0$ is
(1) $\{-6,2\}$      (3) $\{-4,2\}$
(2) $\{4,2\}$      (4) $\{4,-2\}$      34._____

35 The sum of $\sqrt{2}$ and $3\sqrt{2}$ is
(1) $3\sqrt{2}$      (3) $3\sqrt{4}$
(2) $4\sqrt{2}$      (4) $4\sqrt{4}$      35._____

### PART TWO

DIRECTIONS (36-42): *Answer four questions from this part. Show all work unless otherwise directed.*

36 On the same set of coordinate axes, graph the following system of inequalities and label the solution set $S$.

$$y > x + 1$$
$$x \leq -1 \qquad [8,2]$$

37 Solve algebraically and check:
$$2c - d = -1$$
$$c + 3d = 17 \qquad [8,2]$$

38 Jim bought 3 packets of vegetable seeds: beans, carrots, and radishes; and two packets of flower seeds: marigolds and petunias. Finding that his garden was too small, he decided to give away one packet of vegetable seeds and one packet of flower seeds, each selected randomly.

   *a* Draw a tree diagram or list all possible pairs of packets in the sample space that he might select to give away.　　[4]

   *b* Find the probability that he did *not* give away the packet of bean seeds.　　[2]

   *c* Find the probability that he gave away two packets of vegetable seeds.　　[2]

   *d* Find the probability that he gave away the packet of petunia seeds.　　[2]

39 The length of a rectangle is 3 more than three times the width. The perimeter of the rectangle is 62.

   *a* Find the length and width of the rectangle. [*Only an algebraic solution will be accepted.*]　　[4,4]

   *b* Find the area of the rectangle.　　[2]

40 The sum of the squares of two consecutive positive even integers is 52. Find the integers. [*Only an algebraic solution will be accepted.*]　　[4,6]

41 Answer *both a and b.*

   *a* Given the inequality: $8x \geq 3(x - 5)$

     (1) Solve for $x$.   [4]

     (2) Choose one value of $x$ from your solution in part (1), and show that it makes the inequality $8x \geq 3(x - 5)$ true.   [2]

   *b* On your answer paper, copy and complete the truth table for the statement $(p \rightarrow q) \leftrightarrow (p \vee q)$.   [4]

| $p$ | $q$ | $p \rightarrow q$ | $p \vee q$ | $(p \rightarrow q) \leftrightarrow (p \vee q)$ |
|-----|-----|-------------------|------------|-----------------------------------------------|
| T | T | | | |
| T | F | | | |
| F | T | | | |
| F | F | | | |

42 The points scored by Rosa in twenty basketball
games are 35, 33, 27, 35, 29, 37, 32, 35, 35,
32, 23, 37, 32, 29, 26, 30, 28, 31, 29, 35.

a Find the mode.  [2]

b On your answer paper, copy and complete
the table below.  [2]

| Interval | Tally | Frequency |
|----------|-------|-----------|
| 35–37 | | |
| 32–34 | | |
| 29–31 | | |
| 26–28 | | |
| 23–25 | | |

c Construct a frequency histogram based on
the table completed in part b.  [4]

d In what interval does the median lie?  [2]

# Answers January, 1983

## Three-Year Sequence for High School Mathematics—Course 1

### ANSWER KEY
### PART ONE

| | | |
|---|---|---|
| 1. 60% | 12. 1 | 25. 4 |
| 2. 4 | 13. $(x - 5)(x - 2)$ | 26. 1 |
| 3. 10 | 14. 40 | 27. 1 |
| 4. 1 | 15. $6x^3 - 15x^2$ | 28. 3 |
| 5. 2 | 16. 90 | 29. 4 |
| 6. $\dfrac{bx + 2}{a}$ | 17. 7 | 30. 4 |
| | 18. $e^3$ | 31. 1 |
| 7. 1,200 | 19. $(3x + 1)(3x - 1)$ | 32. 2 |
| 8. 18 | 20. 9 | 33. 2 |
| 9. $3x + 1$ | 21. 12 | 34. 4 |
| 10. $\dfrac{2}{11}$ | 22. 4 | 35. 2 |
| | 23. 3 | |
| 11. 46 | 24. 2 | |

Part Two—*See answers explained.*

### ANSWERS EXPLAINED
### PART ONE

1. Convert the percent probability to a fraction: $40\% = \dfrac{40}{100}$

Since probability of an event occurring =
$\dfrac{\text{number of favorable cases}}{\text{total possible number of cases}}$, a probability of $\dfrac{40}{100}$ that it will rain may be interpreted as 40 favorable cases (that is, that it will rain) out of a total possible 100 cases (both rain and *no* rain); thus, there must be $100 - 40$, or 60, cases of *no* rain.

The probability that it will *not* rain is: $\dfrac{60}{100}$

Convert the probability of $\dfrac{60}{100}$ to a percent: $\dfrac{60}{100} = 60\%$

The probability that it will *not* rain tomorrow is **60%**.

11

ALTERNATE SOLUTION: It is certain that either it will rain or it will *not* rain tomorrow. Certainty is represented by a probability of 100%. If the probability that it will rain is 40%, then the probability that it will *not* rain is 100% − 40%, or 60%.

**2.**

Remove parentheses by applying the distributive law of multiplication over addition:

Add 3 (the additive inverse of −3) to both sides of the equation:

$$3(y - 1) = 9$$
$$3y - 3 = 9$$
$$\underline{3 = 3}$$
$$3y = 12$$

Multiply both sides of the equation by $\frac{1}{3}$ (the multiplicative inverse of 3):

$$\frac{1}{3}(3y) = \frac{1}{3}(12)$$
$$y = 4$$

The solution for $y$ is **4**.

**3.**

$$\frac{m}{15} = \frac{2}{3}$$

In a proportion, the product of the means equals the product of the extremes (cross-multiply):

$$3m = 15(2)$$
$$3m = 30$$

Multiply both sides of the equation by $\frac{1}{3}$ (the multiplicative inverse of 3):

$$\frac{1}{3}(3m) = \frac{1}{3}(30)$$
$$m = 10$$

The solution for $m$ is **10**.

**4.**

$$\frac{4}{x} + \frac{1}{y}$$

Since it is given that $x = 6$ and $y = 3$, substitute 6 for $x$ and 3 for $y$:

$$\frac{4}{6} + \frac{1}{3}$$

Reduce the left-hand fraction by dividing both numerator and denominator by 2:

$$\frac{2}{3} + \frac{1}{3}$$

The two fractions now have the same denominator. Fractions with the same denominator may be combined by combining their numerators and placing them over the common denominator:

$$\frac{2 + 1}{3}$$

Combine the terms in the numerator:

$$\frac{3}{3}$$

Simplify:

$$1$$

The sum is **1**.

**5.** Let $x$ = the number of meters in the height of the person.

The person and his shadow and the tree and its shadow form the vertical and horizontal legs respectively of two similar right triangles.

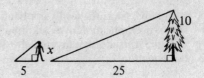

The corresponding sides of two similar triangles are in proportion:

$$\frac{x}{5} = \frac{10}{25}$$

In a proportion, the product of the means equals the product of the extremes (cross-multiply):

$$25x = 5(10)$$
$$25x = 50$$

Multiply both sides of the equation by $\frac{1}{25}$ (the multiplicative inverse of 25):

$$\frac{1}{25}(25x) = \frac{1}{25}(50)$$
$$x = 2$$

The height of the person is **2** meters.

**6.**

$$ay - bx = 2$$

Add $+bx$ (the additive inverse of $-bx$) to both sides of the equation:

$$\frac{+bx = \quad +bx}{ay \quad = 2 + bx}$$

Multiply both sides of the equation by $\frac{1}{a}$ (the multiplicative inverse of $a$):

$$\frac{1}{a}(ay) = \frac{1}{a}(bx + 2)$$
$$y = \frac{bx + 2}{a}$$

The solution is $y = \dfrac{bx + 2}{a}$.

**7.**

$$0.03x = 36$$

Clear decimals by multiplying both sides of the equation by 100:

$$100(0.03x) = 100(36)$$
$$3x = 3,600$$

Multiply both sides of the equation by $\frac{1}{3}$ (the multiplicative inverse of 3:

$$\frac{1}{3}(3x) = \frac{1}{3}(3,600)$$
$$x = 1,200$$

The solution for $x$ is **1,200**.

8. For *each* of the 3 ways to go from A to B, there are 6 ways to go from B to C. Therefore, there are 3 times 6, or 18, ways to go from A to B to C.

The total number of ways is **18**.

9. To add two binomials, write one binomial under the other with like terms in the same column:

$$\begin{array}{r} 4x - 2 \\ -x + 3 \\ \hline 3x + 1 \end{array}$$

Add the terms in each column algebraically:

The sum is $3x + 1$.

10. Probability of an event occurring =
$$\frac{\text{number of favorable cases}}{\text{total possible number of cases}}.$$
Since there are 2 green marbles in the bag, the number of favorable cases for picking a green marble in a random draw is 2.

2 green, 4 blue, and 5 red marbles make a total of 11 marbles in the bag. Thus, the total possible number of cases in a random draw is 11.

The probability of drawing a green marble = $\frac{2}{11}$.

The probability is $\frac{2}{11}$.

11. $\angle AOB$ is a central angle since its vertex is the center of the circle and its sides are radii.

The measure of a central angle is equal to the measure of its intercepted arc:
$$m\angle AOB = m\widehat{AB}$$
$$m\angle AOB = 46°$$

The measure of angle $AOB$ is **46°**.

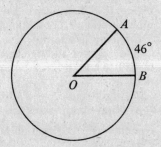

12.

$$\begin{array}{r} 3x + y = 5 \\ 2x - y = 0 \\ \hline 5x \qquad = 5 \end{array}$$

Adding the equations together will eliminate $y$:

Multiply both sides of the equation by $\frac{1}{5}$ (the multiplicative inverse of 5):

$$\frac{1}{5}(5x) = \frac{1}{5}(5)$$
$$x = 1$$

The solution for $x$ is **1**.

**13.** The given expression is a *quadratic trinomial*:

$$x^2 - 7x + 10$$

The factors of a quadratic trinomial are two binomials. The factors of the first term, $x^2$, are $x$ and $x$, and they become the first terms of the binomials:

$$(x \quad )(x \quad )$$

The factors of the last term, $+10$, become the second terms of the binomials but they must be chosen in such a way that the product of the inner terms added to the product of the outer terms equals the middle term, $-7x$, of the original trinomial:

$$-5x = \text{inner product}$$

Try $-5$ and $-2$ as the factors of $+10$:

$$(x - 5)(x - 2)$$

Since $(-5x) + (-2x) = -7x$, these are the correct factors:

$$-2x = \text{outer product}$$
$$(x - 5)(x - 2)$$

The factored form is $(x - 5)(x - 2)$.

**14.** The sum of the measures of the angles of a triangle is 180°. Since the measures of the angles are represented by $x$, $2x$ and $(x + 20)$ respectively:

$$x + 2x + (x + 20) = 180$$

Remove parentheses by applying the distributive law of multiplication over addition:

$$x + 2x + x + 20 = 180$$

Combine like terms:

$$4x + 20 = 180$$

Add $-20$ (the additive inverse of $+20$) to both sides of the equation:

$$\begin{array}{r} -20 = -20 \\ \hline 4x \quad = 160 \end{array}$$

Multiply both sides of the equation by $\frac{1}{4}$ (the multiplicative inverse of 4):

$$\frac{1}{4}(4x) = \frac{1}{4}(160)$$
$$x = 40$$
$$2x = 2(40) = 80$$
$$x + 20 = 40 + 20 = 60$$

The measure of the *smallest* angle of the triangle is **40°**.

· **15.**                                              $3x^2(2x - 5)$

Apply the distributive law of multiplication over addition by multiplying each term within the parentheses by $3x^2$. Remember that when powers of the same base are multiplied, their exponents are added, and note that $x$ has the exponent, 1, understood:                 $6x^3 - 15x^2$

The binomial is **$6x^3 - 15x^2$**.

**16.**  Let $x$ = the number of degrees in the measure of the first angle.

Then $x$ = the number of degrees in the measure of the second angle since the angles are congruent.

If two angles are supplementary, the sum of their measures is 180°:                              $x + x = 180$

Combine like terms:                                  $2x = 180$

Multiply both sides of the equation by $\frac{1}{2}$ (the multiplicative inverse of 2):            $\frac{1}{2}(2x) = \frac{1}{2}(180)$

$$x = 90$$

Each angle has a measure of **90°**.

**17.**  To determine what percent one number is of another, divide the first number by the second. Division may be represented by a fraction having the number to be divided as its numerator and the divisor as its denominator:   $\dfrac{14}{200}$

Reduce the fraction by dividing its numerator and denominator by 2:                                 $\dfrac{7}{100}$

The denominator of the fraction, $\frac{7}{100}$, is 100, so the fraction is 7 hundredths. Percent means hundredths. Therefore:                                          $\dfrac{7}{100} = 7\%$

14 is **7%** of 200.

**18.** The volume of any rectangular solid is equal to its length times it width times its height.

A cube is a rectangular solid with all of its edges equal: length = $e$, width = $e$, height = $e$

Volume = $e \times e \times e = e^3$

The volume of the cube is $e^3$.

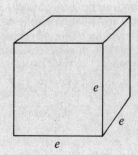

**19.** The given expression is the *difference of two perfect squares*, $9x^2$ and 1:

$$9x^2 - 1$$

To factor it, take the square root of each perfect square:

$$\sqrt{9x^2} = 3x$$
$$\sqrt{1} = 1$$

One factor is the sum of the respective square roots and the other is the difference of the square roots:

$$(3x + 1)(3x - 1)$$

The factored form is $(3x + 1)(3x - 1)$.

**20.** The circumference, $c$, of a circle is given by the formula $c = 2\pi r$ where $r$ is the length of the radius.

It is given that $c = 18\pi$:

$$18\pi = 2\pi r$$

Multiply both sides of the equation by $\frac{1}{2\pi}$ (the multiplicative inverse of $2\pi$):

$$\frac{1}{2\pi}(18\pi) = \frac{1}{2\pi}(2\pi r)$$
$$9 = r$$

The length of the radius is **9**.

**21.** The toss of the fair coin has two possible outcomes: heads or tails. The toss of the fair die has 6 possible outcomes: 1, 2, 3, 4, 5, or 6.

The sample space would show all the possible combinations of outcomes for the coin toss and the die toss. *Each* of the 2 coin toss outcomes may be paired with *each* of the 6 die toss outcomes, making a total of $2 \times 6$, or 12, combination outcomes.

The total number of possible outcomes in the sample space is **12**.

**22.** $\pi$ is an irrational number. An irrational number cannot be represented as the ratio of two integers. Therefore, $\pi$ cannot be equal to a decimal which terminates, since a terminating decimal can always be represented as the ratio of two integers and hence is a rational number. For example, the terminating decimal, 3.14, given in choices (1) and (2), is equal to the ratio $\dfrac{314}{100}$.

The decimal value of $\pi$ is approximately 3.1416 . . ., but the decimal never terminates and never repeats. The decimal, 3.1416 . . ., lies between 3.14 and 3.15. $\pi$ is thus an irrational number between these two values.

The correct choice is (**4**).

**23.**
Add $-1$ (the additive inverse of 1) to both sides of the inequality:

$$\begin{array}{r} 2x + 1 \le 7 \\ \underline{-1 = -1} \\ 2x \quad\;\; \le 6 \end{array}$$

Multiply both sides of the inequality by $\frac{1}{2}$ (the multiplicative inverse of 2):

$$\frac{1}{2}(2x) \le \frac{1}{2}(6)$$
$$x \le 3$$

The solution states that the values of $x$ must be less than or equal to 3. The largest number which meets this requirement is 3.

The correct choice is (**3**).

**24.** $p{\rightarrow}q$ is the *implication*, "If $p$ is true, then $q$ is true."
Since $p$ represents "I am 18" and $q$ represents "I am going to college," $p{\rightarrow}q$ translates into "If I am 18, then I am going to college."

The correct choice is (**2**).

**25.** "It is not winter" is the *negation* of "It is winter."
It is given that $p$ represents "It is cold." Since $q$ represents "It is winter," "It is not winter" is represented by $\sim q$, the negation of $q$.
"It is cold and it is not winter" is the *conjunction* of $p$ and $\sim q$, which is represented by $p{\wedge}{\sim}q$.

The correct choice is (**4**).

**26.** The given implication is $\sim p{\rightarrow}q$. The *inverse* of an implication is another implication which is formed by negating both the *antecedent* (hypothesis or "if clause") and the *consequent* (conclusion or "then clause") of the original implication.

The antecedent of $\sim p \rightarrow q$ is $\sim p$, and its consequent is $q$. The negation of $\sim p$ is $p$ and the negation of $q$ is $\sim q$. Therefore, the inverse of $\sim p \rightarrow q$ is $p \rightarrow \sim q$.

The correct choice is (**I**).

**27.** If the equation of a line is in the form, $y = mx + b$, its slope is represented by $m$.

Examine each choice in turn to see which equation will have a graph with a slope of 2:

(1) $y = 2x - 3$ is in the form, $y = mx + b$, with $m = 2$ and $b = -3$. Therefore, its slope is 2, which is the slope we seek.

(2) $y = -2x + 3$ is in the form, $y = mx + b$, with $m = -2$ and $b = 3$. Its slope is $-2$.

(3) $y = 3x - 2$ is in the form, $y = mx + b$, with $m = 3$ and $b = -2$. Its slope is 3.

(4) $y = -3x + 2$ is in the form, $y = mx + b$, with $m = -3$ and $b = 2$. Its slope is $-3$.

Choice (1) is the only one in which the line has a slope of 2.

The correct choice is (**1**).

**28.** If a point lies on a graph, its coordinates will satisfy the equation of the graph when they are substituted for $x$ and $y$ respectively.

Test the coordinates given in each choice by substituting them in the equation, $x - 2y = 10$:

(1) $(0, -5)$: $0 - 2(-5) \overset{?}{=} 10$
$$0 + 10 \overset{?}{=} 10$$
$$10 = 10 \; \checkmark \; (0, -5) \text{ lies on the line}$$

(2) $(2, -4)$: $2 - 2(-4) \overset{?}{=} 10$
$$2 + 8 \overset{?}{=} 10$$
$$10 = 10 \; \checkmark \; (2, -4) \text{ lies on the line}$$

(3) $(5, 0)$: $\quad 5 - 2(0) \overset{?}{=} 10$
$$5 - 0 \overset{?}{=} 10$$
$$5 \neq 10 \; (5, 0) \text{ does } not \text{ lie on the line}$$

(4) $(6, -2)$: $6 - 2(-2) \overset{?}{=} 10$
$$6 + 4 \overset{?}{=} 10$$
$$10 = 10 \; \checkmark \; (6, -2) \text{ lies on the line}$$

$(5, 0)$ is the only one of the choices that does *not* lie on the line, $x - 2y = 10$.

The correct choice is (**3**).

**29.**   The perimeter of a rectangle is the sum of the lengths of all four sides.

Consider each choice in turn to see whether it must be true if two rectangles have equal perimeters:

(1) Consider the diagram shown as one example of two rectangles with equal perimeters.

Perimeter of Rectangle I = 3 + 5 + 3 + 5 = 16.

Perimeter of Rectangle II = 1 + 7 + 1 + 7 = 16.

The area of a rectangle equals its length times its width. Therefore, the area of Rectangle I = 5 × 3 or 15 and the area of Rectangle II = 7 × 1 or 7.

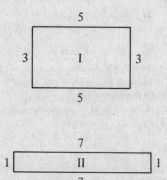

The areas are not equal. Therefore, it is not true that rectangles with equal perimeters *must* have equal areas.

(2) Two rectangles could certainly have equal perimeters without necessarily being squares; they might even be congruent rectangles, for example. Therefore it is not true that rectangles with equal perimeters *must* be squares.

(3) The two rectangles pictured in connection with the discussion of choice (1) have equal perimeters but Rectangle I has a length of 5 while Rectangle II has a length of 7. Thus it is not true that rectangles with equal perimeters *must* have equal lengths.

(4) The perimeter of a rectangle is actually the sum of 2 lengths and 2 widths. The sum of one length and one width would be exactly equal to one-half the perimeter.

If two rectangles have equal perimeters, then halves of their perimeters would also be equal. Hence it *must* be true that the sum of the length and width of one is equal to the sum of the length and width of the other.

The correct choice is (4).

**30.**   Solve the given equation:                                $5x + 10 = 55$

Add −10 (the additive inverse of 10) to both sides of the equation:

$$\begin{aligned} 5x + 10 &= 55 \\ -10 &= -10 \\ \hline 5x\ \ \ \ &= 45 \end{aligned}$$

Multiply both sides of the equation by $\frac{1}{5}$ (the multiplicative inverse of 5):

$$\frac{1}{5}(5x) = \frac{1}{5}(45)$$

$$x = 9$$

The solution set of the given equation is {9}.
Find the solution set of the equation in each choice:

(1)

$$x = 45$$

The solution set of $x = 45$ is {45}. It is *not* the same as that of the given equation.

(2)

$$x + 10 = 11$$

Add $-10$ (the additive inverse of 10) to both sides of the equation:

$$\underline{\phantom{x}-10 = -10}$$
$$x \phantom{++} = 1$$

The solution set is {1} which is *not* the same as the solution set of the given equation.

(3)

$$5x = 65$$

Multiply each side of the equation by $\frac{1}{5}$ (the multiplicative inverse of 5):

$$\frac{1}{5}(5x) = \frac{1}{5}(65)$$

$$x = 13$$

The solution set is {13} which is *not* the same as the solution set of the given equation.

(4)

$$5x + 15 = 60$$

Add $-15$ (the additive inverse of 15) to both sides of the equation:

$$\underline{\phantom{5x}-15 = -15}$$
$$5x \phantom{++} = 45$$

Multiply both sides of the equation by $\frac{1}{5}$ (the multiplicative inverse of 5):

$$\frac{1}{5}(5x) = \frac{1}{5}(45)$$

$$x = 9$$

The solution set is {9} which is the same as the solution set of the given equation.

The correct choice is (**4**).

ALTERNATE SOLUTION: It may be noticed that adding 5 to both sides of the given equation, $5x + 10 = 55$, will produce the equation of choice (4), $5x + 15 = 60$. Since adding the same quantity to both sides of an equation leaves its solution set unchanged, we know immediately that the solution sets of choice (4) and of the given equation are the same, even without solving either of them.

**31.** Find the *mean* of the scores by adding them together and dividing by the number of scores which is 5:

$$\begin{array}{r} 75 \\ 75 \\ 85 \\ 90 \\ \underline{100} \\ 5)\overline{425} \\ \hline 85 \end{array}$$

The *mean* is 85.

Find the *median* of the scores. The median is the middle score when the scores are arranged in order of size. For 75, 75, 85, 90, 100, there are 5 scores so the third one is the median. The *median* is 85.

Find the *mode*. The mode is the score which appears most frequently. Since 75 is the only score which appears more than once, the *mode* is 75.

Examination of the choices indicates that the only one which is true is that the mean, 85, and the median, also 85, are the same.

The correct choice is (**1**).

**32.**
To multiply two monomials, first multiply their numerical coefficients to obtain the numerical coefficient of the product:

$$(3x^2)(-5x^3)$$

$$(3)(-5) = -15$$

Then multiply the literal factors to get the literal factor of the product. Remember that when multiplying powers of the same base, their exponents are added:

$$(x^2)(x^3) = x^5$$

Combine the two results above to form the complete product:

$$-15x^5$$

The correct choice is (**2**).

**33.** The heavy line extends from $-3$ to the right, that is, above $-3$. However, there is a heavy dot at $-3$ which indicates that $-3$ is included in the set. Thus, $-3 \leq x$.

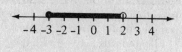

The heavy line extends to the left of 2, that is, below 2. However, the open circle at 2 indicates that 2 is *not* included in the set. Thus, $x < 2$.

Putting the two results together:

$$-3 \leq x < 2$$

The correct choice is (**2**).

**34.**   The given equation is a *quadratic equation*:

$$x^2 - 2x - 8 = 0$$

Factor the *quadratic trinomial* on the left side. The factors of a quadratic trinomial are two binomials. The factors of the first term, $x^2$, are $x$ and $x$, and they become the first terms of the binomials:

$$(x \quad )(x \quad ) = 0$$

The factors of the last term, $-8$, become the second terms of the binomials, but they must be chosen in such a way that the product of the inner terms added to the product of the outer terms equals the middle term, $-2x$, of the original trinomial: Try $-4$ and $+2$ as the factors of $-8$:

$$-4x = \text{inner product}$$
$$(x - 4)(x + 2) = 0$$
$$+2x = \text{outer product}$$

Since $(-4x) + (+2x) = -2x$, these are the correct factors:

$$(x - 4)(x + 2) = 0$$

If the product of two factors equals 0, either factor may equal 0:

$$x - 4 = 0 \quad \text{OR} \quad x + 2 = 0$$

Add the appropriate additive inverse to both sides of each equation, 4 in the case of the left-hand equation, and $-2$ in the case of the right-hand equation:

$$\frac{4 = 4}{x \quad = 4} \qquad \frac{-2 = -2}{x \quad = -2}$$

The solution set is $\{4, -2\}$.

The correct choice is **(4)**.

**35.**   The expressions to be added are *like radicals*:

$$\sqrt{2} + 3\sqrt{2}$$

Like radicals have the same *index* (in this case, 2, representing the square root), and the same *radicand* (the number under the radical sign).

Like radicals may be added by adding their coefficients and placing the sum in front of the common radical. Note that the coefficient of $3\sqrt{2}$ is 3, and that the coefficient of $\sqrt{2}$ is understood to be 1:

$$4\sqrt{2}$$

The correct choice is **(2)**.

### PART TWO

**36.** To draw the graph of the inequality $y > x + 1$, first draw the graph of the equation $y = x + 1$.

Set up a table of values by choosing 3 convenient values for $x$ and substituting in the equation to find the corresponding values of $y$:

| $x$ | $x + 1$ | $= y$ |
|-----|---------|-------|
| $-2$ | $-2 + 1$ | $= -1$ |
| $0$ | $0 + 1$ | $= 1$ |
| $4$ | $4 + 1$ | $= 5$ |

Plot the points $(-2, -1)$, $(0, 1)$, and $(4, 5)$ and draw a *dashed* line through them. The dashed line denotes that points on it are not part of the solution set of the inequality $y > x + 1$; they are on the boundary of the solution set.

The points that satisfy the inequality $y > x + 1$ occupy an entire region (called a *half-plane*) on one side of the dashed line $y = x + 1$. To find out which side of the line represents the half-plane $y > x + 1$, select a test point, say $(0, 0)$, and substitute it in the inequality:

$$0 \overset{?}{>} 0 + 1$$
$$0 \not> 1$$

Therefore, $(0, 0)$ does not lie within the region for which $y > x + 1$. The region for which $y > x + 1$ is on the opposite side of the line from $(0, 0)$ and this region is shaded with cross-hatching extending up and to the right.

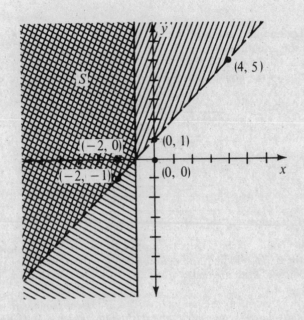

To draw the graph of $x \leq -1$, first draw the graph of the straight line, $x = -1$. A line whose equation is of the form $x = -a$ is parallel to the $y$-axis and $a$ units to the left of the $y$-axis. Since in this case $a = 1$, the graph of $x = -1$ is shown as a solid line parallel to the $y$-axis and 1 unit to the left of it. The solid line denotes that points on it are part of the solution set of $x \leq -1$; they are the part represented by $x = -1$.

To determine on which side of the line $x = -1$ the points representing $x < -1$ lie, choose a test point, say $(-2, 0)$ and substitute its coordinates in the inequality $x < -1$:
$$-2 < -1$$
$$-2 < -1 ✓$$

The side of the line $x = -1$, on which $(-2, 0)$ lies is the solution set of $x < -1$. Shade it with cross-hatching extending down and to the right.

The solution set of the system consists of points which satisfy *both* inequalities. These are the points in the region covered by *both* types of cross-hatching, including that part of the solid line which is a boundary of this region. The region representing the solution set of the system is labeled **S**.

**37.**

$$2c - d = -1$$
$$c + 3d = 17$$

Multiply each term on both sides of the first equation by 3:

$$3(2c) + 3(-d) = 3(-1)$$
$$6c - 3d = -3$$

Add the second equation to the result:
This eliminates $d$:

$$\underline{c + 3d = 17}$$
$$7c \qquad = 14$$

Multiply both sides of the equation by $\frac{1}{7}$ (the multiplicative inverse of 7):

$$\frac{1}{7}(7c) = \frac{1}{7}(14)$$
$$c = 2$$

Substitute 2 for $c$ in the original first equation:

$$2(2) - d = -1$$
$$4 - d = -1$$

Add 1 (the additive inverse of $-1$) and also add $d$ (the additive inverse of $-d$) to both sides of the equation:

$$\frac{1 + d = 1 + d}{5 \qquad = \qquad d}$$

CHECK: The supposed solution, $c = 2$, $d = 5$, is checked by substituting these values in *both* of the *original* equations to see if they are satisfied:

$$2c - d = -1 \qquad\qquad c + 3d = 17$$
$$2(2) - 5 \stackrel{?}{=} -1 \qquad\qquad 2 + 3(5) \stackrel{?}{=} 17$$
$$4 - 5 \stackrel{?}{=} -1 \qquad\qquad 2 + 15 \stackrel{?}{=} 17$$
$$-1 = -1 \;✔ \qquad\qquad 17 = 17 \;✔$$

The solution is $c = 2$, $d = 5$.

**38a.** The tree diagram will contain 3 branches leading from START to represent the 3 possibilities (beans, carrots, or radishes) for selecting a vegetable seed packet to give away. For each of these "first step" branches representing a vegetable seed choice, there are 2 "second step" branches representing the possibilities of selecting either marigolds or petunias as the flower seed packet to give away.

The sample space may also be shown by listing all possible pairs. Each of the three possible choices of a vegetable seed packet is listed twice so that it can be paired with each of the two possible choices of a flower seed:

Sample space:

| Vegetable | Flower |
|-----------|--------|
| BEANS | MARIGOLDS |
| BEANS | PETUNIAS |
| CARROTS | MARIGOLDS |
| CARROTS | PETUNIAS |
| RADISHES | MARIGOLDS |
| RADISHES | PETUNIAS |

**b.** Probability of an event occurring

$$= \frac{\text{number of favorable cases}}{\text{total possible number of cases}}.$$

Using the tree diagram, there are 3 possible paths from START to the vegetable choice, followed in each case by 2 possible paths to the flower choice—for a total possible number of 6 paths. Using the sample space list, there are 6 possible pairs shown. The total possible number of give-away combinations is thus 6.

The probability of *not* giving away the packet of bean seeds is wanted. This means that on the tree diagram the favorable cases are represented by those paths that go from START through CARROTS or RADISHES to a flower choice. There are 4 such favorable cases. In the sample space, the favorable cases are the 4 lines that do not contain BEANS.

The probability of *not* giving away the bean seeds is $\frac{4}{6}$.

**c.** Jim gave away only *one* packet of vegetable seeds and *one* of flower seeds. There are *no* paths from START through to the second choice which involve the selection of two packets of vegetable seeds. Similarly, the sample space list contains *no* lines with 2 vegetables. Therefore, out of the total of 6 possible cases, there are 0 favorable cases for a choice of 2 vegetable seed packets.

The probability of giving away 2 packets of vegetable seeds $= \frac{0}{6} = 0$.

**d.**  The favorable cases for the giving away of the packet of petunia seeds are represented on the tree diagram by the 3 paths which begin at START and end up with PETUNIAS. Thus, out of the 6 possible paths, there are 3 favorable cases. Similarly, the sample space list shows 3 of its 6 lines involving PETUNIAS.

The probability that he gave away the packet of petunia seeds $= \frac{3}{6}$.

**39a.**  Let $x$ = the width of the rectangle.
Then $3x + 3$ = the length of the rectangle.

$$3x + 3$$

$$x \qquad \qquad x$$

$$3x + 3$$

The perimeter of a rectangle is the sum of the lengths of all four sides. Since the perimeter is 62, the equation to use is:     $x + (3x + 3) + x + (3x + 3) = 62$
Remove parentheses by applying the distributive law of multiplication over addition:     $x + 3x + 3 + x + 3x + 3 = 62$
Combine like terms:     $8x + 6 = 62$
Add $-6$ (the additive inverse of 6) to both sides of the equation:

$$\begin{array}{r} -6 = -6 \\ \hline 8x \quad = 56 \end{array}$$

Multiply both sides of the equation by $\frac{1}{8}$ (the multiplicative inverse of 8):     $\frac{1}{8}(8x) = \frac{1}{8}(56)$

$$x = 7$$

Evaluate $3x + 3$:     $3x + 3 = 3(7) + 3 = 21 + 3 = 24$

The width is **7** and the length is **24**.

**b.**  The area of a rectangle is equal to the product of its length and width:

$$\text{Area} = 24(7)$$
$$\text{Area} = 168$$

The area is **168**.

**40.** Let $x$ = the first positive even integer.

Then $x + 2$ = the next consecutive even integer.

The sum of the squares of the two integers is 52; therefore, the equation to use is:

$$x^2 + (x + 2)^2 = 52$$

Square $x + 2$:

$$
\begin{array}{r}
x + 2 \\
x + 2 \\
\hline
x^2 + 2x \\
+ 2x + 4 \\
\hline
x^2 + 4x + 4
\end{array}
$$

Combine like terms:

$$x^2 + x^2 + 4x + 4 = 52$$
$$2x^2 + 4x + 4 = 52$$

This is a *quadratic equation*. Rearrange it so that all terms are on one side equal to 0 by adding $-52$ (the additive inverse of 52) to both sides:

$$
\begin{array}{r}
-52 = -52 \\
\hline
2x^2 + 4x - 48 = 0
\end{array}
$$

Simplify the equation by dividing all terms on both sides by 2:

$$x^2 + 2x - 24 = 0$$

Factor the *quadratic trinomial* on the left side. The factors of a quadratic trinomial are 2 binomials. The factors of the first term, $x^2$, are $x$ and $x$, and they become the first terms of the binomials:

$$(x \quad )(x \quad ) = 0$$

The factors of the last term, $-24$, become the second terms of the binomials, but they must be chosen in such a way that the product of the inner terms added to the product of the outer terms equals the middle term, $+2x$, of the original trinomial. Try $+6$ and $-4$ as the factors of $-24$:

$$+6x = \text{inner product}$$
$$(x + 6)(x - 4) = 0$$
$$-4x = \text{outer product}$$

Since $(+6x) + (-4x) = +2x$, these are the correct factors:

$$(x + 6)(x - 4) = 0$$

If the product of two factors is 0, either factor may equal 0:

$$x + 6 = 0 \quad \text{OR} \quad x - 4 = 0$$

Add the appropriate additive inverse, $-6$ in the case of the left-hand equation and 4 in the case of the right-hand equation:

$$x + 6 = 0 \qquad x - 4 = 0$$
$$\underline{-6 = -6} \qquad \underline{4 = 4}$$
$$x \quad = -6 \qquad x \quad = 4$$

Reject the $-6$ since the question asks for positive integers:

$$x = 4$$
$$x + 2 = 6$$

The consecutive positive even integers are **4** and **6**.

**41a.**    (1)    $8x \geq 3(x - 5)$

Remove parentheses by applying the distributive law of multiplication over addition:

$$8x \geq 3x - 15$$

Add $-3x$ (the additive inverse of $3x$) to both sides of the inequality:

$$\underline{-3x = -3x}$$
$$5x \geq \quad - 15$$

Multiply both sides of the inequality by $\frac{1}{5}$ (the multiplicative inverse of 5):

$$\frac{1}{5}(5x) \geq \frac{1}{5}(-15)$$
$$x \geq -3$$

The solution set is $\{x | x \geq -3\}$.

(2) The solution set consists of all values of $x$ which are greater than or equal to $-3$. One such value is $x = 0$. To show that 0 makes the inequality, $8x \geq 3(x - 5)$, true, substitute 0 for $x$ to see if the inequality is satisfied:

$$8(0) \overset{?}{\geq} 3(0 - 5)$$
$$0 \overset{?}{\geq} 3(-5)$$
$$0 \geq -15 ✔$$

**b.**

| $p$ | $q$ | $p \rightarrow q$ | $p \vee q$ | $(p \rightarrow q) \longleftrightarrow (p \vee q)$ |
|---|---|---|---|---|
| T | T | T | T | T |
| T | F | F | T | F |
| F | T | T | T | T |
| F | F | T | F | F |

The columns for $p$ and $q$ are already filled in with all possible combinations of their truth values, T for true and F for false.

STEP 1: $(p \rightarrow q)$ is the *implication*, $p$ implies $q$. Fill in each line of the column headed $(p \rightarrow q)$ with T or F, determining the proper entry according to the truth values of $p$ and $q$ in the first two columns. $(p \rightarrow q)$ has the value T whenever $q$ is T and also when $p$ and $q$ are both F; it has the value F when $p$ is T and $q$ is F.

STEP 2: $(p \lor q)$ is the *disjunction* of $p$ and $q$. Fill in each line of the column headed $(p \lor q)$ with T or F, again determining the entry according to the truth values of $p$ and $q$ in the first two columns. The disjunction of $p$ and $q$ is T when either $p$ or $q$ or both are T; it is F if both are F.

STEP 3: $(p \rightarrow q) \longleftrightarrow (p \lor q)$ is an *equivalence relation* between $(p \rightarrow q)$ and $(p \lor q)$. Fill in the truth values for this column, determining the proper entry according to the truth values in the columns for $(p \rightarrow q)$ and $(p \lor q)$. When the truth values of both of the latter are the same, that is, both T or both F, the truth value of the equivalence is T; otherwise it is F.

**42a.** The *mode* is the most frequently occurring score.

The score, 35, occurs 5 times; 29 occurs 3 times, 32 occurs 3 times, and 37 occurs 2 times. All other scores occur only once. Therefore, 35 is the mode.

The mode is **35**.

**b.** Tally the scores, using a diagonal line to represent the fifth tally in any one interval:

The frequency is the number of tallies on each line.

| Interval | Tally | Frequency |
|----------|-------|-----------|
| 35-37 | ~~1111~~ 11 | 7 |
| 32-34 | 1111 | 4 |
| 29-31 | ~~1111~~ | 5 |
| 26-28 | 111 | 3 |
| 23-25 | 1 | 1 |
| Total | | 20 |

**c.**

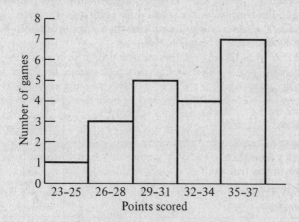

**d.** The *median* is the middle score when the scores are arranged in order of size.

Since there are 20 scores in all, the median lies between the 10th and 11th score; there are 10 scores above it and 10 scores below it.

Using the frequency distribution, count down from the highest score. There are 7 scores in the 35–37 interval, so 3 more are needed to reach the 10th score and 4 more are needed to reach the 11th score. After the first 7 scores, the next 4 all lie within the 32–34 interval, so both the 10th score and the 11th score lie within that interval. Therefore, the median must also lie within that interval.

The median lies in the **32–34** interval.

## SELF-ANALYSIS CHART — January 1983

| Topic | Question Numbers | Number of Points | Your Points | Your Percentage |
|---|---|---|---|---|
| 1. Numbers (rat'l, irrat'l); Percent | 17, 22 | $2 + 2 = 4$ | | |
| 2. Properties of No. Systems | — | 0 | | |
| 3. Operations on Rat'l Nos. and Monomials | 4, 32 | $2 + 2 = 4$ | | |
| 4. Operations on Polynomials | 9, 15 | $2 + 2 = 4$ | | |
| 5. Square root; Operations involving Radicals | 35 | 2 | | |
| 6. Evaluating Formulas and Expressions | — | 0 | | |
| 7. Linear Equations (simple cases incl. parentheses) | 2, 30 | $2 + 2 = 4$ | | |
| 8. Linear Equations containing Decimals or Fractions | 3, 7 | $2 + 2 = 4$ | | |
| 9. Graphs of Linear Functions (slope) | 27, 28 | $2 + 2 = 4$ | | |
| 10. Inequalities | 23, 33, 41a(1), (2) | $2 + 2 + 4 + 2 = 10$ | | |
| 11. Systems of Eqs. & Inequal. (alg. & graphic solutions) | 12, 36, 37 | $2 + 10 + 10 = 22$ | | |
| 12. Factoring | 13, 19 | $2 + 2 = 4$ | | |
| 13. Quadratic Equations | 34 | 2 | | |
| 14. Verbal Problems | 39a, 40 | $8 + 10 = 18$ | | |
| 15. Variation | — | 0 | | |
| 16. Literal Eqs.; Expressing Relations Algebraically | 6, 18 | $2 + 2 = 4$ | | |
| 17. Factorial n | — | 0 | | |

| Topic | Question Numbers | Number of Points | Your Points | Your Percentage |
|---|---|---|---|---|
| 18. Areas, Perims., Circums., Vols. of Common Figures | 20, 29, 39b | $2 + 2 + 2 = 6$ | | |
| 19. Geometry ($\cong$, $\angle$ meas., ‖ lines, compls., suppls., const.) | 11, 14, 16 | $2 + 2 + 2 = 6$ | | |
| 20. Ratio & Proportion (incl. similar triangles) | 5 | 2 | | |
| 21. Pythagorean Theorem | — | 0 | | |
| 22. Logic (symbolic rep., logical forms, truth tables) | 24, 25, 26, 41b | $2 + 2 + 2 + 4 = 10$ | | |
| 23. Probability (incl. tree diagrams & sample spaces) | 1, 10, 21, 38a, 38b, 38c, 38d | $2 + 2 + 2 + 4 + 2 + 2 + 2 = 16$ | | |
| 24. Combinations (arrangements, per-mutations) | 8 | 2 | | |
| 25. Statistics (central tend., freq. dist., his-tograms) | 31, 42a, 42b, 42c, 42d | $2 + 2 + 2 + 4 + 2 = 12$ | | |

# Examination June, 1983

## Three-Year Sequence for High School Mathematics—Course I

### PART ONE

DIRECTIONS: *Answer 30 questions from this part. Each correct answer will receive 2 credits. No partial credit will be allowed. Write your answers in the spaces provided. Where applicable, answers may be left in terms of $\pi$ or in radical form.*

1 Solve for $x$:  $2(x - 3) = 8$

1 __7__

2 If a certain number is decreased by 9, the result is 24. What is the number?

2 __33__

3 If one card is drawn from a standard deck of 52 playing cards, what is the probability the card is a red seven?

3 __$\frac{2}{52}$__

4 The selling price of a radio is $50, not including a sales tax at the rate of 7%. What is the sales tax on the purchase of the radio?

$3.50

4 _____

1

5 In the accompanying diagram, $\overleftrightarrow{AB} \parallel \overleftrightarrow{CD}$, and $\overleftrightarrow{EF}$ intersects $\overleftrightarrow{AB}$ at $G$ and $\overleftrightarrow{CD}$ at $H$. If the degree measure of $\angle AGH$ is $(3x - 10)$ and the degree measure of $\angle GHD$ is 80, find the value of $x$.

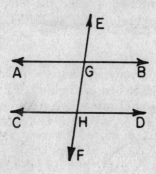

*x=30*

5_____

6 Express as a trinomial: $(3x - 1)(x + 2)$

*$3x^2 + 5x - 2$*

6_____

7 Let $p$ represent "I will go roller skating" and let $q$ represent "The sun is shining." Using $p$ and $q$, write in symbolic form: "I will go roller skating if and only if the sun is shining."

*$p \Leftrightarrow q$*

7_____

8 The side of a square is represented by $(x + 3)$. Express the perimeter of the square in terms of $x$.

*$4x + 12$*

8_____

9 Factor: $64 - x^2$

*$(8 + x)(8 - x)$*

9_____

10 Solve for $x$: $0.25x + 2 = 6$

*$-2 \quad -2$*

*$\dfrac{}{0.25} = 4$*

10___6___

11 What is the $y$-intercept of the graph of the equation $y = 3x - 5$?

$y = 3(0) - 5$

$y = -5$

11 $-5$

12 The lengths of the sides of $\triangle ABC$ are 14, 11, and 4 centimeters. The longest side of similar triangle $RST$ is 28 centimeters. Find the length in centimeters of the shortest side of $\triangle RST$.

12 $8$

13 As shown in the accompanying figure, equilateral triangle $ABC$ is inscribed in circle $O$. Find the measure in degrees of minor arc $AB$.

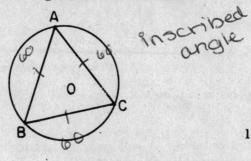

inscribed angle

13 $120$

14 The degree measures of the angles of a triangle are represented by $2x$, $3x$, and $4x$. Find the number of degrees in the *smallest* angle.

14 $40$

15 The following data are numbers of minutes a student spent on homework: 25, 35, 30, 50, and 38. What is the median of the data?

15 $35$

16 Solve for $E$ in terms of $I$ and $R$:

$$\frac{E}{I} = R$$

16 $IR$

17 The lengths of the legs of a right triangle are 3 and 6. Find, in radical form, the length of the hypotenuse of the right triangle.

*Pythagorean $a^2 x b^2 = c^2$*

17 $\sqrt{45}$

18 Solve for $a$: $\dfrac{a + 2}{12} = \dfrac{5}{3}$

18 $18$

19 The circumference of a circle is $8\pi$. What is the radius of the circle?

*Radius is half the circumference*

19 $4$

20 The accompanying histogram shows the distribution of student ages in a ninth grade class. Which age is the mode?

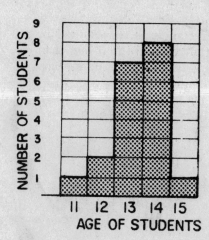

NUMBER OF STUDENTS

AGE OF STUDENTS

20 $14$

21 Express as a trinomial:
$(5x^2 + 2x - 3) - (2x^2 - 3x + 7)$

$3x^2 + 5x - 10$

21 _____

*change terms after ( )*

DIRECTIONS (22-34): *For each question chosen, write in the space provided the numeral preceding the word or expression that best completes the statement or answers the question.*

22 On a test the probability of getting the correct answer to a certain question is represented by $\frac{x}{7}$. Which can *not* be a value of $x$?

(1) 1        (3) 0

(2) −1       (4) 7        22 __2__

23 The expression $(-2)^2(\frac{1}{2})^3$ is equivalent to

(1) −2        (3) $\frac{1}{2}$

(2) 2         (4) $\frac{1}{32}$       23 __1__

$$(4)\left(\frac{1}{8}\right) = \frac{1}{2}$$

24 The length of a rectangle is represented by $x$. If the width of the rectangle is 3 less than its length, which expression represents the area of the rectangle?

(1) $x(x - 3)$        (3) $2x - 6$

(2) $x^2 - 3$        (4) $2x + 6$     24 __2__

25 The value of 4! is

(1) 1        (3) 24

(2) 12       (4) 4        25 __3__

26 The expression $18x^6 \div 3x^3$ is equivalent to

(1) $15x^2$        (3) $6x^2$

(2) $15x^3$        (4) $6x^3$     26 __3__

27 Which is the converse of the statement
$p \rightarrow \sim q$?
(1) $p \rightarrow \sim q$          (3) $q \rightarrow \sim p$
(2) $\sim p \rightarrow \sim q$          (4) $\sim q \rightarrow p$          27 _4_

28 Which graph represents the solution set of
$x \geq 2$?

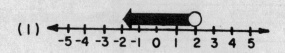

**(1)** -5 -4 -3 -2 -1  0  1  2  3  4  5

**(2)** -5 -4 -3 -2 -1  0  1  2  3  4  5

**(3)** -5 -4 -3 -2 -1  0  1  2  3  4  5

**(4)** -5 -4 -3 -2 -1  0  1  2  3  4  5          28 _3_

2

29 An equation of the line which is parallel to the
$x$-axis and 3 units below the $x$-axis is
(1) $y = -3$          (3) $x = 3$
(2) $y = 3$          (4) $x = -3$          29 _4_

30 The area of a rectangle is represented by
$x^2 + 2x - 3$. If the width of the rectangle is
represented by $(x - 1)$, the length may be represented by
(1) $(x - 3)$          (3) $(x + 3)$
(2) $(x - 2)$          (4) $(x + 4)$          30 _4_

3

31 What is the solution of the system of equations whose graphs are shown below?

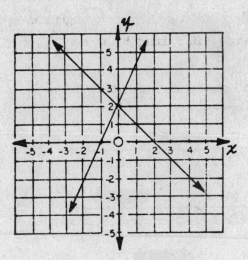

(1) ( 1,2)  (3) (2,0)
(2) (0,2)  (4) (2,−1)

31

32 Which ordered pair is *not* in the solution set of $x - 2y \leq 6$?

(1) (2,−2)  (3) (0,0)
(2) (5,1)  (4) (1,−6)

32 ___4___

33 For which value of $x$ is the expression $\dfrac{x - 4}{x + 3}$ undefined?

(1) −4  (3) 3
(2) −3  (4) 4

33

34 Which statement is false when $p$ is false and $q$ is false?

(1) $p \wedge q$  (3) $\sim p \rightarrow \sim q$
(2) $p \rightarrow q$  (4) $p \leftrightarrow q$

34 ___1___

DIRECTIONS (35): *Use the compasses and straightedge. Leave all construction lines on your answer.*

35 *On the answer sheet,* construct an angle congruent to angle *ABC,* using $\overrightarrow{RS}$ as one ray of the angle.

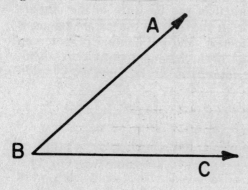

**PART TWO**

DIRECTIONS (36-42): *Answer four questions from this part. Show all work unless otherwise directed.*

36 *a* On the same set of coordinate axes, graph the following system of inequalities:

$$y > -2x + 7$$
$$y \le 3x - 3$$

[8]

*b* Write the coordinates of a point in the solution set of this system. [2]

37 The measure of the base of a parallelogram is 5 meters more than the measure of the altitude to that base. If the area of the parallelogram is 36 square meters, find the number of meters in the measures of the base and altitude. [*Only an algebraic solution will be accepted.*] [5,5]

38 For a class picnic, the school cafeteria prepared a box lunch for each student, consisting of a sandwich and a cookie. The sandwiches were tuna, ham, or peanut butter and the cookies were oatmeal or chocolate chip.

*a* Draw a tree diagram or list a sample space showing all possible combinations of one sandwich and one cookie that could be in the boxes. [4]

*b* If each combination was equally likely to be in any one of the boxes, what is the probability that a box chosen at random contains:

(1) a peanut butter sandwich and an oatmeal cookie [2]

(2) a ham sandwich [2]

(3) a sandwich that is *not* tuna [2]

39 Solve the following system of equations algebraically and check:

$$3x + y = 4$$
$$x - 2y = 6$$

[8,2]

40 In the diagram below, triangle *ABC* is a right triangle with the right angle at *C*. Segment *DE* is perpendicular to $\overline{AC}$ at *E*, *BC* = 8, *AC* = 6, and *DE:BC* = 1:2.

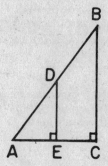

*a* Find *DE*.     [1]
*b* Find *AB*.     [2]
*c* Find *AE*.     [2]
*d* Find the area of △*ABC*.     [2]
*e* Find the area of trapezoid *ECBD*.  - [3]

41 The table below shows the distribution of scores of 30 students on a test.

| Scores | Frequency | Cumulative Frequency |
|--------|-----------|----------------------|
| 91–100 | 3 | 3 |
| 81–90 | 11 | 14 |
| 71–80 | 8 | 22 |
| 61–70 | 6 | 28 |
| 51–60 | 1 | 29 |
| 41–50 | 1 | 30 |

a Using the data in the Frequency column of
   the table, draw a frequency histogram.    [4]

b *On your answer paper*, copy the table and
   complete the column for Cumulative Frequency.    [2]

c Using the data in the Cumulative Frequency
   column of the table, draw a cumulative frequency histogram.    [4]

42 a *On your answer paper*, copy and complete
     the truth table for the statement
     $\sim(p \lor q) \leftrightarrow (\sim p \land \sim q)$.    [8]

| $p$ | $q$ | $p \lor q$ | $\sim(p \lor q)$ | $\sim p$ | $\sim q$ | $(\sim p \land \sim q)$ | $\sim(p \lor q) \leftrightarrow (\sim p \land \sim q)$ |
|---|---|---|---|---|---|---|---|
| T | T | | | | | | |
| T | F | | | | | | |
| F | T | | | | | | |
| F | F | | | | | | |

b Is $\sim(p \lor q) \leftrightarrow (\sim p \land \sim q)$ a tautology?    [1]

c Justify the answer you gave in part b.    [1]

# Answers June, 1983

## Three-Year Sequence for High School Mathematics—Course I

### ANSWER KEY

### PART ONE

| | | | | | |
|---|---|---|---|---|---|
| 1. | 7 | 12. | 8 | 24. | (1) |
| 2. | 33 | 13. | 120 | 25. | (3) |
| 3. | $\frac{2}{52}$ | 14. | 40 | 26. | (4) |
| | | 15. | 35 | 27. | (4) |
| 4. | $3.50 or 3.50 | 16. | $IR$ | 28. | (2) |
| 5. | 30 | 17. | $\sqrt{45}$ | 29. | (1) |
| 6. | $3x^2 + 5x - 2$ | 18. | 18 | 30. | (3) |
| 7. | $p \leftrightarrow q$ | 19. | 4 | 31. | (2) |
| 8. | $4x + 12$ | 20. | 14 | 32. | (4) |
| 9. | $(8 + x)(8 - x)$ | 21. | $3x^2 + 5x - 10$ | 33. | (2) |
| 10. | 16 | 22. | (2) | 34. | (1) |
| 11. | −5 | 23. | (3) | | |

**Part Two**—*See answers explained.*

### ANSWERS EXPLAINED

### PART ONE

**1.**

Remove parentheses by applying the distributive law of multiplication over addition:

Add +6 (the additive inverse of −6) to both sides of the equation:

$$2(x - 3) = 8$$

$$2x - 6 = 8$$

$$+6 = +6$$

$$2x = 14$$

Divide both sides of the equation by 2:

$$\frac{2x}{2} = \frac{14}{2}$$

$$x = 7$$

The solution for $x$ is 7.

12

2. Let $x$ = the number.
The number decreased by 9 equals 24.

| | | | |
|---|---|---|---|
| ↓ | ↓ | ↓ | ↓ |
| $x$ | $-$ | 9 | $= 24$ |

The equation to use is: $\qquad x - 9 = 24$

Add +9 (the additive inverse of $-9$) to both sides of the equation:

$$+9 = +9$$
$$x = 33$$

The number is **33**.

3. Probability of an event occurring =

$$\frac{\text{number of favorable cases}}{\text{total possible number of cases}}.$$

There are two red sevens (the 7 of diamonds and the 7 of hearts) in a deck of cards. Therefore, there are 2 favorable cases for drawing a red seven. The total possible number of cases in a draw from a standard deck is 52, the total number of cards in the deck.

The probability of drawing a red seven is $\frac{2}{52}$.

The probability is $\frac{2}{52}$.

4. The sales tax is determined by multiplying the selling price, $50, by the tax rate, 7%. The rate, 7%, expressed as a decimal is 0.07:

$$50 \times 0.07 = 3.50$$

The sales tax is **$3.50**.

5. $\angle AGH$ and $\angle GHD$ are alternate interior angles for the parallel lines, $\overleftrightarrow{AB}$ and $\overleftrightarrow{CD}$.

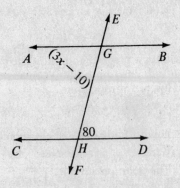

If two parallel lines are cut by a transversal, the measures of a pair of alternate interior angles are equal:

$$3x - 10 = 80$$

Add +10 (the additive inverse of −10) to both sides of the equation:

$$\underline{+10 = +10}$$
$$3x = 90$$

Divide both sides of the equation by 3:

$$\frac{3x}{3} = \frac{90}{3}$$
$$x = 30$$

The value of $x$ is **30**.

**6.**

$$(3x - 1)(x + 2)$$

To express this as a trinomial, multiply the two binomials together:

$$3x - 1$$
$$\underline{x + 2}$$

Multiply each term of $3x - 1$ by $x$, the first term of $x + 2$:

$$3x^2 - x$$

Multiply each term of $3x - 1$ by +2, the second term of $x + 2$, placing like terms under one another:

Add the partial products:

$$\underline{\phantom{3x^2 + 5x} 6x - 2}$$
$$3x^2 + 5x - 2$$

The trinomial is $3x^2 + 5x - 2$.

**7.** $p = $ "I will go roller skating"
    $q = $ "the sun is shining"

"I will go roller skating if and only if the sun is shining" is an *equivalence relation* between the statement "I will go roller skating" and the statement "the sun is shining." In symbolic form it is represented by $p \longleftrightarrow q$.

The symbolic form is $p \longleftrightarrow q$.

**8.** The perimeter of a square is the sum of the lengths of all four sides. Since all sides of a square are equal in length, its perimeter is 4 times the length of any one side:

$$\text{perimeter} = 4(x + 3)$$

Remove parentheses by applying the distributive law of multiplication over addition:

$$\text{perimeter} = 4x + 12$$

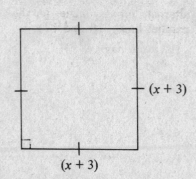

$(x + 3)$

$(x + 3)$

The perimeter is $4x + 12$.

9. The given expression is the *difference between two perfect squares*, 64 and $x^2$:

$$64 - x^2$$

Take the square root of each perfect square:

$$\sqrt{64} = 8; \sqrt{x^2} = x$$

The factors of the difference of two perfect squares are two binomials; one is the sum of their square roots and the other is the difference of their square roots:

$$(8 + x)(8 - x)$$

The factors are $(8 + x)(8 - x)$.

10.

$$0.25x + 2 = 6$$

Clear decimals by multiplying each term on both sides of the equation by 100:

$$100(0.25x) + 100(2) = 100(6)$$
$$25x + 200 = 600$$

Add $-200$ (the additive inverse of $+200$) to both sides of the equation:

$$\underline{-200 = -200}$$
$$25x \qquad\quad = 400$$

Divide both sides of the equation by 25:

$$\frac{25x}{25} = \frac{400}{25}$$
$$x = 16$$

The solution is **16**.

11. The $y$-intercept of the graph of an equation is the value of $y$ where the graph crosses the $y$-axis. At the point where the graph crosses the $y$-axis the value of $x$ is 0. Therefore, substitute 0 for $x$ in the equation to find the corresponding value of $y$:

$$y = 3x - 5$$
$$y = 3(0) - 5$$
$$y = 0 - 5$$
$$y = -5$$

The $y$-intercept is **−5**.

**12.**

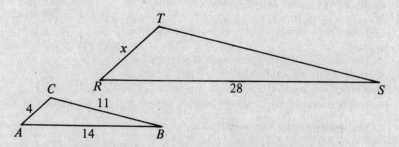

Since △RST is similar to △ABC, the longest side of △RST, 28, must correspond to 14, which is the longest side of △ABC.

Let $x$ = the length of the shortest side of △RST.

$x$ must correspond to the shortest side, 4, of △ABC.

Corresponding sides of similar triangles are in proportion:

$$\frac{28}{14} = \frac{x}{4}$$

Reduce the fraction on the left side by dividing numerator and denominator by 14:

$$\frac{2}{1} = \frac{x}{4}$$

In a proportion the product of the means equals the product of the extremes (cross-multiply):

$$x = 2(4)$$
$$x = 8$$

The shortest side of △RST is **8** centimeters.

**13.** The measure of each angle of an equilateral triangle is 60°. Therefore, m∠C = 60°.

∠C is an *inscribed angle* which intercepts minor arc AB.

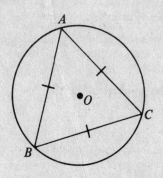

The measure of an inscribed angle is equal to one-half the measure of its intercepted arc:

$$m\angle C = \frac{1}{2}\ m\overset{\frown}{AB}$$

$$60 = \frac{1}{2}\ m\overset{\frown}{AB}$$

Multiply both sides of the equation by 2:

$$2(60) = 2(\frac{1}{2}m\overset{\frown}{AB})$$

$$120 = m\overset{\frown}{AB}$$

The measure of $\overset{\frown}{AB}$ is **120°**.

14.

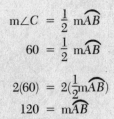

The sum of the measures of the three angles of a triangle is 180°:

Combine like terms:

Divide both sides of the equation by 9:

$$2x + 3x + 4x = 180$$
$$9x = 180$$
$$\frac{9x}{9} = \frac{180}{9}$$
$$x = 20$$

The measure of the *smallest* angle is 2x:

$$2x = 2(20) = 40$$

The number of degrees in the *smallest* angle is **40**.

15. Arrange the data in ascending order:   25, 30, 35, 38, 50

The *median* is the middle term when the data are arranged in order. Since there are 5 terms, the median is the third term, or 35.

The median is **35**.

16.

Clear fractions by multiplying both sides of the equation by $I$:

$$\frac{E}{I} = R$$

$$I(\frac{E}{I}) = I(R)$$

$$E = IR$$

The solution for $E$ is **IR**.

17. Let $x$ = the length of the hypotenuse.

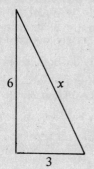

By the Pythagorean Theorem, the square of the length of the hypotenuse of a right triangle is equal to the sum of the squares of the lengths of the legs:

$$x^2 = 3^2 + 6^2$$
$$x^2 = 9 + 36$$

Combine like terms:
$$x^2 = 45$$

Take the square root of both sides of the equation:
$$x = \pm \sqrt{45}$$

Reject the negative root as meaningless for a length:
$$x = \sqrt{45}$$

The length of the hypotenus is $\sqrt{45}$.

18. The equation is in the form of a proportion:
$$\frac{a + 2}{12} = \frac{5}{3}$$

In a proportion, the product of the means equals the product of the extremes (cross-multiply):
$$3(a + 2) = 5(12)$$

Remove parentheses on the left by applying the distributive law of multiplication over addition:
$$3a + 6 = 60$$

Add $-6$ (the additive inverse of $+6$) to both sides of the equation:
$$-6 = -6$$
$$\overline{3a \qquad = 54}$$

Divide both sides of the equation by 3:
$$\frac{3a}{3} = \frac{54}{3}$$
$$a = 18$$

The solution for $a$ is **18**.

**19.** The circumference, $c$, of a circle is given by the formula, $c = 2\pi r$, where $r$ is the length of the radius.

It is given that the circumference is $8\pi$: $\qquad 8\pi = 2\pi r$

Divide both sides of the equation by $2\pi$: $\qquad \dfrac{8\pi}{2\pi} = \dfrac{2\pi r}{2\pi}$

$$4 = r$$

The radius of the circle is **4**.

**20.** The *mode* is the age which occurs with the greatest frequency.

The mode is 14; it occurs 8 times, which is more frequent than any other age.

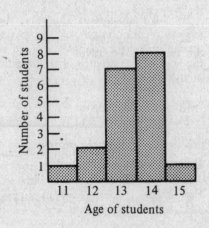

The mode is **14**.

**21.** $\qquad\qquad\qquad (5x^2 + 2x - 3) - (2x^2 - 3x + 7)$

Remove parentheses. To remove the parentheses preceded by the minus sign, change the sign of each term within the parentheses (the preceding minus sign is equivalent to multiplying the expression in parentheses by $-1$):

$$5x^2 + 2x - 3 - 2x^2 + 3x - 7$$

Combine like terms: $\qquad\qquad\qquad 3x^2 + 5x - 10$

The trinomial is $3x^2 + 5x - 10$.

*change terms after ( )

ALTERNATE SOLUTION: $(5x^2 + 2x - 3) - (2x^2 - 3x + 7)$ can be considered as the subtraction of the trinomial in the second parentheses from the trinomial in the first parentheses. Write the second trinomial under the first with like terms in the same column:

$$5x^2 + 2x - 3$$
$$2x^2 - 3x + 7$$

Rewrite the example, changing the signs in each term of the *subtrahend* (the lower trinomial):

$$5x^2 + 2x - 3$$
$$-2x^2 + 3x - 7$$

Add each column algebraically:

$$3x^2 + 5x - 10$$

**22.** A probability is always a number from 0 to 1 inclusive. It can never be negative.

If the probability of getting the correct answer is $\frac{x}{7}$, *then* $x$ represents the number of favorable cases (correct answers) out of a total possible number of 7 responses to the question, since the

$$\text{probability of an event occurring} = \frac{\text{number of favorable cases}}{\text{total possible number of cases}}.$$

Thus, $x$ could be any number from 0 to 7 inclusive; the numbers 1, 0 and 7, which are listed as choices, are thus possible values of $x$. The choice, $-1$, however, is not possible.

$-1$ is the only choice which can *not* be a value of $x$.

The correct choice is **(2)**.

**23.** $(-2)^2(\frac{1}{2})^3$

Since $(-2)^2 = (-2)(-2) = 4$, and

$(\frac{1}{2})^3 = (\frac{1}{2}) (\frac{1}{2}) (\frac{1}{2}) = \frac{1}{8}$, the expression becomes: $(4)(\frac{1}{8})$

Multiply: $\frac{1}{2}$

The correct choice is **(3)**.

**24.** If the width is 3 less than the length, $x$, then the width is $x - 3$.

The area of a rectangle is the product of its length and width:

$$\text{Area} = x(x - 3)$$

The correct choice is **(1)**.

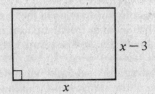

**25.** 4! stands for *factorial* 4.

By definition, $n! = n(n - 1)(n - 2)(n - 3) \ldots (3)(2)(1)$. Therefore, $4! = (4)(3)(2)(1) = (12)(2) = 24$.

The correct choice is **(3)**.

**26.**

To divide two monomials, first divide their numerical coefficients to find the numerical coefficient of the quotient:

Next divide the literal factors to find the literal factor of the quotient. Remember that when dividing powers of the same base exponents are subtracted to produce the exponent of that base in the quotient:

Put the two results together to get the complete quotient:

$$18x^6 \div 3x^3$$

$$18 \div 3 = 6$$

$$x^6 \div x^3 = x^3$$

$$18x^6 \div 3x^3 = 6x^3$$

The correct choice is **(4)**.

**27.** The statement, $p \rightarrow \sim q$, is the *implication*, "If $p$ is true, then the *negation* of $q$ is true (that is, if $p$ is true, then $q$ is not true)." The *hypothesis* ("given" or "if clause") of this implication is "$p$ is true." The *conclusion* ("to prove" or "then clause") of the implication is "the negation of $q$ is true."

The *converse* of a statement is formed by interchanging the hypothesis and conclusion of the original statement. Thus, the converse of $p \rightarrow \sim q$ is $\sim q \rightarrow p$.

The correct choice is **(4)**.

**28.** The solution set of $x \geq 2$ consists of all values of $x$ greater than or equal to 2.

Choices (1) and (3) can immediately be ruled out as representing the solution set because they represent values *less than* 2.

Choices (2) and (4) both consist of the numbers greater than 2, but the solid circle at the number 2 in choice (2) indicates that this choice includes 2, while the open unshaded circle at the number 2 in choice (4) indicates that 2 is *not* included. $x \geq 2$ requires that 2 be included.

The correct choice is **(2)**.

(1)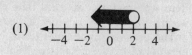

(2)

(3)

(4)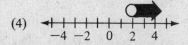

**29.** An equation of a line parallel to the $x$-axis and $b$ units above it is of the form $y = b$.

For the line parallel to the $x$-axis and 3 units below it, $b = -3$, and an equation of the line is $y = -3$.

The correct choice is **(1)**.

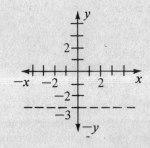

**30.** The area of a rectangle is the product of its length and width. If $x^2 + 2x - 3$ represents the area of a rectangle and $(x - 1)$ represents its width, then $(x - 1)$ must represent one of the factors of $x^2 + 2x - 3$ and the other factor must represent the length. Factor $x^2 + 2x - 3$ to find the other factor.

The given expression is a *quadratic trinomial*:    $x^2 + 2x - 3$

The factors of a quadratic trinomial are two binomials. The factors of its first term, $x^2$, are $x$ and $x$, and they become the first terms of the binomials:       $(x \quad )(x \quad )$

The factors of the last term, −3, become the second terms of the binomials, but they must be chosen in such a way that the product of the inner terms added to the product of the outer terms equals the middle term, +2$x$, of the original trinomial. Try + 3 and −1 as the factors of −3:

$$+3x = \text{inner product}$$

$$(x + 3)(x - 1)$$

$$-x = \text{outer product}$$

Since $(+3x) + (-x) = +2x$, these are the correct factors:

$$(x + 3)(x - 1)$$

Since the factor, $(x - 1)$, represents the width, the other factor, $(x + 3)$, must represent the length.

The correct choice is (3).

ALTERNATE SOLUTION: Since a rectangle's area is the product of its length and width, if the area and width are both known, then the length may be obtained by dividing the area by the width:

$$
\begin{array}{r}
x + 3 \\
x - 1 \overline{)x^2 + 2x - 3} \\
\underline{- \quad +} \\
\oplus x^2 \ominus x \\
3x - 3 \\
\underline{3x - 3}
\end{array}
$$

The quotient of the division, $x + 3$, represents the length.

31. The solution set of the system of equations whose graphs are shown is represented by the coordinates of their point of intersection. The graphs shown intersect at (0,2), so the solution set to the system is (0,2).

The correct choice is (2).

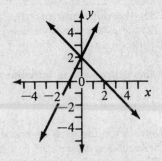

**32.**
$$x - 2y \leq 6$$
Test the ordered pair in each choice by substituting its coordinates for $x$ and $y$ respectively to see if the inequality is satisfied:

(1) $(2, -2)$:  $2 - 2(-2) \overset{?}{\leq} 6$

$2 + 4 \overset{?}{\leq} 6$

$6 \leq 6 \; ✔$

(2) $(5, 1)$:  $5 - 2(1) \overset{?}{\leq} 6$

$5 - 2 \overset{?}{\leq} 6$

$3 \leq 6 \; ✔$

(3) $(0, 0)$:  $0 - 2(0) \overset{?}{\leq} 6$

$0 - 0 \overset{?}{\leq} 6$

$0 \leq 6 \; ✔$

(4) $(1, -6)$:  $1 - 2(-6) \overset{?}{\leq} 6$

$1 + 12 \overset{?}{\leq} 6$

$13 \not\leq 6$

The only ordered pair which is *not* in the solution set of $x - 2y \leq 6$ is $(1, -6)$.

The correct choice is **(4)**.

**33.**
$$\frac{x - 4}{x + 3}$$
Since division by 0 is undefined, the expression will be undefined if its denominator, $x + 3$, is equal to 0.

Set the denominator equal to 0:  $x + 3 = 0$

Add $-3$ (the additive inverse of $+3$) to both sides of the equation:

$$\underline{-3 = -3}$$
$$x \qquad = -3$$

The expression is undefined if $x = -3$.

The correct choice is **(2)**.

**34.** Examine each choice in turn to see which is false when $p$ is false and $q$ is false:

(1) $p \wedge q$ is the *conjunction*, "p is true and $q$ is true." If $p$ and $q$ are both false, then $p \wedge q$ is false. The conjunction, $p \wedge q$, is true only when $p$ and $q$ are both true.

(2) $p \rightarrow q$ is the *implication*, "If $p$ is true, then $q$ is true." If $p$ and $q$ are both false, however, the implication may still be true.

(3) $\sim p \rightarrow \sim q$ is the *implication*, "If $p$ is false, then $q$ is false." This implication is obviously true if $p$ and $q$ are both false.

(4) $p \leftrightarrow q$ is the *equivalence relation*, "$p$ and $q$ are both false or both true." If $p$ and $q$ are both false, this equivalence relation will be true.

Among the choices, the only statement which is false is $p \wedge q$.

The correct choice is **(1)**.

35.

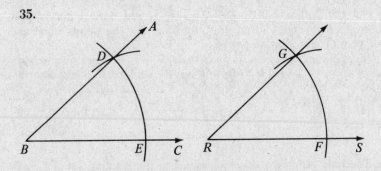

STEP 1: With $B$ as center and with any convenient radius, construct an arc cutting $\overrightarrow{BA}$ at $D$ and $\overrightarrow{BC}$ at $E$.

STEP 2: With the same radius as used in STEP 1 and with $R$ as center, construct an arc cutting $\overrightarrow{RS}$ at $F$.

STEP 3: With $E$ as center, use the compasses to measure the distance between points $E$ and $D$. With $F$ as center and with a radius equal to $\overline{ED}$, mark off a point $G$ on the arc drawn in STEP 2.

STEP 4: Draw $\overrightarrow{RG}$ through point $G$.

$\angle GRS \cong \angle ABC$.

## PART TWO

36 a. STEP 1: In order to draw the graph of the inequality, $y > -2x + 7$, we first draw the graph of the equation, $y = -2x + 7$.

Prepare a table of pairs of values by selecting any 3 convenient values for $x$ and substituting in the equation to calculate the corresponding values of $y$:

| $x$ | $-2x + 7$ | $= y$ |
|-----|-----------|-------|
| $-2$ | $-2(-2) + 7 = 4 + 7$ | $= 11$ |
| $0$ | $-2(0) + 7 = 0 + 7$ | $= 7$ |
| $3$ | $-2(3) + 7 = -6 + 7$ | $= 1$ |

Plot the points $(-2,11)$, $(0,7)$, and $(3,1)$ and draw a *dotted* line through them. The dotted line indicates that the points on it are *not* part of the solution set of $y > -2x + 7$.

The solution set of the inequality, $y > -2x + 7$ lies on one side of the line, $y = -2x + 7$. To find out on which side of the line the solution set lies, choose a convenient test point, say $(0,0)$, and substitute its values for $x$ and $y$ in the inequality: $y > -2x + 7$

$$0 \overset{?}{>} -2(0) + 7$$

$$0 \overset{?}{>} 0 + 7$$

$$0 \not> 7$$

Since $(0,0)$ does not satisfy the inequality, it does not lie in the solution set of $y > -2x + 7$. Therefore shade the *opposite* side of the line, $y = -2x + 7$, with cross-hatching extending up and to the right to indicate that it contains the points whose coordinates represent $y > -2x + 7$.

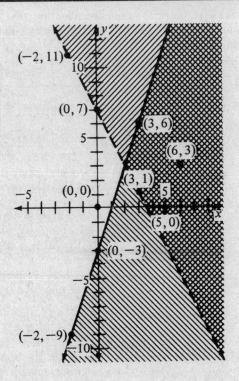

STEP 2: In order to draw the graph of the inequality, $y \le 3x - 3$, we first draw the graph of the equation, $y = 3x - 3$.

Prepare a table of pairs of values by selecting any 3 convenient values for $x$ and substituting in the equation to calculate the corresponding values of $y$:

| $x$ | $3x - 3$ | $= y$ |
|---|---|---|
| $-2$ | $3(-2) - 3 = -6 - 3$ | $= -9$ |
| $0$ | $3(0) - 3 = 0 - 3$ | $= -3$ |
| $3$ | $3(3) - 3 = 9 - 3$ | $= 6$ |

Plot the points $(-2, -9)$, $(0, -3)$, and $(3,6)$ and draw a *solid* line through them. The solid line indicates that the points on $y = 3x - 3$ are part of the solution set of $y \le 3x - 3$.

The part of the solution set represented by $y < 3x - 3$ lies on one side of the line, $y = 3x - 3$. To find out which side, choose a convenient test point, say $(5,0)$, and substitute in $y < 3x - 3$ to see if it is satisfied:

$$0 \overset{?}{<} 3(5) - 3$$

$$0 \overset{?}{<} 15 - 3$$

$$0 < 12 \; ✔$$

Since $(5,0)$ satisfies the inequality, it lies on the side of the line $y = 3x - 3$, which contains the points which satisfy $y < 3x - 3$. Shade this side with cross-hatching extending down and to the right.

**b.** The solution set of the system is represented by those points within the area covered by *both* types of cross-hatching, including that portion of the solid line which forms a boundary of that area.

The coordinates of one point in the solution set are (**6,3**).

**37.** Let $x$ = the measure of the altitude of the parallelogram.
Then $x + 5$ = the measure of the base.

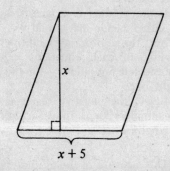

$x$

$x + 5$

The area of a parallelogram is equal to the product of the measures of its base and altitude to that base. Since the area is 36 square units, the equation to use is:

$$x(x + 5) = 36$$

Remove parentheses by applying the distributive law of multiplication over addition:

$$x^2 + 5x = 36$$

This is a *quadratic equation*; rearrange it so that all terms are on one side equal to 0 by adding $-36$ (the additive inverse of $+36$) to both sides:

$$\underline{-36 = -36}$$
$$x^2 + 5x - 36 = 0$$

The left side is a *quadratic trinomial* which can be factored into 2 binomials. The factors of the first term, $x^2$, are $x$ and $x$, and they become the first terms of the binomials:

$$(x \quad )(x \quad ) = 0$$

The factors of the last term, $-36$, become the second terms of the bionomials, but they must be chosen in such a way that the product of the inner terms added to the product of the outer terms equals the middle term, $+5x$, of the original trinomial. Try $+9$ and $-4$ as the factors of $-36$:

$+9x$ = inner product

$$(x + 9)(x - 4) = 0$$

Since the sum of $+9x$ and $-4x$ is $+5x$, these are the correct factors:

$-4x$ = outer product

$$(x + 9)(x - 4) = 0$$

If the product of 2 factors is 0, either factor may equal 0:

$$x + 9 = 0 \quad \text{OR} \quad x - 4 = 0$$

Add the appropriate additive inverse in each equation, $-9$ for the left one and $+4$ for the right one:

$$\frac{-9 = -9}{x \quad = -9} \qquad \frac{+4 = +4}{x \quad = 4}$$

Reject the negative result as meaningless for the measure of a length:

$$x = 4$$
$$x + 5 = 9$$

The measure of the altitude is **4** meters; the measure of the base is **9** meters.


**38 a.** <u>Tree Diagram</u>: The tree diagram contains a branching from the start in 3 directions to indicate the 3 choices of sandwiches: tuna, ham or peanut butter. Each of the 3 initial branches then divides into a second set of 2 branches to indicate the 2 choices of cookies: oatmeal or chocolate chip.

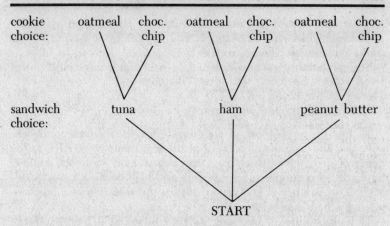

START

Sample Space: The sample space requires one column to list the types of sandwiches and another column to list the types of cookies. Since each of the 3 types of sandwiches may be paired on one line with one of the 2 types of cookies, 2 lines must be provided for each sandwich type:

| Sandwich choice | Cookie choice |
|---|---|
| tuna | oatmeal |
| tuna | chocolate chip |
| ham | oatmeal |
| ham | chocolate chip |
| peanut butter | oatmeal |
| peanut butter | chocolate chip |

**b.**  Apply the definition:

$$\text{Probability of an event occurring} = \frac{\text{number of favorable cases}}{\text{total possible number of cases}}.$$

In each of the three probability problems below, the total possible number of cases is 6: In the tree diagram, there are 6 different paths possible from START through the sandwich choice to the final cookie choice; in the sample space, there are 6 different lines each pairing a sandwich choice with a cookie choice.

(1) If a random choice is to pick a box containing a peanut butter sandwich and an oatmeal cookie, there is only one path in the tree diagram from START that passes through both of these choices. Likewise in the sample space, there is only one line pairing a pea-

nut butter sandwich and an oatmeal cookie. Therefore the number of favorable cases for choosing a box containing a peanut butter sandwich and an oatmeal cookie is 1.

The probability of choosing a box containing a peanut butter sandwich and an oatmeal cookie is $\frac{1}{6}$.

The probability is $\frac{1}{6}$.

(2) For the probability of choosing a box with a ham sandwich, note that the tree diagram has 2 possible paths from START to the final cookie choice which pass through a ham sandwich choice. Similarly, the sample space has 2 lines which contain a ham sandwich. The number of favorable cases for the selection of a box containing a ham sandwich is 2.

The probability of choosing a box containing a ham sandwich is $\frac{2}{6}$.

The probability is $\frac{2}{6}$.

(3) For choosing a box containing a sandwich that is *not* tuna, the tree diagram shows 4 possible paths from START to the final cookie choice which pass through sandwich choices that do *not* involve a tuna sandwich. Similarly, in the sample space, there are 4 lines which do *not* contain a tuna sandwich. The number of favorable cases for *not* choosing a tuna sandwich is therefore 4.

The probability of choosing a box *not* containing a tuna sandwich is $\frac{4}{6}$.

The probability is $\frac{4}{6}$.

**39.** The given system of equations is:

$$3x + y = 4$$
$$x - 2y = 6$$

Multiply each term of the first equation by 2:

$$2(3x) + 2(y) = 2(4)$$

Add the original second equation to it, thus eliminating $y$:

$$6x + 2y = 8$$
$$x - 2y = 6$$

$$\overline{7x \qquad = 14}$$

Divide both sides of the equation by 7:

$$\frac{7x}{7} = \frac{14}{7}$$

$$x = 2$$

Substitute 2 for $x$ in the first original equation:

$$3(2) + y = 4$$
$$6 + y = 4$$

Add $-6$ (the additive inverse of 6) to both sides of the equation:

$$-6 \qquad = -6$$

$$\overline{\qquad y = -2}$$

CHECK: The supposed solution, $x = 2$ and $y = -2$, must satisfy *both original* equations when these values are substituted for the variables:

$$3x + y = 4 \qquad\qquad x - 2y = 6$$
$$3(2) + (-2) \overset{?}{=} 4 \qquad\qquad 2 - 2(-2) \overset{?}{=} 6$$
$$6 - 2 \overset{?}{=} 4 \qquad\qquad 2 + 4 \overset{?}{=} 6$$
$$4 = 4 \;✓ \qquad\qquad 6 = 6 \;✓$$

The solution is $x = 2$, $y = -2$.

**40**    **a.**   Let $x = DE$.

It is given that   $\dfrac{DE}{BC} = \dfrac{1}{2}$:      $\dfrac{x}{8} = \dfrac{1}{2}$

Multiply both sides of the equation by 8 to clear of fractions:   $8\left(\dfrac{x}{8}\right) = 8\left(\dfrac{1}{2}\right)$

$$x = 4$$

$DE = 4$.

**b.**   By the Pythagorean Theorem, in a right triangle the square of the length of the hypotenuse equals the sum of the squares of the lengths of the legs:    $(AB)^2 = (AC)^2 + (BC)^2$

It is given that $AC = 6$ and $BC = 8$:    $(AB)^2 = 6^2 + 8^2$

$$(AB)^2 = 36 + 64$$

Combine like terms:    $(AB)^2 = 100$

Take the square root of both sides of the equation:    $AB = \pm\sqrt{100}$

Reject the negative value as meaningless for the length of a hypotenuse:    $AB = 10$

$AB = 10$.

**c.**   Since $\overline{DE}$ is perpendicular to $\overline{AC}$, $\angle DEA$ is a right angle. Since $\angle C$ is given to be a right angle, $\angle DEA \cong \angle C$.

Both $\triangle ADE$ and $\triangle ABC$ contain $\angle A$. Since the triangles contain 2 pairs of congruent angles, the right angles and $\angle A$, $\triangle ADE$ and $\triangle ABC$ are similar.

Corresponding sides of similar triangles are in proportion:    $\dfrac{DE}{BC} = \dfrac{AE}{AC}$

It is given that $\dfrac{DE}{BC} = \dfrac{1}{2}$ and that $AC = 6$:    $\dfrac{1}{2} = \dfrac{AE}{6}$

To clear of fractions, multiply both sides of the
equation by 6:

$$6\left(\frac{1}{2}\right) = 6\left(\frac{AE}{6}\right)$$

$$3 = AE$$

$AE = 3.$

**d.**   The area of a right triangle is equal to one half the product
of the lengths of its legs:

$$\text{Area of } \triangle ABC = \frac{1}{2}(AC)(BC)$$

$$\text{Area of } \triangle ABC = \frac{1}{2}(6)(8)$$

$$\text{Area of } \triangle ABC = \frac{1}{2}(48)$$

$$\text{Area of } \triangle ABC = 24$$

The area of $\triangle ABC$ is **24.**

**e.**   First find the area of $\triangle ADE$, using the same principle as in
part d above:

$$\text{Area of } \triangle ADE = \frac{1}{2}(AE)(DE)$$

From part c, $AE = 3$; from part a, $DE = 4$:

$$\text{Area of } \triangle ADE = \frac{1}{2}(3)(4)$$

$$\text{Area of } \triangle ADE = \frac{1}{2}(12)$$

$$\text{Area of } \triangle ADE = 6$$

The area of trapezoid $ECBD$ equals the area of $\triangle ABC$ minus the
area of $\triangle ADE$:         Area of trapezoid $ECBD = 24 - 6$
                                 Area of trapezoid $ECBD = 18$

The area of trapezoid $ECBD = $ **18.**

ALTERNATE SOLUTION: $\overline{DE}$ and $\overline{BC}$ are the bases of trapezoid
$ECBD$ since they are parallel. $\overline{EC}$ is the altitude of the trapezoid
since it is perpendicular to both bases.

The area, $A$, of a trapezoid is given by the formula, $A = \frac{1}{2}h(b_1 + b_2)$
where $h$ is the length of the altitude and $b_1$ and $b_2$ are the lengths of the
bases.

For trapezoid $ECBD$, $h = EC = AC - AE = 6 - 3 = 3$
                      $b_1 = DE = 4; b_2 = BC = 8$

$$A = \frac{1}{2}(3)(4 + 8)$$

$$A = \frac{1}{2}(3)(12)$$

$$A = \frac{1}{2}(36)$$

$$A = 18$$

**41 a.**

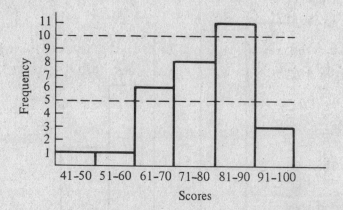

**b.** The cumulative frequency for the first group is the same as the frequency, 3. Thereafter, the entry for the cumulative frequency column is determined by adding the frequency for that line to the preceding cumulative frequency (for example, the cumulative frequency for the second line is 14, obtained by adding the frequency, 11, to the preceding cumulative frequency, 3).

| Scores | Frequency | Cumulative Frequency |
|--------|-----------|---------------------|
| 91-100 | 3 | 3 |
| 81-90 | 11 | 14 |
| 71-80 | 8 | 22 |
| 61-70 | 6 | 28 |
| 51-60 | 1 | 29 |
| 41-50 | 1 | 30 |

c.

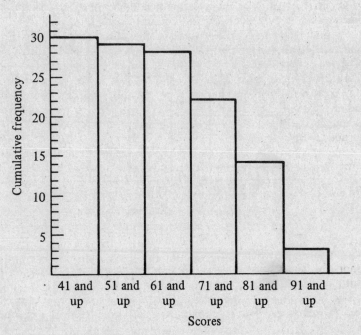

42 a.

| $p$ | $q$ | $p \vee q$ | $\sim (p \vee q)$ | $\sim p$ | $\sim q$ | $(\sim p \wedge \sim q)$ | $\sim (p \vee q) \leftrightarrow (\sim p \wedge \sim q)$ |
|---|---|---|---|---|---|---|---|
| T | T | T | F | F | F | F | T |
| T | F | T | F | F | T | F | T |
| F | T | T | F | T | F | F | T |
| F | F | F | T | T | T | T | T |

$p \vee q$ is the *disjunction* of $p$ and $q$. The disjunction has truth value, T, when either $p$ or $q$ or both have the truth value, T. It has the truth value, F, when both $p$ and $q$ have the truth value, F. Use these facts and the truth values of $p$ and $q$ in the first two columns to determine the entry for each line of the column headed "$p \vee q$."

$\sim(p \lor q)$ is the *negation* of the disjunction, $p \lor q$. The truth value for each line of the column headed "$\sim(p \lor q)$" is the *opposite* of the truth value for the column headed "$p \lor q$."

$\sim p$ and $\sim q$ represent the *negations* of $p$ and $q$ respectively. Each line of the column for $\sim p$ is filled in with the *opposite* truth value of that in the column for $p$, and each line of the column for $\sim q$ is filled in with the *opposite* truth value of that in the column for $q$.

$(\sim p \land \sim q)$ is the *conjunction* of $\sim p$ and $\sim q$. The conjunction has the truth value, T, only when both $\sim p$ and $\sim q$ have the truth value, T. If either $\sim p$ or $\sim q$ or both have the truth value, F, then so does $(\sim p \land \sim q)$.

$\sim(p \lor q) \leftrightarrow (\sim p \land \sim q)$ is an *equivalence relation* between $\sim(p \lor q)$ and $(\sim p \land \sim q)$. The equivalence relation has the truth value, T, whenever the truth values for both $\sim(p \lor q)$ and $(\sim p \land \sim q)$ are the same, that is, both T or both F; if their truth values are different, the equivalence relation has the truth value, F.

**b.** $\sim(p \lor q) \leftrightarrow (\sim p \land \sim q)$ is a tautology. The answer to the question is "**yes**."

**c.** A *tautology* is a statement formed by combining other propositions or statements $(p, q, r, \ldots)$ which is true regardless of the truth or falsity of $p, q, r, \ldots$

The last column of the table in part a shows that $\sim(p \lor q) \leftrightarrow (\sim p \land \sim q)$ is *always* true regardless of the truth or falsity of $p$ and $q$. Therefore, it is a tautology.

## SELF-ANALYSIS CHART — June 1983

| Topic | Question Numbers | Number of Points | Your Points | Your Percentage |
|---|---|---|---|---|
| 1. Numbers (rat'l, irrat'l); Percent | 4 | 2 | | |
| 2. Properties of No. Systems | 33 | 2 | | |
| 3. Operations on Rat'l Nos. and Monomials | 23, 26 | 2 + 2 = 4 | | |
| 4. Operations on Polynomials | 6, 21 | 2 + 2 = 4 | | |
| 5. Square root; Operations involving Radicals | — | 0 | | |
| 6. Evaluating Formulas and Expressions | — | 0 | | |
| 7. Linear Equations (simple cases incl. parentheses) | 1 | 2 | | |
| 8. Linear Equations containing Decimals or Fractions | 10, 18 | 2 + 2 = 4 | | |
| 9. Graphs of Linear Functions (slope) | 11, 29 | 2 + 2 = 4 | | |
| 10. Inequalities | 28, 32 | 2 + 2 = 4 | | |
| 11. Systems of Eqs. & Inequal. (alg. & graphic solutions) | 31, 36a, 36b, 39 | 2 + 8 + 2 + 10 = 22 | | |
| 12. Factoring | 9 | 2 | | |
| 13. Quadratic Equations | — | 0 | | |
| 14. Verbal Problems | 2, 37 | 2 + 10 = 12 | | |
| 15. Variation | — | 0 | | |
| 16. Literal Eqs.; Expressing Relations Algebraically | 8, 16, 24, 30 | 2 + 2 + 2 + 2 = 8 | | |
| 17. Factorial n | 25 | 2 | | |

| Topic | Question Numbers | Number of Points | Your Points | Your Percentage |
|---|---|---|---|---|
| 18. Areas, Perims., Circums., Vols. of Common Figures | 19, 40d, 40e | $2 + 2 + 3 = 7$ | | |
| 19. Geometry ($\cong$, $\angle$ meas., ‖ lines, compls., suppls., const.) | 5, 13, 14, 35 | $2 + 2 + 2 + 2 = 8$ | | |
| 20. Ratio & Proportion (incl. similar triangles) | 12, 40a, 40c | $2 + 1 + 2 = 5$ | | |
| 21. Pythagorean Theorem | 17, 40b | $2 + 2 = 4$ | | |
| 22. Logic (symbolic rep., logical forms, truth tables) | 7, 27, 34, 42a, 42b, 42c | $2 + 2 + 2 + 8 + 1 + 1 = 16$ | | |
| 23. Probability (incl. tree diagrams & sample spaces) | 3, 22, 38a, 38b(1), (2), (3) | $2 + 2 + 4 + 2 + 2 + 2 = 14$ | | |
| 24. Combinations (arrangements, permutations) | — | 0 | | |
| 25. Statistics (central tend., freq. dist., histograms) | 15, 20, 41a, 41b, 41c | $2 + 2 + 4 + 2 + 4 = 14$ | | |

# Examination January, 1984

## Three-Year Sequence for High School Mathematics—Course I

### PART ONE

DIRECTIONS: *Answer 30 questions from this part. Each correct answer will receive 2 credits. No partial credit will be allowed. Write your answers in the spaces provided. Where applicable, answers may be left in terms of π or in* radical form.

1 Express the sum of $(2y + 3)$ and $(3y - 4)$ as a binomial.

*[handwritten: $5y-1$]*

1 _____

2 Solve for $x$:  $x - 0.2 = 1.8$

*[handwritten: $2.0$]*

2 _____

3 There are 3 entrances to a school and there are 2 stairways that go to the second floor. In how many different ways can a student enter the school and go to the second floor?

*[handwritten: $6$]*

3 _____

4 Express, in radical form, the length of the hypotenuse of a right triangle whose legs have lengths of 1 and 3.

*[handwritten: $\sqrt{10}$]*

4 _____

5 Solve for $x$:  $2(x + 3) = x + 7$

*[handwritten: $1$]*

5 _____

1

6 In the diagram below of $\triangle ABC$, $m\angle A = 70$ and $m\angle B = 30$. Find the measure of exterior angle $BCD$.

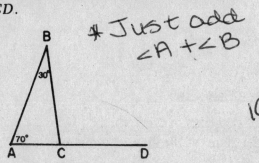

*Just add $\angle A + \angle B$*

100

6 $\underline{\quad 100 \quad}$

7 As shown in the accompanying diagram, $\overleftrightarrow{AB}$ and $\overleftrightarrow{CD}$ intersect at point $E$. If the degree measures of vertical angles $AED$ and $CEB$ are represented by $(3x + 20)$ and $(8x - 5)$, find the value of $x$.

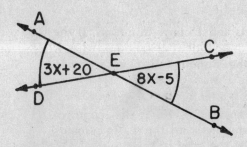

7 $\underline{\quad 5 \quad}$

8 The measures of two complementary angles are in the ratio 2:3. Find the measure of the *larger* angle.

$3x + 2x = 90$

$5x = 90$

$3(18) = 54$         $x = 18$

54

8 $\underline{\quad 30 \quad}$

9 If the mean of four positive integers is exactly 10, find the sum of the four numbers.

9 $\underline{\quad 40 \quad}$

10 Find the value of the expression $3x^3$ when
$x = -2$.

10 _-24_

11 Solve for $x$: $\dfrac{x+1}{8} = \dfrac{1}{2}$

11 _3_

(2x-3)

~12 Factor: $4x^2 - 9$

12 _(2x+3)_

13 Find the slope of the line whose equation is
$y = -2x - 4$.

13 _-2_

14 Thirty percent of what number is 12?

14 _40_

15 Let $p$ represent "I passed the test" and let $q$
represent "I feel proud." Using $p$ and $q$, write
in symbolic form, "I did not pass the test and I
do not feel proud."

~p∧~q

15 _____

16 There are 14 girls and 15 boys in a class. If the
teacher calls on one student at random, what is
the probability the student called on is a girl?

$\frac{14}{29}$

16 _____

32

17 A rectangle has an area of 16. If the length of
the rectangle is <u>doubled</u> and the <u>width</u> remains
the same, what is the area of the new
rectangle?

17 _32_

18 A box of plant food recommends adding $1\frac{1}{2}$
ounces of plant food to every 4 quarts of water.
How many ounces of plant food should be
added to 16 quarts of water?

6

18 _4½_

19 Express as a single fraction: $\dfrac{x}{3} + \dfrac{x}{5}$   $\dfrac{8x}{15}$   19 $\cancel{\dfrac{8}{15}}$

20 Express the product $(2x - 5)(4x + 5)$ as a trinomial.   $8x^2 - 10x - 25$

20____

21 Find the mode of the following group of numbers:   8, 8, 9, 10, 11

21 $8$

22 Factor:   $x^2 - x - 12$

$(x - 4)$

22 $(x + 3)$

23 The inverse of a statement is $p \rightarrow \sim q$. What is the statement?

$\sim p \rightarrow q$

23 $\cancel{True}$

24 Solve the following system of equations for $x$:

$$x + y = 7$$
$$x - y = 1$$

24 $4$

$$2x = 8$$
$$x = 4$$

DIRECTIONS (25-34):   *For each question chosen, write in the space provided the* numeral *preceding the word or expression that best completes the statement or answers the question.*

25 If $x$ represents a number, which expression represents a number which is 5 less than 3 times $x$?

(1) $5x - 3$          (3) $3x - 5$
(2) $5 - 3x$          (4) $3 - 5x$

$3$

25 $\cancel{\varnothing}$

26 Which is logically equivalent to $p \rightarrow q$?

  (1) $\sim q \rightarrow \sim p$        (3) $q \rightarrow p$

  (2) $\sim p \rightarrow \sim q$        (4) $p \wedge \sim q$

26 _2_

27 The length of a rectangle is three times its width. If the width is represented by $x$, which expression represents the perimeter of the rectangle?

  (1) $6x$        (3) $3x^2$

  (2) $8x$        (4) $4x$

27 _1_

28 The accompanying diagram shows the graph of which inequality?

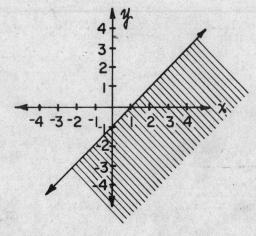

  (1) $y > x - 1$        (3) $y < x - 1$

  (2) $y \geq x - 1$        (4) $y \leq x - 1$

28 _4_

29 The graph of the equation $y = 5$ intersects the $y$-axis at the point whose coordinates are

  (1) $(-5,5)$        (3) $(5,0)$

  (2) $(0,5)$        (4) $(5,5)$

29 _1_

30 If the area of a circle is $16\pi$, the circumference
of the circle is
(1) $8\pi$                     (3) $4\pi$
(2) 8                          (4) 4                        30 __2__ ¹

31 If $x = 1$ and $y = -2$, which expression has a
value of 3?
(1) $x + y$                    (3) $xy$
(2) $x - y$                    (4) $y - x$                  31 __2__

32 The length of an edge of a cube is represented
by $5x$. Which expression represents the volume
of the cube?
(1) $10x^2$                    (3) $5x^3$                   4
(2) $25x^2$                    (4) $125x^3$                 32 __3__

33 Which point does *not* lie on the graph of the
equation $2x + y = 3$?
(1) $(-1,-1)$                  (3) $(0,3)$
(2) $(-1,5)$                   (4) $(\frac{1}{2},2)$        33 __2__ ¹

34 Patty needs a total of $80 to buy a bicycle. She
has already saved $35. If she saves $10 a week
from her earnings, what is the *least* number of
weeks she must work to have enough money to
buy the bicycle?
(1) 5                          (3) 3
(2) 8                          (4) 4                        34 __1__

DIRECTIONS (35):   *Use the compasses and straightedge. Leave all construction lines on your answer.*

35 *On the answer sheet,* construct triangle $A'B'C'$
congruent to $\triangle ABC$, using $\overline{B'C'}$ as one side.

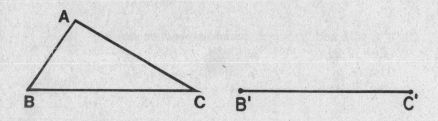

**PART TWO**

DIRECTIONS (36-42):   *Answer four questions from this part. Show all work unless otherwise directed.*

36 Solve the following system of equations
graphically and check:

$$x + y = -3$$
$$2x - y = 6 \qquad [8,2]$$

37 One number is 4 times another. The sum of
the two numbers is less than 12. Find the
largest possible values for the two numbers if
both are integers. [*Only an algebraic solution
will be accepted.*]     [6,4]

38 A garden is in the shape of a square. The
length of one side of the garden is increased by
3 feet and the length of an adjacent side is increased by 2 feet. The garden now has an area
of 72 square feet. What is the measure of a side
of the original square garden? [*Only an algebraic solution will be accepted.*]     [5,5]

39 In the diagram below, △ABC is inscribed in circle O. Triangle ABC is isosceles with $\overline{AB} \cong \overline{BC}$. Line EF, which contains point B, is parallel to line AC. The degree measure of arc BC is 150.

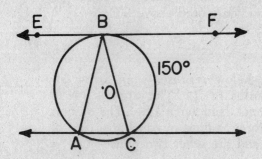

Find:

a the measure of ∠BAC [2]
b the measure of ∠EBA [2]
c the measure of ∠ABC [2]
d the measure of arc AC [2]
e the measure of ∠ABF [2]

40 The table below gives the distribution of test scores for a class of 20 students.

| Test Score Interval | Number of Students (frequency) |
|---|---|
| 91–100 | 1 |
| 81–90 | 3 |
| 71–80 | 3 |
| 61–70 | 7 |
| 51–60 | 6 |

a Draw a *frequency* histogram for the given data.   [4]

b Which interval contains the median?   [2]

c Which interval contains the lower quartile? [2]

d What is the probability that a student selected at random scored above 90?   [2]

41 The diagram below represents an arrow attached to a cardboard disc. The arrow is free to spin, but cannot land on a line. The disc is divided into three regions of equal area, one of which is red and the other two blue.

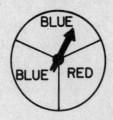

a For any one spin, what is the probability of the arrow:
(1) landing on red   [1]
(2) landing on blue   [1]

b The arrow is spun twice and each outcome is recorded. What is the probability of the arrow:
(1) landing on red on the first spin and blue on the second spin   [2]
(2) landing on blue on both spins   [2]
(3) *not* landing on blue on either spin   [2]
(4) landing on the same color on both spins [2]

42 *a On your answer paper,* copy and complete
the truth table for the statement
$[p \vee (p \wedge q)] \rightarrow \sim q.$    [8]

| $p$ | $q$ | $p \wedge q$ | $[p \vee (p \wedge q)]$ | $\sim q$ | $[p \vee (p \wedge q)] \rightarrow \sim q$ |
|---|---|---|---|---|---|
| T | T | | | | |
| T | F | | | | |
| F | T | | | | |
| F | F | | | | |

*b* Is $[p \vee (p \wedge q)] \rightarrow \sim q$ a tautology?    [1]

*c* Justify the answer you gave in part *b*.    [1]

# Answers January, 1984

## Three-Year Sequence for High School Mathematics—Course I

### ANSWER KEY

### PART ONE

| | | | | | |
|---|---|---|---|---|---|
| 1. | $5y - 1$ | 12. | $(2x - 3)(2x + 3)$ | 24. | 4 |
| 2. | 2 | 13. | $-2$ | 25. | (3) |
| 3. | 6 | 14. | 40 | 26. | (1) |
| 4. | $\sqrt{10}$ | 15. | $\sim p \wedge -q$ | 27. | (2) |
| 5. | 1 | 16. | $\dfrac{14}{29}$ | 28. | (4) |
| 6. | 100 | | | 29. | (2) |
| 7. | 5 | 17. | 32 | 30. | (1) |
| 8. | 54 | 18. | 6 | 31. | (2) |
| 9. | 40 | 19. | $\dfrac{8x}{15}$ | 32. | (4) |
| 10. | $-24$ | | | 33. | (1) |
| 11. | 3 | 20. | $8x^2 - 10x - 25$ | 34. | (1) |
| | | 21. | 8 | | |
| | | 22. | $(x - 4)(x + 3)$ | | |
| | | 23. | $\sim p \rightarrow q$ | | |

**Part Two**—*See answers explained.*

### ANSWERS EXPLAINED

### PART ONE

1. To add two binomials write one of them under the other with like terms in the same column:

$$2y + 3$$
$$\underline{3y - 4}$$

Find the sum of each column by adding the numerical coefficients algebraically and writing the total in front of the literal factor:

$$5y - 1$$

The sum is $5y - 1$.

**2.**
$$x - 0.2 = 1.8$$

Clear decimals by multiplying all terms on both sides of the equation by 10:

$$10(x) - 10(0.2) = 10(1.8)$$
$$10x - 2 = 18$$

Add +2 (the additive inverse of −2) to both sides of the equation:

$$\underline{+\ 2 = +2}$$
$$10x\qquad = 20$$

Divide both sides of the equation by 10:

$$\frac{10x}{10} = \frac{20}{10}$$
$$x = 2$$

The solution is $x = 2$.

**3.**   For each of the entrances, there are two ways to get to the second floor since there are two stairways from which to choose.

For 3 entrances, there are $3 \times 2$, or 6, different ways to enter and go to the second floor.

**6 different ways.**

**4.**   Let $x =$ the length of the hypotenuse.

By the Pythagorean Theorem, the square of the length of the hypotenuse of a right triangle equals the sum of the squares of the lengths of the legs:

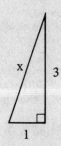

$$x^2 = 1^2 + 3^2$$

Square 1 and square 3:
$$x^2 = 1 + 9$$

Combine like terms:
$$x^2 = 10$$

Take the square root of both sides of the equation:
$$x = \pm\sqrt{10}$$

Reject the negative value as meaningless for a length:
$$x = \sqrt{10}$$

The length of the hypotenuse is $\sqrt{10}$.

**5.**
$$2(x + 3) = x + 7$$

Remove the parentheses by applying the distributive law of multiplication over addition:
$$2x + 6 = x + 7$$

Add $-x$ (the additive inverse of $x$) and also add $-6$ (the additive inverse of $+6$) to both sides of the equation:

$$-x - 6 = -x - 6$$
$$x = 1$$

The solution is $x = 1$.

6.   The measure of an exterior angle of a triangle equals the sum of the measures of the two remote interior angles:   $m\angle BCD = m\angle A + m\angle B$
$m\angle BCD = 70° + 30°$
$m\angle BCD = 100°$
$m\angle BCD = 100°$.

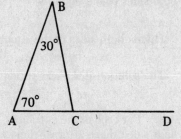

ALTERNATE SOLUTION:   By making use of the fact that the sum of the measures of the three angles of a triangle is $180°$, $m\angle BCA$ can be found to be $80°$. $\angle BCD$ and $\angle BCA$ are supplementary angles. Since the sum of two supplementary angles is $180°$, $m\angle BCD$ must be $100°$.

7.   Vertical angles are congruent:

$$m\angle AED = m\angle CEB$$
$$3x + 20 = 8x - 5$$

Add $-3x$ (the additive inverse of $3x$) and also add $+5$ (the additive inverse of $-5$) to both sides of the equation:

$$-3x + 5 = -3x + 5$$
$$25 = 5x$$

Divide both sides of the equation by 5:

$$\frac{25}{5} = \frac{5x}{5}$$
$$5 = x$$

The value of $x$ is 5.

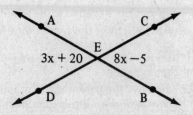

8. Since the measures of the angles are in the ratio 2:3,
let $2x$ = the measure of one angle
then $3x$ = the measure of the other angle
The sum of the measures of two complementary angles is 90°:

$$3x + 2x = 90$$

Combine like terms:

$$5x = 90$$

Divide both sides of the equation by 5:

$$\frac{5x}{5} = \frac{90}{5}$$

$$x = 18$$

$$3x = 3(18) = 54$$

The measure of the *larger* angle is **54°**.

9. Let $x$ = the sum of the four numbers.
The mean of four positive numbers is equal to their sum divided by 4:

$$\text{mean} = \frac{x}{4}$$

It is given that the mean is 10:

$$10 = \frac{x}{4}$$

Multiply both sides of the equation by 4:

$$4(10) = 4\left(\frac{x}{4}\right)$$

$$40 = x$$

the sum is **40**.

10. To find the value of $3x^3$ when $x = -2$, substitute $-2$ for $x$ in the expression:

$$3(-2)^3$$

Cube $-2$; $(-2)(-2)(-2) = -8$:

$$3(-8)$$

Perform the indicated multiplication:

$$-24$$

The value is **−24**.

11. The given equation is a fractional equation:

$$\frac{x+1}{8} = \frac{1}{2}$$

Clear fractions by multiplying both sides of the equation by 8:

$$8\left(\frac{x+1}{8}\right) = 8\left(\frac{1}{2}\right)$$

$$x + 1 = 4$$

Add $-1$ (the additive inverse of 1) to both sides of the equation:

$$\underline{-1 = -1}$$

$$x = 3$$

The solution for $x$ is **3**.

**12.** The given expression is the *difference of two perfect squares*, $4x^2$ and 9:

$$4x^2 - 9$$

Take the positive square root of each perfect square:

$$\sqrt{4x^2} = 2x; \sqrt{9} = 3$$

The factors are two binomials; one is the sum of the square roots and the other is the difference of the square roots:

$$(2x + 3)(2x - 3)$$

The factored form is $(2x + 3)(2x - 3)$.

**13.** If the equation of a line is in the form $y = mx + b$, $m$ represents the slope and $b$ represents the $y$-intercept.

The equation, $y = -2x - 4$, is in the form $y = mx + b$ with $m = -2$ and $b = -4$. Therefore, the slope of $y = -2x - 4$ is $-2$.

The slope is **$-2$**.

**14.** Let $x = $ the number.

30% is represented as a decimal as 0.30.

30% of the number is 12:

$$0.30x = 12$$

To clear decimals, multiply both sides of the equation by 100:

$$100(0.30x) = 100(12)$$
$$30x = 1200$$

Divide both sides of the equation by 30:

$$\frac{30x}{30} = \frac{1200}{30}$$
$$x = 40$$

The number is **40**.

**15.** $p = $ "I passed the test"

$q = $ "I feel proud"

"I did not pass the test" is the *negation* of $p$, and is represented by $\sim p$.

"I do not feel proud" is the *negation* of $q$, and is represented by $\sim q$.

"I did not pass the test and I do not feel proud" is the *conjunction* of the negation of $p$ with the negation of $q$; this conjunction is represented by $\sim p \wedge \sim q$.

The symbolic form is $\sim p \wedge \sim q$.

**16.** The probability of an event occurring $=$ $\dfrac{\text{the number of favorable cases}}{\text{total possible number of cases}}$.

Since there are 14 girls in the class, the number of favorable cases for calling on a girl if a student is picked at random is 14.

Since there are 14 girls and 15 boys, or a total of 29 pupils, the total possible number of cases for calling on a student at random is 29.

The probability of calling on a girl = $\frac{14}{29}$.

The probability is $\frac{14}{29}$.

**17.** If the length of the rectangle is doubled but the width remains the same, the new rectangle is equivalent to two of the old rectangles placed side by side along one of the widths.

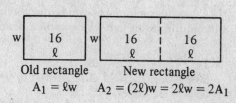

Old rectangle      New rectangle

$A_1 = \ell w$      $A_2 = (2\ell)w = 2\ell w = 2A_1$

The area of the new rectangle will be twice the area of the old rectangle:

The area will be **32**.

$$\text{Area} = 2(16) = 32$$

**18.** Let $x$ = the number of ounces of plant food to be added to 16 quarts of water.

Form a proportion; $x$ ounces bears the same ratio to 16 quarts of water as $1\frac{1}{2}$ ounces does to 4 quarts:

$$\frac{x}{16} = \frac{1\frac{1}{2}}{4}$$

In a proportion, the product of the means equals the product of the extremes (cross-multiply):

$$4x = 16\left(1\frac{1}{2}\right)$$

Change $1\frac{1}{2}$ to an improper fraction:

$$4x = 16\left(\frac{3}{2}\right)$$

$$4x = 8(3)$$

$$4x = 24$$

Divide both sides of the equation by 4:

$$\frac{4x}{4} = \frac{24}{4}$$

$$x = 6$$

**6** ounces must be added.

**19.** The given fractions have unlike denominators: $\frac{x}{3} + \frac{x}{5}$
Find the least common denominator (L.C.D.); the
L.C.D. is the smallest number into which all of the de-
nominators will divide evenly: The L.C.D. for 3 and 5 is 15.

Change $\frac{x}{3}$ into an equivalent fraction having 15 as its denominator by multiplying it by 1 in the form $\frac{5}{5}$, and change
$\frac{x}{5}$ to an equivalent fraction having 15 as its denominator by
multiplying it by 1 in the form $\frac{3}{3}$:

$$\frac{5(x)}{5(3)} + \frac{3(x)}{3(5)}$$

$$\frac{5x}{15} + \frac{3x}{15}$$

Since the fractions now have the same denominator,
they may be combined by combining their numerators and
placing the result over the common denominator:

$$\frac{5x + 3x}{15}$$

Combine like terms:
The single fraction is $\frac{8x}{15}$.

$$\frac{8x}{15}$$

**20.**
$$(2x - 5)(4x + 5)$$

To multiply two binomials, apply the distributive
law by multiplying each term of the first binomial by
each term of the second binomial and combining any
like terms that result:

$$
\begin{array}{r}
2x - 5 \\
4x + 5 \\
\hline
8x^2 - 20x \\
+ 10x - 25 \\
\hline
8x^2 - 10x - 25
\end{array}
$$

The trinomial is $8x^2 - 10x - 25$.

**21.** The *mode* of a group of numbers is the number that occurs most
frequently.
The mode for 8, 8, 9, 10, 11 is 8; 8 occurs twice, and each of the other
numbers occurs only once.
The mode is **8**.

**22.** The given expression is a *quadratic trinomial:*

$$x^2 - x - 12$$

The factors of a quadratic trinomial are two binomials. The factors of the first term, $x^2$, are $x$ and $x$, and they become the first terms of the binomials:

$$(x \quad )(x \quad )$$

The factors of the last term, $-12$, become the second terms of the binomials, but they must be chosen in such a way that the product of the inner terms added to the product of the outer terms equals the middle term, $-x$, of the original trinomial. Try $-4$ and $+3$ as the factors of $-12$:

$$-4x = \text{inner product}$$

$$(x - 4)(x + 3)$$

Since $(-4x) + (+3x) = -x$, these are the correct factors:

$$+3x = \text{outer product}$$

$$(x - 4)(x + 3)$$

The factored form is $(x - 4)(x + 3)$.

**23.** Since $p \rightarrow \sim q$ is the inverse of the statement to be found, the statement to be found is the inverse of $p \rightarrow \sim q$.

The *inverse* of a statement is formed by *negating* both its antecedent (hypothesis) and consequent (conclusion). In the statement, $p \rightarrow \sim q$, the antecedent (the hypothesis or "if clause") is $p$, and the consequent (the conclusion or "then clause") is $\sim q$. The negation of $p$ is $\sim p$, and the negation of $\sim q$ is $q$. Therefore, the inverse of $p \rightarrow \sim q$ is $\sim p \rightarrow q$.

The inverse is $\sim p \rightarrow q$.

**24.** The given system of equations is:

$$x + y = 7$$
$$x - y = 1$$

Adding the two equations will eliminate $y$:

$$2x = 8$$

Divide both sides of the equation by 2:

$$\frac{2x}{2} = \frac{8}{2}$$

$$x = 4$$

The solution for $x$ is **4**.

**25.** $x =$ a number.

To represent "5 less than 3 times $x$" requires that we start with $3x$ and subtract 5 from it:

$$3x - 5$$

The correct choice is **(3)**.

**26.** The *contrapositive* of a proposition is always logically equivalent to it.

The contrapositive of a proposition is formed by negating both the antecedent (hypothesis or "if clause") and the consequent (conclusion or "then clause") of the proposition and then interchanging them.

The antecedent (hypothesis) of $p \rightarrow q$ is $p$, and the consequent (conclusion) is $q$. The negation of $p$ is $\sim p$, and the negation of $q$ is $\sim q$. Therefore, the contrapositive of $p \rightarrow q$ is $\sim q \rightarrow \sim p$, which is choice (1).

Choice (2), $\sim p \rightarrow \sim q$, is the *inverse* of $p \rightarrow q$ since it has been formed by negating both the antecedent and consequent of $p \rightarrow q$. However, the inverse of a true proposition may or may not be true, so they are not logically equivalent.

Choice (3), $q \rightarrow p$, is the *converse* of $p \rightarrow q$ since it has been formed by interchanging the antecedent and consequent of $p \rightarrow q$. However, the converse of a true proposition may or may not be true, so they are not logically equivalent.

Choice (4), $p \wedge \sim q$, is the *conjunction* of $p$ with the *negation* of $q$. It asserts that $p$ and "not $q$" are both true, that is, that $p$ is true and $q$ is false. But this would contradict the original implication, $p \rightarrow q$, which states that if $p$ is true, $q$ must be true. Thus, they are not logically equivalent.

The correct choice is (**1**).

**27.** Let $x =$ the width of the rectangle.

Since the length is 3 times the width, then $3x =$ the length of the rectangle.

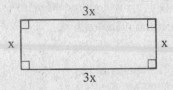

The perimeter of a rectangle is the sum of the lengths of all 4 sides:

Combine like terms:

The correct choice is (**2**).

perimeter $= x + 3x + x + 3x$
perimeter $= 8x$

**28.** The equation, $y = x - 1$, is in the form, $y = mx + b$, with $m = 1$ and $b = -1$. In this form, $m$ represents the slope of the graph of the equation and $b$ represents its $y$-intercept.

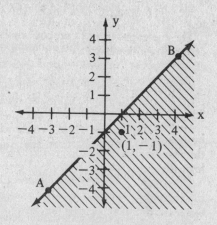

The slope is 1 and the $y$-intercept is $-1$. The line $\overline{AB}$ shown in the graph has a slope of 1 and a $y$-intercept of $-1$ and hence is the graph of $y = x - 1$. The fact that it is shown as a *solid line* indicates that points on it are included in the set whose inequality is to be found.

This immediately rules out choice (1), $y > x - 1$, and choice (3), $y < x - 1$, as possible answers since they do *not* include points on the line, $y = x - 1$.

Choose a test point, say $(1, -1)$ within the shaded area. Substitute its coordinates in the inequalities of choices (2) and (4):

| | |
|---|---|
| (2) $y \geq x - 1$ | (4) $y \leq x - 1$ |
| $-1 \overset{?}{\geq} 1 - 1$ | $-1 \overset{?}{\leq} 1 - 1$ |
| $-1 \neq 0$ | $-1 \leq 0$ |

The test point satisfies the inequality of choice (4) but not the inequality of choice (2). Therefore, the graph is the graph of the inequality, $y \leq x - 1$.

The correct choice is **(4)**.

**29.** A graph whose equation is of the form $y = b$ is a line parallel to the $x$-axis and $b$ units above it. Thus, the graph of $y = 5$ is a line parallel to the $x$-axis and 5 units above it.

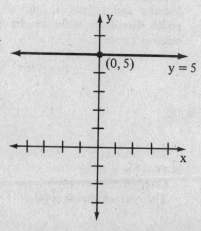

The $x$-coordinate of any point on the $y$-axis is $\emptyset$. The intersection of $y = 5$ with the $y$-axis is the point $(0, 5)$.

The correct choice is **(2)**.

**30.** The area, $A$, of a circle whose radius is $r$ is given by the formula, $A = \pi r^2$:

Divide both sides of the equation by $\pi$:

$$16\pi = \pi r^2$$
$$\frac{16\pi}{\pi} = \frac{\pi r^2}{\pi}$$
$$16 = r^2$$

Take the square root of both sides of the equation: $\pm\sqrt{16} = r$
Reject the negative value as meaningless for a length:

$$4 = r$$

The circumference, $C$, of a circle whose radius is $r$ is given by the formula, $C = 2\pi r$; since $r = 4$:

$$C = 2\pi(4)$$
$$C = 8\pi$$

The correct choice is (**1**).

**31.** To see which expression has the value 3, test each choice by substituting 1 for $x$ and $-2$ for $y$:

(1) $x + y \overset{?}{=} 3$  (2) $x - y \overset{?}{=} 3$  (3) $xy \overset{?}{=} 3$  (4) $y - x \overset{?}{=} 3$
$\quad 1 - 2 \overset{?}{=} 3 \qquad 1 - (-2) \overset{?}{=} 3 \qquad (1)(-2) \overset{?}{=} 3 \qquad -2 - 1 \overset{?}{=} 3$
$\quad\quad -1 \neq 3 \qquad\quad 1 + 2 \overset{?}{=} 3 \qquad\quad -2 \neq 3 \qquad\quad -3 \neq 3$
$\qquad\qquad\qquad\qquad\quad 3 = 3 \; ✔$

The correct choice is (**2**).

**32.** The volume, $V$, of any rectangular solid (including a cube) is equal to the product of its length, width, and height. In a cube, the length, width, and height are all equal. Therefore, if the length of the edge of a cube is $e$: $V = e^3$
$$V = (5x)^3$$
$$V = 125x^3$$

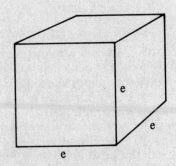

Here, $e = 5x$:
$(5x)(5x)(5x) = 125x^3$:
The correct choice is (**4**).

**33.** Coordinates of points which lie on the graph will satisfy the equation of the graph. Test each point by substituting its coordinates for $x$ and $y$ in the equation, $2x + y = 3$:

(1) $(-1, -1)$: $2(-1) + (-1) \stackrel{?}{=} 3$
$$-2 - 1 \stackrel{?}{=} 3$$
$$-3 \neq 3 \qquad (-1, -1) \text{ does } not \text{ lie on the graph.}$$

(2) $(-1, 5)$: $2(-1) + 5 \stackrel{?}{=} 3$
$$-2 + 5 \stackrel{?}{=} 3$$
$$3 = 3 \; \vee \quad (-1, 5) \text{ lies on the graph.}$$

(3) $(0, 3)$: $2(0) + 3 \stackrel{?}{=} 3$
$$0 + 3 \stackrel{?}{=} 3$$
$$3 = 3 \; \vee \quad (0, 3) \text{ lies on the graph.}$$

(4) $\left(\frac{1}{2}, 2\right)$: $2\left(\frac{1}{2}\right) + 2 \stackrel{?}{=} 3$
$$1 + 2 \stackrel{?}{=} 3$$
$$3 = 3 \; \vee \quad \left(\frac{1}{2}, 2\right) \text{ lies on the graph.}$$

The only point that does *not* lie on the graph is $(-1, -1)$.
The correct choice is **(1)**.

**34.** Let $x$ = the *least* number of weeks Patty must work. then $10x$ = the total savings from earnings for $x$ weeks.

$$\underbrace{\text{Savings}\atop\text{already made}}_{35} \; \text{plus} \atop + \; \underbrace{\text{savings}\atop\text{from earnings}}_{10x} \; \underbrace{\text{equals or exceeds}}_{\geq} \; \underbrace{\text{bicycle cost}}_{80}$$

The inequality to use is: $\qquad\qquad\qquad 35 + 10x \geq 80$
Add $-35$ (the additive inverse of 35) to both sides of the inequality: $\qquad\qquad \underline{-35 \qquad\qquad = -35}$
$$10x \geq 45$$
Divide both sides of the inequality by 10: $\qquad \dfrac{10x}{10} \geq \dfrac{45}{10}$
$$x \geq 4.5$$

The *lease* whole number value of $x$ that will satisfy $x \geq 4.5$ is 5.
The correct choice is **(1)**.

35.

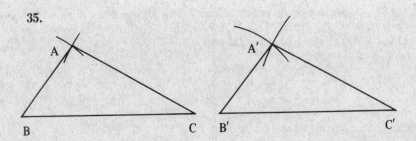

STEP 1: Open the compasses to the length of the segment $\overline{AB}$. With $B'$ as center, swing an arc whose radius equals the length of $\overline{AB}$.

STEP 2: Open the compass to the length of segment $\overline{CA}$. With $C'$ as center, swing an arc whose radius equals the length of $\overline{CA}$.

STEP 3: Label the point of intersection of the two arcs $A'$, and draw $\overline{B'A'}$ and $\overline{C'A'}$.

$\triangle A'B'C'$ is the required triangle congruent to $\triangle ABC$.

## PART TWO

36. To draw the graph of $x + y = -3$, first rearrange the equation so that it is solved for $y$; add $-x$ (the additive inverse of $x$) to both sides:

$$x + y = -3$$
$$\underline{-x \qquad = \qquad -x}$$
$$y = -3 - x$$

Choose any 3 convenient values of $x$ and substitute them in the equation to find the corresponding values of $y$:

| $x$ | $-3 - x$ | $= y$ |
|---|---|---|
| 3 | $-3 - 3$ | $= -6$ |
| 0 | $-3 - 0$ | $= -3$ |
| $-2$ | $-3 - (-2) = -3 + 2$ | $= -1$ |

Plot the points $(3, -6)$, $(0, -3)$, and $(-2, -1)$ and draw a straight line through them. This straight line is the graph of $x + y = -3$.

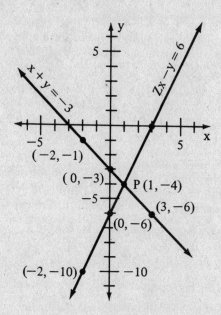

To draw the graph of $2x - y = 6$, first rearrange the equation so that it is solved for $y$; add $y$ (the additive inverse of $-y$) and also add $-6$ (the additive inverse of $6$) to both sides of the equation:

$$2x - y = 6$$
$$\underline{-6 \quad +y = -6 + y}$$
$$2x - 6 = \qquad y$$

Choose any 3 convenient values of $x$ and substitute them in the equation to find the corresponding values of $y$:

| $x$ | $2x - 6$ | $= y$ |
|---|---|---|
| 3 | $2(3) - 6 = 6 - 6$ | $= 0$ |
| 0 | $2(0) - 6 = 0 - 6$ | $= -6$ |
| -2 | $2(-2) - 6 = -4 - 6$ | $= -10$ |

Plot the points $(3, 0)$, $(0, -6)$, and $(-2, -10)$ and draw a straight line through them. This straight line is the graph of $2x - y = 6$.

The solution to the system is represented by the coordinates of the point $P(1, -4)$ where the two graphs intersect.

The solution is $x = 1$, $y = -4$.

CHECK: The solution is checked by substituting the values of $x$ and $y$ in *both original* equations to see if both are satisfied:

$$x + y = -3 \qquad\qquad 2x - y = 6$$
$$1 + (-4) \overset{?}{=} -3 \qquad 2(1) - (-4) \overset{?}{=} 6$$
$$1 - 4 \overset{?}{=} -3 \qquad\qquad 2 + 4 \overset{?}{=} 6$$
$$-3 = -3 ✔ \qquad\qquad 6 = 6 ✔$$

37. Let $x =$ one number.
Then $4x =$ the other number.
The sum of the two numbers is less than 12: $\qquad x + 4x < 12$
Combine like terms: $\qquad\qquad\qquad\qquad\qquad\qquad\qquad 5x < 12$

Divide both sides of the inequality by 5: $\qquad\qquad \dfrac{5x}{5} < \dfrac{12}{5}$

$$x < 2\tfrac{2}{5}$$

The solution to the inequality states that $x$ must be less than $2\tfrac{2}{5}$.

Since $x$ must also be an integer, the largest possible value of $x$ is 2. The corresponding value of $4x$ is $4(2)$ or 8.
The largest values for the two nunbers are 2 and 8.

38. Let $x =$ the length of the side of the square forming the original garden.
Then $x + 3 =$ the length of the enlarged garden.
And $x + 2 =$ the width of the enlarged garden.

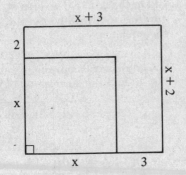

The enlarged garden is a rectangle. The area of a rectangle equals the product of its length and width:
Multiply together the two binomials on the left side of the equation by multiplying each term of $x + 3$ by each

$$(x + 3)(x + 2) = 72$$

term of $x + 2$ and combining any like terms which result:

$$x + 3$$
$$x + 2$$
$$\overline{x^2 + 3x}$$
$$+ 2x + 6$$
$$\overline{x^2 + 5x + 6}$$
$$x^2 + 5x + 6 = 72$$

The equation is a *quadratic equation*; re-arrange it so that all terms are on one side equal to 0 by adding $-72$ (the additive inverse of 72) to both sides:

$$-72 = -72$$
$$\overline{x^2 + 5x - 66 = 0}$$

The left side is a *quadratic trinomial* which can be factored into the product of two bino-mials. The factors of the first term, $x^2$, are $x$ and $x$, and they become the first terms of the binomials:

$$(x \quad)(x \quad) = 0$$

The factors of the last term, $-66$, become the second terms of the binomials but they must be chosen in such a way that the product of the inner terms added to the product of the outer terms equals the middle term, $+5x$, of the original trinomial:

$$+11x = \text{inner product}$$
$$(x + 11)(x - 6) = 0$$

Since $(+11x) + (-6x)$ equals $+5x$, these are the correct factors:

$$-6x = \text{outer product}$$
$$(x + 11)(x - 6) = 0$$

If the product of two factors is 0, either factor may equal 0:

$$x + 11 = 0 \quad \text{OR} \quad x - 6 = 0$$

Add the appropriate additive in-verse to both sides of the equation, $-11$ in the case of the left equation, and $+6$ in the case of the right:

$$-11 = -11 \qquad +6 = +6$$
$$\overline{x \quad = -11} \qquad \overline{x \quad = 6}$$

Reject the negative value as meaningless for a length:

$$x = 6$$

The length of the side of the original square is **6** feet.

**39 a.** $\angle BAC$ is an *inscribed angle*. The measure of an inscribed angle is equal to one-half the measure of its intercepted arc:

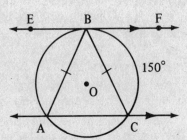

$$m\angle BAC = \frac{1}{2}m\widehat{BC}$$

$$m\angle BAC = \frac{1}{2}(150°)$$

$$m\angle BAC = 75°$$

$m\angle BAC = \textbf{75°}$.

**b.**   In an isosceles triangle, the base angles are congruent:

Since $\angle BCA$ is also an inscribed angle (see part **a**):

$$m\angle BCA = m\angle BAC = 75°$$

$$m\angle BCA = \frac{1}{2}m\widehat{BA}$$

$$75° = \frac{1}{2}m\widehat{BA}$$

Multiply both sides of the equation by 2:

$$2(75°) = 2\left(\frac{1}{2}m\widehat{BA}\right)$$

$$150° = m\widehat{BA}$$

$\angle EBA$ is an *angle formed by a tangent and a secant drawn to a circle from an outside point.* The measure of an angle formed by a tangent and a secant drawn to a circle from an outside point is equal to one-half the difference of the measures of the intercepted arcs:

$$m\angle EBA = \frac{1}{2}m\widehat{BA}$$

$$m\angle EBA = \frac{1}{2}(150°)$$

$$m\angle EBA = 75°$$

$m\angle EBA = \textbf{75°}$.

**c.**   The sum of the measures of the three angles of a triangle is 180°:

$$m\angle BAC + m\angle ABC + m\angle BCA = 180°$$

$$75° + m\angle ABC + 75° = 180°$$

$$m\angle ABC + 150° = 180°$$

Combine like terms:
Add $-150°$ (the additive inverse of $+150°$) to both sides of the equation:

$$\frac{-150° = -150°}{m\angle ABC \qquad = 30°}$$

$m\angle ABC = \textbf{30°}$.

**d.** The sum of the measures of all the arcs comprising a circle is 360°:

$$m\widehat{BA} + m\widehat{AC} + m\widehat{BC} = 360°$$
$$150° + m\widehat{AC} + 150° = 360°$$

Combine like terms:

$$m\widehat{AC} + 300° = 360°$$

Add −300° (the additive inverse of +300°) to both sides of the equation:

$$\underline{\quad\quad - 300° = -300°}$$
$$m\widehat{AC} \qquad = 60°$$

$m\widehat{AC} = 60°$.

**e.** $\angle ABF$ is an *angle formed by a tangent and a chord drawn to the point of contact* (see part **b**):

$$m\angle ABF = \frac{1}{2} m\widehat{BCA}$$

But $\widehat{BCA} = \widehat{BC} + \widehat{CA}$:

$$m\angle ABF = \frac{1}{2}(m\widehat{BC} + m\widehat{CA})$$

From part **d**, $m\widehat{CA} = 60°$; it is given that $m\widehat{BC} = 150°$:

$$m\angle ABF = \frac{1}{2}(150° + 60°)$$

Combine like terms:

$$m\angle ABF = \frac{1}{2}(210°)$$
$$m\angle ABF = 105°$$

$m\angle ABF = 105°$.

ALTERNATE SOLUTION: $\angle ABF$ and $\angle EBA$ together form a straight angle. A straight angle has a measure of 180°:

$$m\angle ABF + m\angle EBA = 180°$$

From part **b**, $m\angle EBA = 75°$:

$$m\angle ABF + 75° = 180°$$

Add −75° (the additive inverse of +75°) to both sides of the equation:

$$\underline{\quad\quad - 75° = -75°}$$
$$m\angle ABF \qquad = 105°$$

**40  a.**

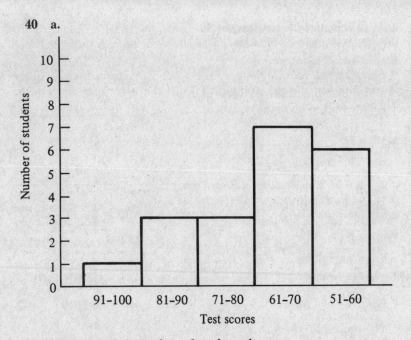

**b.** Find the total number of students by adding all the frequencies: $1 + 3 + 3 + 7 + 6 = 20$

If the scores are arranged in order of size, the *median* is the middle score if the number of scores is odd; or, if there is an even number of scores (as is the case here), the median is the score midway between the two middle scores. Since there are 20 scores, the median score will lie midway between the $10^{th}$ and $11^{th}$ scores.

Counting up from the bottom, there are 6 scores in the 51–60 interval. To count up to the $10^{th}$ score, 4 more are needed from the next interval (the 61–70 interval); 5 more are needed from the same interval to reach the $11^{th}$ score. Both the $10^{th}$ and $11^{th}$ scores are in the 61–70 interval. The score midway between them (the median) must also lie in this interval.

The **61–70** interval contains the median.

**c.** The *lower quartile* is the score separating the lowest one-quarter of all scores from the remaining three-quarters.

Since there are 20 scores in all and $\frac{1}{4}(20) = 5$, the lowest 5 scores comprise the lowest one-quarter; the remaining 15 scores comprise the upper three-quarters. The lower quartile is the score midway between the $5^{th}$ and $6^{th}$ scores.

Counting up from the bottom, the $5^{th}$ and $6^{th}$ scores both lie in the lowest interval, the 51–60 interval. Thus, the lower quartile is in the 51–60 interval.

The **51–60** interval contains the lower quartile.

**d.** The probability of an event occurring =

$$\frac{\text{the number of favorable cases}}{\text{the total possible number of cases}}.$$

Since there is only one score in the 91–100 interval, there is only one favorable case for the random selection of a student with a score above 90.

Since any student may be chosen, the total possible number of cases in a random selection is the total number of students, 20.

The probability of a random selection of a student with a score > 90 is $\frac{1}{20}$.

The probability is $\frac{1}{20}$.

**41 a.** The probability of an event occurring =

$$\frac{\text{the number of favorable cases}}{\text{the total possible number of cases}}.$$

(1) The number of favorable areas for landing on red is 1. The total possible number of areas is 3. Therefore, the probability of landing on a red area is $\frac{1}{3}$.

Probability = $\frac{1}{3}$.

(2) The number of favorable areas for landing on blue is 2. The total possible number of areas is 3. Therefore, the probability of landing on a blue area is $\frac{2}{3}$.

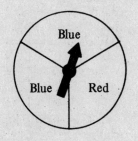

Probability = $\frac{2}{3}$.

**b.** The probability of two independent events occurring is the product of their separate probabilities.

(1) Since the probability of landing on red is $\frac{1}{3}$ and the probability of landing on blue is $\frac{2}{3}$, the probability of a landing on red followed by a landing on blue is $\frac{1}{3} \times \frac{2}{3} = \frac{2}{9}$.

Probability $= \frac{2}{9}$.

(2) The probability of a landing on blue followed by another landing on blue is $\frac{2}{3} \times \frac{2}{3} = \frac{4}{9}$.

Probability $= \frac{4}{9}$.

(3) The probability of *not* landing on blue on either spin is the same as the probability of landing on red on the first spin followed by landing on red on the second spin; this probability is $\frac{1}{3} \times \frac{1}{3} = \frac{1}{9}$.

Probability $= \frac{1}{9}$.

(4) The probability of one of two mutually exclusive events occurring is the sum of their separate probabilities. The probability of landing on the same color on both of two spins is therefore the sum of the probability of landing on blue both times and the probability of landing on red both times. The probability of landing on the same color both times is $\frac{4}{9} + \frac{1}{9} = \frac{5}{9}$.

Probability $= \frac{5}{9}$.

**42 a.**

| $p$ | $q$ | $p \wedge q$ | $[p \vee (p \wedge q)]$ | $\sim q$ | $[p \vee (p \wedge q)] \rightarrow \sim q$ |
|---|---|---|---|---|---|
| T | T | T | T | F | F |
| T | F | F | T | T | T |
| F | T | F | F | F | T |
| F | F | F | F | T | T |

$p \wedge q$ is the *conjunction* of $p$ and $q$. Use the truth values of $p$ and $q$ in the first two columns to determine what entry to make on each line for the truth value of $p \wedge q$. $p \wedge q$ has the truth value, T, if both $p$ and $q$ have truth values of T; in all other cases, the truth value of $p \wedge q$ is F.

$[p \vee (p \wedge q)]$ is the *disjunction* between $p$ and $(p \wedge q)$. Use the truth values of $p$ and $p \wedge q$ to determine the truth value entry on each line of $[p \vee (p \wedge q)]$. The disjunction has truth value, T, if either $p$ or $(p \wedge q)$ or both have truth value, T; its truth value is F when both $p$ and $(p \wedge q)$ have truth value, F.

$\sim q$ is the *negation* of $q$. The truth value on each line of $\sim q$ will be the opposite of the truth value of $q$ on that line.

$[p \vee (p \wedge q)] \to \sim q$ is the *implication* that if $[p \vee (p \wedge q)]$ is true, then $\sim q$ is true. The implication has the value, T, if both $[p \vee (p \wedge q)]$ and $\sim q$ have the same truth value (either both T or both F). It also has the truth value, T, when $\sim q$ is T and $[p \vee (p \wedge q)]$ is F. It has the truth value, F, when $[p \vee (p \wedge q)]$ is T and $\sim q$ is F.

**b.** $[p \vee (p \wedge q)] \to \sim q$ is *not* a tautology.

**c.** A tautology is a proposition formed by combining other propositions $(p, q, r, \ldots)$ which is true regardless of the truth or falsity of $p, q, r, \ldots$

The implication, $[p \vee (p \wedge q)] \to \sim q$ is not a tautology since the last column of the table in part **a** shows that it is sometimes true and sometimes false, depending on the truth values of $p$ and $q$.

## SELF-ANALYSIS CHART — January 1984

| Topic | Question Numbers | Number of Points | Your Points | Your Percentage |
|---|---|---|---|---|
| 1. Numbers (rat'l, irrat'l); Percent | 14 | 2 | | |
| 2. Properties of No. Systems | — | 0 | | |
| 3. Operations on Rat'l Nos. and Monomials | 19 | 2 | | |
| 4. Operations on Polynomials | 1, 20 | 2 + 2 = 4 | | |
| 5. Square root; Operations involving Radicals | — | 0 | | |
| 6. Evaluating Formulas and Expressions | 10, 31 | 2 + 2 = 4 | | |
| 7. Linear Equations (simple cases incl. parentheses) | 5 | 2 | | |
| 8. Linear Equations containing Decimals or Fractions | 2, 11 | 2 + 2 = 4 | | |
| 9. Graphs of Linear Functions (slope) | 13, 29, 33 | 2 + 2 + 2 = 6 | | |
| 10. Inequalities | 28 | 2 | | |
| 11. Systems of Eqs. & Inequal. (alg. & graphic solutions) | 24, 36 | 2 + 10 = 12 | | |
| 12. Factoring | 12, 22 | 2 + 2 = 4 | | |
| 13. Quadratic Equations | — | 0 | | |
| 14. Verbal Problems | 34, 37, 38 | 2 + 10 + 10 = 22 | | |
| 15. Variation | 17 | 2 | | |
| 16. Literal Eqs.; Expressing Relations Algebraically | 25, 27, 32 | 2 + 2 + 2 = 6 | | |
| 17. Factorial n | — | 0 | | |

33

| Topic | Question Numbers | Number of Points | Your Points | Your Percentage |
|---|---|---|---|---|
| 18. Areas, Perims., Circums., Vols. of Common Figures | 30 | 2 | | |
| 19. Geometry (≅, ∠ meas., ‖ lines, compls., suppls., const.) | 6, 7, 8, 35, 39a, 39b, 39c, 39d, 39e | 2 + 2 + 2 + 2 + 2 + 2 + 2 + 2 + 2 = 18 | | |
| 20. Ratio & Proportion (incl. similar triangles) | 18 | 2 | | |
| 21. Pythagorean Theorem | 4 | 2 | | |
| 22. Logic (symbolic rep., logical forms, truth tables) | 15, 23, 26, 42a, 42b, 42c | 2 + 2 + 2 + 8 + 1 + 1 = 16 | | |
| 23. Probability (incl. tree diagrams & sample spaces) | 16, 40d, 41a(1), (2), 41b(1), (2), (3), (4) | 2 + 2 + 1 + 1 + 2 + 2 + 2 + 2 = 14 | | |
| 24. Combinations (arrangements, permutations) | 3 | 2 | | |
| 25. Statistics (central tend., freq. dist., histograms) | 9, 21, 40a, 40b, 40c | 2 + 2 + 4 + 2 + 2 = 12 | | |

# Examination June, 1984
## Three-Year Sequence for High School Mathematics—Course I

### PART ONE

DIRECTIONS: *Answer 30 questions from this part. Each correct answer will receive 2 credits. No partial credit will be allowed. Write your answers in the spaces provided. Where applicable, answers may be left in terms of   or in radical form.*

1 Solve for $m$:  $\dfrac{m}{4} = \dfrac{5}{2}$

1 __10__

2 Solve for $x$:  $5 + 3(x + 2) = 14$

2 __1__

3 Find the value of $3x^2y$ if $x = -2$ and $y = 3$.

3 ~~108~~ 36

4 Jean is making sandwiches for a class picnic. She is using 4 different fillings with 2 different kinds of bread. How many different kinds of sandwiches can she make using one kind of filling on one kind of bread for each sandwich?

4 __8__

5 If all seven of the letters of the word "REGENTS" were placed in a hat, what would be the probability of drawing an E at random on the first draw?

5 __2/7__

6 In the accompanying diagram, $\overleftrightarrow{AB} \parallel \overleftrightarrow{CD}$, $\overleftrightarrow{HG}$ intersects $\overleftrightarrow{AB}$ at $E$ and $\overleftrightarrow{CD}$ at $F$. If $m\angle CFE = 95$ and $m\angle BEF = 3x + 5$, find $x$.

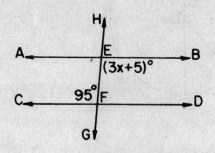

6_ 30

7 A student received test scores of 89, 86, 81, 94, and 75. Find the mean score.

7_ 79   85

8 If a card is drawn at random from a standard deck of 52 cards, what is the probability that the card is a red queen?

8_ $\dfrac{2}{52}$

9 The measure of each base angle of an isosceles triangle is 15°. Find the number of degrees in the measure of the vertex angle.

9_ 150

10 Solve the following system of equations for $x$:

$$4x - y = 10$$
$$x + y = 5$$

10_ 3

11 In the accompanying diagram of circle $O$, diameters $AB$ and $CD$ intersect at $O$. If the measure of arc $AC$ is 40°, find the number of degrees in the measure of angle $COB$.

140

11_ 80°

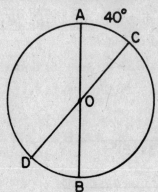

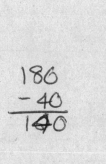

186
− 40
140

12 Factor:    $x^2 + 5x - 6$

12 $(x+6)(x-1)$

13 Solve for $x$:    $0.4x - 1.7 = 0.7$

13 6

14 Solve for $x$:    $\dfrac{x}{3} - 2 = 10$

36

14 ~~40~~

15 In the accompanying diagram, triangle $ABC$ is similar to triangle $XYZ$, with $\angle A \cong \angle X$, $\angle B \cong \angle Y$, and $\angle C \cong \angle Z$. If $AB = 35$, $XY = 7$, $BC = 10$, and $YZ = 2$, how many times larger is side $AC$ than side $XZ$?

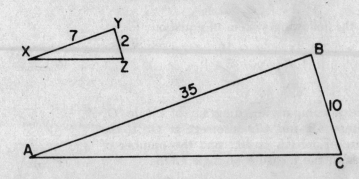

15 5

16 In the accompanying diagram, $\triangle ABC$ is a right triangle with the right angle at $C$. If $AB = 10$ and $BC = 6$, find $AC$.

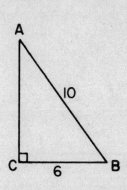

$$c^2 + a^2 = b^2$$
$$x^2 + 36 = 100$$
$$x^2 = \sqrt{64}$$

$\cdot 8$

16_$\cancel{36}$_

17 Write, in symbolic form, using $p$ and $q$, the converse of $\sim p \rightarrow \sim q$.

$\sim q \rightarrow \sim p$

17_____

18 What is the slope of the graph of the equation $y = -x + 1$?

18_$-1$_

19 From $3x^2 + x - 2$ subtract $x^2 - 2x + 3$.

$2x^2 + 3x - 5$

19_____

Add

20 Find the positive root of the equation $x^2 - 25 = 0$.

$+25 \; +25$

$x^2 = \sqrt{25}$

⑤

20_$5$_

21 Two complementary angles are in the ratio of 8:1. Find the number of degrees in the measure of the smaller angle.

21_$10$_

22 In the accompanying diagram, $\angle ACD$ is an exterior angle of triangle $ABC$. If $m\angle A = 40$ and $m\angle B = 60$, find $m\angle ACD$.

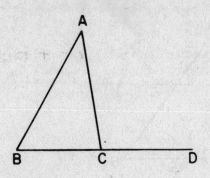

22 $\underline{100}$

DIRECTIONS (23-35): *For each question chosen, write in the space provided the numeral preceding the word or expression that best completes the statement or answers the question.*

23 The statement, "$x$ is odd and $x$ is greater than 2," is true when $x$ equals

(1) 1  (3) 3
(2) 2  (4) 4

23 $\underline{3}$

24 Let $s$ represent "You score at least 65," and let $p$ represent "You pass the exam." Which is the symbolic representation of the statement, "If you do not score at least 65, then you do not pass the exam"?

(1) $\sim s \wedge \sim p$  (3) $s \rightarrow p$
(2) $\sim s \rightarrow \sim p$  (4) $\sim p \rightarrow \sim s$

24 $\underline{2}$

25 If $n$ represents an odd integer, which represents the next larger consecutive odd integer?

(1) $n - 1$  (3) $n + 2$
(2) $2n$  (4) $n + 1$

25 $\underline{3}$

26 For the set of data, 9, 9, 10, 11, 16, which statement is true?
(1) mean > median
(3) median < mode
(2) mean < mode
(4) mean = mode

26 __1__

27 What are the coordinates of the $y$-intercept for the equation $y + 3x = 6$?
(1) (0,6)
(3) (0,3)
(2) (0,−6)
(4) (0,−3)

27 __3__

28 The value of 6! is
(1) 6
(3) $\frac{1}{6}$
(2) 30
(4) 720

28 __4__

29 The circumference of a circle is $20\pi$. What is the area of the circle?
(1) $10\pi$
(3) $100\pi$
(2) $20\pi$
(4) $400\pi$

29 __3__

30 Given four geometric figures: a square, a rectangle, a trapezoid, and a circle. If one figure is selected at random, what is the probability that the figure has four right angles?

(1) $\frac{1}{4}$
(3) $\frac{3}{4}$
(2) $\frac{1}{2}$
(4) 0

30 __2__

31 Which are factors of $15y^2 - 5y$?
(1) $5y - 1$ and $3y + 5$
(2) $5y$ and $3y - 1$
(3) $5y$ and $3y$
(4) $5y - y$ and $3y + 5$

31 __4__

32 A triangle has a base of 12 centimeters and an area of 24 square centimeters. What is the height of the triangle?
(1) 6 cm          (3) 3 cm
(2) 2 cm          (4) 4 cm

32 _2_

33 Which inequality is equivalent to $2x - 1 > 5$?
(1) $x > 6$          (3) $x < 3$
(2) $x > 2$          (4) $x > 3$

33 _4_

34 The sum of $6\sqrt{6}$ and $\sqrt{54}$ equals
(1) $3\sqrt{6}$          (3) $9\sqrt{6}$
(2) $6\sqrt{60}$          (4) $15\sqrt{6}$

34 _3_

35 In the truth table below, which is a correct heading for column III?

| Column I | Column II | Column III |
|----------|-----------|------------|
| $p$ | $q$ | ? |
| T | T | T |
| T | F | F |
| F | T | F |
| F | F | T |

(1) $p \rightarrow q$          (3) $p \wedge \sim q$
(2) $p \leftrightarrow q$          (4) $\sim p \vee q$

35 _2_

**PART TWO**

DIRECTIONS (36-42): *Answer four questions from this part. Show all work unless otherwise directed.*

36 Solve the following system of equations graphically and check:
$$x + y = 1$$
$$2x - y = 8 \qquad [8,2]$$

37 Find the three largest consecutive integers whose sum is less than 86. [*Only an algebraic solution will be accepted.*]  [5,5]

38 The frequency histogram below shows the distribution of scores on a math test.

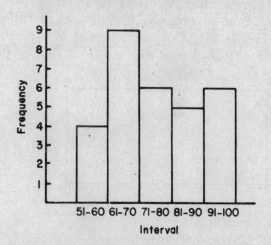

*a* On *your answer paper*, copy and complete the table.  [2]

| Scores | Frequency | Cumulative Frequency |
|--------|-----------|----------------------|
| 51–60 | 4 | 4 |
| 61–70 | 9 | 13 |
| 71–80 | 6 | 19 |
| 81–90 | 5 | 24 |
| 91–100 | 6 | 30 |

*b* How many students took the math test?  [2]

*c* How many students scored above 80?  [2]

*d* Using the table completed in part *a*, draw a cumulative frequency histogram.  [4]

39 One positive number is 5 more than another. The sum of their squares is 53. Find both numbers. [*Only an algebraic solution will be accepted.*] [5,5]

40 In the accompanying diagram, *ABCD* is a rectangle and *AGE* is an isosceles triangle with *AG* = *EG*, $\overline{GF} \perp \overline{AD}$, *E* is the midpoint of $\overline{AD}$, *AF* = *FE*, *AB* = 8, and *AD* = 24.

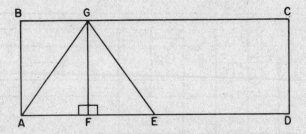

*a* What is the length of $\overline{AE}$? [2]

*b* What is the length of $\overline{AF}$? [2]

*c* What is the length of $\overline{AG}$? [2]

*d* What is the area of triangle *AGE*? [2]

*e* What is the area of trapezoid *ADCG*? [2]

41 The letters *A*, *E*, *N*, *T* are written on four individual cards and placed in a container. Each has an equal likelihood of being drawn. One card is drawn from the container, the letter noted, and then the card is returned to the container. A second card is drawn and the letter noted.

*a* Make a tree diagram or list the sample space showing all possible outcomes after both drawings. [4]

*b* Find the probability that:

(1) both letters drawn are the same  [2]
(2) the first letter drawn is *A* and the second letter is *T*  [2]
(3) for both drawings the letter *N* does not appear  [2]

42 *a* On your answer paper, copy and complete the truth table for the statement
$[(p \rightarrow q) \wedge \sim p] \rightarrow \sim q$.  [8]

| $p$ | $q$ | $p \rightarrow q$ | $\sim p$ | $\sim q$ | $(p \rightarrow q) \wedge \sim p$ | $[(p \rightarrow q) \wedge \sim p] \rightarrow \sim q$ |
|---|---|---|---|---|---|---|
| T | T | | | | | |
| T | F | | | | | |
| F | T | | | | | |
| F | F | | | | | |

*b* Using your results from part *a*, is
$[(p \rightarrow q) \wedge \sim p] \rightarrow \sim q$ a tautology?  [1]
*c* Justify the answer you gave in part *b*.  [1]

# Answers June 1984

## Three-Year Sequence for High School Mathematics—Course I

### ANSWER KEY

### PART ONE

| | | | | | |
|---|---|---|---|---|---|
| 1. | 10 | 12. | $(x + 6)(x - 1)$ | 25. | (3) |
| 2. | 1 | 13. | 6 | 26. | (1) |
| 3. | 36 | 14. | 36 | 27. | (1) |
| 4. | 8 | 15. | 5 | 28. | (4) |
| 5. | $\dfrac{2}{7}$ | 16. | 8 | 29. | (3) |
| | | 17. | $\sim q \rightarrow \sim p$ | 30. | (2) |
| 6. | 30 | 18. | $-1$ | 31. | (2) |
| 7. | 85 | 19. | $2x^2 + 3x - 5$ | 32. | (4) |
| 8. | $\dfrac{2}{52}$ | 20. | 5 | 33. | (4) |
| | | 21. | 10 | 34. | (3) |
| 9. | 150 | 22. | 100 | 35. | (2) |
| 10. | 3 | 23. | (3) | | |
| 11. | 140 | 24. | (2) | | |

Part Two—*See answers explained.*

### ANSWERS EXPLAINED

### PART ONE

**1.**
The smallest number into which both denominators will divide evenly is 4. Multiply both sides of the equation by 4 to clear fractions:

$$\frac{m}{4} = \frac{5}{2}$$

$$4\left(\frac{m}{4}\right) = 4\left(\frac{5}{2}\right)$$

$$m = 2(5)$$

$$m = 10$$

The value of $m$ is 10.

**2.**
Remove parentheses by applying the distributive law of multiplication over addition:

Combine like terms:

Add $-11$ (the additive inverse of 11) to both sides of the equation:

Divide both sides of the equation by 3:

$$5 + 3(x + 2) = 14$$

$$5 + 3x + 6 = 14$$
$$3x + 11 = 14$$
$$\underline{\quad -11 = -11}$$
$$3x \quad\quad = 3$$

$$\frac{3x}{3} = \frac{3}{3}$$

$$x = 1$$

The value of $x$ is 1.

**3.** The given expression is:
Since $x = -2$ and $y = 3$, substitute $-2$ for $x$ and 3 for $y$:

Square $-2$:
,Perform the indicated multiplication:

$$3x^2y$$
$$3(-2)^2(3)$$
$$3(4)(3)$$
$$36$$

The value is **36**.

**4.** Each of the 4 fillings may be used with each of the 2 kinds of bread. Thus there are $4 \times 2$ or 8 different kinds of sandwiches possible.

8 kinds of sandwiches.

**5.** The probability of an event occurring =

$$\frac{\text{number of favorable cases}}{\text{total possible number of cases}}.$$

"REGENTS" contains 2 E's, so there are 2 favorable cases for drawing an E at random.

"REGENTS" contains 7 letters in all so the total possible number of cases is 7.

The probability of drawing an E at random is thus $\frac{2}{7}$.

The probability is $\frac{2}{7}$.

6.  $\overleftrightarrow{AB} \parallel \overleftrightarrow{CD}$. If two lines are parallel, a transversal to them makes a pair of alternate interior angles equal in measure. Therefore,

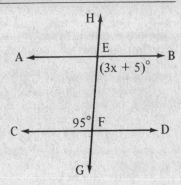

$m\angle BEF = m\angle CFE$:
   Add $-5$ (the additive inverse of 5) to both sides of the equation:

$$3x + 5 = 95$$

$$\underline{-5 = -5}$$

$$3x\quad = 90$$

   Divide both sides of the equation by 3:

$$\frac{3x}{3} = \frac{90}{3}$$

$$x = 30$$

$x = 30$.

7.  The mean is obtained by adding the individual scores and dividing by the number of them.

```
        89
        86
        81
        94
        75
     5) 425
        85
```

The mean score is **85**.

8.  The probability of an event occurring = 

number of favorable cases
──────────────────────────
total possible number of cases.

   There are 2 red queens: the queen of diamonds and the queen of hearts. Thus, there are 2 favorable cases for drawing a red queen.
   The total possible number of cases is the number of cards in a standard deck: 52.

The probability of drawing a red queen at random is $\dfrac{2}{52}$.

The probability is $\dfrac{2}{52}$.

9. Let $x$ = number of degrees in the measure of the vertex angle.

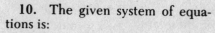

The sum of the measures of the angles of a triangle is 180°:

Combine like terms:

Add $-30$ (the additive inverse of 30) to both sides of the equation:

$$x + 15 + 15 = 180$$
$$x + 30 = 180$$
$$\underline{\phantom{xxxxxx} -30 = -30}$$
$$x \phantom{xxx} = 150$$

The measure of the vertex angle is **150°**.

10. The given system of equations is:

Add the two equations to eliminate $y$:

Divide both sides of the equation by 5:

$$4x - y = 10$$
$$\underline{x + y = 5}$$
$$5x \phantom{xx} = 15$$
$$\frac{5x}{5} = \frac{15}{5}$$
$$x = 3$$

$x = 3$.

11. Since $\overline{AB}$ is a diameter, arc $ACB$ is a semicircle. The measure of a semicircle is 180°:

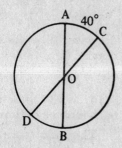

$m\widehat{CB} = m\widehat{ACB} - m\widehat{AC}$:

$$m\widehat{ACB} = 180°$$
$$m\widehat{CB} = 180° - 40°$$
$$m\widehat{CB} = 140°$$

∠*COB* is a *central angle* since its vertex is the center of the circle and its sides are radii. The measure of a central angle is equal to the measure of its intercepted arc:

$$m\angle COB = m\widehat{CB}$$
$$m\angle COB = 140°$$

The measure of ∠*COB* is **140°**.

**12.**  The given expression is a *quadratic trinomial*:

$$x^2 + 5x - 6$$

The factors of a quadratic trinomial are two binomials. The factors of the first term, $x^2$, are $x$ and $x$, and they become the first terms of the binomials:

$$(x \qquad)(x \qquad)$$

The factors of the last term, $-6$, become the second terms of the binomials, but they must be chosen in such a way that the product of the inner terms and the product of the outer terms add up to the middle term, $+5x$, of the original quadratic trinomial. Try $+6$ and $-1$ as the factors of 6:

$$+6x = \text{inner product}$$
$$(x + 6)(x - 1)$$

Since $(+6x) + (-x) = +5x$, these are the correct factors:

$$-x = \text{outer product}$$
$$(x + 6)(x - 1)$$

The factored form is $(x + 6)(x - 1)$.

**13.**
Clear decimals by multiplying each term on both sides of the equation by 10:

$$0.4x - 1.7 = 0.7$$
$$10(0.4x) - 10(1.7) = 10(0.7)$$
$$4x - 17 = 7$$

Add 17 (the additive inverse of $-17$) to both sides of the equation:

$$\underline{17 = 17}$$
$$4x \qquad = 24$$

Divide both sides of the equation by 4:

$$\frac{4x}{4} = \frac{24}{4}$$
$$x = 6$$

$x = 6$.

**14.**  Clear fractions by multiplying each term on both sides of the equation by 3:

$$\frac{x}{3} - 2 = 10$$
$$3\left(\frac{x}{3}\right) - 3(2) = 3(10)$$
$$x - 6 = 30$$

Add 6 (the additive inverse of $-6$) to both sides of the equation:

$$\underline{6 = 6}$$
$$x \qquad = 36$$

$x = 36$.

**15.**  Corresponding sides of similar triangles are in proportion. Since $\triangle ABC$ is similar to $\triangle XYZ$ with $\angle A \cong \angle X$, $\angle B \cong \angle Y$ and $\angle C \cong \angle Z$, then:

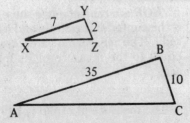

$$\frac{AC}{XZ} = \frac{BC}{YZ}$$

Substitute the numerical values of $BC$ and $YZ$:

$$\frac{AC}{XZ} = \frac{10}{2}$$

Reduce the fraction on the right by dividing its numerator and denominator by 5:

$$\frac{AC}{XZ} = \frac{5}{1}$$

Thus, the ratio of $AC$ to $XZ$ is 5 to 1, or $AC$ is 5 times as large as $XZ$.

5 times as large.

**16.** Let $x = AC$.
By the Pythagorean Theorem, the sum of the squares of the lengths of the legs of a right triangle is equal to the square of the length of the hypotenuse:

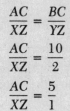

Square 6 and square 10:

$$x^2 + 6^2 = 10^2$$
$$x^2 + 36 = 100$$

Add $-36$ (the additive inverse of 36) to both sides of the equation:

$$\underline{\qquad -36 = -36}$$
$$x^2 \qquad = 64$$

Take the square root of both sides of the equation:

$$x = \pm\sqrt{64}$$

Reject the negative value as meaningless for a length:

$$x = \pm 8$$
$$x = 8$$

$AC = 8$.

**17.** The *converse* of a proposition is formed by interchanging the hypothesis or antecedent (the "if clause") and the conclusion or consequent (the "then clause").
$\sim p \rightarrow \sim q$ is the *implication*, "If $p$ is not true, then $q$ is not true." The hypothesis is $\sim p$ and the conclusion is $\sim q$. Therefore, $\sim q \rightarrow \sim p$ is the converse.

The converse is $\sim q \rightarrow \sim p$.

**18.** If the equation of a line is in the form, $y = mx + b$, $m$ represents the slope and $b$ represents the $y$ intercept.

$y = -x + 1$ is in the form, $y = mx + b$, with $m = -1$ and $b = +1$. Therefore, the slope is $-1$.

The slope is $-1$.

**19.** Write the polynomial to be subtracted under the other polynomial with like terms in the same column:

$$3x^2 + x - 2$$
$$x^2 - 2x + 3$$

Change the signs of each term in the lower polynomial:

$$3x^2 + x - 2$$
$$-x^2 + 2x - 3$$

Add each column algebraically:

$$\overline{2x^2 + 3x - 5}$$

The difference is $2x^2 + 3x - 5$.

**20.**
Add 25 (the additive inverse of $-25$) to both sides of the equation:

$$x^2 - 25 = 0$$
$$25 = 25$$

Take the square root of both sides of the equation:

$$x^2 = 25$$
$$x = \pm\sqrt{25}$$
$$x = \pm 5$$

The positive root is **5.**

**21.** Let $x$ = the measure of the smaller angle.
Then $8x$ = the measure of the larger angle.
The sum of the measures of two complementary angles is $90°$:

$$x + 8x = 90$$

Combine like terms:

$$9x = 90$$

Divide both sides of the equation by 9:

$$\frac{9x}{9} = \frac{90}{9}$$
$$x = 10$$

The measure of the smaller angle is **10°**

**22.** The measure of an exterior angle of a triangle equals the sum of the measures of the two remote interior angles:

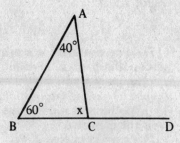

Combine like terms:

$$m\angle ACD = 60 + 40$$
$$m\angle ACD = 100$$

The measure of $\angle ACD$ is **100°**

ALTERNATIVE
SOLUTION: Let $x =$ the
measure of $\angle ACB$.

The sum of the measures of the
angles of a triangle is 180°:

$$x + 60 + 40 = 180$$

Combine like terms:

$$x + 100 = 180$$

Add $-100$ (the additive inverse
of 100) to both sides of the
equation:

$$-100 = -100$$

$\angle ACB = 80°$:

$$x \quad\quad = 80$$

$\angle ACD$ and $\angle ACB$ are *supplementary angles*. The sum of the measures of two supplementary angles
is 180°:

$$m\angle ACD + 80 = 180$$

Add $-80$ (the additive inverse of
80) to both sides of the equation:

$$-80 = -80$$

$$m\angle ACD \quad\quad = 100$$

**23.** In order for the statement to be true, $x$ must be both odd and greater than 2.

Consider each choice in turn:

(1) $x = 1$: Here $x$ is odd but $x$ is not greater than 2. The statement is false.

(2) $x = 2$: Here $x$ is neither odd nor greater than 2. The statement is false.

(3) $x = 3$: Here $x$ is both odd and greater than 2. The statement is true.

(4) $x = 4$: Here $x$ is greater than 2 but it is not odd. The statement is false.

The correct choice is (3).

**24.** $s$ represents "You score at least 65"
$p$ represents "You pass the exam"
"You do not score at least 65" is the *negation* of $s$, which is represented by $\sim s$.

"You do not pass the exam" is the *negation* of $p$, which is represented by $\sim p$.

"If you do not score at least 65, then you do not pass the exam" is the *implication*, $\sim s \rightarrow \sim p$.

The correct choice is (2).

**25.** Consecutive odd integers differ by 2. For example, 3, 5, 7, 9, . . . are consecutive odd integers. Therefore, if $n$ represents an odd integer, the next consecutive odd integer is represented by $n + 2$.

The correct choice is (3).

**26.** The *mean* of 9, 9, 10, 11, and 16 is obtained by adding them and dividing by the number of them, 5:

Mean $= \dfrac{9 + 9 + 10 + 11 + 16}{5} = \dfrac{55}{5} = 11$

The *median* of 9, 9, 10, 11, 16 is the middle item when they are arranged in order of size:

The median is 10.

The *mode* of a set of data is the item appearing most frequently. 9 appears twice and the other items appear only once:

The mode is 9.

Substitute the values for the mean, median and mode in each of the statements to see which is true.

(1) mean > median: $11 > 10$     This is true.
(2) mean < mode: $11 < 9$     This is false.
(3) median < mode: $10 < 9$     This is false.
(4) mean = mode: $11 = 9$     This is false.

The correct choice is (1).

**27.** The $y$ intercept is the point where the graph of the equation intersects the $y$ axis. The $x$ coordinate of every point on the $y$ axis is 0. Therefore, the $x$ coordinate of the $y$ intercept is 0.

Substitute 0 for $x$ in equation, $y + 3x = 6$:     $y + 3(0) = 6$
Perform the indicated multiplication:     $y + 0 = 6$
Thus, the $y$ coordinate of the $y$ intercept is 6.     $y = 6$
The coordinates of the $y$ intercept are $(0,6)$.

The correct choice is (1).

**28.** $n!$ stands for *factorial n*; $n! = n(n - 1)(n - 2)(n - 3) \ldots (3)(2)(1)$

$6! = 6(5)(4)(3)(2)(1)$
$6! = (30)(12)(2)$
$6! = (360)(2)$
$6! = 720$

The correct choice is (4).

**29.** The circumference, $c$, of a circle is given by the formula, $c = 2\pi r$, where $r$ is the length of the radius. Since the circumference is given as $20\pi$:

$$2\pi r = 20\pi$$

Divide both sides of the equation by $2\pi$:

$$\frac{2\pi r}{2\pi} = \frac{20\pi}{2\pi}$$

$$r = 10$$

The area, $A$, of a circle is given by the formula, $A = \pi r^2$, where $r$ is the length of the radius:

$$A = \pi(10)^2$$

Square 10:

$$A = 100\pi$$

The correct choice is (3).

**30.** The probability of an event occurring $= \dfrac{\text{number of favorable cases}}{\text{total possible number of cases}}$.

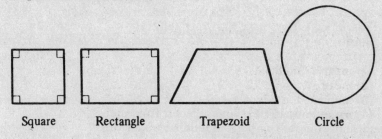

Square     Rectangle     Trapezoid     Circle

Both the square and the rectangle have four right angles. A trapezoid could have two right angles, but never four. A circle certainly does not have four right angles. Thus, the number of favorable cases for the random selection of a figure with four right angles is 2 (the square and the rectangle).

Since there are four figures from which the selection is to be made, the total possible number of cases is 4.

The probability of selecting a figure with four right angles $= \dfrac{2}{4}$ or $\dfrac{1}{2}$.

The correct choice is (2).

**31.** $15y^2 - 5y$ contains a *highest common monomial* factor of $5y$. Determine the other factor by dividing each term of $15y^2 - 5y$ by $5y$, thus applying the distributive law:

$$15y^2 - 5y = 5y(3y - 1)$$

The correct choice is (2).

32. The area, $A$, of a triangle is given by the formula, $A = \dfrac{1}{2}bh$, where $b$ is the length of the base and $h$ is the height or the length of the altitude to that base.

Here, $b = 12$ and $A = 24$: $\qquad 24 = \dfrac{1}{2}(12)h$

Perform the indicated multiplication: $\qquad 24 = 6h$

Divide both sides of the equation by 6: $\qquad \dfrac{24}{6} = \dfrac{6h}{6}$
The height is 4 cm.
$\qquad 4 = h$

The correct choice is (4).

33. The given inequality is: $\qquad 2x - 1 > 5$
Add 1 (the additive inverse of $-1$) to both sides of the inequality:

$$\dfrac{1 = 1}{2x \qquad > 6}$$

Divide both sides of the inequality by 2: $\qquad \dfrac{2x}{2} > \dfrac{6}{2}$

$$x > 3$$

The correct choice is (4).

34. $\qquad\qquad 6\sqrt{6} + \sqrt{54}$

Factor out any perfect square factor from the radicands (the radicand is the number under the radical sign): $\qquad 6\sqrt{6} + \sqrt{9(6)}$

Remove the perfect square factor from under the radical sign by taking its square root and writing it as the coefficient of the radical: $\qquad 6\sqrt{6} + 3\sqrt{6}$

The two terms are now like radicals since each is a multiple of $\sqrt{6}$. Like radicals may be combined by combining their coefficients: $\qquad 9\sqrt{6}$

The correct choice is (3).

35. Examination of Column III shows that it has the truth value T whenever $p$ and $q$ have the same truth value (that is, when both are T or when both are F); Column III has the truth value F whenever $p$ and $q$ have dif-

| Column I | Column II | Column III |
|----------|-----------|------------|
| $p$ | $q$ | ? |
| T | T | T |
| T | F | F |
| F | T | F |
| F | F | T |

ferent truth values (that is, when one of them is T and the other is F). Thus, Column III represents a relationship which has the truth value T whenever $p$ and $q$ agree but has the truth value F when they are different. This relationship is the *equivalence relation*, $p \leftrightarrow q$, which states that $p$ and $q$ are both true or both false.

The correct choice is (2).

## PART TWO

**36.** To draw the graph of $x + y = 1$ it is convenient to solve the equation for $y$. To do so, add $-x$ to each side of the equation:

$$
\begin{array}{rcl}
x + y & = & 1 \\
-x & = & -x \\
\hline
y & = & 1 - x
\end{array}
$$

Prepare a table of values of $x$ and $y$ by choosing any three convenient values for $x$ and substituting them in the equation to determine the corresponding values of $y$:

| $x$ | $1 - x$ | $= y$ |
|-----|---------|-------|
| $-2$ | $1 - (-2) = 1 + 2$ | $= 3$ |
| $0$ | $1 - 0$ | $= 1$ |
| $4$ | $1 - 4$ | $= -3$ |

Plot the points, $(-2, 3)$, $(0, 1)$ and $(4, -3)$ and draw a straight line through them. This straight line is the graph of $x + y = 1$.

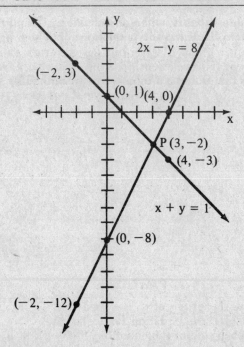

To draw the graph of $2x - y = 8$, it is convenient to solve it for $y$. To do so, add $y$ and also add $-8$ to each side of the equation:

$$2x - y = 8$$
$$-8 \quad + y = -8 + y$$
$$\overline{-8 + 2x \quad = \qquad y}$$

Prepare a table of values of $x$ and $y$ by choosing any three convenient values for $x$ and substituting them in the equation, $-8 + 2x = y$, to determine the corresponding values of $y$:

| $x$ | $-8 + 2x$ | $= y$ |
|-----|-----------|-------|
| $-2$ | $-8 + 2(-2) = -8 - 4$ | $= -12$ |
| $0$ | $-8 + 2(0) = -8 + 0$ | $= -8$ |
| $4$ | $-8 + 2(4) = -8 + 8$ | $= 0$ |

Plot the points $(-2, -12)$, $(0, -8)$ and $(4, 0)$ and draw a straight line through them. This line is the graph of $2x - y = 8$.

The solution to the system is represented by the point, $P$, where the two lines intersect. $P$ is the point $(3, -2)$ or $x = 3, y = -2$.

The solution is $(3, -2)$ or $x = 3, y = -2$.

CHECK: The solution to the system is checked by substituting 3 for $x$ and $-2$ for $y$ in *both* of the *original* equations to see if they are satisfied:

$$\underline{x + y = 1}: 3 + (-2) \overset{?}{\underset{?}{=}} 1 \qquad \underline{2x - y = 8}: 2(3) - (-2) \overset{?}{\underset{?}{=}} 8$$
$$3 - 2 \overset{.}{=} 1 \qquad\qquad\qquad 6 + 2 \overset{.}{=} 8$$
$$1 = 1 \qquad\qquad\qquad\qquad 8 = 8$$

37. Let $x$ = the first consecutive integer.
Then $x + 1$ = the second consecutive integer.
And $x + 2$ = the third consecutive integer.
The sum of the three consecutive integers is less than 86:

$$x + x + 1 + x + 2 < 86$$

Combine like terms:

$$3x + 3 < 86$$

Add $-3$ (the additive inverse of 3) to both sides of the inequality:

$$-3 = -3$$
$$\overline{\phantom{3x}\quad 3x \quad\quad < 83}$$

Divide both sides of the inequality by 3:

$$\frac{3x}{3} < \frac{83}{3}$$

The largest integral value of $x$ for which $x < 27\frac{2}{3}$ is 27:

$$x < 27\frac{2}{3}$$
$$x = 27$$
$$x + 1 = 28$$
$$x + 2 = 29$$

The consecutive integers are 27, 28, and 29.

38.

a. The frequency column is filled in by reading the height of each bar in the frequency histogram. The cumulative frequency column is filled in by beginning with the first frequency, 4, and successively adding each frequency to it:

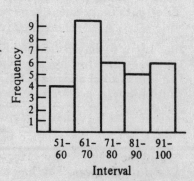

| Scores | Frequency | Cumulative Frequency |
|--------|-----------|----------------------|
| 51–60 | 4 | 4 |
| 61–70 | 9 | 13 |
| 71–80 | 6 | 19 |
| 81–90 | 5 | 24 |
| 91–100 | 6 | 30 |
| | 30 | |

**b.** The number of students who took the math test is equal to the final number in the cumulative frequency column, 30. It is also the sum of all the entries in the frequency column, 30.

**30 students took the test.**

**c.** The number of students who scored above 80 is the sum of the frequencies in the $81 - 90$ interval and in the $91 - 100$ interval: $5 + 6 = 11$

**11 students scored above 80.**

**d.**

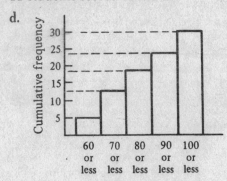

**39.** Let $x$ = the smaller number.
Then $x + 5$ = the larger number.
The sum of their squares is 53:          $x^2 + (x + 5)^2 = 53$
Multiply out $(x + 5)^2$:

$$
\begin{array}{r}
x + 5 \\
x + 5 \\
\hline
x^2 + 5x \\
5x + 25 \\
\hline
x^2 + 10x + 25
\end{array}
$$

$x^2 + x^2 + 10x + 25 = 53$

Combine like terms:                    $2x^2 + 10x + 25 = 53$

This is a *quadratic equation.* Rearrange it so that all terms are on one side equal to 0 by adding −53 (the additive inverse of 53) to both sides:

$$\frac{\phantom{2x^2 + 10x}-53 = -53}{2x^2 + 10x - 28 = 0}$$

Simplify by dividing all terms on both sides of the equation by 2:

$$x^2 + 5x - 14 = 0$$

The left side is a *quadratic trinomial* which can be factored into the product of two binomials. Be sure to check that the sum of the product of the inner terms of the binomials and the product of the outer terms is equal to the middle term, $+5x$, of the trinomial:

$$+7x = \text{inner product}$$
$$(x + 7)(x - 2) = 0$$
$$-2x = \text{outer product}$$
$$(x + 7)(x - 2) = 0$$

Since $(+7x) + (-2x) = +5x$, these are the correct factors:

If the product of two factors equals zero, either factor may equal zero:

$$x + 7 = 0 \quad \text{OR } x - 2 = 0$$

Add the appropriate additive inverse to both sides of each equation, −7 for the left-hand equation and 2 for the right-hand equation:

$$\frac{-7 = -7}{x \quad = -7} \qquad \frac{2 = 2}{x \quad = 2}$$

Reject −7 since the question asks for positive numbers; if $x = -7$, the second number (which we have represented by $x + 5$) would be −2:

$$x = 2$$
$$x + 5 = 7$$

The numbers are **2** and **7**.

40  a.  Since
*E* is the midpoint
of $\overline{AD}$,

$$AE = \frac{1}{2}(AD) =$$

$$\frac{1}{2}(24) = 12$$

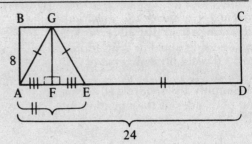

The length of
$\overline{AE}$ is **12**.

b.  Since $AF = FE$, $AF = \frac{1}{2}(AE) = \frac{1}{2}(12) = 6$

The length of $\overline{AF}$ is **6**.

c.  Since $ABCD$ is given to be a rectangle, $\angle BAF$ and $\angle B$ are right angles. Since $\overline{GF} \perp \overline{AD}$, $\angle AFG$ is also a right angle. Thus, $ABGF$ is also a rectangle and its opposite sides are equal; $GF = AB = 8$.

In $\triangle AFG$, use the Pythagorean Theorem to determine the length of $\overline{AG}$. In a right triangle, the square of the length of the hypotenuse equals the sum of the squares of the lengths of the legs:

$$(AG)^2 = (AF)^2 + (GF)^2$$
$$(AG)^2 = 6^2 + 8^2$$
$$(AG)^2 = 36 + 64$$
$$(AG)^2 = 100$$

Take the square root of both sides of the equation:

$$AG = \pm\sqrt{100}$$
$$AG = \pm 10$$

Reject the negative value as meaningless for a length.

$$AG = 10$$

The length of $\overline{AG}$ is **10**.

d.  The area, *A*, of a triangle is given by the formula, $A = \frac{1}{2}bh$, where *b* is the length of the base and *h* is the length of the altitude to that base.

For $\triangle AGE$, $b = AE = 12$, and $h = GF = 8$:

$$A = \frac{1}{2}(12)(8)$$
$$A = 6(8)$$
$$A = 48$$

The area of $\triangle AGE$ is **48**.

e. The area, $A$, of a trapezoid is given by the formula, $A = \dfrac{1}{2}$ $h(b_1 + b_2)$, where $h$ is the length of the altitude and $b_1$ and $b_2$ are the lengths of the bases of the trapezoid.

For trapezoid $ADCG$, $h = GF = 8$, $b_1 = GC = FE + ED = 6 +$

12 = 18, and $b_2 = AD = 24$:

$$A = \frac{1}{2}(8)(18 + 24)$$
$$A = 4(42)$$
$$A = 168$$

The area of trapezoid $ADCG$ is **168**.

**41  a.**  Tree Diagram: There are four possible results for the first drawing: $A$, $E$, $N$, or $T$, so four branches are drawn from START. Each of the four first drawing results can be followed by one of the four possible results, $A$, $E$, $N$, or $T$, for the second drawing. Thus, four branches radiate from each of the first drawing results to represent the second drawing results:

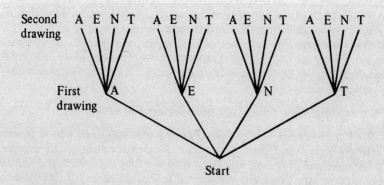

Sample Space: The sample space must contain 16 lines in all. Each of the four first drawing results, $A$, $E$, $N$, or $T$, may be paired with each of the four second drawing results:

| First Drawing | Second Drawing |
|:---:|:---:|
| A | A |
| A | E |
| A | N |
| A | T |
| E | A |
| E | E |
| E | N |
| E | T |
| N | A |
| N | E |
| N | N |
| N | T |
| T | A |
| T | E |
| T | N |
| T | T |

**b.**   The probability of an event occurring =
number of favorable cases

total possible number of cases.

(1) 4 pathways that pass through two letters that are the same go from START on the tree diagram through the second drawing: AA, EE, NN, and TT. Correspondingly, the sample space contains 4 lines in which both of the letters are the same. Thus the number of favorable cases for drawing two letters that are the same is 4.

The total possible number of pathways from START to the second drawing on the tree diagram is 16. Correspondingly, the total number of lines in the sample space is 16. Thus, the total possible number of cases is 16.

The probability of drawing both letters the same = $\dfrac{4}{16}$.

(2) There is only one pathway on the tree diagram which passes through A first and then through T. Correspondingly, the sample space contains only one line with A in the first column and T in the second column. Thus, the number of favorable cases for drawing an A first and then a T is 1.

The total possible number of cases is again 16.

The probability of drawing an A first and then a T is $\dfrac{1}{16}$.

(3) On the tree diagram, three paths which do not go through $N$ may be taken from START. Each of these paths may continue along three possible paths which do not go through $N$ for the second drawing. Thus there are $3 \times 3$ or 9 paths which do not go through an $N$. Correspondingly, the sample space contains 9 lines which do not contain $N$ in either the first or second column. Thus, the number of favorable cases for not having an $N$ appear in both drawings is 9.

The probability that $N$ does not appear in both drawings $= \dfrac{9}{16}$.

42   a

| $p$ | $q$ | $p \to q$ | $\sim p$ | $\sim q$ | $(p \to q)$ $\wedge \sim p$ | $[(p \to q)$ $\wedge \sim p] \to \sim q$ |
|---|---|---|---|---|---|---|
| T | T | T | F | F | F | T |
| T | F | F | F | T | F | T |
| F | T | T | T | F | T | F |
| F | F | T | T | T | T | T |

For each column in the table above, the truth values, T or F, are filled in according to the values of $p$ and $q$ on the line.

$p \to q$ is the *implication*, if $p$ is true, then $q$ is true. It has the truth value, T, whenever $q$ has the truth value, T, or whenever $p$ and $q$ both have the value, F; it has the truth value, F, when $p$ is T and $q$ is F.

The column headed $\sim p$ is the *negation* of $p$, or "not $p$." The truth value for each line is the opposite of the truth value on that line for $p$.

The column headed $\sim q$ is the *negation* of $q$, or "not $q$." The truth values in this column are the opposites of those on the same line for $q$.

$(p \to q) \wedge \sim p$ is the *conjunction* of $(p \to q)$ and $\sim p$. The conjunction has the truth value, T, only when $(p \to q)$ and $\sim p$ both have the truth value, T; in all other cases, the conjunction has the truth value, F.

$[(p \to q) \wedge \sim p] \to \sim q$ is the *implication*, if the conjunction of $(p \to q)$ and the negation of $p$ is true, then the negation of $q$ is true. The implication has the truth value, T, whenever $\sim q$ has the truth value, T, or whenever $(p \to q) \wedge \sim p$ and $\sim q$ both have the truth value, F; it has the truth value, F when $(p \to q) \wedge \sim p$ is T and $\sim q$ is F.

  **b.** $[(p \rightarrow q) \wedge \sim p] \rightarrow \sim q$ is **not a tautology.**

  **c.** A tautology is a proposition formed by combining other propositions $(p, q, r, \ldots)$ which is true regardless of the truth or falsity of $p, q, r, \ldots$

  Since $[(p \rightarrow q) \wedge \sim p] \rightarrow \sim q$ has the truth value, F, for certain values of $p$ and $q$ (notably when $p$ is F and $q$ is T), it is not a tautology.

| Topic | Question Numbers | Number of Points | Your Points | Your Percentage |
|---|---|---|---|---|
| 1. Numbers (rat'l, irrat'l); percent | — | 0 | | |
| 2. Properties of No. Systems | 23 | 2 | | |
| 3. Operations on Rat'l Nos. and Monomials | — | 0 | | |
| 4. Operations on Polynomials | 19 | 2 | | |
| 5. Square root; Operations involving Radicals | 34 | 2 | | |
| 6. Evaluating Formulas and Expressions | 3 | 2 | | |
| 7. Linear Equations (simple cases incl. parentheses) | 2 | 2 | | |
| 8. Linear Equations containing Decimals or Fractions | 1, 13, 14 | 2+2+2=6 | | |
| 9. Graphs of Linear Functions (slope) | 18, 27 | 2+2=4 | | |
| 10. Inequalities | 33 | 2 | | |
| 11. Systems of Eqs. & Inequal. (alg. & graphic solutions) | 10, 36 | 2+10=12 | | |
| 12. Factoring | 12, 31 | 2+2=4 | | |
| 13. Quadratic Equations | 20 | 2 | | |
| 14 Verbal Problems | 37, 39 | 10+10=20 | | |
| 15 Variation | — | 0 | | |
| 16. Literal Eqs.; Expressing Relations Algebraically | 25 | 2 | | |
| 17. Factorial n | 28 | 2 | | |

| Topic | Question Numbers | Number of Points | Your Points | Your Percentage |
|---|---|---|---|---|
| 18. Areas, Perims., Circums., Vols. of Common Figures | 29, 32, 40d, 40e | 2+2+2+2= 8 | | |
| 19. Geometry (≅, ∠ meas., ‖ lines, compls., suppls., const.) | 6, 9, 11, 21, 22, 40a, 40b | 2+2+2+2+ 2+2+2= 14 | | |
| 20. Ratio & Proportion (incl. similar triangles) | 15 | 2 | | |
| 21. Pythagorean Theorem | 16, 40c | 2+2=4 | | |
| 22. Logic (symbolic rep., logical forms, truth tables) | 17, 24, 35, 42a, 42b, 42c | 2+2+2+8+ 1+1=16 | | |
| 23. Probability (incl. tree diagrams & sample spaces) | 5, 8, 30, 41a, 41b(1), (2), (3) | 2+2+2+4+ 2+2+2= 16 | | |
| 24 Combinations (arrangements, permutations) | 4 | 2 | | |
| 25. Statistics (central tend., freq. dist., histograms) | 7, 26, 38a, 38b, 38c, 38d | 2+2+2+2+ 2+4=14 | | |

# Examination January 1985

## Three-Year Sequence for High School MATHEMATICS—Course I

### PART ONE

DIRECTIONS: *Answer 30 questions from this part. Each correct answer will receive 2 credits. No partial credit will be allowed. Write your answers in the spaces provided. Where applicable, answers may be left in terms of π or in radical form.*

1 A car rental agency has 5 compact cars, 3 regular size cars, and 2 station wagons for rent. If a car is rented at random, what is the probability it is a compact?

1 $\frac{5}{10}$

2 In the accompanying diagram, $\overleftrightarrow{AB}$ and $\overleftrightarrow{CD}$ intersect at $E$, and $m\angle AEC = 24$. If $m\angle DEB = 2x - 6$, find $x$.

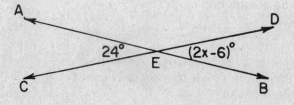

2 $15$

3 If the mean of four scores is 85, what is the total of the four scores?

3 $340$

4 Evaluate: 5!

4 $120$

1

5 The ratio of Tom's shadow to Emily's shadow is 3 to 2. If Tom is 180 centimeters tall, how many centimeters tall is Emily?

5 _120_

6 If Pat correctly answered 24 out of 30 questions, what percent of the questions did she answer correctly?

6 _80_

7 Express, in cubic feet, the volume of a room whose dimensions are 12 feet long by 10 feet wide by 8 feet high.

7 _____

8 If $a = 1$ and $b = -2$, find the value of $(a + b)^2$.

8 _____

9 A single six-sided die is rolled. What is the probability that the outcome is a number less than 12?

9 _1_

10 Solve the following system of equations for $x$:

$$x + y = 4$$
$$5x - y = 20$$

10 _4_

11 Solve for $x$ in terms of $a$, $b$, and $c$:

$$ax + b = c$$

$X = c - b$

11 _a_

12 Simplify by combining like terms:

$$(3a + b) - (a + b)$$

12 _____

13 Two angles of a right triangle are congruent. What is the number of degrees in the measure of each of these angles?

13 _____

14 Solve for $x$:   $2x - 4 = 4x + 4$

14 _____

15 Solve for $x$:   $x + \frac{1}{2} = \frac{10}{4}$

15 _____

16 A rectangle has an area of $x^2 - 4$. If its length is $x + 2$, express its width in terms of $x$.

16 _____

17 Solve for $y$: $0.02y - 1.5 = 8$

17 $\underline{475}$

18 Factor: $x^2 - x - 6$

18 _____

19 In the accompanying diagram of circle $O$, m$\angle ABC = 30$. Find the number of degrees in the measure of acute angle $AOC$.

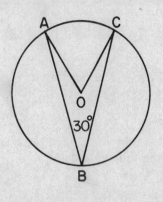

Add*
Inscribed

19 $\underline{60}$

20 What is the perimeter, in centimeters, of a square whose area is 36 square centimeters?

20 $\underline{24}$

21 In the accompanying diagram, angle $BCD$ is an exterior angle of triangle $ABC$. If the measure of angle $A$ is $25°$ and the measure of angle $B$ is $85°$, find the number of degrees in the measure of angle $BCD$.

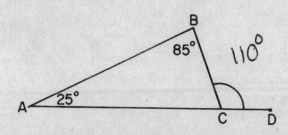

110°

21 _____

DIRECTIONS (22-35): *For each question chosen, write in the space provided the* numeral *preceding the word or expression that best completes the statement or answers the question.*

22 Given the true statement: "If John lives in Buffalo, then he lives in New York State."

If John does not live in New York State, which statement is a logical conclusion?
(1) He does not live in Buffalo.
(2) He might still live in Buffalo.
(3) He lives in Chicago.
(4) He does not live in the United States.    22_____

23 The expression "$p$ and $q$" may be written as
(1) $p \lor q$      (3) $p \leftrightarrow q$
(2) $p \rightarrow q$      (4) $p \land q$    23_____

24 What is the mode for the following data?
$$19, 8, 38, 41, 8, 16, 3$$
(1) 7      (3) 16
(2) 8      (4) 19    24_____

25 Which expression is equivalent to $6x + 6y$?
(1) $12xy$      (3) $6xy$
(2) $6(x + y)$      (4) $6x + y$    25_____

26 The product of $5x^2$ and $3x^5$ is
(1) $8x^7$      (3) $15x^7$
(2) $8x^{10}$      (4) $15x^{10}$    26_____

27 Which is an equation of a line whose slope is $-2$?
(1) $y = 2x - 1$      (3) $y = x - 2$
(2) $y = -2x + 1$      (4) $y - 2x = 4$    27_____

28 As shown on the accompanying graph, what is the solution of the system of equations $y = 2x + 1$ and $x + y = 1$?

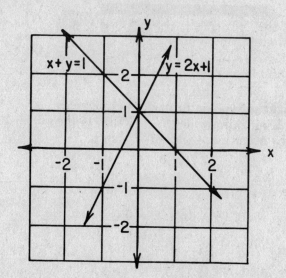

(1) $(1,0)$          (3) $(0,1)$
(2) $(-1,0)$        (4) $(0,-1)$                28____

29 The coordinates of the vertices of a triangle are $(1,1)$, $(3,1)$, and $(3,5)$. The triangle formed is

(1) a right triangle
(2) an obtuse triangle
(3) an isosceles triangle
(4) an equilateral triangle                29____

30 Which is undefined when $x = 2$?

(1) $x - 2$                    (3) $\dfrac{x}{2}$

(2) $\dfrac{1}{x - 2}$              (4) $x^0$

                                            30____

31 Which inequality is the solution set of the graph shown below?

(1) $-2 < x < 4$        (3) $-2 \le x \le 4$
(2) $-2 \le x < 4$        (4) $-2 < x \le 4$        31_____

32 The length of the hypotenuse of a right triangle is 7 and the length of one leg is 4. What is the length of the other leg?

(1) 11        (3) 3
(2) $\sqrt{65}$        (4) $\sqrt{33}$        32_____

33 The solution set of $x^2 - 3x + 2 = 0$ is

(1) $\{2,1\}$        (3) $\{-2,1\}$
(2) $\{-2,-1\}$        (4) $\{2,-1\}$        33_____

34 Which of the following is true when $p$ is false and $q$ is false?

(1) $p \lor q$        (3) $p \leftrightarrow q$
(2) $p \land q$        (4) $\sim(\sim p)$        34_____

35 The expression $\sqrt{150}$ is equivalent to

(1) $5\sqrt{6}$        (3) $25\sqrt{6}$
(2) $15\sqrt{10}$        (4) 75        35_____

## PART TWO

DIRECTIONS (36-42):   *Answer four questions from this part. Show all work unless otherwise directed.*

36 Solve the following system of equations graphically and check:

$$x + y = 12$$
$$y = 3x$$

[8,2]

37 One integer is 3 more than twice another integer.
The sum of these integers is greater than 24.
Find the *smallest* values for these integers. [*Only
an algebraic solution will be accepted.*]      [5,5]

38 In the diagram below, $\overline{PR}$ is a diameter of
circle $O$. The measure of $\angle QOR$ is $(4x - 10)°$
and the measure of $\angle QOP$ is $(x + 50)°$.

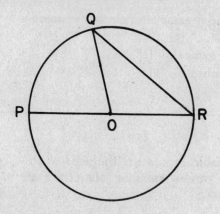

a What is the value of $x$?      [3]
b How many degrees are in the measure of
minor arc $QP$?   [2]
c How many degrees are in the measure of
$\angle QRP$?   [2]
d If the area of circle $O$ is $16\pi$, find the circumference in terms of $\pi$.   [3]

39 In triangle $ABC$, the ratio of the measure of
angle $A$ to the measure of angle $B$ is 3:5. The
measure of angle $C$ is 20 more than the sum of
the measures of angles $A$ and $B$. What is the
measure of each angle in triangle $ABC$? [*Only an
algebraic solution will be accepted.*]    [5,5]

40 A softball team plays two games each weekend, one on Saturday and the other on Sunday. The probability of winning on Saturday is $\frac{3}{5}$ and the probability of winning on Sunday is $\frac{4}{7}$.

What is the probability of:
a losing a Saturday game [2]
b losing a Saturday game and winning a Sunday game [2]
c winning a Sunday game after already winning a Saturday game [2]
d winning both games [2]
e losing both games [2]

41 The following table represents the ages of students hired for various summer jobs at a State park in New York:

| Age Interval | Cumulative Frequency |
|---|---|
| 11–12 | 2 |
| 13–14 | 6 |
| 15–16 | 9 |
| 17–18 | 15 |
| 19–21 | 20 |

a Draw a cumulative frequency histogram. [4]
b What was the total number of students hired? [2]
c In which interval does the median lie? [2]
d How many students age 13 or 14 were hired? [2]

42 *a* Complete the truth table for the statement

$\sim(p \rightarrow q) \leftrightarrow (p \wedge \sim q)$. [8]

| $p$ | $q$ | $\sim q$ | $p \rightarrow q$ | $\sim(p \rightarrow q)$ | $p \wedge \sim q$ | $\sim(p \rightarrow q) \leftrightarrow (p \wedge \sim q)$ |
|---|---|---|---|---|---|---|
| T | T | | | | | |
| T | F | | | | | |
| F | T | | | | | |
| F | F | | | | | |

*b* What is logically equivalent to the negation of:
   "If I receive a scholarship, then I will go to college"?   [2]
   (1) If I do not receive a scholarship, then I will not go to college.
   (2) I receive a scholarship and I will not go to college.
   (3) It is not the case that I receive a scholarship and I go to college.
   (4) If I do not go to college, then I did not receive a scholarship.

# Answers January 1985

## Three-Year Sequence for High School Mathematics—Course I

**ANSWER KEY**

**PART ONE**

1. $\dfrac{5}{10}$
2. 15
3. 340
4. 120
5. 120
6. 80
7. 960
8. 1
9. 1
10. 4
11. $\dfrac{c - b}{a}$

12. $2a$
13. 45
14. $-4$
15. 2
16. $x - 2$
17. 475
18. $(x - 3)(x + 2)$
19. 60
20. 24
21. 110
22. (1)
23. (4)
24. (2)

25. (2)
26. (3)
27. (2)
28. (3)
29. (1)
30. (2)
31. (4)
32. (4)
33. (1)
34. (3)
35. (1)

**Part Two**—*See answers explained.*

**ANSWERS EXPLAINED**

**PART ONE**

1. Probability of an event occurring =

$$\dfrac{\text{number of favorable cases}}{\text{total possible number of cases}}.$$

Since there are 5 compact cars, the number of favorable cases for renting a compact is 5.

Since there are 5 compacts, 3 regular size cars, and 2 station wagons, the total possible number of cases is $5 + 3 + 2 = 10$.

The probability of renting a compact is $\dfrac{5}{10}$.

The probability is $\dfrac{5}{10}$.

**2.** When two lines intersect, a pair of vertical angles formed are equal in measure:

$2x - 6 = 24$

Add $+6$, the additive inverse of $-6$, to both sides of the equation:

$$\dfrac{+6 = +6}{2x \quad = 30}$$

Divide both sides of the equation by 2:

$$\dfrac{2x}{2} = \dfrac{30}{2}$$

$$x = 15$$

$x = \mathbf{15}.$

**3.** Let $x$ = the total of the 4 scores.
The *mean* is the total of the four scores divided by 4; since the mean is 85:

$$\dfrac{x}{4} = 85$$

Multiply both sides of the equation by 4:

$$4\left(\dfrac{x}{4}\right) = 4(85)$$

The total is **340.**

$$x = 340$$

**4.** 5! stands for *factorial* 5.
$$n! = n(n-1)(n-2)(n-3)\ldots(2)(1):$$

$5! = 5(4)(3)(2)(1)$
$5! = 20(6)$
$5! = 120$

$5! = \mathbf{120}.$

**5.**  Let $x$ = the number of centimeters in Emily's height.

The ratio of the lengths of their
shadows is 3 to 2: Let $3y$ = the
number of centimeters in the length
of Tom's shadow. Then $2y$ = the
number of centimeters in the length
of Emily's shadow.

TOM

EMILY

180

$x$

3y        2y

Tom and his shadow and Emily
and her shadow form the legs of two
similar right triangles.  The measures

of the corresponding sides of two similar triangles are
in proportion:

$$\frac{180}{x} = \frac{3y}{2y}$$

Reduce the fraction on the right by dividing both
numerator and denominator by $y$:

$$\frac{180}{x} = \frac{3}{2}$$

In a proportion, the product of the means equals
the product of the extremes (cross multiply):

$$3x = 2(180)$$
$$3x = 360$$

Divide both sides of the equation by 3:

$$\frac{3x}{3} = \frac{360}{3}$$
$$x = 120$$

Emily is **120** centimeters tall.

**6.**  The percent answered correctly is the number answered correctly divided by the total number of questions:

$$\frac{24}{30}$$

Reduce the fraction by dividing both numerator and denominator by 6:

$$\frac{4}{5}$$

$\frac{4}{5}$ is equivalent to 80 percent; the decimal equivalent may
also be obtained by dividing 4.00 by 5:

$$5)\overline{4.00}^{\,.80}$$
$$\underline{40}$$

**80** percent were answered correctly.

**7.**  The vol-
ume, $V$, of a room
is obtained by
multiplying the
length by the
width by the
height:

$$V = 12(10)(8)$$
$$V = 12(80)$$
$$V = 960$$

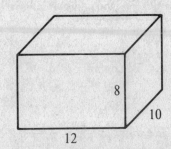

8

10

12

The volume is **960** cubic feet.

8.   $a = 1, b = -2$                                                           $(a + b)^2$
The value of $(a + b)^2$ is obtained by substituting 1 for $a$
and $-2$ for $b$ in the expression:                                    $(1 - 2)^2$
  Combine like terms:                                                      $(-1)^2$
  Square $-1$:                                                                      1

The value is 1.


9.   Probability of an event occurring $=$

$$\frac{\text{number of favorable cases}}{\text{total possible number of cases}}$$

A die has six sides, numbered 1, 2, 3, 4, 5, and 6, respectively. All
sides are numbers less than 12; the number of favorable cases for an
outcome less than 12 is 6.
The total possible number of cases is the total number of sides or 6.

The probability of rolling a number less than 12 is $\frac{6}{6}$ or 1.

The probability is 1.


ALTERNATIVE SOLUTION: It is certain that on rolling a die the
outcome will be a number less than 12 since there are no other possibilities.
  Certainty is represented by a probability of 1.


10.   The given system of equations is                  $x + y = 4$
                                                                            $5x - y = 20$
Adding the equations will eliminate $y$:            $\overline{6x \quad\quad = 24}$

Divide both sides of the equation by 6:             $\dfrac{6x}{6} = \dfrac{24}{6}$

The value of $x$ is 4.                                           $x = 4$


11.   The given equation is a *literal* equation:   $ax + b = c$
Add $-b$, the additive inverse of $b$, to both sides
of the equation:
                                                                            $\underline{-b = -b}$
                                                                    $ax \quad = c - b$

Divide both sides of the equation by $a$:           $\dfrac{ax}{a} = \dfrac{c - b}{a}$

                                                                            $x = \dfrac{c - b}{a}$

The solution is $x = \dfrac{c - b}{a}$.

**12.**

$$(3a + b) - (a + b)$$

Remove parentheses. When removing parentheses preceded by a plus sign, the signs of the terms inside the parentheses remain unchanged; when removing parentheses preceded by a minus sign, the signs of the terms inside the parentheses are changed:

$$3a + b - a - b$$

Combine like terms:

$$2a$$

The correct answer is **2a**.

**13.**   Let $x =$ the measure of each of the congruent angles.

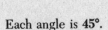

The sum of the measures of the 3 angles of a triangle is 180°:

$$x + x + 90 = 180$$

Combine like terms:

$$2x + 90 = 180$$

Add $-90$, the additive inverse of $+90$, to both sides of the equation:

$$\begin{aligned} -90 &= -90 \\ \hline 2x &= 90 \end{aligned}$$

Divide both sides of the equation by 2:

$$\frac{2x}{2} = \frac{90}{2}$$

$$x = 45$$

Each angle is **45°**.

**14.**

$$2x - 4 = 4x + 4$$

Add, $-2x$, the additive inverse of $2x$, and also add $-4$, the additive inverse of $+4$, to both sides of the equation:

$$\begin{aligned} -2x - 4 &= -2x - 4 \\ \hline -8 &= 2x \end{aligned}$$

Divide both sides of the equation by 2:

$$\frac{-8}{2} = \frac{2x}{2}$$

$$-4 = x$$

The solution is $x = -4$.

**15.**

$$x + \frac{1}{2} = \frac{10}{4}$$

The least common multiple (L.C.M.) of a set of numbers is the smallest number into which they all divide evenly. The L.C.M. for denominators 2 and 4 is 4. Multiply each term on both sides of the equation by 4:

$$4(x) + 4\left(\frac{1}{2}\right) = 4\left(\frac{10}{4}\right)$$
$$4x + 2 = 10$$

Add $-2$, the additive inverse of $+2$, to both sides of the equation:

$$\frac{-2 = -2}{4x \quad = 8}$$

Divide both sides of the equation by 4:

$$\frac{4x}{4} = \frac{8}{4}$$
$$x = 2$$

The solution is $x = 2$.

**16.**   Let $y =$ the width of the rectangle.

The area of a rectangle equals the product of its length and width:
$$x^2 - 4 = y(x + 2)$$
To solve for $y$, divide both sides of the equation by $(x + 2)$:
$$\frac{x^2 - 4}{(x + 2)} = \frac{y(x + 2)}{(x + 2)}$$

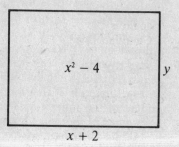

$x^2 - 4$ is the *difference of two perfect squares.* The difference of two perfect squares can be factored into two factors; one is the sum of the square roots of the perfect squares, and the other is the difference of the square roots:
$$\frac{(x + 2)(x - 2)}{(x + 2)} = \frac{y(x + 2)}{(x + 2)}$$
Cancel like factors which appear in numerator and denominator in each fraction:
$$\frac{\cancel{(x + 2)}(x - 2)}{\cancel{(x + 2)}} = \frac{y\cancel{(x + 2)}}{\cancel{(x + 2)}}$$
$$x - 2 = y$$

The width of the rectangle is $x - 2$.

**17.**

$$0.02y - 1.5 = 8$$

To clear decimals, multiply each term on both sides of the equation by 100:

$$100(0.02y) - 100(1.5) = 100(8)$$
$$2y - 150 = 800$$

Add $+150$, the additive inverse of $-150$, to both sides of the equation:

$$
\begin{array}{r}
+150 = +150 \\
\hline
2y \quad\ = 950
\end{array}
$$

Divide both sides of the equation by 2:

$$\frac{2y}{2} = \frac{950}{2}$$
$$y = 475$$

The solution is **$y = 475$**.

**18.** The given expression is a *quadratic trinomial*:

$$x^2 - x - 6$$

A quadratic trinomial may be factored into the product of two binomials. The factors of the first term, $x^2$, are $x$ and $x$, and they become the first terms of the binomials:

$$(x \quad )(x \quad )$$

The factors of the last term, $-6$, are the last terms of the binomials, but they must be chosen in such a way that the product of the inner terms added to the product of the outer terms equals the middle term, $-x$, of the original trinomial. Try $-3$ and $+2$ as the factors of $-6$:

$$-3x = \text{inner product}$$
$$(x - 3)(x + 2)$$
$$+2x = \text{outer product}$$

Since $(-3x) + (+2x) = -x$, these are the correct factors:

$$(x - 3)(x + 2)$$

The factored form is **$(x - 3)(x + 2)$**.

**19.** $\angle ABC$ is an *inscribed angle*. The measure of an inscribed angle is equal to one-half the measure of its intercepted arc:

$$m\angle ABC = \frac{1}{2}\, m\widehat{AC}$$

$$30 = \frac{1}{2}\, m\widehat{AC}$$

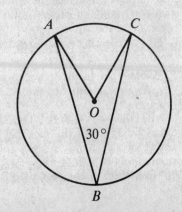

Multiply both sides of the equation by 2:

$$2(30) = 2\left(\frac{1}{2}\, m\widehat{AC}\right)$$
$$60 = m\widehat{AC}$$

$\angle AOC$ is a *central angle*. The measure of a central angle is equal to the measure of its intercepted arc:

$$m\angle AOC = m\widehat{AC}$$
$$m\angle AOC = 60$$

The measure of $\angle AOC$ is **60°**.

**20.** Let $x =$ the length in centimeters of one side of the square.

The area of a square equals the square of the length of one side:

$$36 = x^2$$

Take the square root of both sides of the equation:     $\pm\sqrt{36} = x$

Reject the negative value as meaningless for a length:     $6 = x$

The perimeter of a square is the sum of the lengths of all 4 equal sides:     Perimeter $= 4(6)$

                    Perimeter $= 24$

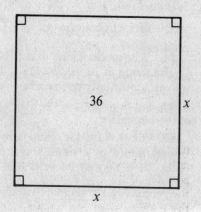

The perimeter is **24** cm.

**21.** The measure of an exterior angle of a triangle equals the sum of the measures of the two remote interior angles:

$$m\angle BCD = m\angle A + m\angle B$$
$$m\angle BCD = 25 + 85$$
$$m\angle BCD = 110$$

$$m\angle BCD = \textbf{110°.}$$

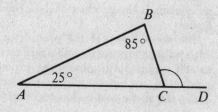

ALTERNATIVE SOLUTION: The third angle of the triangle may be found by applying the fact that the sum of the measures of the three angles of a triangle is 180°; this gives $\angle BCA = 70°$. $\angle BCD$ is the supplement of $\angle BCA$; therefore, $m\angle BCD$ may be found by subtracting 70° from 180°, giving 110°.

**22.** "If John lives in Buffalo, then he lives in New York State" is a proposition whose hypothesis (given) is "John lives in Buffalo" and whose conclusion (to prove) is "he lives in New York State."

If a proposition is true, then its *contrapositive* is also true. The contrapositive of a proposition is formed by negating the hypothesis and conclusion of the original proposition and then interchanging them. The contrapositive of "If John lives in Buffalo, then he lives in New York State" is "If John does not live in New York State, then he does not live in Buffalo."

The correct choice is **(1)**.

**23.** "*p* and *q*" is the *conjunction* of *p* with *q* which is symbolized by "$p \wedge q$."

The correct choice is **(4)**.

**24.** The *mode* of a set of data is the item appearing most frequently. The mode of 19, 8, 38, 41, 8, 16, 3 is 8. It appears twice; all other values appear only once each.

The correct choice is **(2)**.

**25.** $6x + 6y$ has a *common monomial factor* of 6. The other factor is determined by dividing 6 into each of the terms of $6x + 6y$ in turn. Thus, $6x + 6y$ may be written in factored form as $6(x + y)$.

The correct choice is **(2)**.

**26.** The product of the two monomials may be expressed as:

$$(5x^2)(3x^5)$$

The numerical coefficient of the product of two monomials is the product of their numerical coefficients:

$$(5)(3) = 15$$

The literal factor of the product of two monomials is the product of their literal factors; remember to add exponents to obtain the exponent for the product of two powers of the same base:

$$(x^2)(x^5) = x^7$$

Put the above two results together:

$$(5x^2)(3x^5) = 15x^7$$

The correct choice is **(3)**.

**27.** If an equation of a line is in the form, $y = mx + b$, then $m$ represents the slope of the line.

Examine each of the choices in turn:

(1) $y = 2x - 1$ is in the form, $y = mx + b$, with $m = 2$. Its slope is 2.

(2) $y = -2x + 1$ is in the form, $y = mx + b$, with $m = -2$. Its slope is $-2$.

(3) $y = x - 2$ is in the form, $y = mx + b$, with $m = 1$. Its slope is 1.

(4) $y - 2x = 4$ can be rearranged so that it is in the form, $y = mx + b$, by adding $+2x$ to both sides of the equation:

$$\begin{array}{rl} y - 2x &= 4 \\ +2x &= \phantom{2x+} +2x \\ \hline y &= 2x + 4 \end{array}$$

$y = 2x + 4$ is in the form, $y = mx + b$, with $m = 2$. Its slope is 2.

The correct choice is **(2)**.

**28.** The solution to a system of equations is represented by the coordinates of the point where their graphs intersect.

The graphs of $y = 2x + 1$ and $x + y = 1$ intersect at the point $(0, 1)$. Their solution is therefore $(0, 1)$.

The correct choice is **(3)**.

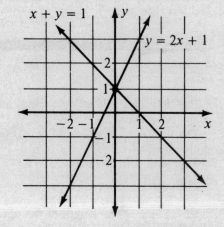

**29.** Plot the points $A(1, 1)$, $B(3, 1)$, and $C(3, 5)$ and draw the triangle for which they represent the vertices.

The line $\overline{AB}$ is parallel to the $x$ axis and the line $\overline{BC}$ is parallel to the $y$ axis. Hence, $\overline{AB}$ and $\overline{BC}$ are perpendicular to one another, thus making triangle $ABC$ a right triangle.

The correct choice is **(1)**.

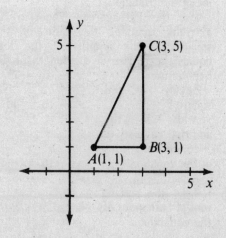

**30.**   Evaluate the expression given in each choice by substituting 2 for $x$:

(1) $x - 2$: $2 - 2 = 0$

(2) $\dfrac{1}{x-2}$: $\dfrac{1}{2-2} = \dfrac{1}{0}$. This is undefined since division by 0 is undefined.

(3) $\dfrac{x}{2}$: $\dfrac{2}{2} = 1$

(4) $x^0$: $2^0 = 1$

The correct choice is (**2**).

**31.**   The graph shown includes numbers which are greater than $-2$ and less than 4.

The dark, shaded circle at 4 indicates that the value, 4, is included in the inequality.

The unshaded, open circle at $-2$ indicates that $-2$ is not included in the inequality.

Therefore, the inequality is $-2 < x \le 4$.

The correct choice is (**4**).

**32.**   Let $x =$ the length of the other leg of the triangle.

Use the Pythagorean Theorem: In a right triangle, the sum of the squares of the lengths of the legs equals the square of the length of the hypotenuse:       $x^2 + 4^2 = 7^2$

Square 4 and square 7:       $x^2 + 16 = 49$

Add $-16$, the additive inverse of $+16$, to both sides of the equation:

$$\begin{array}{r} -16 = -16 \\ \hline x^2 \quad\;\; = 33 \end{array}$$

Take the square root of both sides of the equation:       $x = \pm \sqrt{33}$

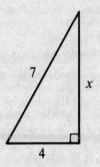

Reject the nega-
tive value as mean-
ingless for a length:          $x = $     $\sqrt{33}$

The correct choice is **(4)**.

**33.** The given equation is a
*quadratic equation:*                          $x^2 - 3x + 2 = 0$

The left side is a *quadratic trinomial* which can be factored into
the product of two binomials. The
factors of the first term, $x^2$, are $x$
and $x$, and they become the first
terms of the binomials:                      $(x \quad )(x \quad ) = 0$

The factors of the last term, $+2$,
become the second terms of the
binomials, but they must be chosen in such a way that the sum of
the inner product and the outer
product equals the middle term,          $-2x = $ inner product
$-3x$, of the original trinomial. Try    $(x - 2)(x - 1) = 0$
$-2$ and $-1$ as the factors of $+2$:           $-x = $ outer product
Since $(-2x) + (-x) = -3x$,
these are the correct factors:              $(x - 2)(x - 1) = 0$
If the product of two factors is
0, either factor may equal 0:       $x - 2 = 0$   OR   $x - 1 = 0$
Add the appropriate additive
inverse, $+2$ in the case of the left
equation and $+1$ in the case of the
right equation:                      $\underline{+2 = +2}$          $\underline{+1 = +1}$
The solution set is $\{2, 1\}$.       $x \quad = 2$       $x \quad = 1$

The correct choice is **(1)**.

**34.**  Examine each of the choices in turn:
(1) $p \lor q$ is the *disjunction* of $p$ and $q$. The disjunction is true if
either $p$ is true or $q$ is true or both are true. Since $p$ and $q$ are both
false, $p \lor q$ is false.
(2) $p \land q$ is the *conjunction* of $p$ and $q$. The conjunction is true only
when both $p$ and $q$ are true; it is false if either is false. Since $p$ and $q$
are both false, $p \land q$ is false.
(3) $p \leftrightarrow q$ is the *equivalence relation* between $p$ and $q$. The equivalence relation is true if both $p$ and $q$ are true or if both $p$ and $q$ are
false. Since $p$ and $q$ are both false, $p \leftrightarrow q$ is true.

(4) $\sim (\sim p)$ is the *negation* of $\sim p$, that is, it is the negation of the negation of $p$. Since $p$ is false, $\sim p$, which is the negation of $p$, is true. $\sim (\sim p)$, or the negation of $\sim p$, is then false.

The correct choice is **(3)**.

**35.**                                              $\sqrt{150}$

Factor out any perfect square factor contained in the radicand:                                    $\sqrt{25(6)}$

Remove the perfect square factor from under the radical sign by taking its square root and writing it as a coefficient of the radical:                                           $5\sqrt{6}$

The correct choice is **(1)**.

## PART TWO

**36.** STEP 1: To draw the graph of $x + y = 12$, first rearrange the equation so that it is solved for $y$. Add $-x$ to each side of the equation:

$$x + y = 12$$
$$\underline{-x \qquad = \qquad -x}$$
$$y = 12 - x$$

Choose any 3 convenient values for $x$. Substitute them in the equation and calculate the corresponding values of $y$:

| $x$ | $12 - x$ | $= y$ |
|---|---|---|
| $-2$ | $12 - (-2) = 12 + 2$ | $= 14$ |
| $0$ | $12 - 0$ | $= 12$ |
| $4$ | $12 - 4$ | $= 8$ |

Plot the points, $(-2, 14)$, $(0, 12)$, and $(4, 8)$, and draw a straight line through them. This line is the graph of $x + y = 12$.

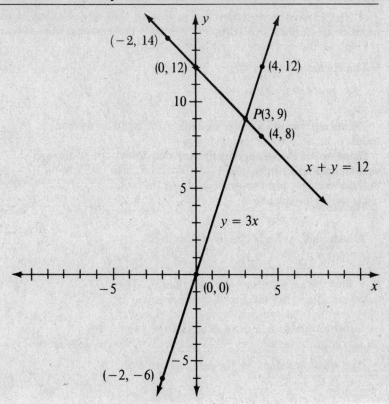

STEP 2: To plot the graph of $y = 3x$, choose any 3 convenient values for $x$. Substitute them in the equation and calculate the corresponding values of $y$:

| $x$ | $3x$ | $= y$ |
|---|---|---|
| $-2$ | $3(-2)$ | $= -6$ |
| $0$ | $3(0)$ | $= 0$ |
| $4$ | $3(4)$ | $= 12$ |

Plot the points, $(-2, -6)$, $(0, 0)$, and $(4, 12)$, and draw a straight line through them. This line is the graph of $y = 3x$.

STEP 3: The solution to the system is represented by the coordinates of the point, $P$, where the two graphs intersect. $P$ is the point $(3, 9)$.

The solution is $(3, 9)$ or $x = 3$, $y = 9$.

CHECK: Substitute 3 for $x$ and 9 for $y$ in *both* of the *original* equations to see if both are satisfied:

$$\underline{x + y = 12} \qquad\qquad \underline{y = 3x}$$
$$3 + 9 \overset{?}{=} 12 \qquad\qquad 9 \overset{?}{=} 3(3)$$
$$12 = 12 \checkmark \qquad\qquad 9 = 9 \checkmark$$

**37.** Let $x$ = the smaller integer.
Then $2x + 3$ = the larger integer.
The sum of the integers is greater than 24: $\qquad x + 2x + 3 > 24$
Combine like terms: $\qquad\qquad\qquad\qquad\qquad 3x + 3 > 24$
Add $-3$, the additive inverse of $+3$, to both sides of the inequality:

$$\dfrac{\phantom{3x}\quad -3 = -3}{3x \qquad\quad > 21}$$

Divide both sides of the inequality by 3: $\qquad \dfrac{3x}{3} > \dfrac{21}{3}$

$$x > 7$$

$x$ may be any integer greater than 7. The *smallest* value that satisfies this requirement is 8: $\qquad\qquad\qquad\qquad\qquad\qquad$ Let $x = 8$.

Substitute 8 for $x$ in $2x + 3$ to find the value of the larger integer: $\qquad 2x + 3 = 2(8) + 3 = 16 + 3 = 19$

The *smallest* values for the integers are **8** and **19**.

**38a.** $\angle QOR$ and $\angle QOP$ are supplementary angles. Therefore, the sum of their measures is 180°:

$4x - 10 + x + 50 = 180$
Combine like terms:
$\qquad\qquad 5x + 40 = 180$
Add $-40$, the additive inverse of $+40$, to both sides of the equation:

$$\dfrac{\quad -40 = -40}{5x \quad = 140}$$

Divide both sides of the equation by 5: $\dfrac{5x}{5} = \dfrac{140}{5}$

$$x = 28$$

$x = 28$.

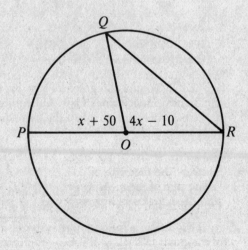

**b.** From part **a**, $x = 28$.    $m\angle QOP = x + 50 = 28 + 50 = 78$
$\angle QOP$ is a *central angle*. The measure of a central angle is equal to the measure of its intercepted arc:

$$m\angle QOP = m\overset{\frown}{QP}$$
$$78 = m\overset{\frown}{QP}$$

The measure of $\overset{\frown}{QP}$ is **78°**.

**c.** $\angle QRP$ is an *inscribed angle*. The measure of an inscribed angle is equal to one-half the measure of its intercepted arc:

$$m\angle QRP = \frac{1}{2}\, m\overset{\frown}{QP}$$

From part **b**, $m\overset{\frown}{QP} = 78°$:

$$m\angle QRP = \frac{1}{2}\,(78)$$

The measure of $\angle QRP$ is **39°**.

$$m\angle QRP = 39$$

**d.** The area, $A$, of a circle is given by the formula, $A = \pi r^2$, where $r$ is the length of the radius. $A$ is given to be $16\pi$:

$$16\pi = \pi r^2$$
$$\frac{16\pi}{\pi} = \frac{\pi r^2}{\pi}$$

Divide both sides of the equation by $\pi$:

$$16 = r^2$$

Take the square root of both sides of the equation:
Reject the negative value as meaningless for a length:

$$\pm\sqrt{16} = r$$
$$4 = r$$

The circumference, $c$, of a circle is given by the formula, $c = 2\pi r$, where $r$ is the length of the radius. Since $r = 4$:

$$c = 2\pi(4)$$

The circumference is **8π**.

$$c = 8\pi$$

**39.** Let $3x$ = the measure of $\angle A$.

Then $5x$ = the measure of $\angle B$.

And $3x + 5x + 20$, or $8x + 20$ = the measure of $\angle C$.

The sum of the measures of the three angles of a triangle is 180°:

$3x + 5x + 8x + 20 = 180$

Combine like terms:

$16x + 20 = 180$

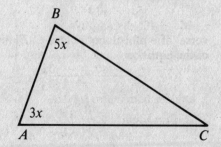

Add $-20$, the additive inverse of $+20$, to both sides of the equation:

$$\frac{-20 = -20}{16x \qquad = \quad 160}$$

Divide both sides of the equation by 16: $\dfrac{16x}{16} = \dfrac{160}{16}$

$$x = 10$$

$m\angle A$: $3x = 3(10) = 30$
$m\angle B$: $5x = 5(10) = 50$
$m\angle C$: $8x + 20 = 8(10) + 20 = 80 + 20 = 100$

$m\angle A = 30°$; $m\angle B = 50°$; $m\angle C = 100°$.

**40.** The probability of winning =

$$\frac{\text{the number of games won}}{\text{the total number of games played}}.$$

**a.** Since the probability of winning a Saturday game is $\dfrac{3}{5}$, 3 games are won for every 5 games played. Thus, $5 - 3$, or 2 games, are lost for every 5 games played.

The probability of losing = $\dfrac{\text{the number of games lost}}{\text{the total number of games played}}$.

The probability of losing a Saturday game is $\dfrac{2}{5}$.

The probability is $\dfrac{2}{5}$.

**b.** The probability of losing a Saturday game and winning a Sunday game is the product of the respective probabilities of these events:

$$\frac{2}{5} \times \frac{4}{7} = \frac{8}{35}$$

The probability is $\dfrac{8}{35}$.

**c.** The probability of winning a Sunday game is $\dfrac{4}{7}$, no matter what the result of the preceding Saturday game. Therefore, the probability of winning on Sunday after already winning a Saturday game is still $\frac{4}{7}$.

The probability is $\frac{4}{7}$.

**d.** The probability of winning both games is the product of the respective probabilities of winning on Saturday and winning on Sunday:

$$\frac{3}{5} \times \frac{4}{7} = \frac{12}{35}$$

The probability of winning both games is $\frac{12}{35}$.

**e.** Since the probability of winning on Sunday is $\frac{4}{7}$, 4 games are won on Sunday for every 7 games played. Therefore, 7 − 4, or 3 games, are lost on Sunday for every 7 games played. The probability of losing a Sunday game is thus $\frac{3}{7}$.

The probability of losing both games is the product of the respective probabilities of losing on Saturday and losing on Sunday: $\frac{2}{5} \times \frac{3}{7} = \frac{6}{35}$

The probability of losing both games is $\frac{6}{35}$.

**41a.** Prepare a third column for the table to be headed "Frequency." The cumulative frequency shown for any interval of ages is the sum of the frequency for that interval and the cumulative frequency shown for the preceding lower age interval. To obtain the frequency for each interval, subtract the preceding cumulative frequency from the cumulative frequency for that interval.

| Age Interval | Cumulative Frequency | Frequency |
|:---:|:---:|:---:|
| 11–12 | 2 | 2 |
| 13–14 | 6 | 4 |
| 15–16 | 9 | 3 |
| 17–18 | 15 | 6 |
| 19–21 | 20 | 5 |
| | | 20 |

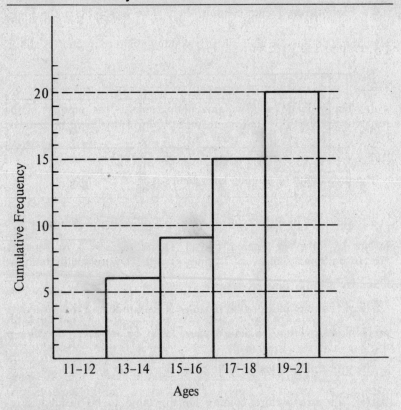

**b.** The total number of students hired is the final cumulative frequency figure, 20.

**20** students were hired.

**c.** The *median* is the middle value of a set of numbers when they are arranged in order of size; one-half of the numbers lie above the median, and one-half lie below it. Since there is a total of 20 students, the median lies halfway between the 10th and 11th student. From the Cumulative Frequency column it is apparent that the first three age intervals together contain 9 students. Thus, one more is needed to reach the 10th student and 2 more are needed to reach the 11th. Since the next interval (ages 17–18) contains 6 students, both the 10th and 11th students in order of age are in the 17–18 interval. Thus, the median also lies in this interval.

The median lies in the **17–18** interval.

**d.**  From the frequency column, there were 4 students in the 13–14 age group.

4 students age 13 or 14 were hired.

42a.

| $p$ | $q$ | $\sim q$ | $p \to q$ | $\sim(p \to q)$ | $p \wedge \sim q$ | $\sim(p \to q) \leftrightarrow (p \wedge \sim q)$ |
|---|---|---|---|---|---|---|
| T | T | F | T | F | F | T |
| T | F | T | F | T | T | T |
| F | T | F | T | F | F | T |
| F | F | T | T | F | F | T |

$\sim q$ is the *negation* of $q$. Fill in each line of the column for $\sim q$ with a truth value opposite to that of the truth value shown on that line for $q$. $p \to q$ is the *implication*, $p$ implies $q$. $p \to q$ has the truth value, T, whenever $q$ has the value, T, and also whenever $p$ and $q$ both have the value, F; it has the value, F, when $p$ is T and $q$ is F.

$\sim(p \to q)$ is the *negation* of the implication, $(p \to q)$. $\sim(p \to q)$ has a truth value on each line which is opposite to that for $(p \to q)$.

$p \wedge \sim q$ is the *conjunction* between $p$ and $\sim q$. $p \wedge \sim q$ has the truth value, T, only when $p$ and $\sim q$ have the truth value, T. If either $p$ or $\sim q$ or both have the truth value, F, then so does $p \wedge \sim q$.

$\sim(p \to q) \leftrightarrow (p \wedge \sim q)$ is an *equivalence relation* between $\sim(p \to q)$ and $(p \wedge \sim q)$. The equivalence relation has the truth value, T, whenever the truth values for $\sim(p \to q)$ and $(p \wedge \sim q)$ are the same, that is, both T or both F; if their truth values are different, the equivalence relation has the truth value, F.

**b.**  Let $p$ = "I receive a scholarship"
   Let $q$ = "I will go to college"

Then the given proposition, "If I receive a scholarship, then I will go to college," is represented by the implication, $p \to q$, and its negation is represented by the statement, $\sim(p \to q)$.

Examine each of the choices:

(1) "If I do not receive a scholarship, then I will not go to college" is represented by the *implication*, $\sim p \to \sim q$.

(2) "I receive a scholarship and I will not go to college" is represented by the *conjunction*, $p \wedge \sim q$.

(3) "It is not the case that I receive a scholarship and I go to college" is represented by the *negation* of the *conjunction* of $p$ and $q$, that is, by $\sim(p \wedge q)$.

(4) "If I do not go to college, then I did not receive a scholarship" is represented by the *implication*, $\sim q \to \sim p$.

Using four lines to list all possible combinations of the truth values of $p$ and $q$, prepare a table to list the corresponding truth values of $p \to q$, $\sim(p \to q)$, $\sim p$, $\sim q$, $\sim p \to \sim q$ (choice 1), $p \wedge \sim q$ (choice 2), $p \wedge q$, $\sim(p \wedge q)$ (choice 3), and $\sim q \to \sim p$ (choice 4):

| $p$ | $q$ | Orig. Prop. $p \to q$ | Negation of Orig. $\sim(p \to q)$ | $\sim p$ | $\sim q$ | (1) $\sim p \to \sim q$ | (2) $p \wedge \sim q$ | $p \wedge q$ | (3) $\sim(p \wedge q)$ | (4) $\sim q \to \sim p$ |
|---|---|---|---|---|---|---|---|---|---|---|
| T | T | T | F | F | F | T | F | T | F | T |
| T | F | F | T | F | T | T | T | F | T | F |
| F | T | T | F | T | F | F | F | F | T | T |
| F | F | T | F | T | T | T | F | F | T | T |

Since the truth values in the column for $\sim(p \to q)$, or the negation of the original proposition, and the column for $p \wedge \sim q$, or choice (2), are identical, $\sim(p \to q)$ and $p \wedge \sim q$ are logically equivalent.

The correct choice is (**2**).

ALTERNATIVE SOLUTION: The solution may be shortened somewhat by noting that choice (1), $\sim p \to \sim q$, is the *inverse* of the original proposition since $p$ and $q$, the respective hypothesis and conclusion of the original, have been negated to form it. If a proposition is true, its inverse may or may not be true. Therefore, there is no logical relationship between (1) and the original or between (1) and the negation of the original. Thus, choice (1) may immediately be ruled out.

Choice (4), $\sim q \to \sim p$, is the *contrapositive* of the original proposition since $p$ and $q$, the respective hypothesis and conclusion of the original, have been negated and interchanged to form it. A proposition and its contrapositive are logically equivalent, that is, they always have the same truth values. Therefore, the contrapositive will have the opposite truth values to the negation of the proposition and certainly will not be logically equivalent. Thus, choice (4) may immediately be ruled out.

Examination need only be made of the truth values of choices (2) and (3) for all combinations of the truth values of $p$ and $q$ to determine which is the correct choice. The correct choice must have truth values which agree in all instances with the corresponding truth values of $\sim(p \to q)$.

## SELF-ANALYSIS CHART—January 1985

| Topic | Question Numbers | Number of Points | Your Points | Your Percentage |
|---|---|---|---|---|
| 1. Numbers (rat'l, irrat'l); Percent | 6 | 2 | | |
| 2. Properties of No. Systems | 30 | 2 | | |
| 3. Operations on Rat'l Nos. and Monomials | 12, 26 | 2 + 2 = 4 | | |
| 4. Operations on Polynomials | — | 0 | | |
| 5. Square root; Operations involving Radicals | 35 | 2 | | |
| 6. Evaluating Formulas and Expressions | 8 | 2 | | |
| 7. Linear Equations (simple cases incl. parentheses) | 14 | 2 | | |
| 8. Linear Equations containing Decimals or Fractions | 15, 17 | 2 + 2 = 4 | | |
| 9. Graphs of Linear Functions (slope) | 27 | 2 | | |
| 10. Inequalities | 31 | 2 | | |
| 11. Systems of Eqs. & Inequal. (alg. & graphic solutions) | 10, 28, 36 | 2 + 2 + 10 = 14 | | |
| 12. Factoring | 18, 25 | 2 + 2 = 4 | | |
| 13. Quadratic Equations | 33 | 2 | | |
| 14. Verbal Problems | 37, 39 | 10 + 10 = 20 | | |
| 15. Variation | — | 0 | | |
| 16. Literal Eqs.; Expressing Relations Algebraically | 11, 16 | 2 + 2 = 4 | | |
| 17. Factorial $n$ | 4 | 2 | | |
| 18. Area, Perims., Circums., Vols. of Common Figures | 7, 20, 38d | 2 + 2 + 3 = 7 | | |
| 19. Geometry ($\cong$, $\angle$ meas., $\parallel$ lines, compls., suppls., const.) | 2, 13, 19, 21, 29, 38a, 38b, 38c | 2 + 2 + 2 + 2 + 2 + 3 + 2 + 2 = 17 | | |
| 20. Ratio & Proportion (incl. similar triangles) | 5 | 2 | | |
| 21. Pythagorean Theorem | 32 | 2 | | |
| 22. Logic (symbolic rep., logical forms, truth tables) | 22, 23, 34, 42a, 42b | 2 + 2 + 2 + 8 + 2 = 16 | | |
| 23. Probability (incl. tree diagrams & sample spaces) | 1, 9, 40a, 40b, 40c, 40d, 40e | 2 + 2 + 2 + 2 + 2 + 2 + 2 = 14 | | |
| 24. Combinations (arrangements, permutations) | — | 0 | | |
| 25. Statistics (central tend., freq. dist., histograms) | 3, 24, 41a, 41b, 41c, 41d | 2 + 2 + 4 + 2 + 2 + 2 = 14 | | |

# Examination June 1985

## Three-Year Sequence for High School Mathematics—Course I

### PART ONE

DIRECTIONS: *Answer 30 questions from this part. Each correct answer will receive 2 credits. No partial credit will be allowed. Write your answers in the spaces provided. Where applicable, answers may be left in terms of π or in radical form.*

1 A letter is chosen at random from the letters of the word "DIGIT." What is the probability that the letter chosen is an "I"?

1_____

2 Solve for $x$:  $58 = 10x - 2$

2_____

3 The measure of the vertex angle of an isosceles triangle is 100. Find the measure of one of the base angles of the triangle.

3_____

4 There are 5 entrances and 3 exits to a large parking lot. Find the total number of different ways a driver can enter and exit the parking lot.

4_____

5 If the perimeter of a square is 32, find the area of the square.

5_____

6 In the accompanying diagram, parallel lines $\overleftrightarrow{AB}$ and $\overleftrightarrow{CD}$ are intersected by transversal $\overleftrightarrow{EF}$ at R and S, respectively. If m∠BRS = 110, find m∠RSD

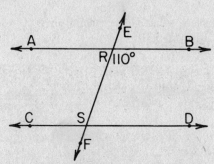

6____

7 The statement, "If I pass this test, then I will celebrate," is represented symbolically by $p \rightarrow q$. Using $p$ and $q$, express the statement, "If I do not celebrate, then I did not pass this test."

7____

8 Solve for $x$:    $0.02x + 6 = 6.24$

8____

9 On a math test, a score of 60 was the lower quartile (25th percentile). If 20 students took the test, how many received scores of 60 or below?

9____

10 Solve for $a$:    $\dfrac{3a + 1}{4} = \dfrac{5}{2}$

10____

11 If the square of a positive number is decreased by 10, the result is 6. Find the number.

11____

12 The ages of five students are 14, 17, 17, 15, and 16. What is the median age?

12____

13 Solve the following system of equations for $x$:

$$6x + y = 15$$
$$x + y = 5$$

13_____

14 If two coins are tossed, what is the probability of getting one head and one tail?

14_____

15 If $x = 3$ and $y = -2$, find the value of $4xy^2$.

15_____

16 What is the diameter of a circle whose circumference is equal to $20\pi$?

16_____

17 Evaluate:   $\dfrac{5!}{2!}$

17_____

18 Solve for $x$:   $5x + 2 = 3(x - 2)$

18_____

19 In the accompanying diagram, $\triangle ABC$ is a right triangle with the right angle at $C$. If $AC = 8$ and $BC = 6$, find $AB$.

19_____

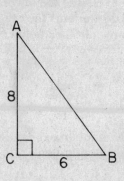

20 Express the product $(x - 3)(x + 8)$ as a trinomial.        20_____

21 Solve for $R$ in terms of $I$, $P$, and $T$:

$$I = PRT$$

21_____

22 Factor: $9x^2 - 16$

22_____

23 From $2x^2 - 3x - 5$ subtract $x^2 - x - 6$.

23_____

DIRECTIONS (24-35): *For each question chosen, write in the space provided the* numeral *preceding the word or expression that best completes the statement or answers the question.*

24 Which polygon is *not* a quadrilateral?
   (1) rectangle          (3) trapezoid
   (2) square             (4) hexagon                24_____

25 A root of the equation $x^2 + 2x - 15 = 0$ is
   (1) 0                  (3) 3
   (2) −2                 (4) 5                       25_____

26 The product of $3x^5$ and $2x^4$ is
   (1) $5x^9$             (3) $5x^{20}$
   (2) $6x^9$             (4) $6x^{20}$               26_____

27 The measures of two supplementary angles are in
   the ratio 5:1. What is the measure of the *smaller*
   angle?
   (1) 150                (3) 30
   (2) 75                 (4) 15                      27_____

28 An equation of the line with a slope of −2 and a
   $y$-intercept of 3 is
   (1) $y = -2x + 3$      (3) $y = 2x + 3$
   (2) $y = 3x - 2$       (4) $y = -2x - 3$           28_____

29 When drawn on the same set of axes, the graphs of the equations $y = x - 1$ and $x + y = 5$ intersect at the point whose coordinates are

(1) $(-5,6)$  (3) $(3,2)$
(2) $(2,1)$  (4) $(4,1)$

29_____

30 If $p \rightarrow q$ is false, then
(1) both $p$ and $q$ are true
(2) $p$ is true and $q$ is false
(3) both $p$ and $q$ are false
(4) $p$ is false and $q$ is true

30_____

31 Which inequality is represented by the graph below?

(1) $-2 \leq x < 3$  (3) $-2 \leq x \leq 3$
(2) $-2 < x \leq 3$  (4) $x < 3$

31_____

32 In the accompanying diagram of circle $O$, triangle $ROS$ *must* be which type of triangle?

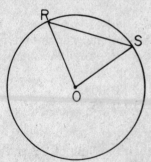

(1) equilateral  (3) scalene
(2) isosceles  (4) right

32_____

33 The inverse of a statement is $\sim p \to q$. Which is the statement?

(1) $q \to \sim p$          (3) $p \to q$

(2) $\sim q \to p$          (4) $p \to \sim q$          33____

34 The expression $\sqrt{48} + \sqrt{27}$ is equivalent to

(1) $7\sqrt{3}$          (3) $6\sqrt{3}$

(2) $\sqrt{75}$          (4) $4\sqrt{6}$          34____

35 In the accompanying diagram, what is the ratio of the measure of angle $ACB$ to the measure of angle $AOB$?

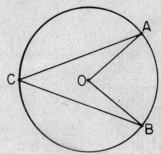

(1) 1:1          (3) 3:1

(2) 2:1          (4) 1:2          35____

## PART TWO

DIRECTIONS (36–42): *Answer four questions from this part. Show all work unless otherwise directed.*

36 Solve graphically and check:

$$y = 2x - 1$$
$$x + y = 2$$          [8,2]

37 Answer *both* *a* and *b*.

  *a* In triangle *ABC*, the measure of angle *B* is twice as large as the measure of angle *A*. The measure of angle *C* is 20 less than the measure of angle *A*. Find the measure of angle *A*. [*Only an algebraic solution will be accepted.*]  [5]

  *b* Eight more than six times *x* is less than 39. Find the largest integer for *x*. [*Only an algebraic solution will be accepted.*]  [5]

38 In the accompanying diagram, $\triangle RST$ is inscribed in circle *O* with diameter $\overline{RT}$. Radius $\overline{OS}$ is an altitude of $\triangle RST$ and $OS = 4$.

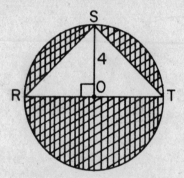

  *a* Find *RT*.  [2]

  *b* Express, in terms of $\pi$, the area of circle *O*. [2]

  *c* Find the area of $\triangle RST$.  [2]

  *d* Express, in terms of $\pi$, the area of the shaded region.  [2]

  *e* Find *RS*. [Answer may be left in radical form.] [2]

39 Find three consecutive odd integers such that the sum of the first and twice the second is 6 more than the third. [*Only an algebraic solution will be accepted.*]  [5,5]

40 In the accompanying diagram, *ABCD* is a rectangle and *DEFG* is a square. The area of *ABCD* is 80, *CG* = 8, and *AE* = 6. Find the length of the side of square *DEFG*. [*Only an algebraic solution will be accepted.*] [5,5]

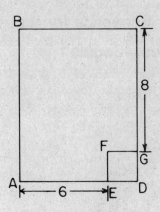

41 A penny, a nickel, and a dime are in a box. Bob randomly selects a coin, notes its value and returns it to the box. He randomly selects another coin from the box.

*a* Draw a tree diagram or list the sample space showing all possible outcomes. [4]

*b* What is the probability that a nickel will be drawn *at least* once? [3]

*c* What is the probability that the total value of both coins which were selected will *exceed* 11¢? [3]

42 *On your answer paper*, construct a truth table for the statement ~($p$ → ~$q$) ↔ ($p$ ∧ $q$). [10]

# Answers    June 1985

## Three-Year Sequence for High School Mathematics—Course I

### ANSWER KEY
### PART ONE

1. $\frac{2}{5}$

2. 6

3. 40

4. 15

5. 64

6. 70

7. $\sim q \rightarrow \sim p$

8. 12

9. 5

10. 3

11. 4

12. 16

13. 2

14. $\frac{1}{2}$

15. 48

16. 20

17. 60

18. −4

19. 10

20. $x^2 + 5x - 24$

21. $\dfrac{I}{PT}$

22. $(3x + 4)(3x - 4)$

23. $x^2 - 2x + 1$

24. (4)

25. (3)

26. (2)

27. (3)

28. (1)

29. (3)

30. (2)

31. (1)

32. (2)

33. (4)

34. (1)

35. (4)

Part Two—*See* Answers Explained.

### ANSWERS EXPLAINED
### PART ONE

1.  Probability of an event occurring

$$= \frac{\text{number of favorable cases}}{\text{total possible number of cases}}.$$

The word "DIGIT" contains two "I"s, so the number of favorable cases for choosing an "I" is 2.

The word "DIGIT" contains a total of five letters, so the total possible number of choices is 5.

The probability of choosing an "I" from the letters of the word "DIGIT" is $\frac{2}{5}$.

The probability is $\frac{2}{5}$.

**2.** The given equation is:

Add +2 (the additive inverse of −2) to both sides of the equation:

$$58 = 10x - 2$$

$$\underline{+2 = \qquad\qquad +2}$$

$$60 = 10x$$

Divide both sides of the equation by 10:

$$\frac{60}{10} = \frac{10x}{10}$$

$$6 = x$$

$x = 6.$

**3.** The two base angles of an isosceles triangle are equal in measure.

Let $x$ = the measure of each base angle.

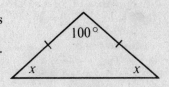

The sum of the measures of the three angles of a triangle is 180°:

Combine like terms:

$$x + x + 100 = 180$$
$$2x + 100 = 180$$

Add −100 (the additive inverse of +100) to both sides of the equation:

$$\underline{-100 = -100}$$
$$2x \qquad = 80$$

Divide both sides of the equation by 2:

$$\frac{2x}{2} = \frac{80}{2}$$

$$x = 40$$

The measure of one of the base angles is **40°**.

**4.** Since there are 5 entrances to the parking lot, a driver has 5 different ways of entering it.

Since there are 3 exists, a driver can leave in 3 different ways.

Each of the 5 ways of entering the parking lot can be combined with any of the 3 ways for exiting. Therefore the total number of different ways a driver can enter and exit is $5 \times 3$ or 15.

The total number of different ways is **15**.

**5.** All sides of a square are equal in length.

Let $x =$ the length of one side of the square.

The perimeter of a square equals the sum of the lengths of the four sides:    $4x = 32$

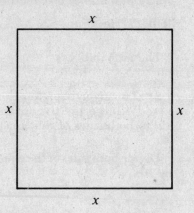

Divide both sides of the equation by 4:

$$\frac{4x}{4} = \frac{32}{4}$$
$$x = 8$$

The area, $A$, of a square is equal to the square of the length of one side:    $A = x^2$

Since $x = 8$:
$$A = 8^2$$
$$A = 64$$

The area is **64**.

**6.** $\overrightarrow{AB}$ and $\overrightarrow{CD}$ are parallel. If two parallel lines are cut by a transversal, then a pair of alternate interior angles are equal in measure. Therefore:

$$m\angle CSR = m\angle BRS$$

It is given that $m\angle BRS = 110°$:

$$m\angle CSR = 110°$$

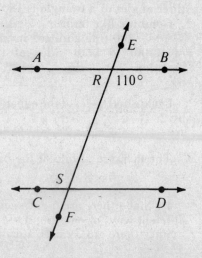

Angles $RSD$ and $CSR$ are supplementary since together they form the straight $\angle CSD$. The sum of the measures of two supplementary angles is 180°:

$$m\angle RSD + m\angle CSR = 180$$
$$m\angle RSD + 110 = 180$$

Add −110 (the additive inverse of +110)

to both sides of the equation:

$$\underline{-110 = -110}$$
$$m\angle RSD \quad = 70$$

$m\angle RSD = 70°$.

7.   Since $p \to q$ represents the statement "If I pass this test, then I will celebrate," then $p$ represents "I pass this test" and $q$ represents "I will celebrate."

"I do not celebrate" is the *negation* of $q$, which is represented by $\sim q$.

"I did not pass this test" is the *negation* of $p$, which is represented by $\sim p$.

"If I do not celebrate, then I did not pass this test" is the *implication* represented by $\sim q \to \sim p$.

The correct expression is $\sim q \to \sim p$.

8.   The given equation contains decimal coefficients:

$$0.02x + 6 = 6.24$$

Clear the decimals by multiplying each term on both sides of the equation by 100:

$$100(0.02x) + 100(6) = 100(6.24)$$
$$2x + 600 = 624$$

Add −600 (the additive inverse of +600) to both sides of the equation:

$$\underline{-600 = -600}$$
$$2x \quad = 24$$

Divide both sides of the equation by 2:

$$\frac{2x}{2} = \frac{24}{2}$$
$$x = 12$$

$x = 12$.

9.   The lower quartile (or 25th percentile) is the score at or below which one quarter of all the scores lie.

If 20 students took the test and the lower quartile was 60, then $\frac{1}{4} \times 20$ or 5 students received scores of 60 or below.

5 students scored 60 or below.

**10.** The given equation is a *fractional* equation:

$$\frac{3a+1}{4}=\frac{5}{2}$$

Clear fractions by multiplying both sides of the equation by the least common denominator (L.C.D.). The L.C.D. is the least number into which all denominators will divide evenly; the L.C.D. for 4 and 2 is 4:

$$4\left(\frac{3a+1}{4}\right)=4\left(\frac{5}{2}\right)$$
$$3a+1=2(5)$$
$$3a+1=10$$

Add −1 (the additive inverse of +1) to both sides of the equation:

$$\frac{-1=-1}{3a\phantom{+1}=9}$$

Divide both sides of the equation by 3:

$$\frac{3a}{3}=\frac{9}{3}$$
$$a=3$$

$a = 3$.

**11.** Let $x =$ the positive number.
The square of the positive number decreased by 10 is 6.

$$x^2 \qquad - \qquad 10 = 6$$

The equation to use is:

$$x^2-10=6$$

Add +10 (the additive inverse of −10) to both sides of the equation:

$$\frac{+10=+10}{x^2\phantom{aa}=16}$$

Take the square root of both sides of the equation:

$$x=\pm\sqrt{16}$$
$$x=\pm4$$

Reject the negative value since the question calls for a positive number:

$$x=4$$

The number is **4**.

**12.** The ages of the students are given
as 14, 17, 17, 15, and 16.

Rearrange the ages in order of size:      14, 15, 16, 17, 17

The *median* of a set of numbers is the
middle number when they are arranged
in order of size. One-half of the numbers
lie below the median and one-half lie
above the median. In this case the median
is:       16

The median age is **16**.

**13.** The given system is:

$$6x + y = 15$$
$$x + y = 5$$

Subtracting the second equation
from the first will eliminate $y$:    $5x \quad = 10$

Divide both sides of the equation
by 5:

$$\frac{5x}{5} = \frac{10}{5}$$
$$x = 2$$

$x = 2$.

**14.** Probability of an event occurring

$$= \frac{\text{number of favorable cases}}{\text{total possible number of cases}}.$$

For tossing two coins there is a total of four possible results:

Both heads:        H–H

Both tails:         T–T

First coin head, second coin tail:   H–T

First coin tail, second coin head:   T-H

There are two favorable cases for getting
one head and one tail:     H–T and T–H.

The probability of getting one head and
one tail when two coins are tossed is:   $\frac{2}{4}$ or $\frac{1}{2}$

The probability is $\frac{1}{2}$.

ALTERNATIVE SOLUTION: It does not matter what the result of the
first coin toss is; it could be either a head or a tail. Whatever the
result (either head or tail), the result of the second coin toss must
be the opposite in order to get one head and one tail. There is one

favorable case for getting the opposite out of the two possible

outcomes, so the probability is $\frac{1}{2}$.

**15.**  The given expression is:                            $4xy^2$
To evaluate this expression when
$x = 3$ and $y = -2$, substitute 3 for $x$
and $-2$ for $y$:                                           $4(3)(-2)^2$
  Square $-2$:                                              $4(3)(4)$
  Multiply together the remaining
factors:                                                    $12(4)$
                                                            $48$

The value is **48**.

**16.**  The circumference, $c$, of a circle is given by the formula
$c = 2\pi r$, where $r$ is the length of the radius.
  The circumference is $20\pi$:                     $20\pi = 2\pi r$
  Divide both sides of the equation
by $2\pi$:
$$\frac{20\pi}{2\pi} = \frac{2\pi r}{2\pi}$$
$$10 = r$$

  The length of the diameter, $d$, of
a circle is twice the length of the
radius:                                             $d = 2r$
  Since $r = 10$:                                   $d = 2(10)$
                                                    $d = 20$

The diameter is **20**.

**17.**  *Factorial n*, or $n!$, is defined as the product
$n(n-1)(n-2) \ldots (3)(2)(1)$.
Therefore:                                  $\dfrac{5!}{2!} = \dfrac{(5)(4)(3)(2)(1)}{(2)(1)}$

  Cancel the factors that appear in                         $1$
both the numerator and the
denominator:                                $\dfrac{5!}{2!} = \dfrac{(5)(4)(3)(\cancel{2})(1)}{(\cancel{2})(1)}$
  Multiply together the remaining
factors in the numerator, and also                          $1$
multiply together the remaining
factors in the denominator:                 $\dfrac{5!}{2!} = \dfrac{60}{1} = 60$

The value is **60**.

**18.** The given equation is:

$$5x+2=3(x-2)$$

Remove the parentheses on the right side by multiplying each term within the parentheses by 3:

$$5x+2=3x-6$$

Add $-3x$ (the additive inverse of $3x$) and also add $-2$ (the additive inverse of 2) to both sides of the equation:

$$\frac{-3x-2=-3x-2}{2x\quad=\quad-8}$$

Divide both sides of the equation by 2:

$$\frac{2x}{2}=\frac{-8}{2}$$
$$x=-4$$

$x=-4.$

**19.** Let $x=AB$.

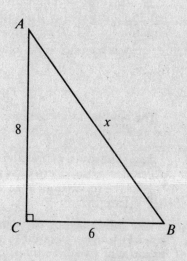

By the Pythagorean Theorem, in a right triangle the square of the length of the hypotenuse equals the sum of the squares of the lengths of the legs:

Square 8 and square 6:

Combine like terms:

$$x^2=8^2+6^2$$
$$x^2=64+36$$
$$x^2=100$$

Take the square root of both sides of the equation:

$$x=\pm\sqrt{100}$$

Reject the negative value as meaningless for a length:

$$x=10$$

$AB=10.$

**20.**   The indicated product is:                              $(x-3)(x+8)$

Write one binomial factor under the other:                  $x-3$
Multiply each term of $x-3$ by the first                    $x+8$
term, $x$, of the lower binomial:                           $x^2-3x$

Then multiply each term of $x-3$ by the
second term, $+8$, of the lower binomial,
writing like terms in the same column:                      $\underline{+8x-24}$
Add the columns to obtain the product:                      $x^2+5x-24$

The product as a trinomial is $x^2+5x-24$.

**21.**   The given equation is:                                $I = PRT$
To isolate $R$ on one side of the
equation, divide both sides of the
equation by $PT$:

$$\frac{I}{PT} = \frac{PRT}{PT}$$

$$\frac{I}{PT} = R$$

$$R = \frac{I}{PT}.$$

**22.**   The given expression is the
*difference of two perfect squares*:                        $9x^2-16$
Take the square root of each per-
fect square:                                                $\sqrt{9x^2}=3x; \sqrt{16}=4$

The difference of two perfect
squares can be factored into the
product of two binomials; one
binomial is the sum of the square
roots of the perfect squares and
the other is the difference of the
square roots:                                               $(3x+4)(3x-4)$
The factored form is $(3x+4)(3x-4)$.

**23.**   Write the polynomial to be subtracted underneath the polynomial from which it is to be subtracted, keeping like terms in the
same column:                                $2x^2-3x-5$
                                            $\underline{x^2-\ \ x-6}$

Rewrite, changing the sign of each term in the subtrahend (the polynomial being subtracted):

Combining each column algebraically:

$$2x^2 - 3x - 5$$
$$\underline{-x^2 + \ x + 6}$$
$$x^2 - 2x + 1$$

The difference is $x^2 - 2x + 1$.

**24.** A *quadrilateral* is a polygon that has four sides.

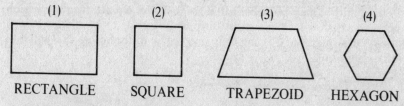

(1) RECTANGLE  (2) SQUARE  (3) TRAPEZOID  (4) HEXAGON

A rectangle, square, and trapezoid all have four sides each; a hexagon is a polygon that has six sides. Only the hexagon is *not* a quadrilateral.

The correct choice is **(4)**.

**25.** The given equation is a *quadratic equation*:

$$x^2 + 2x - 15 = 0$$

The left side is a *quadratic trinomial* which can be factored into the product of two binomials. The factors of the first term, $x^2$, are $x$ and $x$ and they become the first terms of the binomials:

$$(x \qquad)(x \qquad) = 0$$

The factors of the last term, $-15$, become the second terms of the binomials, but they must be chosen in such a way that the product of the inner terms added to the product of the outer terms equals the middle term, $+2x$, of the original trinomial. Try $+5$ and $-3$ as the factors of $-15$:

$$+5x = \text{inner product}$$
$$(x + 5)(x - 3) = 0$$
$$-3x = \text{outer product}$$

Since $(+5x) + (-3x) = +2x$, these are the correct factors:

If the product of two factors

$$(x + 5)(x - 3) = 0$$

equals zero, either factor may equal zero:

$$x+5=0 \quad \text{OR} \quad x-3=0$$

Add the appropriate additive inverse to both sides of the equations, $-5$ for the left equation and $+3$ for the right equation:

$$\frac{-5=-5}{x \quad =-5} \qquad \frac{+3=+3}{x \quad =3}$$

The roots are 3 and $-5$.
The correct choice is (3).

ALTERNATIVE SOLUTION: Each of the choices given for roots, 0, $-2$, 3, and 5, may be substituted for $x$ in the equation to see which choice satisfies it. Four substitutions will have to be made. It will be determined that 3 is the only one of the four choices that satisfies the equation.

26. The product may be represented as:

$$(3x^5)(2x^4)$$

To find the numerical coefficient of the product of two monomials, multiply their numerical coefficients together:

$$3 \cdot 2 = 6$$

Multiply the literal factors together to obtain the literal factor of the product. Remember that, when multiplying powers of the same base, the exponents are added to find the exponent of the product:

$$x^5 \cdot x^4 = x^9$$

Combine the above two results:

$$(3x^5)(2x^4) = 6x^9$$

The correct choice is (2).

27. Let $x =$ the measure of the *smaller* angle.
Then $5x =$ the measure of the larger angle (since their measures are in the ratio $5:1$).

Supplementary angles are two angles the sum of whose measures in $180°$:

$$x + 5x = 180$$

Combine like terms:

$$6x = 180$$

Divide both sides of the equation by 6:

$$\frac{6x}{6} = \frac{180}{6}$$

$$x = 30$$

The measure of the *smaller* angle is $30°$
The correct choice is (3).

**28.** If the equation of a line is in the form $y = mx + b$, its slope is represented by $m$ and its $y$-intercept is represented by $b$. Use these facts to examine each of the choices:

(1) $y = -2x + 3$ is in the form $y = mx + b$ with $m = -2$ and $b = 3$. Therefore, its slope is $-2$ and its $y$-intercept is 3. This is the correct choice.

(2) $y = 3x - 2$ is in the form $y = mx + b$ with $m = 3$ and $b = -2$. Therefore, its slope is 3 and its $y$-intercept is $-2$.

(3) $y = 2x + 3$ is in the form $y = mx + b$ with $m = 2$ and $b = 3$. Therefore, its slope is 2 and its $y$-intercept is 3.

(4) $y = -2x - 3$ is in the form $y = mx + b$ with $m = -2$ and $b = -3$. Therefore, its slope is $-2$ and its $y$-intercept is $-3$.

The correct choice is **(1)**.

**29.** If the graphs of two equations intersect, the coordinates of the point of intersection must satisfy both equations and therefore represent their common solution.

Find the common solution for $y = x - 1$ and $x + y = 5$ by substituting $x - 1$ for $y$ in the second equation:

$$x + x - 1 = 5$$

Combine like terms:

$$2x - 1 = 5$$

Add $+1$ (the additive inverse of $-1$) to both sides of the equation:

$$\frac{+1 = +1}{2x \quad = 6}$$

Divide both sides of the equation by 2:

$$\frac{2x}{2} = \frac{6}{2}$$

$$x = 3$$

To find the value of $y$, substitute 3 for $x$ in $y = x - 1$:

$$y = 3 - 1$$
$$y = 2$$

The coordinates of the intersection point are $(3, 2)$.

The correct choice is **(3)**.

ALTERNATIVE SOLUTION: The values of $x$ and $y$ given in each choice may be substituted in *both* equations to see which pair of values satisfies *both*. This method requires eight checks (four pairs of values must be substituted in each of the two equations).

**30.** The *implication* $p \to q$ means that $p$ implies $q$, that is, when $p$ is true, $q$ is true.

If $p \to q$ is false, then it is *not* true that, when $p$ is true, $q$ is true; in other words, if $p$ is true, $q$ is false.

The correct choice is **(2)**.

**31.** The dark line indicates that the inequality covers numbers from −2 to 3.

The shaded circle at −2 indicates that −2 is included in the inequality.

The open, unshaded circle at 3 indicates that 3 is *not* included in the inequality.

Therefore, the inequality is $-2 \leq x < 3$.

The correct choice is (1).

**32.** $\overline{OR}$ and $\overline{OS}$ are radii of the circle. Since radii of the same circle are congruent, $\overline{OR} \cong \overline{OS}$.

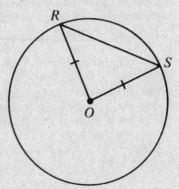

A triangle with two congruent sides is isosceles; therefore, $\triangle ROS$ *must* be isosceles.

The correct choice is (2).

**33.** In the statement $\sim p \rightarrow q$, the hypothesis (or antecedent) is $\sim p$ and the conclusion (or consequent) is $q$.

The *inverse* of a statement is the statement formed by *negating* the hypothesis and conclusion of the original statement. The *negation* of $\sim p$ is $p$, and the *negation* of $q$ is $\sim q$. Therefore, the inverse of $\sim p \rightarrow q$ is $p \rightarrow \sim q$.

The correct choice is (4).

**34.** The given expression is:

$$\sqrt{48}+\sqrt{27}$$

Simplify the *radicands* (numbers under the radical sign) by factoring out any perfect square factors:

$$\sqrt{16(3)}+\sqrt{9(3)}$$

Remove the perfect square factor from under the radical sign by taking its square root and writing it as the numerical coefficient outside the radical sign:

$$4\sqrt{3}+3\sqrt{3}$$

The radicals are now *like radicals* since they have the same index (both are square roots) and the same radicand (in this case, 3). Like radicals may be combined by combining their numerical coefficients:

$$7\sqrt{3}$$

The correct choice is (**1**).

**35.** Angle *ACB* is an *inscribed angle*. The measure of an inscribed angle is equal to one-half the measure of its intercepted arc:

$$\text{m}\angle ACB = \frac{1}{2}\text{m}\widehat{AB}$$

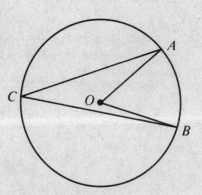

Angle *AOB* is a *central angle*. The measure of a central angle is equal to the measure of its intercepted arc:

$$\text{m}\angle AOB = \text{m}\widehat{AB}$$

Therefore, $\text{m}\angle ACB : \text{m}\angle AOB = 1:2$.

The correct choice is (**4**).

**PART TWO**

**36.** STEP 1: To draw the graph of $y = 2x - 1$, select any three convenient values for $x$, and substitute them in the equation to determine the corresponding values of $y$:

| $x$ | $2x-1$ | $=y$ |
|-----|--------|------|
| $-2$ | $2(-2)-1=-4-1$ | $=-5$ |
| $0$ | $2(0)-1=0-1$ | $=-1$ |
| $3$ | $2(3)-1=6-1$ | $=5$ |

Plot the points $(-2, 5)$, $(0, -1)$, and $(3, 5)$, and draw a straight line through them. This line is the graph of $y = 2x - 1$.

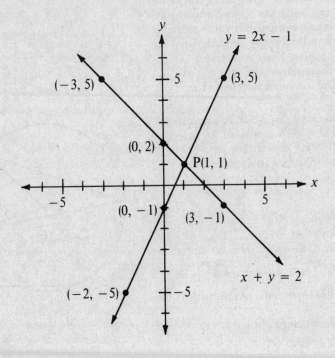

STEP 2: To draw the graph of $x + y = 2$ it is convenient to first rearrange the equation so that it is solved for $y$:

Add $-x$ (the additive inverse of $x$) to both sides of the equation:

$$x + y = 2$$

$$\underline{-x \quad = \quad -x}$$
$$y = 2 - x$$

Choose any three convenient values for $x$, and substitute them in the equation to determine the corresponding values of $y$:

| $x$ | $2-x$ | $=y$ |
|---|---|---|
| $-3$ | $2-(-3)=2+3$ | $=5$ |
| $0$ | $2-0$ | $=2$ |
| $3$ | $2-3$ | $=-1$ |

Plot the points $(-3, 5)$, $(0, 2)$, and $(3, -1)$, and draw a straight line through them. This line is the graph of $x+y=2$.

STEP 3: The coordinates of the point of intersection of the two lines represent the solution to the system of equations. The graphs intersect at the point $P(1, 1)$.

The solution is $\{1, 1\}$ or $x=1$, $y=1$.

CHECK: To check, substitute 1 for $x$ and 1 for $y$ in *both original* equations to see whether both are satisfied:

$$y=2x-1 \qquad x+y=2$$
$$1 \stackrel{?}{=} 2(1)-1 \qquad 1+1 \stackrel{?}{=} 2$$
$$1 \stackrel{?}{=} 2-1 \qquad\quad 2=2\checkmark$$
$$1=1\checkmark$$

**37. a.**  Let $x=$ the measure of $\angle A$.
Then $2x=$ the measure of $\angle B$.
And $x-20=$ the measure of $\angle C$.

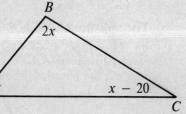

The sum of the measures of the three angles of a triangle is $180°$:

$$x+2x+x-20=180$$

Combine like terms:

$$4x-20=180$$

Add $+20$ (the additive inverse of $-20$) to both sides of the equation:

$$\frac{+20=+20}{4x \quad = 200}$$

Divide both sides of the equation by 4:

$$\frac{4x}{4}=\frac{200}{4}$$
$$x=50$$

$m\angle A=\mathbf{50°}.$

**b.**   8 more than 6 times $x$ is less than 39

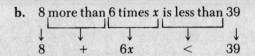

$$8 \quad + \quad 6x \quad < \quad 39$$

The inequality to use is:                         $8 + 6x < 39$

Add −8 (the additive inverse of
8) to both sides of the inequality:       **b.**  $\dfrac{-8 \quad\quad = -8}{6x < 31}$

Divide   both   sides   of   the
inequality by 6:                              $\dfrac{6x}{6} < \dfrac{31}{6}$

$$x < 5\frac{1}{6}$$

Since $x$ must be less than $5\dfrac{1}{6}$, the largest integer for $x$ is 5.

The largest integer for $x$ is **5**.

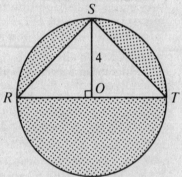

**38. a.**  It is given that radius
$OS = 4$. But all radii of the same
circle are congruent. Therefore:

$$OR = OT = OS = 4$$
$$RT = RO + OT$$
$$RT = 4 + 4$$
$$RT = 8$$

The measure of $RT$ is **8**.

**b.**  The area, $A$, of a circle is
given by this formula:                      $A = \pi r^2$
where $r$ is the length of the radius.
Here, $r = 4$:                                 $A = \pi(4)^2$
Square 4:                                       $A = 16\pi$
The area of circle $O$ is **16π**.

**c.**  The area, $A$, of a triangle is
one-half the product of its base and
altitude:                                        $A = \dfrac{1}{2}(RT)(OS)$

Since $RT = 8$ and $OS = 4$:              $A = \dfrac{1}{2}(8)(4)$

$$A = \frac{1}{2}(32)$$

The area of $\triangle RST$ is **16**.        $A = 16$

**d.**  The area of the shaded region is the area of circle $O$ minus the area of $\triangle RST$. Using the results of parts b and c for the area of circle $O$ and the area of $\triangle RST$, we find that the area of the shaded region $= 16\pi - 16$.
The area of the shaded region is **$16\pi - 16$.**

**e.**  Since $\overline{OS}$ is an altitude, $\angle SOR$ is a right angle and $\triangle SOR$ is a right triangle whose hypotenuse is $\overline{RS}$.
By the Pythagorean Theorem, in a right triangle the square of the length of the hypotenuse equals the sum of the squares of the lengths of the legs:

$$(RS)^2 = (OR)^2 + (OS)^2$$

Since $OR = 4$ and $OS = 4$: $\quad (RS)^2 = 4^2 + 4^2$

Square 4: $\quad (RS)^2 = 16 + 16$

Combine like terms: $\quad (RS)^2 = 32$

Take the square root of both sides of the equation:

$$RS = \pm\sqrt{32}$$

Reject the negative value as meaningless for a length:

$$RS = \sqrt{32}$$

The value $\sqrt{32}$ may be simplified by factoring out a perfect square factor from the radicand:

$$RS = \sqrt{16(2)}$$

Remove the perfect square factor from under the radical sign by taking its square root and writing it outside the radical sign as a numerical coefficient:

$$RS = 4\sqrt{2}$$

$RS = \sqrt{32}$ or $4\sqrt{2}$.

**39.**  Let $x =$ the first consecutive odd integer.
Then $x + 2 =$ the second consecutive odd integer.
And $x + 4 =$ the third consecutive odd integer.
The first added to twice the second is 6 more than the third.

$$x \qquad + \qquad 2(x+2) \qquad = 6 \qquad + \qquad x+4$$

The equation to use is: $\qquad x + 2(x+2) = 6 + x + 4$
Remove the parentheses by multiplying each term within them by 2: $\qquad x + 2x + 4 = 6 + x + 4$

Combine like terms:

Add $-x$ (the additive inverse of $x$) and also add $-4$ (the additive inverse of $+4$) to both sides of the equation:

Divide both sides of the equation by 2:

$$3x + 4 = 10 + x$$

$$\dfrac{-x - 4 = -4 - x}{2x \;\;\;\; = 6}$$

$$\frac{2x}{2} = \frac{6}{2}$$

$$x = 3$$
$$x + 2 = 5$$
$$x + 4 = 7$$

The three consecutive odd intergers are **3, 5, and 7.**

**40.**  Let $x =$ the length of a side of square *DEFG*.
Then $CD = GD + CG = x + 8.$

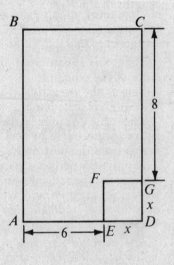

And $AD = ED + AE = x + 6.$
The area of a rectangle is the product of its length and width. Since the area of rectangle *ABCD* is given as 80:
Multiply out $(x + 8)(x + 6)$:

$$(x + 8)(x + 6) = 80$$

$$\begin{array}{r} x + 8 \\ x + 6 \\ \hline x^2 + 8x \\ 6x + 48 \\ \hline x^2 + 14x + 48 \end{array}$$

$$x^2 + 14x + 48 = 80$$

This is a *quadratic equation.* Rearrange it so that all terms are on one side equal to 0 by adding $-80$ (the additive inverse of 80) to both sides:

$$\dfrac{-80 = -80}{x^2 + 14x - 32 = 0}$$

The left side is a *quadratic trinomial,* which can be factored into the product of two binomials. The factors of the first term, $x^2$, are $x$ and $x$, and they become the first terms of the binomials:

$$(x \quad )(x \quad ) = 0$$

The factors of the last term, $-32$, become the second terms of the binomials, but they must be chosen in such a way that the product of the inner terms added to the product of the outer terms equals the middle term, $+14x$, of the original trinomial. Try $+16$ and $-2$ as the factors of $-32$:

Since $(+16x) + (-2x) = +14x,$

$$+16x = \text{inner product}$$
$$(x + 16)(x - 2) = 0$$
$$-2x = \text{outer product}$$

these are the correct factors:

$$(x + 16)(x - 2) = 0$$

If the product of two factors equals zero, either factor may equal zero:

$$x + 16 = 0 \quad \text{OR} \quad x - 2 = 0$$

Add the appropriate additive inverse for each equation, $-16$ for the left equation and $+2$ for the right equation:

$$\frac{-16 = -16}{x \quad = -16} \qquad \frac{+2 = +2}{x \quad = 2}$$

Reject the negative value as meaningless for a length:

$$x = 2$$

The length of the side of the square is **2**.

**41**   **a.**   The tree diagram will have three primary branches radiating from START and representing the selections of a penny, a nickel, and a dime for the first selection. Each primary branch will have three secondary branches since a penny, a nickel, or a dime may be chosen on the second selection:

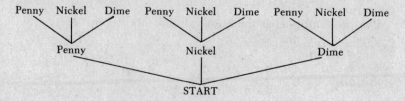

The sample space will have nine lines since each of the three possible first selections (penny, nickel, or dime) may be paired with each of the three possible second selections (penny, nickel, or dime):

| First Selection | Second Selection |
|---|---|
| Penny | Penny |
| Penny | Nickel |
| Penny | Dime |
| Nickel | Penny |
| Nickel | Nickel |
| Nickel | Dime |
| Dime | Penny |
| Dime | Nickel |
| Dime | Dime |

**b.** Probability of an event occurring

$$= \frac{\text{number of favorable cases}}{\text{total possible number of cases}}.$$

There are nine lines in the sample space and nine complete paths from START through the second selection of a coin in the tree diagram. Thus, the total possible number of cases for the selection of two coins is 9.

Of the lines in the sample space, five contain *at least* one nickel. Similarly, five complete paths in the tree diagram have *at least* one nickel: penny–nickel, nickel–penny, nickel–nickel, nickel–dime, and dime–nickel.

The probability that a nickel will be drawn *at least* once is $\frac{5}{9}$.

The probability is $\frac{5}{9}$.

**c.** In the tree diagram, the paths involving two coin selections whose total value will *exceed* 11¢ are nickel–dime, dime–nickel, and dime–dime. There are thus three favorable cases. Similarly, the sample space contains just three lines where the total value of both coins *exceeds* 11¢.

The probability that the total value of both coins selected will *exceed* 11¢ is $\frac{3}{9}$.

The probability is $\frac{3}{9}$.

**42.** The truth table must begin with columns for $p$ and $q$. There are four possible combinations of truth values $T$ (true) and $F$ (false) for $p$ and $q$, so the table must have four lines. In order to get values for $p \to \sim q$ it is desirable to first prepare a column of values for $\sim q$. The column for $p \to \sim q$ is needed to determine values for $\sim(p \to \sim q)$. Similarly, a column for $p \wedge q$ is needed to determine values for the final column, $\sim(p \to \sim q) \leftrightarrow (p \wedge q)$.

| $p$ | $q$ | $\sim q$ | $p \to \sim q$ | $\sim(p \to \sim q)$ | $p \wedge q$ | $\sim(p \to \sim q) \leftrightarrow (p \wedge q)$ |
|---|---|---|---|---|---|---|
| $T$ | $T$ | $F$ | $F$ | $T$ | $T$ | $T$ |
| $T$ | $F$ | $T$ | $T$ | $F$ | $F$ | $T$ |
| $F$ | $T$ | $F$ | $T$ | $F$ | $F$ | $T$ |
| $F$ | $F$ | $T$ | $T$ | $F$ | $F$ | $T$ |

The columns for $p$ and $q$ are filled in with all possible combinations of their truth values, $T$ for true and $F$ for false.

$\sim q$ (the third column) represents the *negation* of $q$. The truth value on each line of $\sim q$ is the opposite of that for $q$.

$p \to \sim q$ is the *implication* $p$ implies "not $q$." $p \to \sim q$ has the value $T$ whenever $\sim q$ is $T$ and also when $p$ and $\sim q$ are both $F$; it has the value $F$ when $p$ is $T$ and $\sim q$ is $F$.

$\sim(p \to \sim q)$ is the *negation* of $p \to \sim q$. The truth value on each line for $\sim(p \to \sim q)$ is the opposite of that for $p \to \sim q$ on that line.

$p \wedge q$ is the *conjunction* of $p$ and $q$. The conjunction has the truth value $T$ only when $p$ and $q$ both have the truth value $T$; in all other cases, the conjunction has the truth value $F$.

$\sim(p \to \sim q) \leftrightarrow (p \wedge q)$ is an *equivalence relation* between $\sim(p \to \sim q)$ and $(p \wedge q)$. When the truth values of $\sim(p \to \sim q)$ and $(p \wedge q)$ are the same, that is, both $T$ or both $F$, the truth value of the equivalence relation is $T$; otherwise it is $F$.

## SELF-ANALYSIS CHART     June 1985

| Topic | Question Numbers | Number of Points | Your Points | Your Percentage |
|---|---|---|---|---|
| 1. Numbers (rat'l, irrat'l); Percent | — | 0 | | |
| 2. Properties of No. Systems | — | 0 | | |
| 3. Operations on Rat'l Nos. and Monomials | 26 | 2 | | |
| 4. Operations on Multinomials | 20, 23 | 2 + 2 = 4 | | |
| 5. Square root; Operations Involving Radicals | 34 | 2 | | |
| 6. Evaluating Formulas and Expressions | 15 | 2 | | |
| 7. Linear Equations (simple cases incl. parentheses) | 2, 18 | 2 + 2 = 4 | | |
| 8. Linear Equations Containing Decimals or Fractions | 8, 10 | 2 + 2 = 4 | | |
| 9. Graphs of Linear Functions (slope) | 28 | 2 | | |
| 10. Inequalities | 31 | 2 | | |
| 11. Systems of Eqs. & Inequal. (alg. & graphic solutions) | 13, 29, 36 | 2 + 2 + 10 = 14 | | |
| 12. Factoring | 22 | 2 | | |
| 13. Quadratic Equations | 25 | 2 | | |
| 14. Verbal Problems | 37a, 37b, 39, 40 | 5 + 5 + 10 + 10 = 30 | | |
| 15. Variation | — | 0 | | |
| 16. Literal Eqs.; Expressing Relations Algebraically | 21 | 2 | | |
| 17. Factorial $n$ | 17 | 2 | | |

| Topic | Question Numbers | Number of Points | Your Points | Your Percentage |
|---|---|---|---|---|
| 18. Areas, Perims., Circums., Vols. of Common Figures | 5, 38a, 38b, 38c, 38d | $2+2+2+2 +2 = 10$ | | |
| 19. Geometry ($\cong$, $\angle$ meas., $\parallel$ lines, compls., suppls., const.) | 3, 6, 16, 24, 32 | $2+2+2+2 +2 = 10$ | | |
| 20. Ratio & Proportion (incl. similar triangles) | 27, 35 | $2+2 = 4$ | | |
| 21. Pythagorean Theorem | 19, 38e | $2+2 = 4$ | | |
| 22. Logic (symbolic rep., logical forms, truth tables) | 7, 30, 33, 42 | $2+2+2+10 = 16$ | | |
| 23. Probability (incl. tree diagrams & sample spaces) | 1, 14, 41a, 41b, 41c | $2+2+4+3 +3 = 14$ | | |
| 24. Combinations (arrangements, permutations) | 4 | 2 | | |
| 25. Statistics (central tend., freq. dist., histograms) | 9, 12 | $2+2 = 4$ | | |

# Examination January 1986

## Three-Year Sequence for High School Mathematics—Course I

### PART ONE

DIRECTIONS: *Answer 30 questions from this part. Each correct answer will receive 2 credits. No partial credit will be allowed. Write your answers in the spaces provided. Where applicable, answers may be left in terms of π or in radical form.*

1 Solve for $x$:  $\dfrac{4}{6} = \dfrac{x}{15}$

1____

2 Let $p$ represent "He is able" and let $q$ represent "He will win." Using $p$ and $q$, write in symbolic form: "He is able and he will win."

2____

3 If 4 more than twice a number is 18, find the number.

3____

4 Solve for $x$:  $1.5x = 30$

4____

5 A man has 8 shirts, 5 pairs of pants, and 6 ties. Find the total number of possible outfits he can wear consisting of a shirt, a pair of pants, and a tie.

5____

6 Solve for $x$:  $5x + 7 = 2x - 2$

6____

7 Given the formula $P = K^2W$, find the value of $P$ if $K = 5$ and $W = -3$.

7____

1

8 Express as a single fraction in simplest form:

$$\frac{a}{3} + \frac{2a}{5}$$

8___

9 Solve the following system of equations for $x$:

$$x + y = 6$$
$$x - y = 2$$

9___

10 Given the following table, which score is the mode?

| Score | Frequency |
|-------|-----------|
| 98 | 2 |
| 95 | 3 |
| 92 | 2 |
| 87 | 1 |
| 84 | 2 |

10___

11 Factor:  $x^2 + 5x - 24$

11___

12 In the accompanying diagram, transversal $\overleftrightarrow{RS}$ intersects parallel lines $\overleftrightarrow{XY}$ and $\overleftrightarrow{WZ}$ at $E$ and $H$, respectively. If m$\angle HEY$ = 72, what is m$\angle ZHS$?

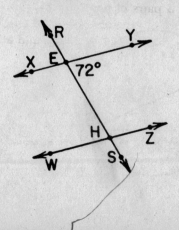

12___

13 If $(k,3)$ is a point on the graph of the equation $x + 2y = 8$, what is the value of $k$?

13_____

14 A tree casts a shadow 24 feet long at the same time a man 6 feet tall casts a shadow 4 feet long. Find the number of feet in the height of the tree.

14_____

15 In how many different ways can the subjects math, English, social studies, and science be scheduled during the first four periods of the school day?

15_____

16 The measure of the vertex angle of an isosceles triangle is 70. Find the measure of a base angle of the triangle.

16_____

17 Find the sum of $5x^3 - 3x^2 + 5$ and $-2x^3 + 6x^2 - 5$.

17_____

18 What is the volume, in cubic centimeters, of a cube whose edge measures 2 centimeters?

18_____

19 Solve for $x$:  $5x - 2(x + 1) = 10$

19_____

20 In the accompanying diagram, the measure of arc $AB$ is 48. What is the measure of inscribed angle $ACB$?

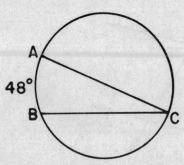

48°

20_____

21 The measures of two supplementary angles are in the ratio of 7:2. Find the measure of the *larger* angle.

21_____

22 Solve for $a$ in terms of $b$ and $c$:

$$3a + 4b = c$$

22_____

DIRECTIONS **(23–35):** *For each question chosen, write in the space provided the* numeral *preceding the word or expression that best completes the statement or answers the question.*

23 If two fair dice are tossed once, the probability of getting 12 is $\frac{1}{36}$. What is the probability of not getting 12?

(1) $\frac{35}{36}$        (3) $\frac{6}{36}$

(2) $\frac{30}{36}$        (4) $\frac{34}{36}$

23_____

24 If $x$ represents an even number, which expression represents an odd number?

(1) $x^3$        (3) $3x$

(2) $x + 3$        (4) $\frac{x}{3}$

24_____

25 Each side of a regular hexagon is represented by $(x + 6)$. Which expression represents the perimeter of the hexagon?

(1) $36x$        (3) $6x + 6$

(2) $5x + 30$        (4) $6x + 36$

25_____

26 From a standard deck of 52 cards, one card is drawn. What is the probability that it will be either a club or a diamond?

(1) $\frac{8}{52}$      (3) $\frac{26}{52}$

(2) $\frac{2}{52}$      (4) $\frac{12}{52}$

26_____

27 The $y$-intercept of the graph of the equation $y = 2x - 3$ is

(1) –2      (3) 3
(2) 2      (4) –3

27_____

28 The inequality $3x + 2 > x + 8$ is equivalent to

(1) $x > -\frac{3}{2}$      (3) $x > 3$

(2) $x > \frac{3}{2}$      (4) $x < 3$

28_____

29 The circumference of a circle is represented by $2\pi r$. If the radius of the circle is doubled, then the circumference is

(1) multiplied by 4      (3) squared
(2) increased by 2      (4) doubled

29 _____

30 The quotient of $\dfrac{-18x^6}{6x^3}$ is equal to

(1) $-3x^3$      (3) $-12x^2$
(2) $-3x^2$      (4) $-12x^3$

30_____

31 What is the converse of the statement $q \rightarrow p$?

(1) $\sim q \rightarrow \sim p$      (3) $q \rightarrow \sim p$
(2) $p \rightarrow q$      (4) $\sim p \rightarrow \sim q$

31_____

32 Which represents an irrational number?
  (1) 0                    (3) $\sqrt{3}$
  (2) $\frac{3}{4}$        (4) $\sqrt{4}$                    32____

33 For which value of $x$ is the expression $\dfrac{x}{x-2}$ undefined?
  (1) 1                    (3) –2
  (2) 2                    (4) 0                            33____

34 Let $p$ represent the statement "$x$ is prime" and let $q$ represent the statement "$x < 10$." If $x = 11$, which statement is true?
  (1) $\sim p \vee q$       (3) $\sim p \to q$
  (2) $p \wedge q$          (4) $p \to q$                   34____

35 The solution set of the equation $x^2 - 4x = 0$ is
  (1) $\{0,4\}$            (3) $\{-4\}$
  (2) $\{4,-4\}$           (4) $\{4\}$                      35____

**PART TWO**

DIRECTIONS: *Answer* four *questions from this part. Show all work unless otherwise directed.*

36 *a* On the same set of coordinate axes, graph the following system of inequalities:

$$y < 2x + 4$$
$$x + y \le 7 \qquad [8]$$

*b* Based on your answer to part *a*, write the coordinates of a point which is *not* in the solution set of the system of inequalities. [2]

37 The square of a positive number decreased by 4 times the number is 12. Find the positive number. [*Only an algebraic solution will be accepted.*] [5,5]

38 The length of a rectangle is 7 more than the side of a square. The width of the rectangle is equal to the side of the square. The area of the square is 56 less than the area of the rectangle. Find the width of the rectangle. [*Only an algebraic solution will be accepted.*] [6,4]

39 Solve the following system of equations algebraically and check:

$$x - 4y = 16$$
$$y = 1 - x$$ [8,2]

40 Let $p$ represent: $x$ is an even integer.
Let $q$ represent: $x$ is a prime number.
Let $r$ represent: $x$ is divisible by 3.

$a$ Write each statement in sentence form:

(1) $\sim r \vee q$ [2]
(2) $p \rightarrow r$ [2]

$b$ Write each statement in symbolic form:

(1) $x$ is an even integer, if and only if $x$ is divisible by 3. [2]
(2) If $x$ is a prime number and $x$ is divisible by 3, then $x$ is an even integer. [2]

$c$ Write in symbolic form the contrapositive of:

If $x$ is not an even number, then $x$ is a prime number. [2]

41 In the accompanying diagram, $\overline{AC}$ and $\overline{BD}$ are diameters of circle $O$ and the measure of $\angle ACB$ is 50.

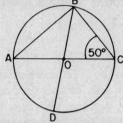

  *a* Find the measure of minor arc $AB$.   [2]
  *b* Find m$\angle BOC$.   [2]
  *c* Find m$\angle BAC$.   [2]
  *d* Find the measure of minor arc $AD$.   [2]
  *e* Find m$\angle ABC$.   [2]

42 The cumulative frequency histogram below shows the number of weeks of annual vacation for workers at a company.

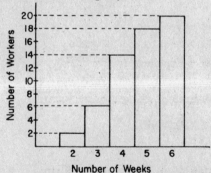

  *a* How many workers are employed by the company?   [2]
  *b* How many workers receive more than 4 weeks of vacation?   [2]
  *c* Find the median number of weeks of vacation.   [2]
  *d* Using the data from parts *a*, *b*, and *c*, draw a frequency histogram on your paper.   [4]

# Answers January 1986

## Three-Year Sequence for High School Mathematics—Course I

**ANSWER KEY**

**PART ONE**

| | | | | | | |
|---|---|---|---|---|---|---|
| 1. | 10 | 13. | 2 | 25. | (4) |
| 2. | $p \wedge q$ | 14. | 36 | 26. | (3) |
| 3. | 7 | 15. | 24 | 27. | (4) |
| 4. | 20 | 16. | 55 | 28. | (3) |
| 5. | 240 | 17. | $3x^3 + 3x^2$ | 29. | (4) |
| 6. | $-3$ | 18. | 8 | 30. | (1) |
| 7. | $-75$ | 19. | 4 | 31. | (2) |
| 8. | $\dfrac{11a}{15}$ | 20. | 24 | 32. | (3) |
| | | 21. | 140 | 33. | (2) |
| 9. | 4 | 22. | $\dfrac{c - 4b}{3}$ | 34. | (3) |
| 10. | 95 | | | 35. | (1) |
| 11. | $(x + 8)(x - 3)$ | 23. | (1) | | |
| 12. | 72 | 24. | (2) | | |

**Part Two—*See* Answers Explained**

**ANSWERS EXPLAINED**

**PART ONE**

1. The given equation is in the form of a proportion: $\dfrac{4}{6} = \dfrac{x}{15}$

In a proportion, the product of the means equals the product of the extremes (cross-multiply):

$$6x = 4(15)$$
$$6x = 60$$

Divide both sides of the equation by 6:

$$\frac{6x}{6} = \frac{60}{6}$$
$$x = 10$$

$x = 10$.

9

**2.** $p$ represents "He is able"

$q$ represents "He will win"

"He is able and he will win" is the *conjunction* of $p$ and $q$, which is represented by $p \wedge q$.

The symbolic form is $p \wedge q$.

**3.** Let $x =$ the number.

| 4 | more than | twice the number | is | 18 |
|---|-----------|------------------|-----|-----|
| ↓ | | | ↓ | ↓ |
| 4 | + | $2x$ | = | 18 |

The equation to use is:

Add $-4$ (the additive inverse of 4) to both sides of the equation:

$$4 + 2x = 18$$
$$\underline{-4 \qquad\quad = -4}$$
$$2x = 14$$

Divide both sides of the equation by 2:

$$\frac{2x}{2} = \frac{14}{2}$$
$$x = 7$$

The number is **7**.

**4.** The given equation contains a decimal coefficient:

$$1.5x = 30$$

Clear decimals by multiplying both sides of the equation by 10:

$$10(1.5x) = 10(30)$$
$$15x = 300$$

Divide both sides of the equation by 15:

$$\frac{15x}{15} = \frac{300}{15}$$
$$x = 20$$

$x = \mathbf{20}$.

**5.** The man has 8 choices for the shirt.

He has 5 choices for the pair of pants.

He has 6 choices for the tie.

To form a complete outfit, he may combine each of the 8 choices for the shirt with each of the 5 choices for the pair of pants, and these combinations may in turn be combined with each of the 6 choices for the tie. The total number of possible outfits consisting of a shirt, a pair of pants, and a tie is thus the product of the number of choices for each element:

$$8 \times 5 \times 6$$
$$40 \times 6$$
$$240$$

The total possible number of outfits is **240**.

**6.**   The given equation is:

$$5x + 7 = 2x - 2$$

Add $-2x$ (the additive inverse of $2x$) and also add $-7$ (the additive inverse of $+7$) to both sides of the equation:

$$\frac{-2x - 7 = -2x - 7}{3x \quad = \quad -9}$$

Divide both sides of the equation by 3:

$$\frac{3x}{3} = \frac{-9}{3}$$

$$x = -3$$

The solution is $x = -3$.

**7.**   The given formula is:

$$P = K^2W$$

Substitute 5 for $K$ and $-3$ for $W$:

$$P = (5)^2(-3)$$

Evaluate the power, $(5)^2$, first:

$$P = 25(-3)$$

Perform the indicated multiplication:

$$P = -75$$

The value of $P$ is $-75$.

**8.**   The given fractions have different denominators:

$$\frac{a}{3} + \frac{2a}{5}$$

In order to combine fractions, they must have a common denominator. The least common denominator (L.C.D.) is the smallest number into which each of the denominators will divide evenly; the L.C.D. for 3 and 5 is 15.

Convert each fraction to an equivalent fraction having the L.C.D. by multiplying the first fraction by 1 in the form $\frac{5}{5}$ and by multiplying the second fraction by 1 in the form $\frac{3}{3}$:

$$\frac{5a}{5(3)} + \frac{3(2a)}{3(5)}$$

$$\frac{5a}{15} + \frac{6a}{15}$$

Fractions having the same denominator may be combined by combining their numerators:

$$\frac{5a + 6a}{15}$$

Combine like terms in the numerator:

$$\frac{11a}{15}$$

The single fraction in simplest form is $\frac{11a}{15}$.

**9.** The given system of equations is:

$$x + y = 6$$
$$x - y = 2$$

Adding the two equations will eliminate $y$:

$$2x = 8$$

Divide both sides of the equation by 2:

$$\frac{2x}{2} = \frac{8}{2}$$

$x = 4$.

$$x = 4$$

**10.**

| Score | Frequency |
|-------|-----------|
| 98 | 2 |
| 95 | 3 |
| 92 | 2 |
| 87 | 1 |
| 84 | 2 |

The *mode* of a set of scores is the score which occurs most frequently. In the given table, 95 occurs three times while all other scores occur either once or twice. The mode is **95**.

**11.** The given expression is a *quadratic trinomial*:

$$x^2 + 5x - 24$$

A quadratic trinomial may be factored into the product of two binomials. The factors of the first term, $x^2$, are $x$ and $x$, and they become the first terms of the binomials:

$$(x \quad )(x \quad )$$

The factors of the last term, $-24$, become the second terms of the binomials, but they must be chosen in such a way that the inner and outer products add up to the middle term, $+5x$, of the original trinomial. Try $+8$ and $-3$ as the factors of $-24$:

Since $(+8x) + (-3x) = +5x$, these are the correct factors:

$$+8x = \text{inner product}$$
$$(x + 8)(x - 3)$$
$$-3x = \text{outer product}$$
$$(x + 8)(x - 3)$$

The factored form is $(x + 8)(x - 3)$.

**12.**
∠ ZHS and ∠ HEY are *corresponding angles* of the parallel lines. If two lines are parallel, a transversal makes a pair of corresponding angles equal in measure:

$$\text{m} \angle ZHS = \text{m} \angle HEY$$
$$\text{m} \angle ZHS = 72$$
$$\text{m} \angle ZHS = 72°.$$

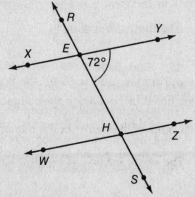

13.    $(k, 3)$ is a point on the graph of:                $x + 2y = 8$

If a point is on the graph of an equation, the coordinates of the point must satisfy the equation:

$k + 2(3) = 8$
$k + 6 = 8$

Add $-6$ (the additive inverse of $+6$) to both sides of the equation:

$$\begin{array}{r} -6 = -6 \\ \hline k = 2 \end{array}$$

The value of $k$ is 2.

14.

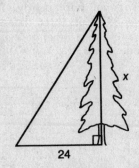

Let $x$ = the number of feet in the height of the tree.

The tree and its shadow and the man and his shadow form the legs of two similar right triangles. In similar triangles, the corresponding sides are in proportion:

In a proportion, the product of the means equals the product of the extremes (cross-multiply):

$$\frac{x}{6} = \frac{24}{4}$$

$4x = 6(24)$
$4x = 144$

Divide both sides of the equation by 4:

$$\frac{4x}{4} = \frac{144}{4}$$

$x = 36$

The tree is **36** feet high.

15.    Since there are four subjects from which to choose (math, English, social studies, and science), the first period may be programmed in 4 different ways.

The second period may then be programmed for any one of the remaining subjects, and hence in 3 different ways.

Similarly, the third period may be programmed in 2 different ways and the fourth period in only 1 way.

The number of different ways for scheduling the

4 subjects in the first four periods is the product of
these ways:

$$4 \times 3 \times 2 \times 1$$
$$24$$

The schedule may be made up in **24** different
ways.

**16.**   Let $x$ = the measure of one of
the base angles of the isosceles triangle.

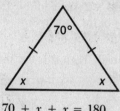

Then $x$ = the measure of the other
base angle, since the base angles of an
isosceles triangle are equal in measure.

The sum of the measures of the three
angles of a triangle is 180°:

Combine like terms:

Add $-70$ (the additive inverse of 70)
to both sides of the equation:

$$70 + x + x = 180$$
$$70 + 2x = 180$$

$$\underline{-70 \qquad = -70}$$
$$2x = 110$$

Divide both sides of the equation by
2:

$$\frac{2x}{2} = \frac{110}{2}$$
$$x = 55$$

The measure of a base angle is **55°**.

**17.**   Write one polynomial under the other with
like terms in the same column:

$$5x^3 - 3x^2 + 5$$
$$\underline{-2x^3 + 6x^2 - 5}$$
$$3x^3 + 3x^2$$

Add the terms in each column algebraically:
The sum is $3x^3 + 3x^2$.

**18.**   The volume of
any rectangular solid is
the product of its length,
width and height:                    $V = lwh$

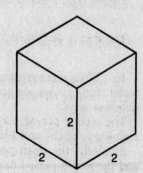

In the case of a cube,
all edges are equal in
length, so the volume is
the cube of the length of
one edge:                           $V = e^3$

In this case, $e = 2$:              $V = 2^3$
                                    $V = 8$

The volume is **8** cubic
centimeters.

**19.** The given equation contains parentheses:

$$5x - 2(x + 1) = 10$$

Remove the parentheses by multiplying each term inside by the coefficient, $-2$,:

$$5x - 2x - 2 = 10$$
$$3x - 2 = 10$$

Combine like terms:

Add $+2$ (the additive inverse of $-2$) to both sides of the equation:

$$\frac{+2 = +2}{3x \quad = 12}$$

Divide both sides of the equation by 3:

$$\frac{3x}{3} = \frac{12}{3}$$
$$x = 4$$

$x = \mathbf{4}$.

**20.** The measure of an inscribed angle is equal to one-half the measure of its intercepted arc:

$$\text{m} \angle ACB = \frac{1}{2} \text{mAB}$$

$$\text{m} \angle ACB = \frac{1}{2} (48)$$

$$\text{m} \angle ACB = 24$$

The measure of angle $ACB$ is **24°**.

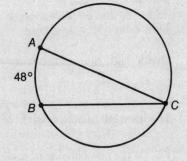

**21.** Let $7x$ = the measure of the *larger* angle.

Then $2x$ = the measure of the *smaller* angle since they are in the ratio $7 : 2$.

The sum of the measures of two supplementary angles is 180°:

$$7x + 2x = 180$$

Combine like terms:

$$9x = 180$$

Divide both sides of the equation by 9:

$$\frac{9x}{9} = \frac{180}{9}$$
$$x = 20$$

The measure of the *larger* angle is $7x$:

$$7x = 7(20) = 140$$

The measure of the *larger* angle is **140°**.

**22.** The given literal equation is:

$$3a + 4b = c$$

Add $-4b$ (the additive inverse of $+4b$) to both sides of the equation:

$$\frac{-4b = \quad -4b}{3a \quad = c - 4b}$$

Divide both sides of the equation by 3: $\dfrac{3a}{3} = \dfrac{c - 4b}{3}$

$$a = \dfrac{c - 4b}{3}$$

The solution for $a$ is $\dfrac{c - 4b}{3}$.

**23.** The probability of an event occurring $=$

$$\dfrac{\text{the number of favorable cases}}{\text{the total possible number of cases}}.$$

If the probability of getting 12 is $\dfrac{1}{36}$, then the number of favorable cases is 1 when the total possible number of cases is 36.

The number of *unfavorable* cases (that is, cases of not getting 12) is $36 - 1$ or 35.

The probability of not getting 12 is: $\dfrac{35}{36}$

The correct choice is **(1)**.

ALTERNATIVE SOLUTION: Certainty is represented by a probability of 1. It is certain that the toss of two fair dice will either result in a 12 or not result in a 12. Therefore the probability of getting a 12 and the probability of not getting a 12 must add up to 1. The probability of not getting a 12 is thus $1 - \dfrac{1}{36}$ or $\dfrac{35}{36}$.

**24.** $x$ represents an even number.
Consider each choice in turn:

(1) $x^3$: $x^3$ means $x \cdot x \cdot x$. The product of three even numbers is an even number.

(2) $x + 3$: If 3 is added to an even number, the sum will be an odd number. Therefore, this is the correct answer.

(3) $3x$: Three times an even number is also an even number.

(4) $\dfrac{x}{3}$: If an even number is divided by 3, the quotient may not be a whole number; therefore, the result cannot be said to be either even or odd. If the quotient did happen to be a whole number, it would be an even number since $x$ is even; dividing an even number by 3 would divide out only the odd factor, 3, leaving one or more even factors.
The correct choice is **(2)**.

**25.** The perimeter of any polygon is the sum of the lengths of all the sides.

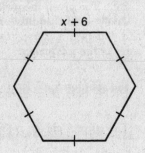

A regular hexagon has 6 sides, all equal in length. The perimeter, $P$, of a regular hexagon would therefore be 6 times the length of one side:

$$P = 6(x + 6)$$

Remove parentheses by multiplying each term inside by the coefficient, 6:

$$P = 6x + 36$$

The perimeter is $6x + 36$.
The correct choice is (4).

**26.** The probability of an event occurring =

$$\frac{\text{the number of favorable cases}}{\text{the total possible number of cases}}.$$

There are 13 clubs and 13 diamonds in a standard deck of 52 cards.
Therefore, the number of favorable cases for drawing either a club or a diamond is 13 + 13, or 26.
The total possible number of cases is the total number of cards in the deck, or 52.

The probability of drawing either a club or a diamond is $\frac{26}{52}$.

The correct choice is (3).

**27.** The given equation is:

$$y = 2x - 3$$

The $y$-intercept of the graph of an equation is the value of $y$ where the equation crosses the $y$-axis. At the point where the graph crosses the $y$-axis, the value of $x$ is 0. Substitute 0 for $x$ in the equation:

$$y = 2(0) - 3$$

Multiply $2(0)$:

$$y = 0 - 3$$
$$y = -3$$

The $y$-intercept is $-3$.
The correct choice is (4).

**28.** The given inequality is:

$$3x + 2 > x + 8$$

Add $-x$ (the additive inverse of $x$) and also add $-2$ (the additive inverse of $+2$) to both sides of the inequality:

$$\frac{-x - 2 = -x - 2}{2x \quad > \quad 6}$$

Divide both sides of the inequality by 2:

$$\frac{2x}{2} > \frac{6}{2}$$

$$x > 3$$

The correct choice is (3).


**29.** If $r$ is the radius of a circle, the circumference, $C$, is given by the formula:

$$C = 2\pi r$$

If the radius, $r$, is doubled, $r$ is replaced by $2r$ in the formula; call the new circumference $C'$:

$$C' = 2\pi(2r)$$

Perform the indicated multiplication:

$$C' = 4\pi r$$

Since $4\pi r$ is double $2\pi r$, the new circumference, $C'$, is double the original circumference, $C$.

The correct choice is (4).

ALTERNATIVE SOLUTION: The question may be solved by choosing a specific numerical value for the radius, $r$, say $r = 3$. Doubling the radius will make the new radius 6. Calculating the circumferences shows the circumference of the original circle to be $2\pi(3)$ or $6\pi$, and the circumference of the new circle to be $2\pi(6)$ or $12\pi$. $12\pi$ is double $6\pi$.


**30.** The given expression is:

$$\frac{-18x^6}{6x^3}$$

To divide monomials, first divide their numerical coefficients to obtain the numerical coefficient of the quotient:

$$(-18) \div (6) = -3$$

Next, divide the literal factors to obtain the literal factor of the quotient. Remember that powers of the same base are divided by subtracting their exponents:

$$x^6 \div x^3 = x^3$$

Combine the above results:

$$\frac{-18x^6}{6x^3} = -3x^3$$

The correct choice is (1).


**31.** The given statement is the implication, $q \rightarrow p$.

The *converse* of a statement is formed by interchanging the hypothesis or antecedent (the given or "if clause") with the conclusion or consequent (the "to prove" or "then clause").

In $q \rightarrow p$, the hypothesis or antecedent is $q$ and the conclusion or consequent is $p$.

The converse of $q \rightarrow p$ is $p \rightarrow q$.

The correct choice is (2).

**32.** An irrational number is a number that cannot be represented as the quotient of two integers.

Consider each of the choices in turn:

(1) 0 can be represented as $\dfrac{0}{3}$. Therefore 0 is not an irrational number.

(2) $\dfrac{3}{4}$ is in the form of the quotient of two integers. Therefore, $\dfrac{3}{4}$ is not irrational.

(3) $\sqrt{3}$ is equivalent to a non-terminating, non-repeating decimal, .1732...... A non-terminating, non-repeating decimal cannot be represented as the quotient of two integers. Therefore, $\sqrt{3}$ is an irrational number.

(4) $\sqrt{4}$ is equivalent to 2, which can be represented as $\dfrac{2}{1}$. Therefore, $\sqrt{4}$ is not an irrational number.

The correct choice is (3).

**33.** Since division by 0 is undefined, the expression $\dfrac{x}{x-2}$ will be undefined if its denominator, $x-2$, equals 0; set the denominator equal to 0:

$$x - 2 = 0$$

Add $+2$ (the additive inverse of $-2$) to both sides of the equation:

$$\underline{+2 = +2}$$
$$x = 2$$

If $x = 2$, $\dfrac{x}{x-2}$ becomes $\dfrac{2}{2-2}$ or $\dfrac{2}{0}$ and is therefore undefined.

The correct choice is (2).

**34.** Given: $p$ represents "$x$ is prime"
$q$ represents "$x < 10$"
$x = 11$

Consider each choice in turn:

(1) $\sim p \vee q$: $\sim p$ is the *negation* of $p$; $\sim p = $ "$x$ is not prime." $\sim p \vee q$ is the *disjunction* of $\sim p$ and $q$, which states that either $x$ is not prime or $x < 10$ or both. Since $x = 11$, $x$ is prime and $x$ is greater than 10, so $\sim p \vee q$ is not true.

(2) $p \wedge q$: $p \wedge q$ is the *conjunction* of $p$ and $q$, which states that $x$ is both prime and less than 10. If $x = 11$, $x$ is not less than 10, so $p \wedge q$ is false.

(3) $\sim p \rightarrow q$: $\sim p \rightarrow q$ is the *implication*, $\sim p$ implies $q$, which states that if $x$ is not prime then $x$ is less than 10. For $x = 11$, "$x$ is not prime" is false and "$x$ is less than 10" is false. If the hypothesis and conclusion of an implication are both false, the implication is true. Therefore, $\sim p \rightarrow q$ is true.

(4) $p \rightarrow q$: $p \rightarrow q$ is the *implication*, $p$ implies $q$, which states that if $x$ is prime then $x$ is less than 10. This is false when $x = 11$, since 11 is prime but is not less than 10.

The correct choice is **(3)**.

**35.** The given equation is a *quadratic equation*:

$$x^2 - 4x = 0$$

Factor out the *common monomial factor* of $x$ on the left side of the equation:

$$x(x - 4) = 0$$

If the product of two factors equals 0, then either of the factors may equal 0:

$$x = 0 \quad \text{OR} \quad x - 4 = 0$$

Add $+4$ (the additive inverse of $-4$) to both sides of the right hand equation:

$$\underline{\qquad\qquad +4 = +4}$$
$$x = 4$$

The solution set is $\{0, 4\}$.
The correct choice is **(1)**.

**PART TWO**

**36.** **a.** STEP 1: To draw the graph of the inequality, $y < 2x + 4$, we first draw the graph of the equation, $y = 2x + 4$.

Prepare a table of values for $x$ and $y$ by selecting any three convenient values for $x$ and substituting them in the equation to calculate the corresponding values of $y$:

| $x$ | $2x + 4$ | $=$ | $y$ |
|---|---|---|---|
| $-3$ | $2(-3) + 4 = -6 + 4$ | $=$ | $-2$ |
| $0$ | $2(0) + 4 = 0 + 4$ | $=$ | $4$ |
| $2$ | $2(2) + 4 = 4 + 4$ | $=$ | $8$ |

Plot the points $(-3, -2)$, $(0, 4)$, and $(2, 8)$ and draw a *broken* line through them. The broken line indicates that points on it are *not* part of the solution set of $y < 2x + 4$.

The solution set of $y < 2x + 4$ lies on one side of the line, $y = 2x + 4$. To find out on which side of the line the solution set lies, choose a convenient test point, say $(0, 0)$, and substitute its coordinates in the inequality to see if it is satisfied:

$$y < 2x + 4$$
$$0 \overset{?}{<} 2(0) + 4$$
$$0 \overset{?}{<} 0 + 4$$
$$0 < 4 \checkmark$$

Since $(0, 0)$ satisfies the inequality, it lies in the solution set of $y < 2x + 4$. Therefore, shade the side of the line, $y = 2x + 4$, which contains $(0, 0)$ with cross-hatching extending to the right and down; the region shaded will contain the points whose coordinates satisfy $y < 2x + 4$.

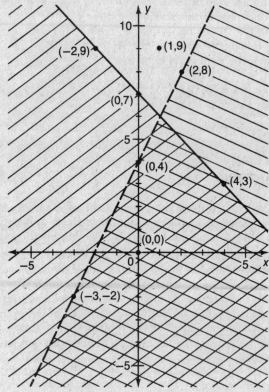

STEP 2: To draw the graph of $x + y \leq 7$, we first draw the graph of the line, $x + y = 7$.

It is convenient to rearrange the equation so that it is solved for $y$ by adding $-x$ to both sides:

$$x + y = 7$$
$$\underline{-x \qquad = \qquad -x}$$
$$y = 7 - x$$

Prepare a table of values for $x$ and $y$ by selecting any three convenient values for $x$ and substituting them in $y = 7 - x$ to determine the corresponding values of $y$:

| $x$ | $7 - x$ | $= y$ |
|-----|---------|-------|
| $-2$ | $7 - (-2) = 7 + 2$ | $= 9$ |
| $0$ | $7 - 0$ | $= 7$ |
| $4$ | $7 - 4$ | $= 3$ |

Plot the points $(-2, 9)$, $(0, 7)$, and $(4, 3)$ and draw a *solid* line through them. The solid line indicates that points on $y = 7 - x$ are part of the solution set of $x + y \leq 7$; they are the part representing $x + y = 7$.

The part of the solution set representing $x + y < 7$ lies on one side of the line $x + y = 7$. To determine which side, choose a test point, say $(0, 0)$, and substitute its coordinates in the inequality to see if they satisfy it:

$$x + y < 7$$
$$0 + 0 \overset{?}{<} 7$$
$$0 < 7 \checkmark$$

Since $(0, 0)$ satisfies $x + y < 7$, it lies on the side of the line, $x + y = 7$, which represents the solution set for $x + y < 7$. Shade this region with cross-hatching extending to the left and down.

**b.** The points which are in the solution set of the system of inequalities are those which lie in the region containing both types of cross-hatching or which lie on the part of the solid line which forms a boundary of this region. Points *not* in the solution set of the system of inequalities lie anywhere except in the region defined above; they may be in a region with no cross-hatching or in one with only one type of cross-hatching.

The point $(1, 9)$ is a point which is *not* in the solution set of the system of inequalities.

37. Let $x$ = the positive number.

The square of a positive number decreased by 4 times the number is 12.

$$x^2 \qquad - \qquad 4x \qquad = 12$$

The equation to use is: $\qquad x^2 - 4x = 12$

The equation is a *quadratic equation*; re-arrange it so that all terms are on one side equal to 0 by adding $-12$ (the additive inverse of 12) to both sides:

$$\underline{\qquad\qquad -12 = -12}$$
$$x^2 - 4x - 12 = 0$$

The left side of the equation is a *quadratic trinomial*. It may be factored into the product of two binomials. The factors of the first term, $x^2$, are $x$ and $x$, and they become the first terms of the binomials:

$$(x\qquad)(x\qquad) = 0$$

The factors of the last term, $-12$, become the second terms of the binomials, but they must be chosen in such a way that the inner product and the outer product add up to the middle term, $-4x$, of the original trinomial. Try $-6$ and $+2$ as the factors of $-12$:

$$-6x = \text{inner product}$$
$$(x - 6)(x + 2) = 0$$
$$+2x = \text{outer product}$$

Since $(-6x) + (+2x) = -4x$, these are the correct factors:

$$(x - 6)(x + 2) = 0$$

If the product of two factors is 0, either factor may equal 0:

$$x - 6 = 0 \quad \text{OR} \quad x + 2 = 0$$

Add the appropriate additive inverses, to both sides of the equations, $+6$ in the case of the left-hand equation and $-2$ in the case of the right-hand equation:

$$\underline{+6 = +6} \qquad\qquad \underline{-2 = -2}$$
$$x = 6 \qquad\qquad\qquad x = -2$$

Reject $-2$ since the question calls for a *positive* number:

$$x = 6$$

The positive number is **6**.

38.

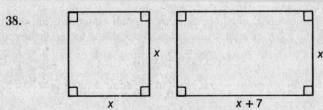

Let $x$ = the length of a side of the square.
Then $x$ = the width of the rectangle.
And $x + 7$ = the length of the rectangle.
The area of the square is equal to the area of the rectangle less 56.

$$x^2 \qquad = \qquad x(x + 7) \qquad - \quad 56$$

The equation to use is: $\qquad\qquad\qquad x^2 = x(x + 7) = 56$

Remove the parentheses by multiplying each term inside them by $x$: $\qquad x^2 = x^2 + 7x - 56$

Add $-x^2$ (the additive inverse of $x^2$) and also add $+56$ (the additive inverse of $-56$) to both sides of the equation:

$$\frac{+56 - x^2 = -x^2 \qquad +56}{56 \qquad = \qquad 7x}$$

Divide both sides of the equation by 7: $\qquad \dfrac{56}{7} = \dfrac{7x}{7}$

$$8 = x$$

The width of the rectangle is 8.

---

**39.**  The given system of equations is:
$$x - 4y = 16$$
$$y = 1 - x$$

Using the expression for $y$ from the second equation, substitute $1 - x$ for $y$ in the first equation: $\qquad\qquad x - 4(1 - x) = 16$

Remove the parentheses by multiplying each term inside them by $-4$: $\qquad x - 4 + 4x = 16$

Combine like terms: $\qquad\qquad\qquad\qquad -4 + 5x = 16$

Add $+4$ (the additive inverse of $-4$) to both sides of the equation:

$$\frac{+4 \qquad\qquad = +4}{5x = 20}$$

Divide both sides of the equation by 5: $\qquad \dfrac{5x}{5} = \dfrac{20}{5}$

$$x = 4$$

Substitute 4 for $x$ in the equation, $y = 1 - x$: $\qquad y = 1 - 4$

$$y = -3$$

The solution is $(4, -3)$ or $x = 4, y = -3$.

CHECK: The solution must satisfy *both original* equations. Substitute 4 for $x$ and $-3$ for $y$ in both of the original equations to see if they are satisfied:

$$x - 4y = 16 \qquad\qquad\qquad y = 1 - x$$
$$4 - 4(-3) \stackrel{?}{=} 16 \qquad\qquad -3 \stackrel{?}{=} 1 - 4$$
$$4 + 12 \stackrel{?}{=} 16 \qquad\qquad -3 = -3 \;\checkmark$$
$$16 = 16 \;\checkmark$$

40.   $p$ represents "$x$ is an even integer."
  $q$ represents "$x$ is a prime number."
  $r$ represents "$x$ is divisible by 3."

  **a.**   (1) $\sim r \vee q$ is the *disjunction* of the *negation* of $r$ with $q$. The negation of $r$ is "$x$ is not divisible by 3." In sentence form, the disjunction states, "**Either $x$ is not divisible by 3 or $x$ is a prime number or both.**"

  (2) $p \rightarrow r$ is the *implication* that if $p$ is true, $r$ is true. In sentence form, it states, "**If $x$ is an even number, then $x$ is divisible by 3.**"

  **b.**   (1) "$x$ is an even integer, if and only if $x$ is divisible by 3" is the *equivalence relation* between $p$ and $r$. In symbolic form, $p \leftrightarrow r$.

  (2) "If $x$ is a prime number and $x$ is divisible by 3, then $x$ is an even integer" is the *implication* that if the *conjunction* of $q$ with $r$ is true, then $p$ is true. In symbolic form, $(q \wedge r) \rightarrow p$.

  **c.**   "If $x$ is not an even number, then $x$ is a prime number" is the *implication* that if the *negation* of $p$ is true, then $q$ is true; symbolically, $\sim p \rightarrow q$.

  The *contrapositive* of a proposition is found by negating the hypothesis (or antecedent) of the proposition and negating the conclusion (or consequent), and then interchanging them.

  The hypothesis of $\sim p \rightarrow q$ is $\sim p$ and the conclusion is $q$. The negation of $\sim p$ is $p$ and the negation of $q$ is $\sim q$. Thus, the contrapositive of $\sim p \rightarrow q$ is $\sim q \rightarrow p$.

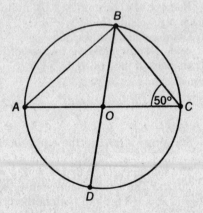

  **41.  a.**   Angle $C$ is an *inscribed angle*. The measure of an inscribed angle is equal to one-half the measure of its intercepted arc:

$$m \angle C = \frac{1}{2}\ m\widehat{AB}$$

$$50 = \frac{1}{2}\ m\widehat{AB}$$

  Multiply both sides of the equation by 2:

$$2(50) = 2\left( \frac{1}{2}\ m\widehat{AB} \right)$$

$$100 = m\widehat{AB}$$

  The measure of $\widehat{AB}$ is **100°**.

**b.** Since $\overline{AC}$ is a diameter, $\overset{\frown}{ABC}$ is a semicircle and m$\overset{\frown}{ABC}$ = 180°:

From part *a*, m$\overset{\frown}{AB}$ = 100°:

Add −100 (the additive inverse of 100) to both sides of the equation:

$$m\overset{\frown}{AB} + m\overset{\frown}{BC} = m\overset{\frown}{ABC}$$
$$100 + m\overset{\frown}{BC} = 180$$

$$\underline{-100 \qquad\qquad = -100}$$
$$m\overset{\frown}{BC} = 80$$

Angle *BOC* is a *central angle*. The measure of a central angle is equal to the measure of its intercepted arc:

$$m \angle BOC = m\overset{\frown}{BC}$$
$$m \angle BOC = 80$$

m $\angle$ *BOC* = **80°**.

**c.** Angle *BAC* is an *inscribed angle*. The measure of an inscribed angle is equal to one-half the measure of its intercepted arc:

From part *b*, m$\overset{\frown}{BC}$ = 80°:

$$m \angle BAC = \frac{1}{2} m\overset{\frown}{BC}$$
$$m \angle BAC = \frac{1}{2} (80)$$
$$m \angle BAC = 40$$

m $\angle$ *BAC* = **40°**.

**d.** Angle *BOC* and angle *AOD* are *vertical angles*. Vertical angles are equal in measure:

From part b, m $\angle$ *BOC* = 80°:

Angle *AOD* is a *central angle*. The measure of a central angle is equal to the measure of its intercepted arc:

$$m \angle AOD = m \angle BOC$$
$$m \angle AOD = 80$$

$$m \angle AOD = m\overset{\frown}{AD}$$
$$80 = m\overset{\frown}{AD}$$

m$\overset{\frown}{AD}$ = **80°**.

**e.** Angle *ABC* is an *inscribed angle*. The measure of an inscribed angle is equal to one-half the measure of its intercepted arc:

Since $\overline{AC}$ is a diameter, $\overset{\frown}{ADC}$ is a semi circle and m$\overset{\frown}{ADC}$ = 180°:

$$m \angle ABC = \frac{1}{2} m\overset{\frown}{ADC}$$
$$m \angle ABC = \frac{1}{2} (180)$$
$$m \angle ABC = 90$$

m $\angle$ *ABC* = **90°**.

**42.** **a.** In the cumulative frequency histogram below, the height of each bar represents the frequency of that number of weeks vacation *added to* the height of the preceding (lower) bar. Thus, the height of each bar really represents the number of workers receiving the number of weeks vacation shown *or less*. The last bar for 6 weeks vacation or less would thus include *all* workers in the company; hence the total number of workers employed is **20**.

CUMULATIVE FREQUENCY HISTOGRAM

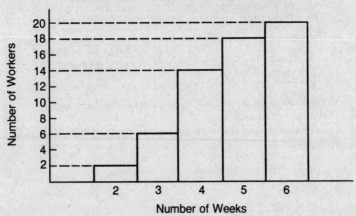

**b.** There are 14 workers having 4 weeks vacation or less. Thus the remainder, 20 − 14, or **6** workers receive more than 4 weeks vacation.

**c.** If the workers are arranged in order according to the lengths of their vacations, the median number of weeks of vacation is the number received by the middle worker. Half of the workers will have fewer weeks of vacation than the median and half will have more.

From part a, the total number of workers is 20. One-half of 20 is 10. To have 10 workers below the median and 10 above, the median must lie between the number of weeks of vacation of the 10th and 11th workers. The 10th and 11th workers are *both* represented in the bar for those having 4 weeks or less. Therefore, the median number of weeks of vacation is **4**.

**d.** Prepare a table showing the cumulative frequencies and the frequencies for each of the vacation lengths.

The *cumulative* frequencies are obtained by reading the heights of the bars in the *cumulative* frequency histogram in terms of the number of workers.

The entries for the frequencies are obtained by subtracting each *cumulative* frequency entry from its successor. The lowest frequency entry (for two weeks of vacation) will be the same as the entry for two weeks of vacation or less in the *cumulative* frequency column. Each succeeding entry is obtained by subtracting the preceding *cumulative* frequency from the *cumulative* frequency shown on that line. For example, the entry for 3 weeks is $6 - 2$, or 4; the entry for 4 weeks is $14 - 6$, or 8.

| Vacation | Cumulative Frequency | Vacation | Frequency |
|---|---|---|---|
| 2 weeks or less | 2 | 2 weeks | 2 |
| 3 weeks or less | 6 | 3 weeks | 4 |
| 4 weeks or less | 14 | 4 weeks | 8 |
| 5 weeks or less | 18 | 5 weeks | 4 |
| 6 weeks or less | 20 | 6 weeks | 2 |

Use the frequency column to plot the height of the bars in the frequency histogram:

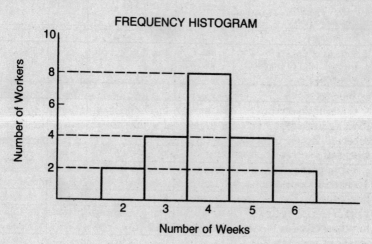

FREQUENCY HISTOGRAM

## SELF-ANALYSIS CHART    January 1986

| Topic | Question Numbers | Number of Points | Your Points | Your Percentage |
|---|---|---|---|---|
| 1. Numbers (rat'l, irrat'l); Percent | 32 | 2 | | |
| 2. Properties of No. Systems | 33 | 2 | | |
| 3. Operations on Rat'l Nos. and Monomials | 8, 30 | 2 + 2 = 4 | | |
| 4. Operations on Multinomials | 17 | 2 | | |
| 5. Square root; Operations Involving Radicals | — | 0 | | |
| 6. Evaluating Formulas and Expressions | 7 | 2 | | |
| 7. Linear Equations (simple cases incl. parentheses) | 6, 19 | 2 + 2 = 4 | | |
| 8. Linear Equations Containing Decimals or Fractions | 1, 4 | 2 + 2 = 4 | | |
| 9. Graphs of Linear Functions (slope) | 13, 27 | 2 + 2 = 4 | | |
| 10. Inequalities | 28 | 2 | | |
| 11. Systems of Eqs. & Inequal. (alg. & graphic solutions) | 9, 36a, 36b, 39 | 2 + 8 + 2 + 10 = 22 | | |
| 12. Factoring | 11 | 2 | | |
| 13. Quadratic Equations | 35 | 2 | | |
| 14. Verbal Problems | 3, 37, 38 | 2 + 10 + 10 = 22 | | |
| 15. Variation | 29 | 2 | | |
| 16. Literal Eqs.; Expressing Relations Algebraically | 22, 24 | 2 + 2 = 4 | | |
| 17. Factorial $n$ | — | 0 | | |
| 18. Areas, Perims., Circums., Vols. of Common Figures | 18, 25 | 2 + 2 = 4 | | |
| 19. Geometry ($\cong$, $\angle$ meas., $\parallel$ lines, compls, suppls, const.) | 12, 16, 20, 21, 41a, b, c, d, e | 2 + 2 + 2 + 2 + 2 + 2 + 2 + 2 + 2 = 18 | | |
| 20. Ratio & Proportion (incl. similar triangles) | 14 | 2 | | |
| 21. Pythagorean Theorem | — | 0 | | |

| Topic | Question Numbers | Number of Points | Your Points | Your Percentage |
|-------|------------------|------------------|-------------|-----------------|
| 22. Logic (symbolic rep., logical forms, truth tables) | 2, 31, 34, 40a(1), (2), 40b(1), (2), 40c | 2 + 2 + 2 + 2 + 2 + 2 + 2 + 2 = 16 | | |
| 23. Probability (incl. tree diagrams & sample spaces) | 23, 26 | 2 + 2 = 4 | | |
| 24. Combinations (arrangements, permutations) | 5, 15 | 2 + 2 = 4 | | |
| 25. Statistics (central tend., freq. dist., histograms) | 10, 42a, b, c, d | 2 + 2 + 2 + 2 + 4 = 12 | | |

# Examination  June 1986

## Three-Year Sequence for High School Mathematics—Course I

### PART ONE

DIRECTIONS: *Answer 30 questions from this part. Each correct answer will receive 2 credits. No partial credit will be allowed. Write your answers in the spaces provided. Where applicable, answers may be left in terms of π or in radical form.*

1 In the accompanying diagram, lines $\overleftrightarrow{AB}$ and $\overleftrightarrow{CD}$ intersect at point $E$. If $m\angle AED = (x + 10)$ and $m\angle CEB = 50$, find $x$.

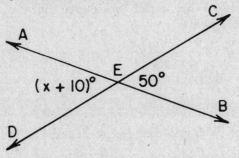

1____

2 Solve for $x$:  $5x - 1 = 3x + 7$

2____

3 Let $p$ represent "I can run," and let $q$ represent "I can walk." Using $p$ and $q$, write in symbolic form: "If I can run, then I can walk."

3____

4 Solve for $x$:  $0.6x + 1.5 = 3.9$

4____

1

5 Find the value of $(x^2 - 5x + 4)$ if $x = 7$. 5____

6 Solve the following system of equations for $x$:

$$3x + y = 9$$
$$2x - y = 6$$
6____

7 In a class of 24 students, 25% of them failed a test. How many students failed the test? 7____

8 On level ground, a person 6 feet tall casts a shadow of 8 feet. At the same time, a nearby tree casts a shadow of 20 feet. Find the number of feet in the height of the tree. 8____

9 From a standard deck of 52 cards, one is drawn at random. What is the probability that the card is *not* a heart? 9____

10 Solve for $x$: $3(x - 8) = x + 4$ 10____

11 In the accompanying diagram, parallel lines $\overleftrightarrow{AB}$ and $\overleftrightarrow{CD}$ are cut by transversal $\overleftrightarrow{GH}$ at $E$ and $F$, respectively. If $m\angle BEF = (3x + 60)$ and $m\angle EFD = 60$, find the value of $x$.

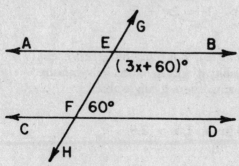

11____

12 Two numbers whose sum is 24 are in the ratio of 1:3. Find the *smaller* number.　　12____

13 Solve for $x$: $\frac{2}{3}x = -12$　　13____

14 Find the sum of $2x^2 - 5x - 2$ and $4x^2 - 6x + 8$.　　14____

15 Solve for $x$ in terms of $b$ and $c$:
$$2x - b = c$$　　15____

16 Find the perimeter of a square whose area is 25.　　16____

17 In the accompanying diagram, right triangle $ABC$ is inscribed in circle $O$ and $\overline{AOB}$ is a diameter. If $AC = 6$ and $BC = 8$, find the length of the radius of the circle.

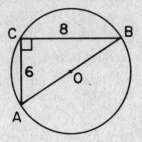

17____

18 Find the measure of a base angle of an isosceles triangle whose vertex angle measures 72.　　18____

19 Express $x^2 + 5x - 6$ as the product of two binomials.　　19____

20 Express $\frac{x}{6} + \frac{x}{8}$ as a single fraction in lowest terms.

20_____

DIRECTIONS (21–35): *For each question chosen, write in the space provided the* numeral *preceding the word or expression that best completes the statement or* answers the question.

21 A bag contains 2 red marbles and 3 blue marbles. If one marble is drawn at random, what is the probability that it is red?

(1) $\frac{1}{5}$          (3) $\frac{3}{5}$

(2) $\frac{2}{5}$          (4) $\frac{4}{5}$      21_____

22 When $x = 2$ and $y = 3$, which expression has the *smallest* value?
(1) $x - y$          (3) $x + y$
(2) $x \cdot y$          (4) $x \div y$      22_____

23 The smallest whole number that satisfies the inequality $3x - 1 > 2$ is
(1) 1          (3) 3
(2) 2          (4) 0      23_____

24 John has 6 pairs of pants and 3 shirts. How many possible outfits consisting of one shirt and one pair of pants can he select?
(1) 9          (3) 12
(2) 2          (4) 18      24_____

25 The product of $3x^2y^3$ and $-4x^3y^4$ is

(1) $-7x^5y^7$  (3) $-12x^5y^7$

(2) $-x^5y^7$  (4) $-12x^6y^{12}$  25____

26 What is the measure of an inscribed angle that intercepts an arc whose measure is 200?

(1) 100  (3) 300

(2) 200  (4) 50  26____

27 Which point satisfies the equation $2x + 3y = 8$?

(1) (1,4)  (3) (−1,3)

(2) (2,2)  (4) (−2,4)  27____

28 For the group of data, 3, 3, 5, 8, 18, which is true?

(1) median > mean  (3) mean > median

(2) mode > mean  (4) median = mode  28____

29 If the length of a rectangular solid is unchanged but the width and height are tripled, then the volume of the original figure is multiplied by a factor of

(1) 6  (3) 3

(2) 9  (4) 27  29____

30 What is the $y$-intercept of the graph of the equation $y = \frac{1}{4}x - \frac{2}{3}$?

(1) $-\frac{2}{3}$  (3) $-\frac{1}{4}$

(2) $\frac{2}{3}$  (4) $\frac{1}{4}$  30____

31 Which is the contrapositive of $\sim p \rightarrow q$?

(1) $p \rightarrow \sim q$     (3) $\sim p \rightarrow q$

(2) $q \rightarrow \sim p$     (4) $\sim q \rightarrow p$     31_____

32 The sum of $\sqrt{18}$ and $6\sqrt{2}$ is

(1) $7\sqrt{20}$     (3) $15\sqrt{2}$

(2) $9\sqrt{2}$     (4) 18     32_____

33 If the replacement set for $x$ is the set of real numbers, which graph represents the inequality $x + 6 \geq 3$?

33_____

34 If $p$ represents "$x$ is prime" and $q$ represents "$2x = 10$," then which statement is true when $x = 3$?

(1) $p \vee q$     (3) $p \rightarrow q$

(2) $p \wedge q$     (4) $q$     34_____

35 How many different ways can 3 students be seated in a row of 3 fixed chairs?

(1) 1     (3) 3

(2) 6     (4) 9     35_____

**PART TWO**

DIRECTIONS: *Answer* four *questions from this part. Show all work unless otherwise directed.*

36 On the same set of coordinate axes, graph the following system of inequalities and label the solution set S:

$$x + y < 3$$
$$y \leq 2x$$

[8,2]

37 The square of a positive number is 12 more than 4 times the number. Find the number. [*Only an algebraic solution will be accepted.*]
[5,5]

38 In the accompanying diagram, circles O and P have diameters $\overline{AD}$ and $\overline{BC}$, respectively, $\overline{AD} \cong \overline{BC}$, AD = 12, ABCD is a rectangle, and side AB = 15. [Answers may be left in terms of $\pi$.]

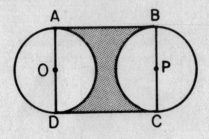

*a* What is the perimeter of rectangle *ABCD*?
[2]
*b* What is the area of rectangle *ABCD*? [2]
*c* What is the length of the radius of circle *O*?
[2]
*d* What is the area of circle *O*? [2]
*e* What is the area of the shaded region in the diagram? [2]

39 Solve the following system of equations algebraically and check:

$$3x + 2y = 6$$
$$5x - 3y = -28 \qquad [8,2]$$

40 The longer leg of a right triangle is 7 more than the shorter leg. The hypotenuse is 8 more than the shorter leg. The perimeter of the triangle is 30.

a Find the length of each leg. [*Only an algebraic solution will be accepted.*]    [8]

b Find the area of the triangle.    [2]

41 Each of 20 students was asked to select *one* number from the following choices: 6, 7, 8, 9, 10. The table below gives the distribution of these selections.

| Number | Frequency |
|--------|-----------|
| 6 | 3 |
| 7 | 10 |
| 8 | 1 |
| 9 | 4 |
| 10 | 2 |

a **Draw** a frequency histogram for the given data.    [4]

b Find the mode.    [2]

    *c* What is the probability that a student selected the number 7? [2]

    *d* What is the probability that a student selected a number less than 6? [2]

42 *a* Complete the truth table for the statement $(p \rightarrow q) \leftrightarrow (\sim p \rightarrow \lor q)$.

| $p$ | $q$ | $\sim p$ | $(p \rightarrow q)$ | $(\sim p \lor q)$ | $(p \rightarrow q) \leftrightarrow (\sim p \lor q)$ |
|-----|-----|----------|---------------------|-------------------|------------------------------------------------------|
| T | | | | | |
| T | | | | | |
| F | | | | | |
| F | | | | | |

  *b* What is logically equivalent to "If Rob can borrow a car, then he will take Susan to the prom"?

    (1) If Rob can not borrow a car, then he will not take Susan to the prom.

    (2) Rob can borrow a car and he will take Susan to the prom.

    (3) It is not the case that Rob will borrow a car or take Susan to the prom.

    (4) Rob can not borrow a car or he will take Susan to the prom.

# Answers   June 1986

## Three-Year Sequence for High School Mathematics—Course I

### ANSWER KEY

### PART ONE

1. 40
2. 4
3. $p \to q$
4. 4
5. 18
6. 3
7. 6
8. 15
9. $\dfrac{39}{52}$
10. 14
11. 20
12. 6

13. $-18$
14. $6x^2 - 11x + 6$
15. $\dfrac{b + c}{2}$
16. 20
17. 5
18. 54
19. $(x + 6)(x - 1)$
20. $\dfrac{7x}{24}$
21. (2)
22. (1)
23. (2)

24. (4)
25. (3)
26. (1)
27. (4)
28. (3)
29. (2)
30. (1)
31. (4)
32. (2)
33. (3)
34. (1)
35. (2)

**Part Two**—*See* **Answers Explained**

### ANSWERS EXPLAINED

### PART ONE

1. Vertical angles are equal in measure:
   Add $-10$ (the additive inverse of $+10$) to both sides of the equation:

$$x + 10 = 50$$
$$\underline{-10 = -10}$$
$$x = 40$$

$x = 40°.$

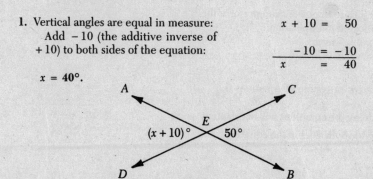

**10**

**2.** The given equation is:

$$5x - 1 = 3x + 7$$

Add $+1$ (the additive inverse of $-1$) and also add $-3x$ (the additive inverse of $+3x$) to both sides of the equation:

$$\frac{-3x + 1 = -3x + 1}{2x \qquad = \qquad 8}$$

Divide both sides of the equation by 2:

$$\frac{2x}{2} = \frac{8}{2}$$

$$x = 4$$

$x = 4.$

**3.** $p =$ "I can run."  $q =$ "I can walk"
"If I can run, then I can walk" is the *implication* which is represented by $p \rightarrow q$.
The symbolic form is $p \rightarrow q$.

**4.** The given equation contains *decimal* coefficients:

$$0.6x + 1.5 = 3.9$$

Clear decimals by multiplying each term on both sides of the equation by 10:

$$10(0.6x) + 10(1.5) = 10(3.9)$$
$$6x + 15 = 39$$

Add $-15$ (the additive inverse of $+15$) to both sides of the equation:

$$\frac{-15 = -15}{6x \quad = \quad 24}$$

Divide both sides of the equation by 6:

$$\frac{6x}{6} = \frac{24}{6}$$

$$x = 4$$

$x = 4.$

**5.** The given expression is:

$$x^2 - 5x + 4$$

To find its value when $x = 7$, substitute 7 for $x$:

$$7^2 - 5(7) + 4$$

First raise to powers and perform the indicated multiplication:

$$49 - 35 + 4$$

Combine terms:

$$18$$

The value is **18**.

**6.** The given system of equations is:

$$3x + y = 9$$
$$\frac{2x - y = 6}{5x \qquad = 15}$$

Adding the equations will eliminate $y$:

Divide both sides of the equation by 5:

$$\frac{5x}{5} = \frac{15}{5}$$

$$x = 3$$

$x = 3.$

7. If 25% of a class of 24 students failed a
test, then the number who failed is
obtained by multiplying 24 by 25%:      24(0.25)

25%, or 0.25, is equivalent to $\frac{1}{4}$:      $24\left(\frac{1}{4}\right)$

**6** students failed the test.

8. Let $x$ = the number of feet in the height of the tree

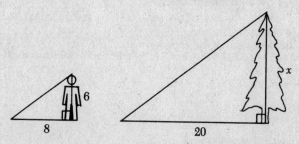

    The tree and its shadow and the
person and his shadow form two similar right triangles. In similar triangles,
corresponding sides are in proportion:      $\dfrac{6}{x} = \dfrac{8}{20}$

    In a proportion, the product of the
means is equal to the product of the
extremes (cross multiply):      $8x = 6(20)$
$$8x = 120$$

Divide both sides of the equation by 8:      $\dfrac{8x}{8} = \dfrac{120}{8}$

$$x = 15$$

The tree is **15** feet high.

9. The probability of an event occurring $= \dfrac{\text{the number of favorable cases}}{\text{the total possible number of cases.}}$

In a standard deck of 52 cards, there are 13 hearts. Therefore there are $52 - 13$ or
39 cards that are *not* hearts.

    The number of favorable cases for drawing a card that is *not* a heart is thus 39
and the total possible number of cases is 52, the total number of cards in the deck.

    The probability of drawing a card that is *not* a heart is $\dfrac{39}{52}$.

    The probability is $\dfrac{39}{52}$.

10. The given equation *contains paren-theses:*

$$3(x - 8) = x + 4$$

To remove the parentheses, apply the distributive law by multiplying each term within the parentheses by 3:

$$3x - 3(8) = x + 4$$
$$3x - 24 = x + 4$$

Add + 24 (the additive inverse of − 24) and also add − x (the additive inverse of x) to both sides of the equation:

$$\underline{-x + 24 = -x + 24}$$
$$2x \quad = \quad 28$$

Divide both sides of the equation by 2:

$$\frac{2x}{2} = \frac{28}{2}$$

$$x = 14$$

*x* = **14.**

11. If two lines are parallel, the measures of their alternate interior angles are equal:

$$m\angle AEF = m\angle EFD$$

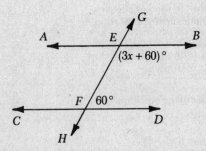

It is given that m∠EFD = 60°: ∠AEF and ∠BEF are supplementary. The sum of the measures of two supplementary angles is 180°:

$$m\angle AEF = \quad 60$$

$$m\angle AEF + m\angle BEF = \quad 180$$
$$60 + 3x + 60 = \quad 180$$

Combine like terms:

$$3x + 120 = \quad 180$$

Add − 120 (the additive inverse of + 120) to both sides of the equation:

$$\underline{-120 = -120}$$
$$3x = \quad 60$$

Divide both sides of the equation by 3:

$$\frac{3x}{3} = \frac{60}{3}$$

$$x = \quad 20$$

*x* = **20.**

12. Let $x$ = the *smaller* number
Since the numbers are in the ratio
1:3, then $3x$ = the *larger* number
The sum of the numbers is 24:

$$x + 3x = 24$$

Combine like terms:

$$4x = 24$$

Divide both sides of the equation
by 4:

$$\frac{4x}{4} = \frac{24}{4}$$

$$x = 6$$

The *smaller* number is **6.**

13. The given equation contains a fraction:

$$\frac{2}{3}x = -12$$

Clear fractions by multiplying each
term of the equation by 3:

$$3\left(\frac{2}{3}x\right) = 3(-12)$$

$$2x = -36$$

Divide both sides of the equation by 2:

$$\frac{2x}{2} = \frac{-36}{2}$$

$$x = -18$$

$x = -18.$

14. To add two polynomials write one
under the other with similar terms in
the same column:

$$2x^2 - 5x - 2$$
$$4x^2 - 6x + 8$$

In each column, add the coefficients to determine the coefficient of
that term in the sum:

$$6x^2 - 11x + 6$$

The sum is $6x^2 - 11x + 6.$

15. The given equation is a *literal equation*:

$$2x - b = c$$

To isolate the term containing $x$ on
one side of the equation, add $+b$ (the
additive inverse of $-b$) to both sides of
the equation:

$$+b = +b$$
$$2x = b + c$$

Divide both sides of the equation by 2:

$$\frac{2x}{2} = \frac{b + c}{2}$$

$$x = \frac{b + c}{2}$$

The solution is $x = \dfrac{b + c}{2}.$

16. Let $x$ = the length of the side of the square

    The area of a square is the square of the length of one side:    $x^2 = 25$

    Take the square root of both sides of the equation:    $x = \pm \sqrt{25}$

    Reject the negative value as meaningless for a length:    $x = 5$

    The perimeter, $P$, of a square is the sum of the lengths of the four sides:

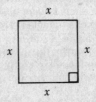

$$P = 4x$$
$$P = 4(5)$$
$$P = 20$$

The perimeter is **20**.

17. Let $x$ = the length of $\overline{AOB}$

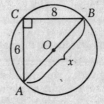

    By the Pythagorean Theorem, in a right triangle the square of the length of the hypotenuse equals the sum of the squares of the lengths of the legs:

$$x^2 = 6^2 + 8^2$$
$$x^2 = 36 + 64$$
$$x^2 = 100$$

    Combine like terms:
    Take the square root of both sides of the equation:    $x = \pm \sqrt{100}$

    Reject the negative value as meaningless for a length:    $x = 10$

   $\overline{AOB}$ is a diameter of the circle. The length of a radius, such as $\overline{OA}$, is

   one-half the length of a diameter:    Length of radius $= \frac{1}{2}(10)$

   Length of radius $= 5$

   The length of the radius is **5**.

18. Let $x$ = the measure of one base angle of the isosceles triangle

    Since the base angles of an isosceles triangle are equal in measure, the measure of the other base angle is also $x$.

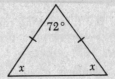

The sum of the measures of the three angles of a triangle is $180°$:

$$x + x + 72 = 180$$

Combine like terms:

$$2x + 72 = 180$$

Add $-72$ (the additive inverse of $+72$) to both sides of the equation:

$$\frac{-72 = -72}{2x \quad = 108}$$

Divide both sides of the equation by 2:

$$\frac{2x}{2} = \frac{108}{2}$$

$$x = 54$$

The measure of a base angle is **54°**.

19. The given expression is a *quadratic trinomial*:

$$x^2 + 5x - 6$$

It can be factored into the product of two binomials. The factors of the first term, $x^2$, are $x$ and $x$, and they become the first terms of the binomials:

$$(x \quad )(x \quad )$$

The factors of the last term, $-6$, become the second terms of the binomials, but they must be chosen in such a way that the sum of the inner product and the outer product of the binomials equals the middle term, $+5x$, of the original trinomial. Try $+6$ and $-1$ as the factors of $-6$:

$+6x =$ inner product

$(x + 6)(x - 1)$

$-x =$ outer product

Since $(+6x) + (-x) = +5x$, these are the correct factors:

$(x + 6)(x - 1)$

The product of two binomials is $(x + 6)(x - 1)$.

20. The given expression contains fractions with *different* denominators:

$$\frac{x}{6} + \frac{x}{8}$$

Determine the least common denominator (L.C.D.). The L.C.D. is the smallest number into which each of the denominators will divide evenly:

The L.C.D. for 6 and 8 is 24

Convert each fraction into an equivalent fraction having the L.C.D. as denominator by multiplying the first fraction by 1 in the form $\frac{4}{4}$ and by multi-

plying the second fraction by 1 in the
form $\frac{3}{3}$ :

$$\frac{4x}{4(6)} + \frac{3x}{3(8)}$$
$$\frac{4x}{24} + \frac{3x}{24}$$

Fractions having the same denominator may be combined by combining
their numerators:

$$\frac{4x + 3x}{24}$$

Combine like terms:

$$\frac{7x}{24}$$

The single fraction is $\frac{7x}{24}$.

21. The probability of an event occurring $= \dfrac{\text{the number of favorable cases}}{\text{the total possible number of cases}}$.

Since there are 2 red marbles in the bag, the number of favorable cases for drawing a red marble is 2.

The total possible number of cases is $2 + 3$ or 5, the number of all the marbles in
the bag.

The probability of drawing a red marble is $\frac{2}{5}$.

The correct choice is (2).

22. If $x = 2$ and $y = 3$, evaluate each choice
by substituting 2 for $x$ and 3 for $y$:
(1) $x - y$ becomes $2 - 3$ or $-1$
(2) $x \cdot y$ becomes $2 \cdot 3$ or 6
(3) $x + y$ becomes $2 + 3$ or 5
(4) $x \div y$ becomes $2 \div 3$ or $\frac{2}{3}$

The *smallest* value is $-1$.
The correct choice is (1).

23. The given inequality is:

$$3x - 1 > 2$$

Add $+1$ (the additive inverse of $-1$) to
both sides of the inequality:

$$\underline{+1 = +1}$$
$$3x > 3$$

Divide both sides of the inequality by 3:

$$\frac{3x}{3} > \frac{3}{3}$$
$$x > 1$$

$x$ must be greater than 1. The smallest
whole number that is greater than 1 is 2.
The correct choice is (2).

24. John has 6 choices for a pair of pants and 3 choices for a shirt. Since he may combine any pair of pants with any shirt to form a possible outfit, he can form $6 \times 3$ or 18 different outfits.

    The correct choice is **(4)**.

25. The product to be simplified is:

    To find the product of two monomials, first find the product of their numerical coefficients:

    Then find the product of their literal factors. Remember that powers of the same literal factor are multiplied by adding their exponents:

    Combine the above two results:

    The correct choice is **(3)**.

$$(3x^2y^3)(-4x^3y^4)$$

$$3(-4) = -12$$

$$(x^2y^3)(x^3y^4) = x^5y^7$$
$$(3x^2y^3)(-4x^3y^4) = -12x^5y^7$$

26. Let $x$ = the measure of the inscribed angle

    The measure of an inscribed angle is equal to one-half the measure of its intercepted arc:

$$x = \frac{1}{2}(200°) = 100°$$

The correct choice is **(1)**.

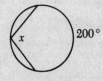

27. If a point satisfies the equation, $2x + 3y = 8$, the equation must balance when the coordinates of the point are substituted for $x$ and $y$ respectively. Test each of the choices in turn:

(1) (1,4): $2(1) + 3(4) \overset{?}{=} 8$
$$2 + 12 \overset{?}{=} 8$$
$$14 \neq 8 \quad \text{(1,4) does not satisfy the equation}$$

(2) (2,2): $2(2) + 3(2) \overset{?}{=} 8$
$$4 + 6 \overset{?}{=} 8$$
$$10 \neq 8 \quad \text{(2,2) does not satisfy the equation}$$

(3) (-1,3): $2(-1) + 3(3) \overset{?}{=} 8$
$$-2 + 9 \overset{?}{=} 8$$
$$7 \neq 8 \quad \text{(-1,3) does not satisfy the equation}$$

(4) $(-2,4)$: $2(-2) + 3(4) \overset{?}{=} 8$
$-4 + 12 \overset{?}{=} 8$
$8 = 8 \;\checkmark\; (-2,4)$ satisfies the equation

The correct choice is **(4)**.

28. The given data are:                                  $3, 3, 5, 8, 18$

    The mean is the sum of all the items divided by the number of them, 5:

$$\text{mean} = \frac{3 + 3 + 5 + 8 + 18}{5}$$

$$\text{mean} = \frac{37}{5} = 7\frac{2}{5}$$

    The median is the middle item when they are arranged in order of size:

$$\text{median} = 5$$

    The mode is the item that appears most frequently:

$$\text{mode} = 3$$

    Test each choice in turn:

(1) median > mean: $5 \not> 7\frac{2}{5}$   this choice is false

(2) mode > mean: $3 \not> 7\frac{2}{5}$   this choice is false

(3) mean > median: $7\frac{2}{5} > 5$ $\checkmark$   this choice is true

(4) median = mode: $5 \neq 3$   this choice is false

The correct choice is **(3)**.

29. Let $l$ = the length, let $w$ = the width, and let $h$ = the height of the original rectangular solid.

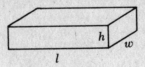

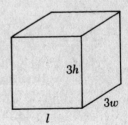

    The volume, V, of a rectangular solid is the product of its length, width and height:   $V = lwh$

    When the length of the rectangular solid remains unchanged but the width and height are tripled, the length, width and height of the resulting new rectangular solid will be $l$, $3w$, and $3h$ respectively.

The volume, $V'$, of the new rectangular solid is:

$$V' = l(3w)(3h)$$
$$V' = 9lwh$$

Therefore, the volume of the new solid is 9 times the volume of the original. The correct choice is **(2)**.

30. The $y$-intercept of a graph is the value of $y$ where the graph crosses the $y$-axis, that is, the value of $y$ when $x = 0$.

To find the $y$-intercept of the graph of $y = \dfrac{1}{4} x - \dfrac{2}{3}$, substitute 0 for $x$:

$$y = \frac{1}{4}(0) - \frac{2}{3}$$
$$y = 0 - \frac{2}{3}$$
$$y = -\frac{2}{3}$$

The correct choice is **(1)**.

31. The contrapositive of a proposition is formed by interchanging the hypothesis or antecedent with the conclusion or consequent, and then negating both of them.

In the proposition, $\sim p \to q$, $\sim p$ is the antecedent and $q$ is the consequent. The negation of $\sim p$ is $p$, and the negation of $q$ is $\sim q$.

Therefore, the contrapositive of $\sim p \to q$ is $\sim q \to p$.

The correct choice is **(4)**.

32. The radicals to be added are *not* like radicals because they have different radicands:

$$\sqrt{18} + 6\sqrt{2}$$

A radical may be simplified by factoring out any perfect square factor in its radicand:

$$\sqrt{9(2)} + 6\sqrt{2}$$

Remove the perfect square factor from under the radical sign by taking its square root and writing it as a coefficient of the radical:

$$3\sqrt{2} + 6\sqrt{2}$$

Both radicals now have the radicand, 2. Like radicals may be combined by combining their coefficients:

$$9\sqrt{2}$$

The correct choice is **(2)**.

33. First solve the given inequality:

Add $-6$ (the additive inverse of $+6$) to both sides of the inequality:

$$x + 6 \geq 3$$
$$\underline{-6 = -6}$$
$$x \geq -3$$

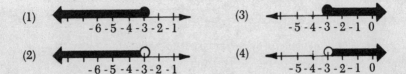

x must be greater than or equal to $-3$. Choices (1) and (2) show $x$ having values less than $-3$. Choice (4) shows values of $x$ greater than $-3$, but the open circle at $x = -3$ indicates that $x = -3$ is not included in the solution set. The solid shading at $x = -3$ in choice (3) indicates that $x = -3$ is part of the solution set; the solid line extending above $-3$ in this choice indicates that all real numbers greater than $-3$ are part of the solution set.

The correct choice is **(3)**.

34. $p =$ "$x$ is prime" $\qquad q =$ "$2x = 10$"

If $x = 3$, $p$ is true since 3 is a prime number, but $q$ is false since $2(3) \neq 10$. Consider each choice in turn:

(1) $p \vee q$ is the *disjunction* of $p$ and $q$. The disjunction is true if $p$ or $q$ or both are true. Hence, $p \vee q$ is true if $x = 3$.

(2) $p \wedge q$ is the *conjunction* of $p$ and $q$. The conjunction is true only if $p$ and $q$ are both true. Hence, $p \wedge q$ is false if $x = 3$.

(3) $p \rightarrow q$ is the *implication* that if $p$ is true, then $q$ is true. The implication is true only if $q$ is true or if $p$ and $q$ are both false. Hence, $p \rightarrow q$ is false if $x = 3$.

(4) $q$ is the statement that $q$ is true. We have seen that $q$ is false if $x = 3$.

The correct choice is **(1)**.

35. The first chair can be filled by any one of the 3 students.

There are then 2 students left as the possible choices for the second chair.

Finally, the one remaining student must be seated in the third chair.

The total number of different ways to seat the students is the product of the ways of filling each chair: $\qquad 3 \times 2 \times 1 = 6$.

They may be seated in 6 ways.

The correct choice is **(2)**.

## PART TWO

36. STEP 1: In order to graph $x + y < 3$, it is convenient to rearrange it into a form in which it is solved for $y$. Add $-x$ (the additive inverse of $+x$) to both sides of the inequality:

$$\begin{aligned} x + y &< 3 \\ -x \quad\quad &= -x \\ \hline y &< 3 - x \end{aligned}$$

To draw the graph of the inequality, $y < 3 - x$, we first draw the graph of the equation, $y = 3 - x$. Prepare a table of pairs of values by selecting any 3 convenient values of $x$ and substituting them in the equation to calculate the corresponding values of $y$:

| $x$ | $3 - x$ | $= y$ |
|---|---|---|
| $-2$ | $3 - (-2) = 3 + 2$ | $= 5$ |
| $0$ | $3 - 0$ | $= 3$ |
| $3$ | $3 - 3$ | $= 0$ |

Plot the points $(-2,5)$, $(0,3)$, and $(3,0)$ and draw a *broken* line through them. The *broken* line indicates that points on it are *not* part of the solution set of $y < 3 - x$.

The solution set of the inequality, $y < 3 - x$, lies on one side of the line, $y = 3 - x$. To find out on which side of the line the solution set lies, choose a convenient test point, say $(0,0)$, and substitute its values for $x$ and $y$ in the inequality:

$$y < 3 - x$$
$$0 \overset{?}{<} 3 - 0$$
$$0 < 3 \checkmark$$

Since $(0,0)$ satisfies the inequality, it lies in the solution set of $y < 3 - x$. Therefore shade the side of the line, $y = 3 - x$, on which $(0,0)$ lies with cross-hatching extending down and to the left to indicate that it is the region containing the points whose coordinates represent $y < 3 - x$.

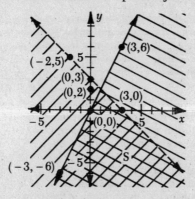

STEP 2: In order to draw the graph of $y \le 2x$, we first draw the graph of the equation, $y = 2x$.

Prepare a table of pairs of values by choosing any 3 convenient values of $x$ and substituting them in the equation to calculate the corresponding values of $y$:

| $x$ | $2x$ | $= y$ |
|---|---|---|
| $-3$ | $2(-3)$ | $= -6$ |
| $0$ | $2(0)$ | $= 0$ |
| $3$ | $2(3)$ | $= 6$ |

Plot the points $(-3, -6)$, $(0,0)$, and $(3,6)$ and draw a *solid* line through them. The *solid* line indicates that points on it are part of the solution set of $y \leq 2x$; it is the part represented by $y = 2x$. The part of the solution set represented by $y < 2x$ lies on one side of the line, $y = 2x$. To find out on which side, select a convenient test point, say $(0,2)$ and substitute its coordinates for $x$ and $y$ in the inequality, $y < 2x$:

$$2 \overset{?}{<} 2(0)$$

$$2 \not< 0$$

Since $(0,2)$ does not satisfy the inequality, it does not lie in the solution set of $y < 2x$. Therefore shade the *opposite* side of the line, $y = 2x$, with cross-hatching extending down and to the right to indicate the points represented by $y < 2x$.

STEP 3: The solution to the system of inequalities is the area labelled S, which consists of the region containing *both* types of cross-hatching and any portion of the *solid* line on its boundary.

37. Let $x$ = the positive number

The square of the positive number is 4 times the number and 12 more.

$$x^2 \qquad = \qquad 4x \qquad + \quad 12$$

The equation to use is: $\qquad\qquad\qquad\qquad\qquad x^2 = 4x + 12$

This is a *quadratic equation*. Rearrange it so that all terms are on one side equal to zero by adding $-4x$ (the additive inverse of $4x$) and $-12$ (the additive inverse of $+12$) to both sides:

$$\underline{-4x - 12 = -4x - 12}$$
$$x^2 - 4x - 12 = 0$$

The left side is a *quadratic trinomial* which can be factored into the product of two binomials. The factors of the first term, $x^2$, are $x$ and $x$, and they become the first terms of the binomials:

$$(x\quad)(x\quad) = 0$$

The factors of the last term, $-12$, become the last terms of the binomials but they must be selected in such a way that the sum of the inner product and the outer product equals the middle term, $-4x$, of the original trinomial. Try $-6$ and $+2$ as the factors of $-12$:

$$-6x = \text{inner product}$$
$$(x - 6)(x + 2) = 0$$

Since $(-6x) + (+2x) = -4x$, these are the correct factors:

$$+2x = \text{outer product}$$
$$(x - 6)(x + 2) = 0$$

If the product of two factors is zero, either factor may equal zero:

$$x - 6 = 0 \ \text{ OR } \ x + 2 = 0$$

Add the appropriate additive inverse to both sides of the equation, $+6$ for the left

equation, and −2 for the right equation:
Reject the negative value since the question calls for a *positive* number:

$$+6 = +6 \qquad -2 = -2$$
$$x \quad = \quad 6 \qquad x \quad = -2$$
$$x = 6$$

The number is 6.

**38 a.** Since $\overline{AD} \cong \overline{BC}$, and $AD = 12$, then $BC = 12$.

Since ABCD is a rectangle, its opposite sides are congruent; therefore $\overline{DC} \cong \overline{AB}$ and $DC = 15$.

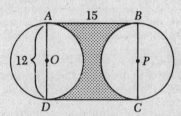

The perimeter of a rectangle is the sum of the lengths of all four sides:

The perimeter of $ABCD = 15 + 12 + 15 + 12 = 54$

The perimeter of rectangle $ABCD$ = **54**.

**b.** The area of a rectangle is equal to the product of its length and width:

Area of $ABCD = 15 \times 12 = 180$

The area of rectangle $ABCD$ = **180**.

**c.** The diameter, $AD$, of circle $O$ is 12. The radius, $OA$, is half the length of the diameter:
The radius = 6

The radius of circle $O$ = **6**.

**d.** The area, $A$, of a circle is given by the formula:
where $r$ is the radius.
From part **c**, $r = 6$:

$$A = \pi r^2$$
$$A = \pi(6)^2$$
$$A = 36\pi$$

The area of circle $O$ is **$36\pi$**.

**e.** The area of the shaded region is the area of rectangle $ABCD$ minus the area of two half-circles. This is equivalent to the area of rectangle $ABCD$ minus the area of one complete circle.

From part **b**, the area of $ABCD = 180$
From part **d**, the area of circle $O = 36\pi$
The area of the shaded region = $180 - 36\pi$
The shaded area = **$180 - 36\pi$**.

**39.** The given system is:

$$3x + 2y = 6$$
$$5x - 3y = -28$$

Multiply each term of the first equation by 3 and each term of the second equation by 2:

$$3(3x) + 3(2y) = 3(6)$$
$$2(5x) - 2(3y) = 2(-28)$$
$$9x + 6y = 18$$
$$10x - 6y = -56$$

Adding the two equations will eliminate $y$:   $19x$   $=$   $-38$

Divide both sides of the equation by 19:   $\dfrac{19x}{19}$   $=$   $\dfrac{-38}{19}$

$x$   $=$   $-2$

Substitute $-2$ for $x$ in the first original equation:   $3(-2) + 2y$   $=$   $6$

$-6 + 2y$   $=$   $6$

Add $+6$ (the additive inverse of $-6$) to both sides of the equation:   $+6$   $=$   $+6$

$2y$   $=$   $12$

Divide both sides of the equation by 2:   $\dfrac{2y}{2}$   $=$   $\dfrac{12}{2}$

$y$   $=$   $6$

The solution is $(-2, 6)$ or $x = -2, y = 6$.

CHECK: The supposed solution, $x = -2, y = 6$, must satisfy *both original* equations when these values are substituted for $x$ and $y$ respectively:

$$3x + 2y = 6 \qquad\qquad 5x - 3y = -28$$

$$3(-2) + 2(6) \overset{?}{=} 6 \qquad\qquad 5(-2) - 3(6) \overset{?}{=} -28$$

$$-6 + 12 \overset{?}{=} 6 \qquad\qquad -10 - 18 \overset{?}{=} -28$$

$$6 = 6 \checkmark \qquad\qquad -28 = -28 \checkmark$$

**40 a.** Let $x =$ the length of the shorter leg

Then $x + 7 =$ the length of the longer leg

And $x + 8 =$ the length of the hypotenuse

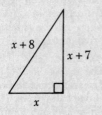

The perimeter of the triangle is 30, that is, the sum of the lengths of the three sides is 30:   $x + x + 7 + x + 8 =$   $30$

Combine like terms:   $3x + 15 =$   $30$

Add $-15$ (the additive inverse of $+15$) to both sides of the equation:   $-15 = -15$

$3x$   $=$   $15$

Divide both sides of the equation by 3:   $\dfrac{3x}{3}$   $=$   $\dfrac{15}{3}$

$x =$   $5$

$x + 7 =$   $12$

The lengths of the legs are **5** and **12**.

**b.** The area, $A$, of a right triangle equals one-half the product of the lengths of the legs:

$$A = \frac{1}{2}(5)(12)$$
$$A = \frac{1}{2}(60)$$
$$A = 30$$

The area of the triangle is **30**.

**41 a.**

| Number | Frequency |
|--------|-----------|
| 6 | 3 |
| 7 | 10 |
| 8 | 1 |
| 9 | 4 |
| 10 | 2 |

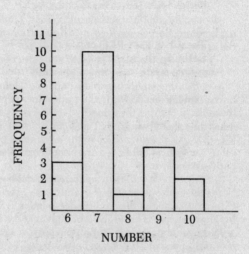

**b.** The mode is the number occurring most frequently; the mode is 7 since 7 occurs 10 times
The mode is **7**.
**c.** The probability of an event occurring $= \dfrac{\text{the number of favorable cases}}{\text{the total possible number of cases}}$.

For choosing a 7, the number of favorable cases is 10 since the frequency with which 7 was selected was 10. The total possible number of cases is the sum of all the frequencies: $3 + 10 + 1 + 4 + 2 = 20$.

The probability of selecting a 7 is $\dfrac{10}{20}$.

The probability is $\dfrac{\mathbf{10}}{\mathbf{20}}$.

**d.** There were no selections of numbers less than 6; therefore the number of favorable cases for choosing a number less than 6 is 0.

The probability of choosing a number less than 6 is $\dfrac{0}{20} = 0$.

The probability is **0**.

**42 a.**

| $p$ | $q$ | $\sim p$ | $(p \to q)$ | $(\sim p \vee q)$ | $(p \to q) \leftrightarrow (\sim p \vee q)$ |
|-----|-----|----------|-------------|-------------------|--------------------------------------------|
| T | T | F | T | T | T |
| T | F | F | F | F | T |
| F | T | T | T | T | T |
| F | F | T | T | T | T |

All possible combinations of truth values, T and F, must be considered for $p$ and $q$. Therefore, the column for $q$ must be filled in with T, F, T, F in that order to match the order of T, T, F, F already filled in for $p$.

$\sim p$ is the *negation* of $p$. The truth values for the column for $\sim p$ are the opposite of those for $p$ on the same line of the table.

$(p \to q)$ is the *implication* that $p$ implies $q$. Determine the proper entries for the $(p \to q)$ column according to the truth values of $p$ and $q$ in the first two columns of the table. $(p \to q)$ has the value T whenever $q$ is T and also when $p$ and $q$ are both F; it has the value F when $p$ is T and $q$ is F.

$(\sim p \vee q)$ is the *disjunction* of the *negation* of $p$ with $q$. The disjunction has the value T whenever either $\sim p$ or $q$ or both have the value T; it has the value F when both $\sim p$ and $q$ are F.

$(p \to q) \leftrightarrow (\sim p \vee q)$ is an *equivalence relation* between $(p \to q)$ and $(\sim p \vee q)$. When the truth values of $(p \to q)$ and $(\sim p \vee q)$ are the same, that is, both T or both F, the truth value of the equivalence relation is T; otherwise it is F.

**b.** This question is best solved by reducing the statements to symbolic form.

The given statement is "If Rob can borrow a car, then he will take Susan to the prom." Represent "If Rob can borrow a car" by $p$, and "He will take Susan to the prom" by $q$. The given statement is then represented by the *implication*, $(p \to q)$.

Consider each choice in turn:

(1) "If Ron can not borrow a car, then he will not take Susan to the prom" is represented by $\sim p \to \sim q$. The hypothesis, $p$, and conclusion, $q$, of the original statement, $p \to q$, have both been negated, so $\sim p \to \sim q$ is the *inverse* of $p \to q$. The inverse of a statement is not logically equivalent to it; for example, if $p$ is F and $q$ is T, then $p \to q$ is T but $\sim p \to \sim q$ is F.

(2) "Rob can borrow a car and he will take Susan to the prom" is represented by the *conjunction*, $p \wedge q$. The conjunction is not logically equivalent to the original statement, $p \to q$; for example, if $p$ and $q$ are both F, then $p \to q$ is T but $p \wedge q$ is F.

(3) "It is not the case that Rob will borrow a car or take Susan to the prom" is represented by the *negation* of the *disjunction* of $p$ and $q$, $\sim (p \vee q)$. $\sim (p \vee q)$ is not equivalent to $(p \to q)$; for example, if $p$ and $q$ are T, then $p \to q$ is T but $\sim (p \vee q)$ is F.

(4) "Rob can not borrow a car or he will take Susan to the prom" is represented by the *disjunction*, $(\sim p \vee q)$. $(\sim p \vee q)$ is the logical equivalent of $(p \to q)$ since the table in part **a** shows the *equivalence relation*, $(p \to q) \leftrightarrow (\sim p \vee q)$, to have the truth value T for all possible values of $p$ and $q$.

The correct choice is **(4)**.

## SELF-ANALYSIS CHART    June 1986

| Topic | Question Numbers | Number of Points | Your Points | Your Percentage |
|---|---|---|---|---|
| 1. Numbers (rat'l, irrat'l); Percent | 7 | 2 | | |
| 2. Properties of No. Systems | — | 0 | | |
| 3. Operations of Rat'l Nos. and Monomials | 20, 25 | $2 + 2 = 4$ | | |
| 4. Operations on Poly-nomials | 14 | 2 | | |
| 5. Square root; Operations involving Radicals | 32 | 2 | | |
| 6. Evaluating Formulas and Expressions | 5, 22 | $2 + 2 = 4$ | | |
| 7. Linear Equations (simple cases incl. parentheses) | 2, 10 | $2 + 2 = 4$ | | |
| 8. Linear Equations contain-ing Decimals or Fractions | 4, 13 | $2 + 2 = 4$ | | |
| 9. Graphs of Linear Functions (slope) | 27, 30 | $2 + 2 = 4$ | | |
| 10. Inequalities | 23, 33 | $2 + 2 = 4$ | | |
| 11. Systems of Eqs. & Inequal. (alg. & graphic solutions) | 6, 36, 39 | $2 + 10 + 10 = 22$ | | |
| 12. Factoring | 19 | 2 | | |
| 13. Quadratic Equations | 37 | 10 | | |
| 14. Verbal Problems | 12, 40a | $2 + 8 = 10$ | | |
| 15. Variation | 29 | 2 | | |
| 16. Literal Eqs.; Expressing Relations Algebraically | 15 | 2 | | |
| 17. Factorial n | — | 0 | | |
| 18. Areas, Perims., Circums., Vols. of Common Figures | 16, 38a,b,c, d,e, 40b | $2 + 2 + 2 + 2 + 2 + 2 + 2 = 14$ | | |
| 19. Geometry ($\cong$, $\angle$ meas., $\parallel$ lines, compls., suppl., const.) | 1, 11, 18, 26 | $2 + 2 + 2 + 2 = 8$ | | |
| 20. Ratio & Proportion (incl. similar triangles) | 8 | 2 | | |
| 21. Pythagorean Theorem | 17 | 2 | | |
| 22. Logic (symbolic rep., logical forms, truth tables) | 3, 31, 34, 42a,b | $2 + 2 + 2 + 8 + 2 = 16$ | | |
| 23. Probability (incl. tree diagrams & sample spaces) | 9, 21, 41c,d | $2 + 2 + 2 + 2 = 8$ | | |
| 24. Combinations (arrange-ments, permutations) | 24, 35 | $2 + 2 = 4$ | | |
| 25. Statistics (central tend., freq. dist., histograms) | 28, 41a,b | $2 + 4 + 2 = 8$ | | |

# Examination   January 1987

## Three-Year Sequence for High School Mathematics — Course I

### PART ONE

DIRECTIONS: *Answer 30 questions from this part. Each correct answer will receive 2 credits. No partial credit will be allowed. Write your answers in the spaces provided. Where applicable, answers may be left in terms of π or in radical form.*

1 Solve for $x$:   $4x - 2 = x + 7$

1_____

2 A cookie jar contains 3 vanilla, 2 chocolate chip, and 7 gingersnap cookies. If one cookie is taken at random from the jar, what is the probability that it will be a vanilla cookie?

2_____

3 In the accompanying diagram of triangle $XYZ$ and triangle $ABC$, $\angle X \cong \angle A$ and $\angle Y \cong \angle B$. If $XY = 5$, $YZ = 12$, and $AB = 15$, what is $BC$?

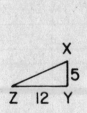 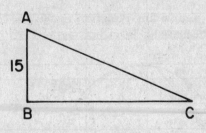

3_____

4 Solve the following system of equations for $x$:

$$2x + 3y = 5$$
$$4x - 3y = 1$$

4_____

1

5 Solve for $x$: $0.4x + 3 = 15$ 5____

6 Solve for $x$: $4(x - 2) - 3 = 9$ 6____

7 In a scale drawing of New York State, 2.5 centimeters represents 10 kilometers. How many kilometers are represented by 10 centimeters? 7____

8 If the product of $4x$ and $5x$ is $ax^2$, find the value of $a$. 8____

9 If $y + 1$ is an even integer, what is the next consecutive even integer? 9____

10 The measures of the angles of a triangle are represented by $4x$, $x + 40$, and $2x$. Find the value of $x$. 10____

11 When a fair die is tossed, what is the probability of getting a number divisible by both 2 and 3? 11____

12 Evaluate the expression $3x^2 + y$ if $x = 1$ and $y = -3$. 12____

13 In the accompanying diagram, $m\overarc{BC} = 120$. Find the measure of inscribed angle $BAC$.

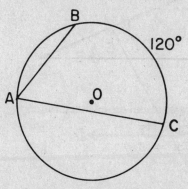

13____

14 If job $A$ can be done in 5 ways and job $B$ can be done in 6 ways, in how many different ways may the two jobs be completed?

14____

15 Solve for $D$ in terms of $C$ and $\pi$: $C = \pi D$

15____

16 Factor: $x^2 - 6x - 7$

16____

17 Solve for $y$: $\dfrac{y}{12} = \dfrac{3}{8}$

17____

18 Find the positive root of the equation $4x^2 - 36 = 0$.

18____

19 Express in simplest form:

$(5a^2 - 3a + 8) + (-4a^2 - 1) + (15a + 11)$

19____

20 In the accompanying diagram, $\overleftrightarrow{AB}$ is parallel to $\overleftrightarrow{CD}$, and $\overleftrightarrow{AB}$ and $\overleftrightarrow{CD}$ are cut by transversal $\overleftrightarrow{EF}$ at points $G$ and $H$, respectively. If $m\angle EGA = (2x + 30)$ and $m\angle EHC = (x + 80)$, find $x$.

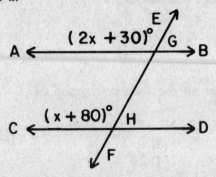

20____

DIRECTIONS (21–34): *For each question chosen, write in the space provided the* numeral *preceding the word or expression that best completes the statement or answers the question.*

21 Let $p$ represent "Jane is a librarian," and let $q$ represent "Jane is a lawyer." Which statement represents "If Jane is not a librarian, then Jane is a lawyer"?

(1) $\sim p \wedge q$      (3) $\sim p \vee q$

(2) $\sim p \rightarrow q$      (4) $\sim(p \rightarrow q)$     21____

22 Pat's grades on Course I tests were 90, 75, 98, 82, 90, and 87. The mode of her grades is

(1) 90      (3) 87

(2) 89      (4) 82     22____

23 The greatest common factor of the numbers 12, 40, and 60 is

(1) 480      (3) 5

(2) 2      (4) 4     23____

24 If $15x^6y$ is divided by $-3x^3$, the quotient is

(1) $-5x^2$      (3) $5x^2$

(2) $-5x^3y$      (4) $5x^3y$     24____

25 Which point satisfies the inequality $2x + y > 10$?

(1) (2,3)      (3) (3,2)

(2) (3,4)      (4) (4,3)     25____

26 What is the median of the following group of numbers?

$$5, 6, 6, 10, 10, 17$$

(1) 6      (3) 9

(2) 8      (4) 10     26____

27 In the accompanying truth table, which statement should be the heading for column 4?

| Column 1 | Column 2 | Column 3 | Column 4 |
|----------|----------|----------|----------|
| $p$ | $q$ | $\sim q$ | ? |
| T | T | F | F |
| T | F | T | T |
| F | T | F | F |
| F | F | T | F |

(1) $p \wedge \sim q$      (3) $p \rightarrow \sim q$

(2) $p \vee \sim q$      (4) $\sim q \rightarrow p$      27____

28 The length of a rectangle is represented by $(x + 4)$ and the width is represented by $(x - 2)$. Which expression represents the area of the rectangle?

(1) $x^2 - 8$      (3) $x^2 + 2x - 8$

(2) $2x + 2$      (4) $4x + 4$      28____

29 What is the perimeter of a square whose area is 64?

(1) 16      (3) 64

(2) 32      (4) 256      29____

30 The graph of the line passing through the points (6,7) and (4,2) has a slope of

(1) $\frac{2}{5}$      (3) $\frac{5}{2}$

(2) $-\frac{5}{2}$      (4) $-\frac{1}{2}$      30____

31 Which is an irrational number?

(1) 0      (3) $-\frac{1}{3}$

(2) $\pi$      (4) $\sqrt{9}$      31____

32 If the lengths of the legs of a right triangle are 5 and 12, what is the length of the hypotenuse?

(1) $\sqrt{119}$          (3) 17

(2) $\sqrt{17}$          (4) 13        32____

33 The accompanying diagram shows the graph of which inequality?

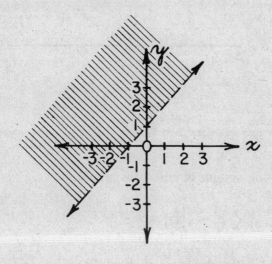

(1) $y < x + 1$        (3) $y \leq x + 1$

(2) $y > x + 1$        (4) $y \geq x + 1$     33____

34 The probability of team $A$ beating team $B$ is $\frac{3}{5}$. What is the probability that team $A$ will win two consecutive games from team $B$?

(1) $\frac{9}{25}$        (3) $\frac{6}{25}$

(2) $\frac{4}{25}$        (4) $\frac{16}{25}$     34____

DIRECTIONS (35): *Leave all construction lines in the answer.*

35 Using point $A$ as an endpoint, construct a line segment $\overline{AB}$ whose length is twice the length of line segment $\overline{CD}$.

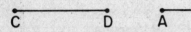

## PART TWO

DIRECTIONS: *Answer four questions from this part. Show all work unless otherwise directed.*

36 Solve the following system of equations graphically and check:
$$3x + y = 3$$
$$y = 2x - 7 \qquad [8,2]$$

37 In the accompanying diagram of circle $O$, diameter $AC = 8$, $\text{m}\widehat{CD}$ and $\text{m}\widehat{BC}$ are in a ratio of 1:2, and $\overline{BO} \perp \overline{CO}$.

a Find $AO$.    [1]
b Find $\text{m}\angle BCA$.    [2]
c Find $\text{m}\widehat{CD}$.    [2]
d Find $\text{m}\angle AOD$.    [2]
e Find $BC$. [Answer may be left in radical form.]    [3]

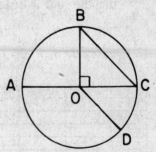

38 One positive number is 8 more than another. The sum of their squares is 130. Find both numbers. [*Only an algebraic solution will be accepted.*] [4,6]

39 Solve the following system of equations algebraically and check:

$$x - \frac{1}{2}y = 4$$
$$x + y = 7$$

[8,2]

40 Ace Construction built five less than twice the number of houses that Ben's Construction built. If the total number of houses built by both firms was 115, how many did each build? [*Only an algebraic solution will be accepted.*] [5,5]

41 A fair die and a fair coin are tossed.
   *a* Draw a tree diagram or list the sample space of all possible pairs of outcomes. [4]
   *b* What is the probability of obtaining a 5 on the die and a tail on the coin? [2]
   *c* What is the probability of obtaining an even number on the die and a head on the coin? [2]
   *d* What is the probability of obtaining an 8 on the die and a head on the coin? [2]

42 *Complete the truth table for the statement* $(p \wedge q) \rightarrow [(p \vee q) \leftrightarrow (p \rightarrow q)]$. [10]

| $p$ | $q$ | $(p \wedge q)$ | $(p \vee q)$ | $(p \rightarrow q)$ | $[(p \vee q) \leftrightarrow (p \rightarrow q)]$ | $(p \wedge q) \rightarrow [(p \vee q) \leftrightarrow (p \rightarrow q)]$ |
|---|---|---|---|---|---|---|
| T | T | | | | | |
| T | F | | | | | |
| F | T | | | | | |
| F | F | | | | | |

## Three-Year Sequence for High School Mathematics—Course I

### ANSWER KEY

#### PART ONE

1. 3
2. $\dfrac{3}{12}$ or $\dfrac{1}{4}$
3. 36
4. 1
5. 30
6. 5
7. 40
8. 20
9. $y + 3$
10. 20
11. $\dfrac{1}{6}$
12. 0

13. 60
14. 30
15. $\dfrac{C}{\pi}$
16. $(x - 7)(x + 1)$
17. $4\dfrac{1}{2}$
18. 3
19. $a^2 + 12a + 18$
20. 50
21. (2)
22. (1)
23. (4)
24. (2)

25. (4)
26. (2)
27. (1)
28. (3)
29. (2)
30. (3)
31. (2)
32. (4)
33. (2)
34. (1)
35. construction

Part Two—*See* Answers Explained.

### ANSWERS EXPLAINED

#### PART ONE

1. The given equation is:

$$4x - 2 = x + 7$$

Add $-x$, the additive inverse of $x$, and also add $+2$, the additive inverse of $-2$, to both sides of the equation:

$$\dfrac{-x + 2 = -x + 2}{3x \quad\quad = \quad\quad 9}$$

Divide both sides of the equation by 3:

$$\dfrac{3x}{3} = \dfrac{9}{3}$$
$$x = 3$$

$x = 3$.

**2.** Probability of an event occurring equals

$$\frac{\text{number of favorable cases}}{\text{total possible number of cases}}.$$

Since there are 3 vanilla cookies in the jar, the number of favorable cases for picking a vanilla cookie at random is 3.

The total possible number of cases is the total number of all cookies, vanilla, chocolate chip, and gingersnap: $3 + 2 + 7 = 12$.

The probability of picking a vanilla cookie is $\frac{3}{12}$ or $\frac{1}{4}$.

The probability is $\frac{3}{12}$ or $\frac{1}{4}$.

**3.** Let $x = BC$.

Since $\angle X \cong \angle A$ and $\angle Y \cong \angle B$, $\triangle XYZ$ is similar to $\triangle ABC$ (two triangles are similar if they agree in two corresponding angles).

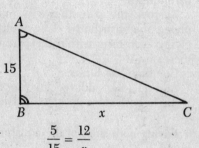

Corresponding sides of similar triangles are in proportion:

$$\frac{5}{15} = \frac{12}{x}$$

In a proportion, the product of the means equals the product of the extremes (cross-multiply):

$$5x = 15(12)$$
$$5x = 180$$

Divide both sides of the equation by 5:

$$\frac{5x}{5} = \frac{180}{5}$$
$$x = 36$$

$BC = 36$.

**4.** The given system of equations is:

$$2x + 3y = 5$$
$$4x - 3y = 1$$

Add the two equations to eliminate $y$:

$$6x = 6$$

Divide both sides of the equation by 6:

$$\frac{6x}{6} = \frac{6}{6}$$
$$x = 1$$

$x = 1$.

**5.** The given equation contains a decimal coefficient:

$$0.4x + 3 = 15$$

Clear decimals by multiplying each term on both sides of the equation by 10:

$$10(0.4x) + 10(3) = 10(15)$$
$$4x + 30 = 150$$

Add $-30$, the additive inverse of $+30$, to both sides of the equation:

$$\underline{\phantom{4x}-30 = -30}$$
$$4x \phantom{==} = 120$$

Divide both sides of the equation by 4:

$$\frac{4x}{4} = \frac{120}{4}$$
$$x = 30$$

$x = 30$.

**6.** The given equation contains parentheses:

$$4(x - 2) - 3 = 9$$

Remove the parentheses by applying the distributive law, multiplying each term within the parentheses by 4:

$$4x - 8 - 3 = 9$$

Combine like terms:

$$4x - 11 = 9$$

Add 11, the additive inverse of $-11$, to both sides of the equation:

$$\underline{\phantom{4x}11 = 11}$$
$$4x \phantom{==} = 20$$

Divide both sides of the equation by 4:

$$\frac{4x}{4} = \frac{20}{4}$$
$$x = 5$$

$x = 5$.

**7.** Let $x$ = the number of kilometers represented by 10 centimeters. On the scale drawing, 2.5 centimeters represents 10 kilometers.

In a scale drawing, the ratio of any real distance to its representation is the same as the ratio of any other real distance to its representation:

$$\frac{10}{2.5} = \frac{x}{10}$$

In a proportion, the product of the means equals the product of the extremes (cross-multiply):

$$2.5x = 10(10)$$
$$2.5x = 100$$

Clear decimals by multiplying both sides of the equation by 10:

$$10(2.5x) = 10(100)$$
$$25x = 1,000$$
$$\frac{25x}{25} = \frac{1,000}{25}$$

Divide both sides of the equation by 25:

10 centimeters represents **40** kilometers.

$$x = 40$$

**8.** The product of $4x$ and $5x$ is $ax^2$:

$$(4x)(5x) = ax^2$$

To multiply the two monomials, $4x$ and $5x$, multiply their coefficients to get the coefficient of the product $(4 \cdot 5 = 20)$, and multiply their literal factors to get the literal factor of the product $(x \cdot x = x^2$ since powers of the same base are multiplied by adding their exponents):

$$20x^2 = ax^2$$

Divide both sides of the equation by $x^2$:

$$\frac{20x^2}{x^2} = \frac{ax^2}{x^2}$$

$a = 20$.

$$20 = a$$

**9.** Consecutive even integers (such as 2, 4, 6, 8, . . .) differ by 2. Therefore the next consecutive even integer after $y + 1$ is $y + 1 + 2$ or $y + 3$.

The next consecutive even integer is $y + 3$.

**10.** The sum of the measures of the angles of a triangle is 180°:

$$4x + x + 40 + 2x = 180$$

Combine like terms:

$$7x + 40 = 180$$

Add $-40$, the additive inverse of $+40$, to both sides of the equation:

$$\frac{-40 = -40}{7x \quad = 140}$$

Divide both sides of the equation by 7:

$$\frac{7x}{7} = \frac{140}{7}$$

$x = 20$.

$$x = 20$$

**11.** Probability of an event occurring equals

$$\frac{\text{number of favorable cases}}{\text{total possible number of cases}}$$

A die contains 6 faces having the numbers 1, 2, 3, 4, 5, and 6. Only one of these numbers, 6, is divisible by both 2 and 3. Thus there is only one favorable case for getting a number divisible by both 2 and 3 in a toss of a fair die.

The total number of possible cases arising from the toss of a die is 6, the total number of faces on a die.

The probability of getting a number divisible by both 2 and 3 is $\frac{1}{6}$.

The probability is $\frac{1}{6}$.

12. The given expression is: $3x^2 + y$

To evaluate the expression if $x = 1$ and $y = -3$, substitute 1 for $x$ and $-3$ for $y$: $3(1)^2 + (-3)$

Square 1: $3(1) - 3$

Remove parentheses by multiplying 1 by 3: $3 - 3$

Combine like terms: $0$

The value of the expression is **0**.

13. The measure of an inscribed angle is equal to one-half the measure of its intercepted arc:

$$m\angle BAC = \frac{1}{2}\, mBC$$

$mBC = 120$:

$$m\angle BAC = \frac{1}{2}\,(120)$$

$$m\angle BAC = 60$$

$m\angle BAC = $ **60**.

14. Each of the 5 ways of doing job $A$ may be combined with each of the 6 ways of doing job $B$. Therefore, the two jobs may be completed in $5 \times 6$ or 30 different ways.

**30 different ways.**

15. The given formula is: $C = \pi D$

To solve for $D$, isolate $D$ on the right side by dividing both sides of the equation by $\pi$:

$$\frac{C}{\pi} = \frac{\pi D}{\pi}$$

$$\frac{C}{\pi} = D$$

$$D = \frac{C}{\pi}.$$

**16.**   The given expression is a *quadratic trinomial*:

$$x^2 - 6x - 7$$

A quadratic trinomial may be factored into the product of two binomials. The factors of the first term, $x^2$, are $x$ and $x$, and they become the first terms of the binomials:

$$(x \quad )(x \quad )$$

The factors of the last term, $-7$, become the second terms of the binomials, but they must be chosen in such a way that the product of the inner terms and the product of the outer terms add up to the middle term, $-6x$, of the original trinomial. Try $-7$ and $+1$ as the factors of $-7$:

$$-7x = \text{inner product}$$
$$(x - 7)(x + 1)$$
$$+x = \text{outer product}$$

Since $(-7x) + (+x) = -6x$, these are the correct factors:

$$(x - 7)(x + 1)$$

The factored form is $(x - 7)(x + 1)$.

**17.**   The given expression has the form of a proportion (two equal ratios):

$$\frac{y}{12} = \frac{3}{8}$$

In a proportion, the product of the means equals the product of the extremes (cross-multiply):

$$8y = 12(3)$$
$$8y = 36$$

Divide both sides of the equation by 8:

$$\frac{8y}{8} = \frac{36}{8}$$

$$y = 4\frac{4}{8} = 4\frac{1}{2}$$

$$y = 4\frac{1}{2}.$$

**18.**   The given equation is:

$$4x^2 - 36 = 0$$

Add $+36$, the additive inverse of $-36$, to both sides of the equation:

$$\frac{+36 = +36}{4x^2 \quad = \quad 36}$$

Divide both sides of the equation by 4:

$$\frac{4x^2}{4} = \frac{36}{4}$$
$$x^2 = 9$$

Take the square root of each side of the equation:

$$x = \pm\sqrt{9}$$
$$x = \pm 3$$

The question calls for the positive root:

$$x = 3$$

The positive root is **3**.

**19.** The given expression is:

$$(5a^2 - 3a + 8) + (-4a^2 - 1) + (15a + 11)$$

Remove parentheses; if parentheses are preceded by a plus (+) sign, the signs of the terms inside the parentheses remain unchanged when the parentheses are removed: $\quad 5a^2 - 3a + 8 - 4a^2 - 1 + 15a + 11$

Combine like terms: $\qquad\qquad\qquad a^2 + 12a + 18$

The simplest form is $a^2 + 12a + 18$.

**20.** $\angle EGA$ and $\angle EHC$ are corresponding angles of the parallel lines $\overleftrightarrow{AB}$ and $\overleftrightarrow{CD}$

If a transversal cuts two parallel lines, the measures of the corresponding angles are equal:

$$m\angle EGA = m\angle EHC$$
$$2x + 30 = x + 80$$

Add $-x$, the additive inverse of $x$, and also add $-30$, the additive inverse of $+30$, to both sides of the equation:

$$\frac{-x - 30 = -x - 30}{x = 50}$$

$x = 50$.

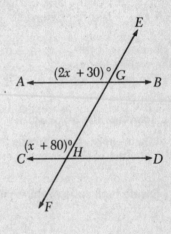

**21.** Given: $p$ = "Jane is a librarian" and $q$ = "Jane is a lawyer".
$\sim p$ is the *negation* of $p$; therefore, $\sim p$ = "Jane is not a librarian".
"If Jane is not a librarian, then Jane is a lawyer" is the *implication*
$\sim p \rightarrow q$.
The correct choice is (2).

**22.** Pat's grades were 90, 75, 98, 82, 90, 87.
The *mode* of a set of numbers is the number that occurs most frequently.
The mode of Pat's grades is 90, which occurs twice; each other grade occurs only once.
The correct choice is (1).

**23.** The greatest common factor of the numbers 12, 40, and 60 is the largest integer that will divide evenly into all of them.

Consider each choice in turn:

(1) 480 is larger than any of the given numbers, so it will not divide into 12, 40, or 60.

(2) 2 will divide into each of 12, 40, and 60.

(3) 5 will not divide evenly into 12.

(4) 4 will divide into each of 12, 40, and 60; also, it is larger than 2, which is also a common factor, and thus it is the greatest common factor.

The correct choice is (4).

**24.** The question is represented by the indicated quotient:

$$\frac{15x^6y}{-3x^3}$$

To divide two monomials, first divide their numerical coefficients to obtain the numerical coefficient of the quotient: $(15) \div (-3) = -5$.

Next divide their literal factors; remember that powers of the same base are divided by subtracting their exponents: $(x^6y) \div (x^3) = x^3y$.

Combine the two results:

$$\frac{15x^6y}{-3x^3} = -5x^3y$$

The correct choice is (2).

**25.** The given inequality is: $\qquad 2x + y > 10$

Test each choice in turn to see which satisfies the inequality:

(1) $(2, 3)$: $2(2) + 3 \overset{?}{>} 10$

$\qquad 4 + 3 \overset{?}{>} 10$

$\qquad 7 \not> 10 \qquad$ $(2, 3)$ does not satisfy the inequality.

(2) $(3, 4)$: $2(3) + 4 \overset{?}{>} 10$

$\qquad 6 + 4 \overset{?}{>} 10$

$\qquad 10 \not> 10 \qquad$ $(3, 4)$ does not satisfy the inequality.

(3) $(3, 2)$: $2(3) + 2 \overset{?}{>} 10$

$\qquad 6 + 2 \overset{?}{>} 10$

$\qquad 8 \not> 10 \qquad$ $(3, 2)$ does not satisfy the inequality.

(4) $(4, 3)$: $2(4) + 3 \overset{?}{>} 10$

$\qquad 8 + 3 \overset{?}{>} 10$

$\qquad 11 > 10 \;\checkmark \quad$ $(4, 3)$ satisfies the inequality.

The correct choice is (4).

**26.** The 6 given numbers are arranged in ascending order: 5, 6, 6, 10, 10, 17.

The *median* is the middle number of a group arranged in order of size if there is an odd number of numbers in the group. If there is an even number of numbers, as is the case here, the median is the average between the two middle numbers.

The third and fourth numbers in the given group are 6 and 10, and their average is

$$\frac{6 + 10}{2} \quad \text{or} \quad \frac{16}{2} \text{ or } 8$$

Thus, the median is 8.

The correct choice is **(2)**.

**27.**

| Column 1 | Column 2 | Column 3 | Column 4 |
|:--------:|:--------:|:--------:|:--------:|
| $p$ | $q$ | $\sim q$ | ? |
| T | T | F | F |
| T | F | T | T |
| F | T | F | F |
| F | F | T | F |

Consider each choice in turn:

(1) $p \wedge \sim q$ is the *conjunction* of $p$ and $\sim q$. The conjunction has the value T if and only if both $p$ and $\sim q$ have the value T. Since Column 4 is T only when both $p$ and $\sim q$ are T, this is the correct choice.

(2) $p \vee \sim q$ is the *disjunction* of $p$ and $\sim q$. The disjunction is T if either $p$ or $\sim q$, or both, have the value T. Since the last line in the table shows Column 4 to be F when $\sim q$ is T, Column 4 cannot be the disjunction.

(3) $p \rightarrow \sim q$ is the *implication* that, if $p$ is true, then $\sim q$ is true. This implication would be T whenever $\sim q$ is T or if both $p$ and $\sim q$ are F. But the last line of Column 4 is F when $\sim q$ is T, so Column 4 is not $p \rightarrow \sim q$.

(4) $\sim q \rightarrow p$ is the *implication* that, if $\sim q$ is true, then $p$ is true. This implication would have the value T whenever $p$ is T or if both $\sim q$ and $p$ are F. The first and third lines of the table contradict this condition, so Column 4 is not the implication $\sim q \rightarrow p$.

The correct choice is **(1)**.

**28.** The area, $A$, of a rectangle is equal to the product of its length and width:
$$A = (x + 4)(x - 2)$$
Multiply $x + 4$ by $x - 2$:

$$
\begin{array}{r}
x + 4 \\
x - 2 \\
\hline
x^2 + 4x \\
-2x - 8 \\
\hline
x^2 + 2x - 8 = A
\end{array}
$$

The correct choice is (3).

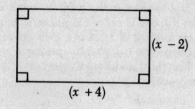

$(x - 2)$

$(x + 4)$

**29.** Let $x$ = the length of a side of the square.

The area, $A$, of a square equals the square of the length of one side: $A = x^2$
The area is 64: $64 = x^2$
Take the square root of each side of the equation: $\pm\sqrt{64} = x$
Reject the negative value as meaningless for a length: $8 = x$
The perimeter, $P$, is the sum of the lengths of all 4 sides:
$$P = 4x$$
$$P = 4(8)$$
$$P = 32$$

The correct choice is (2).

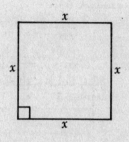

**30.** The slope, $m$, of a line joining the points $(x_1, y_1)$ and $(x_2, y_2)$ is given by the formula:
$$m = \frac{y_2 - y_1}{x_2 - x_1}$$
Let $x_1 = 4$, $y_1 = 2$; and $x_2 = 6$, $y_2 = 7$:
$$m = \frac{7 - 2}{6 - 4}$$
$$m = \frac{5}{2}$$

The slope is $\dfrac{5}{2}$.

The correct choice is (3).

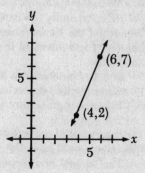

**31.** An irrational number *cannot* be expressed as the quotient of two integers.

Consider each choice in turn:

(1) 0 can be expressed as $\dfrac{0}{8}$, so 0 is rational.

(2) $\pi$ cannot be expressed as the quotient of two integers; it is approximately equal to 3.14159, but the decimal continues without termination and never repeats any pattern of digits. Therefore $\pi$ is irrational.

(3) $-\dfrac{1}{3}$ can be expressed as the quotient $\dfrac{-1}{3}$, so $-\dfrac{1}{3}$ is rational.

(4) $\sqrt{9}$ equals 3, which can be expressed as $\dfrac{3}{1}$; hence $\sqrt{9}$ is rational.

The correct choice is **(2)**.

**32.** Let $x$ = the length of the hypotenuse.

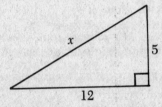

By the Pythagorean Theorem, in a right triangle the square of the length of the hypotenuse equals the sum of the squares of the lengths of the legs:

$$x^2 = 5^2 + 12^2$$

Square 5 and square 12:

$$x^2 = 25 + 144$$

Combine like terms:

$$x^2 = 169$$

Take the square root of each side of the equation:

$$x = \pm\,\sqrt{169}$$

Reject the negative value as meaningless for a length:

$$x = 13$$

The length of the hypotenuse is 13.

The correct choice is **(4)**.

**33.** All 4 choices involve the line $y = x + 1$, as a boundary of the graph. On the graph, the line $y = x + 1$ is shown as a broken line, indicating that points on it are not part of the graph. This rules out choice (3), $y \leq x + 1$, and choice (4), $y \geq x + 1$, in both of which the line $y = x + 1$ would be included as part of the graph.

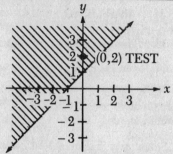

For any given value of $x$, all points on the shaded portion of the graph have $y$-values that are greater than the corresponding $y$-value on the line $y = x + 1$. Hence, for all such points, $y > x + 1$, which is choice 2.

ALTERNATIVE SOLUTION: Choose a test point, say $(0, 2)$, within the shaded portion of the graph, and substitute to see whether its coordinates satisfy choice (1) or choice (2):

(1) $y \overset{?}{<} x + 1$
  $2 \overset{?}{<} 0 + 1$
  $2 \not< 1$ (inequality not satisfied)
The correct choice is (2).

(2) $y \overset{?}{>} x + 1$
  $2 \overset{?}{>} 0 + 1$
  $2 > 1 \checkmark$ (inequality satisfied)

**34.** The probability of two independent events occurring is the product of their separate probabilities. Since the probability of team $A$ beating team $B$ is $\dfrac{3}{5}$, the probability that team $A$ will win two consecutive games from team $B$ is $\dfrac{3}{5} \times \dfrac{3}{5}$ or $\dfrac{9}{25}$

The correct choice is (1).

**35.**

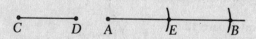

STEP 1: With the point of the compasses on $C$, open the compasses to a radius equal to $CD$.

STEP 2: With the point of the compasses on $A$, and a radius equal to $CD$, describe an arc cutting the ray from $A$ in point $E$.

STEP 3: With the point of the compasses on $E$, and a radius equal to $CD$, describe an arc cutting ray $\overrightarrow{AE}$ at $B$.

$\overline{AB}$ is the required line segment whose length is twice that of $\overline{CD}$.

### PART TWO

**36.**  The given system of equations is:
$$3x + y = 3$$
$$y = 2x - 7$$

STEP 1: Draw the graph of $3x + y = 3$. It is convenient to first solve the equation for $y$ by adding $-3x$, the additive inverse of $3x$, to both sides:

$$3x + y = 3$$
$$\underline{-3x \qquad\;\; = \quad -3x}$$
$$y = 3 - 3x$$

Select any 3 convenient values for $x$, and substitute them in the equation $y = 3 - 3x$ to determine the corresponding values of $y$:

| $x$ | $3 - 3x$ | $=$ | $y$ |
|-----|----------|-----|-----|
| $-2$ | $3 - 3(-2) = 3 + 6$ | $=$ | $9$ |
| $0$ | $3 - 3(0) = 3 - 0$ | $=$ | $3$ |
| $3$ | $3 - 3(3) = 3 - 9$ | $=$ | $-6$ |

Plot the points $(-2, 9)$, $(0, 3)$, and $(3, -6)$, and draw a straight line through them. This line is the graph of $3x + y = 3$.

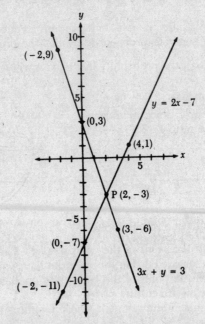

STEP 2: Draw the graph of $y = 2x - 7$. Select any 3 convenient values for $x$, and substitute them in the equation $y = 2x - 7$ to determine the corresponding values of $y$:

| $x$ | $2x - 7$ | $=$ $y$ |
|---|---|---|
| $-2$ | $2(-2) - 7 = -4 - 7$ | $= -11$ |
| $0$ | $2(0) - 7 = \quad 0 - 7$ | $= -7$ |
| $4$ | $2(4) - 7 = \quad 8 - 7$ | $= 1$ |

Plot the points $(-2, -11)$, $(0, -7)$, and $(4, 1)$, and draw a straight line through them. This line is the graph of $y = 2x - 7$.

STEP 3: The coordinates of the point of intersection of the two lines represent the solution to the system of equations. The graphs intersect at the point $P(2, -3)$.

CHECK: To check, substitute 2 for $x$ and $-3$ for $y$ in *both original* equations to see whether each is satisfied:

$$3x + y = 3 \qquad y = 2x - 7$$
$$3(2) - 3 \overset{?}{=} 3 \qquad -3 \overset{?}{=} 2(2) - 7$$
$$6 - 3 \overset{?}{=} 3 \qquad -3 \overset{?}{=} 4 - 7$$
$$3 = 3 \checkmark \qquad -3 = -3 \checkmark$$

The solution is $x = 2$, $y = -3$ or $\{(2, -3)\}$.

**37.** Let $x = m\overset{\frown}{CD}$.

Then $2x = m\overset{\frown}{BC}$ since $m\overset{\frown}{CD}$ and $m\overset{\frown}{BC}$ are in the ratio 1 : 2.

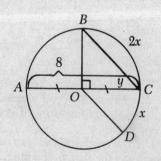

**a.** The length of a radius is one-half the length of a diameter:

$$AO = \frac{1}{2}(AC)$$

It is given that $AC = 8$:

$$AO = \frac{1}{2}(8)$$

$$AO = 4$$

$AO = 4$.

**b.** Radii of the same circle are congruent:

$$CO = OB$$

Therefore right triangle $AOC$ is isosceles.

Let $y = m\angle BCA$; the base angles of an isosceles triangle are congruent:

$$m\angle CBO = y$$

The sum of the measures of the 3 angles of a triangle is 180°:

$$m\angle BCA + m\angle CBO + m\angle BOC = 180$$
$$y + y + 90 = 180$$

Combine like terms:

$$2y + 90 = 180$$

Add $-90$, the additive inverse of 90, to both sides of the equation:

$$\frac{-90 = -90}{2y = 90}$$

Divide both sides of the equation by 2:

$$\frac{2y}{2} = \frac{90}{2}$$

$$m\angle BCA = \mathbf{45}.$$

$$y = 45$$

**c.** The measure of a central angle equals the measure of its intercepted arc:

$$m\angle BOC = m\widehat{BC}$$

$m\angle BOC = 90°$; $m\widehat{BC} = 2x$:

$$90 = 2x$$

Divide both sides of the equation by 2:

$$\frac{90}{2} = \frac{2x}{2}$$

$$45 = x$$

$m\widehat{CD} = x$:

$$m\widehat{CD} = 45$$

$$m\widehat{CD} = \mathbf{45}.$$

**d.** The measure of a central angle equals the measure of its intercepted arc:

$$m\angle COD = m\widehat{CD} = 45$$

$\angle AOD$ and $\angle COD$ are supplementary; the sum of the measures of two supplementary angles is 180°:

$$m\angle AOD + m\angle COD = 180$$
$$m\angle AOD + 45 = 180$$

Add $-45$, the additive inverse of $+45$, to both sides of the equation:

$$\frac{-45 = -45}{m\angle AOD = 135}$$

$$m\angle AOD = \mathbf{135}.$$

e. By the Pythagorean Theorem, in a right triangle the square of the length of the hypotenuse equals the sum of the squares of the lengths of the legs:

$$(BC)^2 = (BO)^2 + (CO)^2$$

From part a, $AO = 4$; radii of the same circle are congruent:

$$BO = CO = AO = 4$$
$$(BC)^2 = (4)^2 + (4)^2$$
$$(BC)^2 = 16 + 16$$
$$(BC)^2 = 32$$

Take the square root of each side of the equation:

$$BC = \pm \sqrt{32}$$

Reject the negative value as meaningless for a length:

$$BC = \sqrt{32}$$

The result may be simplified by factoring out any perfect square factor in the radicand:

$$BC = \sqrt{16(2)}$$

Remove the perfect square factor from under the radical sign by taking its square root and writing it as a coefficient of the radical:

$$BC = 4\sqrt{2}$$

$BC = \sqrt{32}$ or $4\sqrt{2}$.

**38.** Let $x =$ one positive number.

Then $x + 8 =$ the other positive number.

The sum of the squares of the two numbers is 130:

$$x^2 + (x + 8)^2 = 130$$

Simplify $(x + 8)^2$ by multiplying $(x + 8)$ by $(x + 8)$:

$$\begin{array}{r} x + 8 \\ x + 8 \\ \hline x^2 + 8x \\ + 8x + 64 \\ \hline x^2 + 16x + 64 \end{array}$$

Combine like terms:

$$x^2 + x^2 + 16x + 64 = 130$$
$$2x^2 + 16x + 64 = 130$$

This is a *quadratic equation.* Rearrange it so that all terms are on one side, equal to zero, by adding $-130$, the additive inverse of 130, to both sides:

$$\begin{array}{r} -130 = -130 \\ \hline 2x^2 + 16x - 66 = \phantom{-1}0 \end{array}$$

To simplify, divide all terms on both sides of the equation by 2:

$$x^2 + 8x - 33 = 0$$

The left side of the equation is a *quadratic trinomial* which can be factored into the product of two binomials.

The factors of the first term, $x^2$, are $x$ and $x$, and they become the first terms of the binomials:

$$(x \qquad)(x \qquad) = 0$$

The factors of the last term, $-33$, become the second terms of the binomials, but they must be chosen in such a way that the product of the inner terms and the product of the outer terms add up to the middle term, $+8x$, of the original trinomial. Try $+11$ and $-3$ as the factors of $-33$:

$$+11x = \text{inner product}$$
$$(x + 11)(x - 3) = 0$$
$$-3x = \text{outer product}$$

Since $(+11x) + (-3x) = 8x$, these are the correct factors:

$$(x + 11)(x - 3) = 0$$

If the product of two factors equals zero, either factor may equal zero:

$$x + 11 = 0 \quad OR \quad x - 3 = 0$$

Add the appropriate additive inverse to both sides, $-11$ for the left-hand equation and $+3$ for the right-hand equation:

$$\begin{array}{r} -11 = -11 \\ \hline x \phantom{-1} = -11 \end{array} \qquad \begin{array}{r} +3 = +3 \\ \hline x \phantom{-1} = 3 \end{array}$$

Reject the negative root since the problem calls for positive numbers:

$$x = 3$$

$$x + 8 = 11$$

The numbers are **3** and **11**.

**39.** The given system of equations is:

$$x - \frac{1}{2}y = 4$$
$$x + y = 7$$

Multiply each term of the first equation by 2 to clear fractions:

$$2(x) - 2\left(\frac{1}{2}y\right) = 2(4)$$
$$2x - y = 8$$

Adding the original second equation will eliminate $y$:

$$\frac{x + y = 7}{3x \quad = 15}$$

Divide both sides of the equation by 3:

$$\frac{3x}{3} = \frac{15}{3}$$
$$x = 5$$

To solve for $y$, substitute 5 for $x$ in the original second equation:

$$5 + y = 7$$

Add $-5$, the additive inverse of 5, to both sides of the equation:

$$\frac{-5 \qquad = -5}{y = 2}$$

CHECK: To check, substitute 5 for $x$ and 2 for $y$ in *both original* equations to see if each is satisfied:

$$x - \frac{1}{2}y = 4 \qquad\qquad x + y = 7$$

$$5 - \frac{1}{2}(2) \overset{?}{=} 4 \qquad\qquad 5 + 2 \overset{?}{=} 7$$

$$5 - 1 \overset{?}{=} 4 \qquad\qquad\qquad 7 = 7 \checkmark$$

$$4 = 4 \checkmark$$

The solution is $x = 5$, $y = 2$ or $\{(5, 2)\}$.


**40.** Let $x$ = the number of houses built by Ben's Construction. Then $2x - 5$ = the number of houses built by Ace Construction.
The total number of houses built by both was 115:

$$x + 2x - 5 = 115$$

Combine like terms:

$$3x - 5 = 115$$

Add 5, the additive inverse of $-5$, to both sides of the equation:

$$\frac{5 = \quad 5}{3x \qquad = 120}$$

Divide both sides of the equation by 3:

$$\frac{3x}{3} = \frac{120}{3}$$
$$x = 40$$
$$2x - 5 = 2(40) - 5 = 80 - 5 = 75$$

Ace Construction built **75** houses; Ben's Construction built **40**.

**41.**    The toss of the die can produce any one of 6 results: 1, 2, 3, 4, 5, or 6.

The coin toss can result either in heads (H) or tails (T).

Each of the 6 die-toss results can be associated with each of the 2 coin-toss results.

**a.**    Tree diagram:

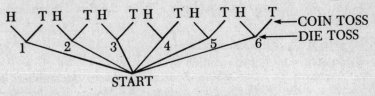

Sample space:

| Die Toss | Coin Toss |
|:---:|:---:|
| 1 | H |
| 1 | T |
| 2 | H |
| 2 | T |
| 3 | H |
| 3 | T |
| 4 | H |
| 4 | T |
| 5 | H |
| 5 | T |
| 6 | H |
| 6 | T |

**b.**    Probability of an event occurring equals

$$\frac{\text{number of favorable cases}}{\text{total possible number of cases}}$$

There is one favorable case for tossing a 5 on a die. The total possible number of cases is 6, since there are 6 faces on a die. Thus, the probability of obtaining a 5 on the toss of a die is $\frac{1}{6}$.

There is one favorable case for obtaining a tail on the toss of a coin. The total possible number of cases is 2, since the coin may land either heads up or tails up. Thus, the probability of obtaining a tail on a toss of a coin is $\frac{1}{2}$.

The probability of the occurrence of two independent events is the product of their separate probabilities. Therefore, the probability of obtaining a 5 on a die and a tail on a coin is $\frac{1}{6} \times \frac{1}{2}$ or $\frac{1}{12}$.

ALTERNATIVE SOLUTION: The problem may be solved by using the tree diagram or the sample space. On the tree diagram, there is a total of 12 pathways from START through the die toss and the branching through the coin toss. Only one of these pathways passes through a die-toss result of "5" and a coin-toss result of "T". Thus, the probability of realizing this pathway is 1 out of 12. In the sample space, there are 12 lines. Only one of them contains both a "5" in the first column and a "T" in the second column.

The probability of a 5 and a tail is $\frac{1}{12}$.

c. There are 3 even numbers, 2, 4, and 6, among the numbers on the faces of a die. With the tree diagram, 3 pathways may be taken from START to an even number. Each of these pathways may be continued on a branching to H (representing heads on a coin). Thus, there are 3 complete pathways through an even number to heads, out of the total possible number of 12 pathways from START through the second branching. With the sample space, 3 lines out of the total of 12 contain an even number and an "H": 2-H, 4-H, and 6-H. Therefore the probability of obtaining an even number and a head is $\frac{3}{12}$ or $\frac{1}{4}$.

ALTERNATIVE SOLUTION: The number of favorable cases for obtaining an even number on a die is 3; the total possible number of cases is 6. Therefore, the probability of obtaining an even number is $\frac{3}{6}$.

The probability of obtaining a head on a toss of a coin is $\frac{1}{2}$.

The probability of two independent events occurring (even number on die, head on coin) is the product of their separate probabilities:

$$\frac{3}{6} \times \frac{1}{2} \text{ or } \frac{3}{12} \text{ or } \frac{1}{4}.$$

The probability of an even number and a head is $\frac{3}{12}$ or $\frac{1}{4}$.

d. There is no 8 on a die. Thus, there are no favorable cases for obtaining an 8. Hence the probability of obtaining an 8 is $\frac{0}{6}$ or 0.

The probability of obtaining a head on a coin toss is $\frac{1}{2}$.

The probability of obtaining an 8 on a die and a head on a coin is the product of their separate probabilities: $0 \times \frac{1}{2} = 0.$

ALTERNATIVE SOLUTION: This result may also be obtained from either the tree diagram or the sample space. On the tree diagram, there is no pathway among the 12 which leads through an "8" to "H". On the sample space, of the 12 lines none contains an "8" and an "H".

The probability of an 8 and a head is **0**.

42.

| $p$ | $q$ | $(p \wedge q)$ | $(p \vee q)$ | $(p \to q)$ | $[(p \vee q) \leftrightarrow (p \to q)]$ | $(p \wedge q) \to [(p \vee q) \leftrightarrow (p \to q)]$ |
|---|---|---|---|---|---|---|
| T | T | T | T | T | T | T |
| T | F | F | T | F | F | T |
| F | T | F | T | T | T | T |
| F | F | F | F | T | F | T |

The truth values, T and F, for any column in the table are filled in according to the values of $p$ and $q$ in the first two columns on the same line.

$(p \wedge q)$ is the *conjunction* of $p$ and $q$. The conjunction has the truth value T only when both $p$ and $q$ have the truth value T; in all other cases, the conjunction has the truth value F.

$(p \vee q)$ is the *disjunction* of $p$ and $q$. The disjunction has the truth value T when either $p$ or $q$, or both, have the value T; the disjunction has the truth value F only when both $p$ and $q$ have the truth value F.

$(p \to q)$ is the *implication* that, if $p$ is true, then $q$ is true. The implication has the truth value T whenever $q$ has the truth value T, or whenever both $p$ and $q$ have the value F; the implication has the value F when $p$ has the value T and $q$ has the value F.

$[(p \vee q) \leftrightarrow (p \to q)]$ is an *equivalence relation* between $(p \vee q)$ and $(p \to q)$. The equivalence relation has the truth value T whenever the truth values of both $(p \vee q)$ and $(p \to q)$ are the same, that is, both T or both F; if their truth values are different, the equivalence relation has the truth value F.

$(p \wedge q) \to [(p \vee q) \leftrightarrow (p \to q)]$ is the *implication* that, if the conjunction of $p$ and $q$ is true, then the equivalence relation between the disjunction of $p$ and $q$ and the implication $(p \to q)$ is true. The implication has the truth value T whenever the equivalence relation has the value T, or when both the disjunction and the equivalence relation have the value F; it has the value F when the disjunction has the value T and the equivalence relation has the value F.

## SELF-ANALYSIS CHART    January 1987

| Topic | Question Numbers | Number of Points | Your Points | Your Percentage |
|---|---|---|---|---|
| 1. Numbers (rat'l, irrat'l); Percent | 31 | 2 | | |
| 2. Properties of No. Systems | — | 0 | | |
| 3. Operations on Rat'l Nos. and Monomials | 8, 23, 24 | 2 + 2 + 2 = 6 | | |
| 4. Operations on Multinomials | 19 | 2 | | |
| 5. Square root; Operations involving Radicals | — | 0 | | |
| 6. Evaluating Formulas and Expressions | 12 | 2 | | |
| 7. Linear Equations (simple cases incl. parentheses) | 1, 6 | 2 + 2 = 4 | | |
| 8. Linear Equations containing Decimals or Fractions | 5, 17 | 2 + 2 = 4 | | |
| 9. Graphs of Linear Functions (slope) | 30, 33 | 2 + 2 = 4 | | |
| 10. Inequalities | 25 | 2 | | |
| 11. Systems of Eqs. & Inequal. (alg. & graphic solutions) | 4, 36, 39 | 2 + 10 + 10 = 22 | | |
| 12. Factoring | 16 | 2 | | |
| 13. Quadratic Equations | 18 | 2 | | |
| 14. Verbal Problems | 40 | 10 | | |
| 15. Variation | — | 0 | | |
| 16. Literal Eqs.; Expressing Relations Algebraically | 9, 15, 28 | 2 + 2 + 2 = 6 | | |
| 17. Factorial $n$ | — | 0 | | |
| 18. Areas, Perims., Circums., Vols. of Common Figures | 29 | 2 | | |
| 19. Geometry ($\cong$, $\angle$ meas., $\parallel$ lines, compls., suppls., const.) | 10, 13, 20, 35, 37a, b, c, d | 2 + 2 + 2 + 2 + 1 + 2 + 2 + 2 = 15 | | |
| 20. Ratio & Proportion (incl. similar triangles) | 3, 7 | 2 + 2 = 4 | | |
| 21. Pythagorean Theorem | 32, 37e | 2 + 3 = 5 | | |
| 22. Logic (symbolic rep., logical forms, truth tables) | 21, 27, 42 | 2 + 2 + 10 = 14 | | |

## SELF-ANALYSIS CHART    January 1987

| Topic | Question Numbers | Number of Points | Your Points | Your Percentage |
|---|---|---|---|---|
| 23. Probability (incl. tree diagrams & sample spaces) | 2, 11, 34, 41a, b, c, d | 2 + 2 + 2 + 4 + 2 + 2 + 2 = 16 | | |
| 24. Combinatorics (arrangements, permutations) | 14 | 2 | | |
| 25. Statistics (central tend., freq. dist., histograms) | 22, 26 | 2 + 2 = 4 | | |

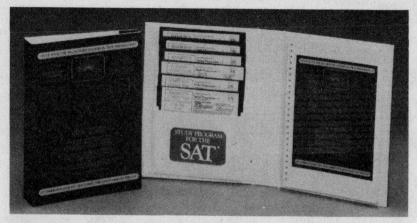

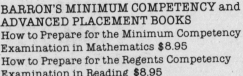

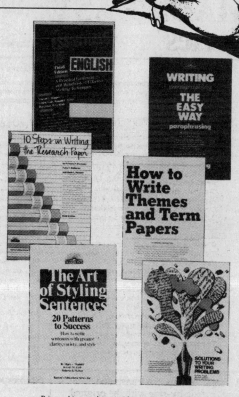

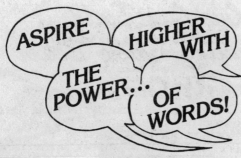

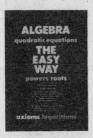

# NOTES